CONSUMERISM
Viewpoints from
Business, Government,
and the Public Interest

CONSUMERISM
Viewpoints from Business, Government, and the Public Interest

Ralph M. Gaedeke
University of Alaska

Warren W. Etcheson
University of Washington

Canfield Press, San Francisco
A Department of Harper & Row, Publishers, Inc.
New York/Evanston/London

CONSUMERISM: VIEWPOINTS FROM BUSINESS, GOVERN-
MENT, AND THE PUBLIC INTEREST

Copyright © 1972 by Ralph M. Gaedeke and Warren W. Etcheson

International Standard Book Number: 0-06-382795-6

Library of Congress Catalog Card Number: 76-189358

73 74 75 987654

Contents

v

Part Three   GOVERNMENT and the CONSUMER   157

Existing Consumer Protection Programs

Consumer Protection Legislation

Consumer Representation

An Appraisal

Part Four   BUSINESS and the CONSUMER   249

The Marketing Challenge

Business Response

Self-Regulation

Recommendations and Prospects

APPENDIXES   371

Texts	(1)	(2)	(3)	(4)	(5)	(6)	(7)
1 Beckman and Davidson, *Marketing*, Eighth ed.	2,38	1-3,7-8, 10,12-13, 19,21,32, 38-39	1,8,19,22, 26,32, 35-36,39		4-6	4-6	4-6,9, 11,27
2 Buskirk, *Principles of Marketing: The Management View*, Third ed.	33				1,7-10, 16,24-26		16
3 Converse, Huggy and Mitchell, *Elements of Marketing*, Seventh ed.	2,3	7-11		4-8	32		
4 Gist, *Marketing and Society: A Conceptual Introduction*	2-3,5,9- 10,12,16, 21,24-26, 28,30,32, 34-36, 38-39	2-3,9-10, 12,16,24- 26,28,30 34-36, 38-39	1-2,7-9, 12,14,16- 17,19-29, 31-34,36, 38-40	1-2,7-9, 12,14,16- 17,19-29, 31-34,36, 38-40	1-2,7-9, 12,14,16, 19-29, 31-34,36, 38-40		4-6,9,15, 17,24,27, 35-36
5 Holloway and Hancock, *Marketing in a Changing Environment*	9-10,12, 16,28, 36,39	10,18,20, 28,31,33, 36-37 39-40		4-6,9,17, 24,27,36	4-6,9,17, 24,27,36	4-6,9,17, 24,27,36	28,30-31, 33,35,39
6 Kotler, *Marketing Management: Analysis, Planning and Control*, Second ed.		33	1-2,16-17, 28,33,39	4-5,36	15	18	
7 Lazer, *Marketing Management*			25,28,38	28	24,26,28, 33,38	28	
8 Lipson and Darling, *Introduction to Marketing: An Administrative Approach*	9-10,12, 16,28,31, 33,36,39	9-10,12, 16,28,31, 33,36,39		10,18,20, 31,37,40	10,18,20, 31,37,40	28,30, 33,35	1-2,7-9, 12,14,16- 17,19-29, 31-36, 38-40
9 McCarthy, *Basic Marketing: A Managerial Approach*, Fourth ed.	9,10,12, 16,28, 36,39	28,31,33, 39,40	1-2,7,9, 12,14,16- 17,19-29, 31-36, 38-39	28,30, 33,35		4-6,9, 17,24,36	3,30
10 Phillips and Duncan, *Marketing Principles and Methods*, Sixth ed.	2,3,11		4,5, 9,33	4,6, 10,33	1,4,6-13, 21,27,33		
11 Stanton, *Fundamentals of Marketing*, Third ed.	9-10,12, 16,28,31, 33,36,39	9-10,12, 16,28,31, 33,36,39	28,30, 33,35	4-6,9, 17,24,36	4-6,9,27	4-6,9,27	4-6,9,27
12 Sturdivant, et al, *Managerial Analysis in Marketing*	1-3,5, 7-10,12, 14,16-17, 19-40		1,2,12, 14,16-17, 19-40	4-6,9,15, 17,24,27	4-6,9,15, 17,24,27	31,33	10-15,20, 22,29-31, 34-36,38

Marketing Textbooks*

(8)	(9)	(10)	(11)	(12)	(13)	(14)	(15)	(16)	
									1
11,16, 19,33	1,4-6,9- 10,12-14, 16-17,19, 24,27	13-14,22, 29,30,35	22	22,29,35					2
			18,21,23, 26,39						3
4-6,9, 15,17,24, 27,35-36	4-6,9, 15,17,24, 27,35-36	4-6,9, 15,17,24, 27,35-36	28,30,33		31,39	10,18,20, 31,37,40	10,18,20, 31,37,40	10,18,20, 31,37,40	4
		1-2,7-10, 12,14,16- 17,19-29, 31-36, 38-40	1-2,7-9, 12,14,16- 17,20-29, 31-36, 38-40				11-15,18, 22,29,31, 34-36,38		5
28,31 33,38		36-37	1	13-14	29-30	18,40	18,31		6
	13,14	14,22,29, 34-35	18,22-23, 29,34-35			15,19-20, 22,30,32, 35,37	15,19,30, 35,37	1,3-6, 9-12,21, 24,33,36	7
1-2,7-9, 12,14,16- 17,19-29, 31-32,34- 36,38-40		4-6,9,17, 24,27,36	4-6,9,17, 24,27,36	15		3,30			8
4-6,9,27	15	10-14,18, 29,31,38	10-12,15, 20,22,29, 31,38		15	11,14, 29-31, 34-36,38	10,18,31, 37,40	10,18, 20,31, 36-37,40	9
			7-8						10
15	10-15, 18,20,22, 29-31, 34-36, 38	10-12,31	10-15,18, 20,22,29- 31,34-36, 38-40	10,18,31, 36-37,40	10,20,31				11
10-13,15, 19-20,22- 23,27,29- 32,35, 37-38	10,40		10,18, 20,31, 36-37,40	10,18, 20,31, 36-37,40	10,18, 20,31, 36-37,40		1,28,33		12

* Top row of numbers represent chapter in each of the marketing texts; numbers in all of the other squares represent readings in *Consumerism*.

Texts	(17)	(18)	(19)	(20)	(21)	(22)	(23)
1 Beckman and Davidson, *Marketing,* Eighth ed.	12-13,29	18,40,	18,40		11,15, 22,30, 32,35,37	11,15,37	
2 Buskirk, *Principles of Marketing: The Management View,* Third ed.		18,40	18,23,40	18,23,40	17,19,30, 32,35,37		15,20, 30,37
3 Converse, Huggy and Mitchell, *Elements of Marketing,* Seventh ed.	31,37						
4 Gist, *Marketing and Society: A Conceptual Introduction*		10-13,18- 20,22-23, 27,29-32, 35,37-38	10-13,15, 18-20, 22-23,27, 29-32, 35,37-38	10-15,18, 20,22, 29-31, 34-36	10,18,40	10,18,40	
5 Holloway and Hancock, *Marketing in a Changing Environment*		10-13,15, 18-20, 22-23,27, 29-32,35, 37-38	10-13,15, 18-20, 22-23,27, 29-32,35, 37-38		3,30	2,5,9,18, 21,24-26, 28,32,34, 35,38,40	
6 Kotler, *Marketing Management: Analysis, Planning and Control,* Second ed.	15,22,30	19-20,23, 27,32,35, 37-38		1		6-12,16- 17,19-27, 34,36-39	3,30
7 Lazer, *Marketing Management*			4-6	4-6, 9-10	1-2,13-14, 24-26,29, 31,38-39	1,11-12, 16-17,21, 25-26,29, 31,38-39	1,3,16- 17,21-23, 25-27,32, 34-36,39
8 Lipson and Darling, *Introduction to Marketing: An Administrative Approach*				10-15,18, 20,22, 29-31, 34-36,38	10,18, 36,40	10,18,20 31,36,40	10-13,15, 18-20, 22-23,27, 29-32, 35,37-38
9 McCarthy, *Basic Marketing: A Managerial Approach,* Fourth ed.				10-13,15, 18-19, 22-23,27, 30-31, 35,37-38	10-11,15, 30-31,38	10-11,15, 20,27,29, 30-32, 35,37,38	10,18,40
10 Phillips and Duncan, *Marketing Principles and Methods,* Sixth ed.					8	29	12-13, 29,30
11 Stanton, *Fundamentals of Marketing,* Third ed.		10,18,40		22		10-13,15, 18-19,23, 27,30-31, 35,37-38	10,15, 30-31,38
12 Sturdivant, et al, *Managerial Analysis in Marketing*							

(24)	(25)	(26)	(27)	(28)	(29)	(30)	(31)	(32)	
							3,26, 33,36		1
	28,31	1,25-26, 28,34, 36,39	25-26,28 32-33, 38,39			18			2
		13-14,22, 29,30	13-14,22		23,40	19,32,37	2-3		3
									4
									5
11,16,17									6
2				7-8,28, 38-39					7
1-2,18, 28,33	5,9,16, 18,21, 24-26,28, 32,34-35, 38,40								8
					1,28,33	2,5,9, 16,18,21, 24-26,28, 31-32,34- 35,38,40			9
			15,30	15,20, 30,40	23,40	23	1,3,11, 19-20, 25-27,29		10
10-11,15, 20,27, 29-32,35, 37-38		3,30		1,28	1,2,7-9, 12,14,16- 17,19-29, 31-36, 38-40	2,5,9, 16,18,21, 24-26,28, 32-35, 38,40,			11
									12

*Top row of numbers represent chapter in each of the marketing texts; numbers in all of the other squares represent readings in *Consumerism.*

Preface

Consumerism, what it is and the response to it, captured the nation's attention in the late 1960s and early 1970s to such an extent that it helped elect sympathetic public officials, launched new public careers, lent support to environmentalists and ecologists when they were struggling for recognition, and bewildered some businessmen who had trouble shifting philosophic gears from *caveat emptor* to *caveat venditor.*

However, in a sense consumerism, or the consumer movement, is very old; in another sense it is quite new. It is old in the sense that there has been concern for the consumer's bargaining position down through the ages—examples include chasing the money lenders from the temples, the general suspicion of coin debasement in medieval times when people bit coins to test their value, the relatively recent spawning of cooperatives in Rochdale, England, in the mid-1850s, and the more recent sound and fury of the muckrakers in this country during the first third of this century. It is new in the sense of its fervor, public consciousness, the number of people actively involved, the charisma of certain of its leaders, and its obvious political appeal.

It is this new consumer movement that this book is all about. The movement is here approached from three perspectives—the perspectives of the two principal parties to marketing transactions, the buyer and the seller, and the perspective of those who advocate greater government involvement in consumer affairs. Positions from within and between these three perspectives are not always in agreement.

Major policy questions and the antecedents of the new consumer movement are traced in Part One to reiterate that there may not be anything new under the sun—only the method of coping with it—and to indicate that the movement is not peculiar to the United States; it is worldwide.

Part Two reviews the background of the consumer movement in the United States and outlines some of the major issues which go to make up the amorphous, yet encompassing thing called consumerism. The current furor over consumer protection, so much in evidence in the press and in the spate of federal, state, and local legislation, is assigned some causes—causes which may not have obtained during earlier concerns about the consumer's welfare.

Part Three examines the positions of the advocates of increased government involvement in consumer protection. These positions progress from the general disenchantment with industrial self-regulation through the claims of inadequacy of administrative action to the various proposals for increasing the role of government in consumer affairs. This section closes with an appraisal of the conflict between the basic desire of government to remain aloof in buyer-seller negotiations and the recognition that a hands-off policy is not the current mood of the country.

Part Four posits the responses of business to the cry for more consumer protection. Selections in this part examine the prospects for achieving a satisfactory detente with consumers through self-regulation. Several selections propose new recommendations for effecting an accommodation with the consumer movement.

An unusual feature of this volume is the set of appendixes. Appendix I is a listing of significant consumer legislation enacted at the federal level during the past century with the title, date, and a short summary of the purpose of each act. To bring the reader up to date on the directions that consumerism has taken most recently, Appendix II is a listing by subject of selected bills introduced in the 92d Congress. Appendix III contains a review of major government-financed or government-sponsored consumer protection activities in ten foreign countries. These examples out of foreign experience provide provocative discussion opportunities regarding "would it work here?"

This collection of readings has been designed to serve several purposes. One obvious one is to supplement an introductory text in marketing. Another is to serve the burgeoning area of consumer economics in schools and departments of business and departments of home economics. Further, departments of business, government, and society will find this collection useful in gaining an understanding of the emerging forces of the buying side of business and in appreciating the conflicting economic, political, and social aspects of consumerism. Finally, any lay student of the role of consumers in the economic affairs of life should find this a contemporary compendium on consumerism.

While researching the literature on consumerism and reviewing our own familiarity with the subject, we were beseeched by colleagues with claims such as "your book won't be complete without this or that article or essay." We admit the merit of these suggestions, but we were faced with exigent space requirements. We submit that this collection, whose authors have our gratitude, is as representative of the various moods and positions regarding consumerism as can be made today and is an accurate statement of the movement, its causes, the design of its current ferment, and its direction. If it isn't, then that is our shortcoming.

Ralph M. Gaedeke
Warren W. Etcheson

Part One

Introduction

The selections chosen for the Introduction provide a frame of reference for the study of consumerism. Included are contributions by Sen. Warren G. Magnuson, the National Goals Research Staff, and Colston E. Warne, President, Consumers Union of the United States.

From the vantage point of Chairman, Senate Commerce Committee,* and Chairman, Subcommittee on Consumer Affairs, Senator Magnuson presents a conceptual foundation of consumerism and a look into the "crystal ball" to see where consumerism is and what its future is likely to be.† Senator Magnuson predicts that industry must eventually submit not only the traditional fiscal audit to stockholders but also a social audit of what contributions its products and services have made to society.

In the second selection, excerpted from *A Report Toward Balanced Growth: Quantity with Quality*, the National Goals Research Staff attempts to put into perspective emerging debates in our society. It outlines the specific areas in which some debates and discussions are taking place and suggests the proposition that our citizens can mold the future of their nation in the direction which they desire. The selection thus serves as a springboard for discussion by stimulating the reader to think more deeply, more cogently, and more analytically about such questions as: Given the

*As Chairman of the Senate Commerce Committee, Senator Magnuson has been instrumental in the passage of numerous consumer protection acts, including the National Traffic and Motor Vehicle Safety Act, the Cigarette Labeling Act, the Fair Packaging and Labeling Act, and the Child Protection Act. (See Appendix I, "Significant Consumer Protection Legislation Enacted.") Legislative bills which he has recently introduced include: S. 983 (Consumer Product Safety Act of 1971), S. 986 (Consumer Products Warranties and Federal Trade Commission Improvements Act of 1971), S. 1222 (Consumer Fraud Prevention Act), and S. 1692 (Consumer Product Test Methods Act).
†Additional insights into consumerism's evolvement are listed in Appendix II, Selected Consumer Bills Introduced in the 92d Congress.

present threat to our natural environment, how should we balance change in patterns of production and consumption with new means of waste disposal or recycling—and how should we allocate the costs? How can consumer protection best be advanced without so interfering with the market mechanism as to leave the consumer worse off in the long run?

The Introduction closes with a selection which examines the global character of consumerism. In his article, "The Worldwide Consumer Movement," Colston Warne describes consumer protection efforts in Western and Eastern Europe, in Asia and in the Pacific area. The author stresses the role of the International Organization of Consumers Unions (IOCU) and points to the unresolved problems in international consumer protection. (A listing of several government-financed consumer protection activities overseas appears in Appendix III, "Major Government Financed Consumer Activities in Nine European Countries and in Canada.")

PART ONE, CONTENTS

1

Consumerism and the Emerging Goals of a New Society

Sen. Warren G. Magnuson

Recent recognition of examples of abuses in the marketplace has unleashed a wave of consumer intolerance that
calls for a redirection of technology and marketing
practices to the satisfaction of redefined goals of society.
Fulfillment of these goals implies that in the future
industry will be required to submit to a social audit in
addition to the traditional fiscal audit.

You can call it consumerism or environmentalism. If you are allergic to it you can denounce it as a sinister foreign "ism"; if you are part of it or partial to it you'll hail it as a 20th century citizen's revolt against the unresponsiveness of both public and private institutions to human needs. But regardless of what you call it, you can no longer evade or ignore its depth and force.

Society has rejected the preeminence of the doctrine of *caveat emptor*. And in its place we see the emergence of a consumers bill of rights. In his first consumer message to the Congress in 1962, President John F. Kennedy enunciated four basic consumer rights:

1) The Right to Safety—to be protected against the marketing of goods which are hazardous to health or life.

Sen. Warren G. Magnuson, Washington, is Chairman of the United States Senate Commerce Committee.

2) The Right to be Informed—to be protected against fraudulent, deceitful, or grossly misleading information, advertising, labeling or other practices, and to be given the facts needed to make an informed choice.

3) The Right to Choose—to be assured, wherever possible, access to a variety of products and services at competitive prices and in those industries in which Government regulations are substituted, an assurance of satisfactory quality and service at fair prices.

4) The Right to be Heard—to be assured that consumer interests will receive full and sympathetic consideration in the formulation of Government policy and fair expeditious treatment in its administrative tribunals.

The legislative program which has subsequently developed is an expression of the Congress' commitment to that bill of rights.

Looking into the crystal ball, beyond today, beyond the different pending consumer protection legislation proposed by either Administration or Congressional consumer advocates, where is consumerism and environmentalism going and why?

To gain perspective, we must look at the seminal auto safety law in 1966. A decade earlier, who would have thought that Congress would place the automobile industry under stringent federal safety regulation? To a large extent that Act reflected a gnawing loss of consumer faith, both in the competence and in the social responsiveness of American business. That faith has been repeatedly jarred by revelations that have progressively tarnished the golden image of American technology and enterprise cherished by our historians and myth makers.

The automobile, which had come to symbolize the brilliance of American manufacturing genius, has progressively been revealed as a surface-styled, poorly-engineered, unsafe, primary polluter of the environment. And as one after another massive recall campaign comes to light, even the Detroit miracle of automotive mass production loses its glow.

But the automobile does not stand alone as an object of consumer wrath. Consumerism has been fueled by a wide range of product flaws and service failures.

The cigarette—a consumer staple descending from the pages of American Colonial history—stands condemned by the medical and scientific community as a lethal health hazard. But the cigarette industry in its desire to maintain sales and profits by attracting women, if not children, beams seductive advertising messages now by magazine, newspapers, point of sale, direct mail and who knows what next week.

These recent changes in consumer consciousness have also unleashed a wave of consumer intolerance. Consumers no longer accept docily their inability to make rational comparisons and judgments in the supermarket and elsewhere. And these fires of discontent have been fueled by skilled advocates. The imagination of the American people has been captured by the spectacle of great corporate Goliaths being toppled by solitary Davids. In many ways the appeal of the consumer revolt to Americans lies as much in its reassertion of the traditional American quality of cantankerous individualism as in the communal loss of faith in the responsiveness of corporate institutions.

In a sports-minded nation whose heart is invariably with the underdog, who can deny the appeal of a contest between Ralph Nader and General Motors or Union Carbide? And who in the general public roots for the giant polluters against the solitary heroes of the Sierra Club?

The best of these crusaders, such as Nader, have been superb publicists and educators. Perhaps the single most significant achievement of Ralph Nader in the auto safety controversy was to redirect the attention of the public from the role of the driver to the role of the vehicle. This focused Congressional awareness as well as public awareness on the concept of packaging people in automobiles so that their human failing need not cause them to be impaled upon the steering column or hurled through a windshield following a crash. There has now emerged a well developed public awareness that products can and ought to be designed to anticipate and guard against misuse as well as the intended use.

In the last year or two both environmental and consumer advocates have made gigantic strides toward institutionalizing their concerns and broadening their base of support and orginizational structure. Traditional groups, such as the Sierra Clubs, and Consumers Union have become more aggressive, more active, their appeal has become broader. There are now several public interest law firms and centers funded by foundations and citizen contributions. There is John Gardner's citizens lobby, Common Cause, and the Consumer Federation of America, a federation of new and old organizations sharing a common interest in consumer legislation. Each of these, while still relatively small and financially undernourished in comparison to industry, has begun to make its presence felt in Washington.

Prospects for substantial growth in the development of these public interest lobbying operations are good. In the state of Oregon, for example, several young lawyers inspired by Nader have helped organize a program involving all eight college campuses in that state. At each school more than fifty percent of the students have signed a petition to the State Board of Education requesting the State Board to add one dollar and fifty cents ($1.50) to each student's fees each semester. The funds raised thereby are to be placed in a fund administered by student elected boards both at the college and state level in an Oregon Student Public Interest Research Group, named: OSPIRG.

Four of the college Presidents in Oregon are actively supporting this project and the prospects of its acceptance by the State Board of Education appear strong. This would provide a fund of perhaps two to three hundred thousand dollars a year, administered by students but carried out by professionals hired by the student boards to act as public interest advocates before local courts and the legislature. Oregon is viewed as but only as a pilot project; just imagine fifty state PIRGS, each financed and directed by students and each sending a lobbyist to Washington!

So the picture is one of anger, frustration, conflicting demands and a growing taste for confrontation in the courts and legislatures, if not physical confrontation on the land.

Beyond laws and regulations, and often in conflict with the obligation to the stockholders, there is growing criticism of companies who fail to meet vague but persistent notions of corporate social responsibility.

Certain clear and powerful trends appear:

First: Mindless product innovation and profitability will no longer satisfy standards of corporate behavior.

Second: Corporate freedom will become increasingly circumscribed by governmental controls reflecting emerging concerns over status, the environment, over consumer rights, even over shifting social values.

Third: Citizen action through the courts and legislatures by increasingly well organized and articulate public interest lobbies and through the politics of confrontation will snowball.

Should industry roll over and play dead until all means of production are centralized in one big federal socialist state? Of course not.

It does not take a learned economist or historian to perceive that only industry has the capacity to marshal the resources and technology needed to satisfy the emerging goals of a new society. Nader and the Sierra Clubs have been remarkably skillful in unmasking its flaws; but they don't have the know-how to cure them. Government can prevent industry from doing things the way they have been done, but Government does not have the capacity to develop socially acceptable, alternative methods of production.

There is a growing recognition both among industry and government scientists that we must soon develop the institutional framework for the process known as technology assessment. Much of the antagonism toward business in this country today stems from the sense that many of our ills are the direct result of a technology run amok without sufficient understanding of secondary and tertiary environmental and social effects.

Government and industry must develop together a system by which technology is evaluated in the light of conflicting or competing social goals so that decisions can be made, based upon the total national fund of knowledge; cooly, deliberately and rationally in furtherance of those goals.

This process clearly involves a surrender of a substantial degree of corporate sovereignty; but it does not mean a surrender of corporate sovereignty to irrational, ill-defined, emotional prejudices against technology and growth.

Today industry must submit annually to a fiscal audit; tomorrow it will undoubtedly be forced to submit, if not done voluntarily, to a new kind of audit: A social audit.

Industry will be asked about not only the contributions made to stockholders in the form of profits and augmented capital investment, but what net contribution to society products or services have made along with the quantification and qualification of such questions as these: Do you products contribute to significant human needs? What are both your short and long term impact on the environment? Are you exploiting or conserving national resources? Do you exceed minimum product safety standards where economical and feasible?

Of course social objectives are more difficult to define than financial objectives. But nevertheless, industry will end up doing this if for no other reason than in self-defense.

The vast power of the consumer, both political and economic, just reaching fulfillment, serves as a warning that Government and industry can never again isolate themselves from the people. For while economic power is political power, the American public has demonstrated that it holds the key to both.

2

Emerging
Debates

National Goals Research Staff

America appears to be at a point of profound change—from
a society which focused on growth for growth's sake to one
dominated by concern for the "quality of life." Consequently, the nation is in a period of marked social change,
one aspect of which is the search for a new growth policy
to guide that change.

In his state of the Union message of January 1970, the President stressed that wealth is
not synonymous with happiness, that economic growth is required not as a thing
desirable in itself, but for the achievement of specific social goals, that our relationship
to the environment must shift from an exploitative mode to one of living in harmony
with the environment. He called for development of a growth policy. In making these
statements, he reiterated an argument that has been expressed somewhat independently in a number of separate institutional areas; i.e., in order for continuing social
transformation to be progressive, its growth processes must be purposeful.

Our country has never dedicated itself solely to conventional economic growth.
Concern about what is now called the "quality of life" is not new in America's life,
and rarely has anyone advocated national policies to promote growth only for its own
sake.

However, ours is a society which, until recently, rarely questioned the virtue of
continued economic growth per se. We were further proud of our ability to generate a
flood of new technology and consumer products, and of our ability to expand our
scientific knowledge and educational resources. But today there is an explicit challenge

Reprinted from *A Report Toward Balanced Growth: Quantity with Quality*, Report of the
National Goals Research Staff (July 4, 1970), pp. 25-35.

8

to the view that we can or should continue to encourage or permit the unfettered growth of our economy, population, technology, use of materials and energy, flow of new products, and even of our scientific knowledge. Some manifestations of this challenge are too sweeping to deserve policy consideration, but others are unquestionably reasonable, and the circumstances precipitating them sufficiently concrete and urgent as to warrant priority attention by public policymakers. Viewed in historical perspective, these challenges signify that a profound re-examination is taking place of man's view of his relationship to nature, to his institutions, and to his fellow man.

The growing challenge to established viewpoints by new concepts is the substance of certain emerging debates that come about not only because of some doubts about the effectiveness of our institutions and the anticipation of worsening future problems, but also because our wealth now provides the latitude and the ability to alter parts of the national life that are found wanting. For example, pollution has become a national problem not only because its symptoms are evident, but also because the promise exists that resources and programs to deal with it may become available; both a visible dissatisfaction *and* the ability to intervene in the causes of dissatisfaction encourage debate.

This call for a growth policy occurs in the midst of a period of rapid social change marked by problems that indicate that even more change is needed. A growth policy in only one element in the total process of social change. It is one set of principles that will influence that change.

The exclusion or inclusion of a topic in this report is not intended to reflect the degree of national priority attached to it. Viewed by the number of people directly affected and by the degree of intensity of the effect, the issues of poverty, minority group status, student unrest, and urban problems are more urgent than, for example, the consumerism movement or the plight of basic natural science—topics that are discussed here.

Important problems, such as equal opportunity and student discontent, are among the driving forces that stimulated the debate over growth policy. While some of these socially urgent issues receive explicit attention in this report, the topics selected for inclusion mainly represent those in which active ongoing debate relevant to a *growth* policy can be identified: population size and distribution, environment, education, basic natural science, technology assessment, and consumerism. These subjects are included because they can be instructive concerning the growth problems—other than that of managing the overall economy—with which we are actually grappling in an effort to reach a policy of balanced growth.

The Debates

The specific issues involved in each of the areas can be outlined as follows:

Population. The traditional view of population growth as a source of national pride and strength is being re-examined. Some authorities argue for zero population growth on the grounds that population stability is imperative for survival, or will improve the quality of our society. (For example, it might enable us to avoid the issue of limitations on the use of energy and materials.)

The merits of sheer size now appear more debatable than heretofore, particularly in the case of large metropolitan areas. Large concentrations of population generate serious pollution problems, traffic congestion, and higher per capita public expenditures. And they are unduly vulnerable to power failures, riots, and other disruptive social action. Thus, major questions are asked: should we limit our population size, and if so, how? And should we redistribute our population, and if so, how?

Environment. Historically, our concern over resources focused on whether there would be enough food, energy, and materials to meet our needs. Today, in the United States, the concern is about the ability of land, air, and water to absorb all the wastes we generate. We already have violated the aesthetic limits of pollution and, from time to time and place to place, we have violated health and survival limits of pollution. Some argue that the long-run issue may well be our survival. Questions often asked are: What can be done to repair the damage already done? To what extent and by what means will future pollution be contained within tolerable limits? Are there fixed limits of environmental tolerance that might make it imperative to limit the size of our population or set per capita quotas on the amount of energy and material we may use?

Education. Throughout its history, America's educational system has had to meet a variety of needs for a growing Nation. Today this system, after a long stretch of phenomenal growth, finds itself the target of deepening dissatisfaction. The nature and degree of the dissatisfaction implies the existence of unmet educational needs in our society. As the education system met earlier needs, a reciprocal relation was formed between our society and the schools. When society needed more skilled citizens it turned to the schools; in turn, the schools raised the knowledge and skill level of society, nurturing additional development in a continuing spiral of mutually supported growth. The question raised in the chapter on education is: What relation might be established between the educational system and a rapidly changing, complex society to achieve balanced growth? A number of specific issues arise, such as whether or not our colleges and universities should assume service roles in society as opposed to the traditional role of discipline-oriented institutions searching for knowledge for its own sake. Also, there are questions relating to individual self-development, equality of opportunity, educational achievement standards, and the financial problems of the schools. And, should we develop a wider diversity of postsecondary opportunities?

Basic Natural Science. To the extent that it was discussed at all in the past, it was generally agreed that science should grow according to its own internal logic as dictated by the structure of evolving knowledge and the criteria and judgments of the scientific community. In America since World War II, basic science continued to develop in its traditional spontaneous fashion because the available funds were so large compared to the capacity of the scientific community that almost everything scientifically worthwhile was funded.

Today, the relationship of the scientific establishment to its funding is being reversed. In relation to the capacity of the research establishment to do research, funds are deficient. Furthermore, many persons, including members of the scientific community, are concerned over the possibility that the knowledge they develop will be used for ends they do not approve. Thus, knowledge no longer is seen as necessarily good. Furthermore, scientists and others have become acutely aware of social and environmental problems for which systematic knowledge may offer solutions, and basic science is asked to address these problems. Thus, the traditional "guidance" mechanism of science is being challenged at a time when funds have declined in relation to the capacity of the scientific community.

Among the questions asked are: To what extent should basic natural science be permitted to develop in a free unguided manner? How much support should the Nation give to development of basic scientific knowledge? To what extent and by what mechanisms should basic science and scientists (whether or not in the capacity for which they were originally trained) be pressed to solve specific social problems?

Technology Assessment. The sophisticated products of our Nation's technologists have been a source of pride and, sometimes, wonder. Largely free of governmental constraint, technology has tended to develop according to the internal logic of its usual industrial, public, and business sponsors. What seemed feasible and profitable was tried. What proved possible and profitable tended to be used. Technology accounts, to a large extent, for the productivity of our economy, our standard of living, our ability to keep a high proportion of the potential work force in school, our achievements in space, and—granting the perils of a nuclear age—our military security. But we have become increasingly aware of technology's adverse effects. Some highly sophisticated drugs produce severe side effects. Airplanes and automobiles make intolerable noise and foul the air. Advanced technology of all sorts produces unexpected and often unwanted indirect consequences. A movement called "technology assessment" now advocates a more pervasive and systematic assessment of the social costs and benefits of both new and existing technology. The main issues are: To what extent should the use of new and old technology be restricted because of adverse side effects? What institutional mechanisms might assess and regulate technology? What effect would such a policy have on economic growth and on the size and nature of our technological and scientific establishments?

Consumerism. While technology is a source of strength in our economy, the abundant flow of new consumer goods has been viewed as a clear indication that the economy brings vast direct benefits to the American people. Yet, in the past decade, this virtue has been questioned. A movement labeled "consumerism" contends that the rapid introduction of new products produces confusion, that the technical complexity of new products makes it impossible to evaluate their benefits or dangers and makes them difficult to repair, and that pressure on business firms to introduce new products and services breeds marketing practices of a dubious nature.

The traditional doctrine of "consumer sovereignty" holds that the consumer is capable of protecting his own interests. Today, the proponents of the consumer movement argue that the consumer does not have the information with which to make an informed choice. The internal guidance system of the marketplace is challenged. The issues include: To what extent and in what ways is the consumer actually the victim of these circumstances? How should he be protected? In the course of this, how can a healthy business environment be maintained?

These are the topics on which the National Goals Research Staff was able to identify an active challenge to traditional views. They are presented in the ensuing chapters in greater detail as problems to be worked on the formulation of a future growth policy, and as the sorts of issues with which we will have to operate in pursuing such a growth policy. The style of presentation is descriptive and analytical. That is to say, it will strive to outline what the issues and options are without presuming to prescribe solutions. These issues challenge many deep-seated values.

In each of the problem areas described here, our institutions have failed to correct fully problems of which we are now clearly aware, and have created many new problems. This report suggests that our concern is leading us to develop a national goal of being more systematic and rational in assessing priorities and solving our problems.

Toward Anticipatory Decisionmaking

What clearly emerges from these debates which have been subsumed under the label of a search for balanced growth is a dissatisfaction with old ways of decisionmaking. The implication is that we wish to shift from a reactive mode of dealing with problems that have forced themselves on us to an anticipatory mode in which we either attempt to prevent their occurrence or are prepared to deal with them as they emerge. The latter mode is necessary and desirable in times of rapid change because of the inertia of large systems. As the President pointed out in announcing the formation of the National Goals Research Staff:

> We can no longer afford to approach the longer-range future haphazardly. As the pace of change accelerates, the process of change becomes more complex. Yet, at the same time an extraordinary array of tools and techniques has been developed by which it becomes increasingly possible to project future trends—and thus to make the kind of informed choices which are necessary if we are to establish mastery over the process of change.

The art of anticipatory decisionmaking in government is one which we are yet far from mastering. Yet, its desirability is so obvious that any move in that direction should be encouraged.

One of the tools for making this shift is, as the President has said, the understanding of the projection of present trends. However, the mere projection of trends can lead to pessimism. They tell us what is most likely to happen if two circumstances prevail: we continue present policies, and events of the rest of the world over which we have no control continue as expected. Frequently the implications are bad.

But the objective of projecting present trends is not primarily to find out what will happen to us if we do nothing to change the trends. It is to give us some clue as to what to do so that our future might be brighter. For this purpose we must imagine which alternative futures are open for us to choose. We must invent feasible and desirable futures and devise policies which will get us there. This is the role of goal setting in national action. It is to enable us to decide where we want to be, and thereby to stimulate us to figure out how to get there.

The acceptance of this mode of national decisionmaking has certain corollaries. One of these, reflected in many arguments related in this study, is that we must evaluate the consequences of our actions on the basis of wider criteria than we have used in the past. For example, the popular phrase "quality versus quantity" has, in some contexts, been taken to imply a turning away from economic goals. This should not be so. There does seem to be, however, a disposition to evaluate our actions and policies in a framework broader than solely technical and immediate economic considerations. Per se, this cannot be said to be new to the American scene. But the emphasis and degree of commitment do seem to be new, and would be a vital ingredient to the adoption of an anticipatory mode of decisionmaking.

Another corollary that flows naturally from our experience and the development of an anticipatory approach to decisionmaking is the acceptance of the complexity of the systems in which we live and on which we act. To say that everything is related to everything else is a true, but sometimes thankless, statement. It is nevertheless true, and to the extent that we cam make our decisions with consideration for the fullest feasible set of interactions that we can visualize, we will be less likely to defeat our own purposes.

The acceptance of the complexities involved in purposive social action will often lead us to the conclusion that the solutions to our problems are more difficult than they appeared to be at first glance. In this circumstance there is both a hope and a danger. The hope is that we will undertake action realistically, and not do so under assumptions that will produce a violation of the public's hopes and expectations. Too often in the past we have attacked problems with the expectation that they could be solved in an unrealistically short time with an unrealistically low estimate of the resources required. The danger is that realism may discourage action. Yet experience shows that when advocates of action exaggerate the ease of success or alternatively overstate the risks of not acting, the consequences are likely to be either disappointment or loss of public support; these can be more discouraging to policy actions than an objective appraisal of the difficulties and the possibilities would warrant.

While we have come to appreciate the complexity of social and environmental processes, our present knowledge of those complex processes is extraordinarily incomplete. From this, it follows that for the long range we must vigorously pursue the extension of our knowledge of these processes. And, for the short range, since our ability to anticipate exactly what will happen is so limited, we must sharpen our ability to detect as rapidly as possible that which has already happened. This requires the development of new, improved methods for the measurement of social change.

Complicating the adoption of such a strategy are the changing roles of citizen and government. This is particularly pertinent since the hope for responding better to long-range matters rests in part on newly evolving techniques of forecasting and planning, the tools largely of specialists. Yet at the same time, citizens are demanding and getting a greater voice in their affairs, and the Federal Government is evolving a new role for itself more as a shaper of policies and less as a doer of things. There is a built-in tension in this situation which one must assume can be resolved with care, patience, and wisdom.

The concepts and tools for developing an anticipatory strategy are still being worked out by analysts and scholars. The methods are being tried with varying degrees of success in both the private and the public sector. The difficulties are enormous. The promise is great. The length of time and the efforts to arrive at such a strategy, and the degree of success we will attain are indeterminate. Yet, we seem to be committing ourselves to trying it.

Premises of the Debates

Our society appears to be one at a point of significant transformation, sometimes described as that from an industrial society to a "post industrial society"—from a society in which production of goods was of primary concern to one dominated more by services and the generation and use of new knowledge. Further, we are in a period of marked social change, one aspect of which is the search for a growth policy that will guide that change.

These developments form the background of the debate over whether growth—in our economy, population, material goods, and even knowledge—is to be valued for its own sake, or whether we should place increased emphasis on more carefully channeling our growing resources to improve the quality of our lives.

The major causes of the debate seem to be:

1. The changing values and a rising level of our expectations concerning the goals that we should set for ourselves in both resolving inequities and improving the quality of our lives.

2. A realization that our resources, although substantial and likely to grow in a generally predictable fashion, are limited, and, therefore, more consideration should be given to the setting of priorities for their use.

3. The development of a wide range of management and planning tools that offer some promise for more rational setting of priorities and for effective action.

Also, as part of the background for the debate, are two additional circumstances:

1. The notion that priority setting, planning, and decisionmaking can remain an isolated "staff" function is not tenable. Such crucial activities on the national level are an integral part of the political process, and probably can work only to the extent that the results are persuasive to citizens who are demanding a more direct representation in decisions affecting their lives.

2. Our model for managing change in complex systems, whether social or environmental, has come to reflect the caution that is appropriate to such complexity. And our society has, in fact, become increasingly complex and interrelated.

These two circumstances, while complicating the task, inject appropriate realism into the process, assuring more acceptability of proposed programs, while reducing the probability of unexpected, unwanted consequences. It must be admitted, however, that it is not yet known how to involve the public most effectively in national decisions. However, in our democracy, decisions in which the public does not concur will be changed emphatically in the privacy of the polling booth.

Constructive public discussion of alternative goals, priorities, and policies, with all groups of people participating, must be initiated. The fruits of this public discussion should be incorporated into policies aimed at alleviating the problems or enhancing the opportunities.

This report is one attempt to contribute to such discussion. The critics seem to be saying that many of our institutions aim at growth for its own sake, but growth now should be directed toward achieving the higher social goal of improving the quality of human life.

SUMMARY

America appears to be at a point of profound change, frequently characterized as that from an industrial society to a "post industrial society"—from a society in which production of goods was of primary concern to one dominated more by services and the generation and use of new knowledge. Consequently, we are in a period of marked social change, one aspect of which is the search for a growth policy to guide that change. This report examines several areas in which the choice of a future growth policy is explicitly or implicitly being debated. Its intent is to use these case examples as a part of a learning experience, as one discrete step in the evolution of a policy of balanced growth, as called for by the President. The approach is analytical and not prescriptive. The purpose is to aid the American people and their representatives in what is assumed to be a long process for evolving a growth policy.

The key substantive areas in which the problem of growth is being debated are: population growth and distribution, environment, education, basic natural science, technology assessment, and consumerism. In general, these topical areas do not correspond to the major social problems with which we are presently concerned, including those of our citics, campus unrest, the Vietnam War, and race relations. These represent dissatisfactions over our performance according to our establish priorities.

Probably the major message that comes from the existing debates over a growth policy is not that our institutions have proven incapable of doing their job. Rather, many of our institutions have performed very well the tasks which we set for them a few decades ago. However, in so doing, they have created unanticipated problems with which we must now deal, and they must be reoriented toward the tasks that are appropriate in a society capable of a new level of performance. The range of criteria whereby we will judge institutional performance will be broader in scope and longer in time perspective. An essential part of this period of transition is the attempt to shift from a reactive form of public decisionmaking, in which we respond to problems when they are forced upon us, to an anticipatory form in which we try either to avoid them or be prepared to deal with them as they emerge.

It is the hallmark of our country that Americans have adjusted to change while preserving the basic qualities of their institutions. This has happened a considerable number of times in our history. In the course of this history, a predominant theme has been one of economic growth, and an accommodation to a larger population. At no time was economic growth considered so dominant a goal that it obscured all other concerns, but neither was the growth per se viewed as other than a good thing.

Today, for the first time, we find the virtues of economic growth questioned, and this issue is put in popular terminology as one of "quantity versus quality." This is, in the view of this report, a false phrasing of the issue, since the new qualitative goals being proposed and the old goals yet unmet can be achieved only if we have continued economic growth. The issue is better put as one of how we can ensure continued economic growth while directing our resources more deliberately to filling our new values.

A large portion of the explanation for this seems to lie in our demonstrated ability to achieve economic stability and growth in the period following the passage of the Employment Act of 1946. Even though our economy is at the moment in a period of transition, the pervading public and official view is that we are a Nation of growing, unprecedented economic resources.

At the same time that we have become a Nation that can afford to care we have also become a Nation that cannot afford not to care. The past decade has been marked by an emerging sense of conscience for the plight of the underprivileged, and awareness of social and economic problems that are the unanticipated consequence of our past actions, a resolution that we can guide our affairs more rationally, and, simultaneously, a broad popular demand for citizen participation in the management of their own fate. While this was happening, we also developed new techniques of decisionmaking whose promise spurred the resolution to run things more rationally, but whose full potential is incompletely understood or tested.

While this resolution to run our affairs both more rationally and more effectively was emerging, two complicating circumstances arose. The Vietnam War placed a strain on our admittedly large resources and belatedly forced us to recognize the necessity of considering priorities more seriously. And, a more complex model of how to go about purposive action evolved in part from the ecologists' experience with the environment, and in part from our increasing knowledge of social science and our mixed experience in attempting social and political reform.

We thus find ourselves at a point at which the following things are true: We have rising expectations and changing values concerning the goals we should set for ourselves both in resolving existing inequities and in improving the quality of our lives. However, while our resources are large and growing, they are finite and we must set priorities more deliberately. In compensation for this complication we have the promise of more rational methods of public decisionmaking as a way of selecting and implementing our priority goals. But, this must be brought about in a context in which there is greater public participation, and greater recognition of the complexities of the world—both social and environmental—in which we live.

3

The Worldwide Consumer Movement

Colston E. Warne

The consumer movement is not novel or peculiar to the
United States and has grown internationally most rapidly in
more advanced nations that have the discipline of quality
control, well-trained government inspection services, and
discerning consumers.

The pattern of consumer protection in Europe bears a remarkable similarity to the
U.S. experience. Industrialized nations on both continents generated extensive brand-
name advertising and were faced with many of the same problems of packaging and of
ensuring the purity of food and drugs. The idea of supplying the consumer with the
results of product testing by brand name crossed the Atlantic following World War II.
Starting in Great Britain, the Netherlands, and Belgium, it spread to the Scandinavian
countries, Austria, West Germany, and France, and was soon exported to Australia,
Japan, and Israel.

Initially, European consumer groups feared the legal consequences of publishing
adverse test results by brand name, even though this had never proved a problem in the
U.S. Nevertheless, the movement, once started, spread so rapidly that in April 1960
the International Organization of Consumers Unions (IOCU) was launched at a
conference in The Hague. The charter members were Consumers Union of U.S., Inc.;
Consumers' Association, London; Australian Consumers' Association; Consumenten
Bond, The Hague; and Association des Consommateurs, Brussels. The IOCU sought to
become an authenticating body that would admit to membership only those organizations that accepted no income from advertising and were financially supported by
either consumers or governments. The IOCU stimulated the interchange of techniques

Reprinted from *1970 Britannica Book of the Year* (The Encyclopaedia Britannica, Inc., 1970), p.
504. Reprinted by permission.

and test results among its affiliates. It provided an interchange of educational materials and established a technical committee to represent consumers on international standardization bodies. It also moved to assist consumers in less developed nations by obtaining consultative status with the Food and Agriculture Organization, the Economic and Social Council, and UNESCO, agencies of the UN concerned with raising living standards in less developed countries.

In Britain the White Paper of the Maloney Committee formed the basis for a revamping of governmental efforts. The privately operated Consumers' Association assumed the exclusive role of consumer testing. Through its grants, the association established a Research Institute for Consumer Affairs, which conducts investigations into governmental, professional, and commercial services. It also established a National Federation of Consumer Groups to assist local consumer groups with such problems as complaints, store services, and price comparisons, and a Consumer Advice Centre in London. As of 1970, it had a membership of 532,000. A new Consumer Council was created by the government in March 1963 as an independent grant-aided body designed to give advice to the consumer and to initiate reforms on his behalf, but it was abolished in 1970 as an economy measure. Weights and measures controls in Britain remain in the hands of local and county authorities. The body mainly responsible for regulating consumer goods and services is the Board of Trade, although the Home Office deals with most of the safety aspects of consumer protection and the Ministry of Health enforces the Food and Drug Act. The British also created Citizens' Advice Bureaux.

Except for Belgium and the Netherlands, European consumer testing organizations have followed the pattern set by the Scandinavian countries rather than by Britain and the U.S. In Norway substantial government grants are given to a consumer organization, Forbrukerradet, operated by representatives of seven leading national organizations. The testing agency also handles complaints and publishes a monthly consumer magazine. An Institute of Informative Labeling has also been established in Norway to foster the growth of quality marks. In Denmark consumer activities are divided between a governmentally operated Household Advice Centre, which undertakes extensive programs in the field of nutrition and household equipment, and a consumer testing organization supported by its individual members as well as some 21 member organizations and the government. Perhaps the most notable of the European efforts is Austria's Verein für Konsumenten-Information. This organization not only issues a monthly testing publication but also operates a demonstration centre in central Vienna where the consumer may view available brands and receive impartial guidance. Member organizations, including the Chamber of Labour, cover 80% of the organization's budget; the government covers 10% and the individual membership, 10%.

A number of coordinating efforts exist among European groups, among them the European Bureau of Consumers Unions, consisting of nine organizations from the six EEC countries; the Contact Committee of Consumers of the European Economic Community; and the International Labeling Centre, which is linked with the International Organization for Standardization and the International Electrical Technical Commission. These efforts were still weak, but it was expected that the Common

Market would inevitably bring increased brand competition between European countries and hence a need for centralized testing. The consumer federations would also enable national groups to act jointly in consultation with the EEC. Similarly, the Scandinavian groups established a Scandinavian Committee on Consumer Matters to coordinate their research and informational efforts. The European consumer protection movement, however, was measurably weakened by the establishment of competitive consumer organizations in many countries, often splitting along political lines. Thus the Belgians had two competing consumer groups, and West Germany had two central organizations, both undertaking consumer testing. The Swiss had four competing consumer groups until the requirements for obtaining a government subsidy induced coordinated effort.

The development of consumer standards and consumer testing also extended into Eastern Europe. Yugoslavia had a federal board on the family and the household to strengthen the role of consumers. Hungary recently entered the consumer testing field. The Soviet Union established a consumer institute which undertakes comparative testing.

In Asia leadership in the testing field belonged to Japan, where there was competition between the Japan Consumer Association, the Japan Housewives Association, and the Japan Consumers Union. Municipal governments also maintained advice centres in Tokyo and Osaka. A number of embryonic movements had been formed in Korea, the Philippines, Malaysia, and India. Perhaps the strongest organizations in the Pacific area, however, were those in Australia and New Zealand. The Consumers Institute of New Zealand received a heavy government subsidy. The Australian movement was independent in character and received no government money. Local consumer movements existed in leading Australian cities, and New South Wales and Victoria had consumer counsels.

In summary, the world consumer movement has grown most rapidly in more advanced nations that have the discipline of quality control, well-trained government inspection services, and discerning consumers. The unresolved problem in international consumer protection is that of discovering methods of aiding the low-income consumers in nations that have never known an honest civil service and that have low levels of business ethics and consumer competence. Through the Codex Alimentarius, the World Food Organization hopes to assist less developed nations by establishing basic food standards. The IOCU has made a beginning in establishing educational seminars for less developed countries. The problem, nonetheless, was that those with low levels of literacy and minimal income were most likely to be deprived of even the elementary protections of honest weights and measures and of purity in food.

Part Two

Consumerism and the Consumer Interest

The objectives of the selections included in Part Two are to provide a theoretical base for viewing the consumer's role in consumerism, to discuss the background of previous consumer movements, and to present some perspectives in and to examine major issues of consumerism.

Contributions by Wesley C. Mitchell, Jerome Rothenberg, and G. William Trivoli provide the theoretical base. In the first article, Mitchell focuses on the "backward art of (consumer) spending" and the consumer's inability to make rational or intelligent choices. His thesis, elucidated in 1912, that the backwardness of the art of spending money is largely due to broad conditions over which the consumer has slight control finds much applicability in today's market arena. The question might be raised: How "backward" is the art of spending in today's era of abundance?

In his paper, "Consumers' Sovereignty Revisited and the Hospitability of Freedom of Choice," Jerome Rothenberg raises some issues connected with the scope of the doctrine of consumers' sovereignty and considers how changes in products and tastes affect the ethical status of the concept. He also questions the extent to which consumers can be truly sovereign and contrasts the doctrine of consumers' sovereignty with the principle of freedom of choice. The thesis of the Trivoli article is a challenge of the frequently voiced contention that consumers are no longer sovereign. The author provides empirical evidence which refutes those who assert that firms are able to manipulate consumers' product desires.

The selections by Ralph M. Gaedeke and Kenneth Dameron discuss the background of previous consumer movements. The reports place the contemporary consumer movement into proper historical perspective. The first selection traces the early beginnings of concern for consumer protection, from the late nineteenth century to the early 1930s. In the second article, Kenneth Dameron outlines the chief objectives and direction of the consumer movement of the 1930s, focusing on government protection, business response, and the role of consumers.

Perspectives in consumerism are presented by Richard H. Buskirk and James T. Rothe, Ralph Gaedeke, and Colston E. Warne, President of Consumers Union. The article by Buskirk and Rothe analyzes underlying causes and implications of consumerism. The authors focus on various market and societal problems that underlie today's consumer protection movement, conclude that it is unlikely that consumerism activity will decline in the future, and make recommendations on what corporations should do in the current situation. Gaedeke's study describes the results of a survey which attempted to ascertain the differences in perceptions among business, government, and consumer spokesmen as they pertain to the nature and causes of consumerism as well as the choice of corrective measures. The study shows that consumerism is of a kaleidoscopic nature. Since Consumers Union is an integral part of consumerism, a selection by the President of Consumers Union is included. In his article, Colston Warne outlines the aims and action programs of Consumers Union and relates them to the need for product testing and information.

A view of the outstanding consumer issues are presented in the last section of Part Two. Although many specific issues are dealt with throughout the text, the selections presented specifically outline the broad underlying issues of consumerism and consider certain issues which are currently being debated in Congress.*

On March 15, 1962, President John F. Kennedy sent to the Congress a "Special Message on Protecting the Consumer Interest." In this message, the President stressed the importance of the long-established role of the federal government in meeting its responsibility to consumers in exercising their rights, which include the "right to (product) safety," the "right to (product) informa-

---

*Recently introduced consumer bills cover such issues as boat safety, consumer education, consumer information, consumer representation, deceptive sales, door-to-door sales, fish inspection, grade labeling, home improvements, product testing, trading stamps, and "truth in warranties."

tion," the "right to (product) choice," and the "right to be heard." The protection and advancement of these rights is, in essence, what consumerism is all about. The first selection of this section on major issues thus elaborates these rights from the perspective of the federal government.

The selection from Ralph Nader's best-selling book, *Unsafe at Any Speed,* shows why values of safety concerning consumers and economic enterprises had not found their way into legislative policy making for safer automobiles prior to the 1966 National Traffic and Motor Vehicle Safety Act. A selection excerpted from the *Final Report of the National Commission on Product Safety* provides additional insights into the safety issue. The excerpt presents a broad perspective on product safety. It identifies not only categories of products harboring unreasonable hazards, but also points to the inadequacies of self-regulation by industry, reports on various shortcomings of common law in the protection of the consumer against such hazards, and proposes recommendations to correct the inadequacy of existing controls on product hazards.

In the article "New Pressures for Consumer Information," the issue of government's sharing its product test data and brand-name comparison studies with the general public is raised.

The three excerpts from the Senate Hearings on the Consumer Protection Act of 1970 represent viewpoints of industry, government, and Ralph Nader on pending consumer legislation, notably class action proposals.

In the next selection, Betty Furness, former Special Assistant to the President for Consumer Affairs, addresses the issue of consumer representation at the federal level of government. Miss Furness recommends a single consumer office, permanently established and given the authority to coordinate the efforts and programs of all interested government agencies.

In the final selection, the issue of disadvantaged low income consumers is discussed. "Exploitation of Disadvantaged Consumers by Retail Merchants," excerpted from the *Reports of the National Advisory Commission on Civil Disorders,* presents the two-sided problem of the merchant-consumer relationship in the ghetto.

PART TWO, CONTENTS

The Theoretical Base

4

The Backward Art of Spending Money

Wesley C. Mitchell

This is a classic statement of the indiscriminate way consumers spend their money. Although the author concentrates perhaps unduly on housewives for his illustrations (which preoccupation might be excused in a sixty-year-old statement), the analysis loses nothing in its cogency.

In the scheme of modern life, making money and spending money are strictly correlative arts. Of the two, spending is rated as both pleasanter and easier to practice. Certainly for most of us it is not less important. A few, indeed, make so much money that they can slight the art of spending without suffering discomfort, but the vast majority would gain as much from wiser spending as from increased earning.

Important as the art of spending is, we have developed less skill in its practice than in the practice of making money. Common sense forbids us to waste dollars earned by irksome efforts; and yet we are notoriously extravagant. Ignorance of qualities, uncertainty of taste, lack of accounting, carelessness about prices—faults which would ruin a merchant—prevail in our housekeeping. Many of us scarcely know what becomes of our money; though well-schooled citizens of a Money Economy ought to plan for their outgoes no less carefully than for their incomes.

For this defect in our way of living we are often taken to task, not only by thrifty souls who feel that waste is sin, but also of late by men of large affairs who wish that we might ask less insistently for higher wages and save more money to invest in their

Reprinted from *American Economic Review*, vol. 2 (June 1912), pp. 269-281. Reprinted by permission.

securities. No doubt there is sufficient reason for faultfinding, and no doubt much of the free advice given on mending our ways is sound. Conscience admits the first, common sense the second. But in our haste to plead guilty we forget certain mitigating circumstances which might go far toward recommending us to the mercy of an impartial court. To spend money is easy, to spend it well is hard. Our faults as spenders are not wholly due to wantonness, but largely to broad conditions over which as individuals we have slight control.

Under the less complicated economic organization of barter and the nascent use of money, the family was the unit in large measure for purposes both of producing and consuming goods. By the time of American colonization, English society had grown out of such simple conditions. But the earlier colonists were forced by their isolation to revert to practices which the mother country had long since abandoned. The family became again a unit of producers, caring for each other's wants. Food-stuffs and other raw materials were produced by the men, assisted by the women and children; these materials were prepared for family use by the women, assisted by the children and men. While this form of organization was transient in any one district, it kept re-appearing upon the frontier, so that for generations production was based in part upon the family as a unit.

Denser settlement would have sufficed by itself to enable Americans to develop division of labor and regular markets corresponding to those of seventeenth and eighteenth-century England. But in addition there came the industrial revolution and the railway. These factors in combination gradually deprived the family of its old importance as a unit for producing goods. For the factory made, the railway brought, the shop kept a great variety of articles which the family once provided for itself. Production was re-organized on the basis of a new unit—the business enterprise—in which the members of many families were employed. And the new unit proved vastly more efficient than the old. It made possible more elaborate specialization of labor and machinery, more perfect coördination of effort and greater reduction of waste than could be attained by the family. There resulted a gigantic increase in the volume of goods produced and in the aggregate incomes earned.

Meanwhile as a unit for consuming goods, for spending money, the family has remained substantially where it was in colonial days. Division of labor in spending has not progressed beyond a rudimentary division between the adult men and women of the family—the women bearing the heavier burden of responsibility. Housework has been lightened by the growth of industry; but housewives still face essentially the same problems of ways and means as did their colonial grandmothers. No trade has made less progress than this, the most important of all trades.

It is because we have not wanted to that we have not developed a larger and more efficient unit for spending money than the family. Our race-old instincts of love between the sexes and parental affection, long since standardized in the institution of monogamy, are a part of experience at once so precious and so respectable that we have looked askance at every relaxation of the family bond, whatever material advantages it has promised. While we have become increasingly dependent upon other men for the goods we buy and for the sale of our services, we have jealously insisted upon maintaining the privacy of family life, its freedom from outside control, so far as our circumstances have permitted. Reluctantly we have let the factory whistle, the timetable, the office hours impose their rigid routine upon our money-making days; but our homes we have tried to guard from intrusion by the world of machinery and business. There are strains in our stock, to be sure, which can adopt themselves more readily to the lock-step of life organized by others; such people fill our family hotels. But most of us still prefer a larger measure of privacy, even though we pay in poor cooking. So long as we cling fondly to home life, so long will the family remain the most important unit for spending money. And so long as the family remains the most important unit for spending money, so long will the art of spending lag behind the art of making money.

The dominance of women in spending, which the family form of organization establishes, may explain the backwardness of the art in some measure. An effective contrast might be drawn between the slipshod shopping of many housewives and the skilful, systematic buying done for business enterprises by men. But the fair comparison is between the housewife's shopping for the family, and her husband's shopping for strictly personal wants. Current opinion certainly represents women as more painstaking than men in making selections, and more zealous in hunting for bargains. Doubtless if men had to do the work they would do it otherwise in some ways, and doubtless they would think their ways better. But if men had to spend money under the limitations now imposed upon women by family life, they would certainly find the task exceedingly difficult. It is the character of the work more than the character of the women which is responsible for poor results. Indeed, the defects of the workers are partly effects of the work. The lack of system, which reduces the efficiency of so many housewives, comes in a measure from the character of their daily tasks, like the pedantry which makes so many teachers uninspiring.

The housewife's tasks are much more varied than the tasks which business organization assigns to most men. She must buy milk and shoes, furniture and meat, magazines and fuel, hats and underwear, bedding and disinfectants, medical services and toys, rugs and candy. Surely no one can be expected to possess expert knowledge of the qualities and prices of such varied wares. The ease with which defects of materials or workmanship can be concealed in finishing many of these articles forces the purchaser often to judge quality by price, or to depend upon the interested assurances of advertisers and shopkeepers. The small scale on which many purchases are made precludes the opportunity of testing before buying, and many articles must be bought hurriedly wherever they are found at whatever price is asked. If this work could be taken over for many families and conducted by a business enterprise it would be subdivided into several departments, and each department would have its own minute division of labor. Then there would be the commisariat with its trained corps of purchasing agents and chemists, each giving his whole working day to the buying or testing of meats, or vegetables, or groceries. Then there would be the departments of building and grounds, of furnishing, of fuel and lighting, of the laundry, of clothing, of the nursery and the like—all bringing specialized knowledge to the solution of their problems, all having time and opportunity to test qualities and find the lowest prices. The single family can no more secure the advantage of such division of labor in caring for its wants as consumers than the frontier family could develop division of labor in production.

Nor can the family utilize labor-saving machinery to reduce the cost of living more effectively than can the very small shop utilize it to reduce the cost of production. The economical use of machinery requires that the work to be done be minutely sub-divided and that each successive operation be standardized. The family unit is so small, the tasks are so various, and the housework is so scattered from cellar to attic as to make machinery more troublesome than useful. Even if a housewife were supplied with an elaborate mechanical equipment, and if she knew how to operate each machine and keep it in order, she could make but brief use of each device as she turned from one of her endless tasks to the next. A machine which is to stand idle ninety-nine hours in a hundred must possess extraordinary advantages, or cost but a trifle to warrant its being installed even in a factory. Hence the equipment which can be employed economically in the household falls into the class of inexpensive utensils and hand tools; even in this age of steam and electricity, a family must be cared for by hand.

Again, the general managers of households, unlike the general managers of business enterprises, are seldom selected upon the basis of efficiency. Indeed there are grounds for believing that in this country less attention is paid than formerly to housewifely capacity in choosing wives. The young farmer going west to take up land knew that his success would depend largely upon the efficiency of his helpmate. Perhaps his grandson exercises as much worldly wisdom in choosing a wife, but he thinks more of how much an available *parti* can add to his income than of the skill with which she can manage what he earns.

However chosen, the young wife seldom approaches her housework in a profes-sional spirit. She holds her highest duty that of being a good wife and a good mother. Doubtless to be a good manager is part of this duty; but the human part of her relationship to husband and children ranks higher than the business part. In a sense the like holds true for the man; but in his case the role of husband and father is separated more sharply from the role of money-maker. The one role is played at home, the other role in the fields, the shop, or the office. This separation helps the man to practice in his own activities a certain division of labor conducive to efficiency in money-making. He can give undivided attention during his working hours to his work. But the woman must do most of her work at home, amidst the countless interruptions of the household, with its endless calls from children and friends. She cannot divide her duties as a human being so sharply from her duties as a worker. Consequently, her housekeeping does not assume objective independence in her thinking, as an occupa-tion in which she must become proficient. Household management, under the condi-tions of family life, is not sufficiently differentiated from other parts of the house-wife's life to be prosecuted with the keen technical interest which men develop in their trades.

Upon the household manager, capable or not as she may be, family life commonly throws an exhausting routine of manual labor. In large business enterprises matters are managed better. The man who makes decisions, who initiates policies, who must exercise sound judgment, does no work with his hands beyond signing his name. He is relieved of all trivial duties, protected from all unnecessary intrusions. One of the handicaps of the small enterprise is that its manager must also keep the books, write the letters, or work in the shop—must disperse his energy over many tasks. In the great majority of homes the housewife labors under a like handicap. If she has no servant, then cooking and sweeping, mending and shopping, tending the children and amusing her husband leave her little leisure and less energy for the work of management proper. Tired people stick in ruts. A household drudge can hardly be a good household manager. Even with one or two servants to assist them, many wives work longer hours than their husbands, and work under conditions which are more nervously exhausting. The number of housewives who have leisure to develop the art of spending money wisely must be a very small percentage.

Though so many conditions of family life conspire to make hard the housewife's task, a surprising number of women achieve individual successes. If housekeeping were organized like business, these efficient managers would rapidly extend the scope of their authority, and presently be directing the work of many others. Then the less capable housewives, like the mass of their husbands, would be employed by these organizing geniuses at tasks which they could perform with credit to themselves and profit to the community. By this system we get the full use of our best brains in making money. But the limitations of family life effectually debar us from making full use of our best domestic brains. The trained intelligence and the conquering capacity of the highly efficient housewife cannot be applied to the congenial task of setting to rights the disordered households of her inefficient neighbors. These neighbors, and even the husbands of these neighbors, are prone to regard critical commentaries upon their slack methods, however pertinent and constructive in character, as meddlesome interferences. And the woman with a consuming passion for good management cannot compel her less progressive sisters to adopt her system against their wills, as an enterprising advertiser may whip his reluctant rivals into line. For the masterful housewife cannot win away the husbands of slack managers as the masterful merchant can win away the customers of the less able. What ability in spending money is developed among scattered individuals, we dam up within the walls of the single household.

There are, however, reasons for the backwardness of the art of spending money other than the organization of expenditure on the basis of the family. Grave technical difficulties inhere in the work itself, difficulties not to be wholly removed by any change of organization.

The rapid progress made and making in the arts of production rests upon progress in scientific knowledge. All the many branches of mechanics and engineering, are branches of the tree of knowledge, nourished by the roots of research. Among the various sciences the most important for industry are physics and chemistry. It is by applying in practice the physical and chemical laws learned in the laboratory that recent generations have been able to develop not only their complicated machinery, but also their effective processes of modifying materials. Now physics and chemistry happen to be the sciences which deal with the subject matter which is simplest, most uniform, and most amenable to experimental control. They are therefore the sciences of which our knowledge is most full, most precise, and most reliable.

In similar fashion, progress in the arts of consumption rests upon progress in science—or rather waits upon progress in science. To secure the better development of our children's bodies we need a better knowledge of food values and digestive processes, just as we need better knowledge of electricity to reduce the waste of energy on long transmission lines. To secure the better development of children's minds we need better knowledge of the order in which their various interests awake, just as we need better knowledge of physical-chemistry to control the noxious fumes of smelting plants.

But, unfortunately for the art of spending money, the sciences of fundamental importance are not physics and chemistry, but physiology and functional psychology. While the latter may be ultimately capable of reduction to a physico-chemical basis, they certainly deal with subject-matters which are far less simple, less uniform, and less amenable to experimental control than physics or chemistry proper. Hence they are in a relatively rudimentary condition. As now written they are easier for the layman to read, they present fewer superficial difficulties; but that is precisely because their real difficulties have not been mastered and elucidated.

Accordingly, even the housewife who is abreast of her time labors under a serious disadvantage in comparison with the manufacturer. The latter can learn from an industrial chemist and a mechanical engineer far more about the materials he uses, the processes at his disposal, the machinery best adapted to his purpose than the housewife could learn from all the living physiologists and psychologists about the scientific laws of bodily and mental development. No doubt the sciences which will one day afford a secure basis of knowledge for bringing up a family are progressing; but it seems probable that they will long lag behind the sciences which serve the same office for industry. Hence the housewife's work presents more unsolved problems, is more a matter of guesswork, and cannot in the nature of things be done as well as the work of making and carrying goods. Until such time as science shall illuminate the housewife's path, she must walk in the twilight of traditional opinion.

If the art of making money has advantages over the art of spending on the side of scientific technique, it has equal advantages on the side of business method. Money making is systematized by accounting in which all the diverse elements in a complicated series of bargains are adequately expressed in terms of one common denominator—the dollar. Thus a business man is enabled to compare the advantage of granting long credits with the advantage of selling on closer margins for cash; he can estimate whether it would be cheaper to buy a higher grade of coal or to let his fire boxes burn out rapidly; he can set off the cost of additional advertising against the cost of more traveling salesmen. And since profits are also expressed in dollars, the business man can control all items of expense on the basis of their estimated contributions toward his gains. In making money, nothing but the pecuniary values of things however dissimilar need be considered, and pecuniary values can always be balanced, compared, and adjusted in an orderly and systematic fashion.

Not so with the housewife's values. A woman can indeed compare costs so long as they consist solely in the money prices she is charged for goods. But she cannot make a precise comparison between the price of a ready-to-wear frock, and the price of the materials plus her own work in making. Still less can she compare costs and gains. For her gains are not reducible to dollars, as are the profits of a business enterprise, but consist in the bodily and mental well-being of her family. For lack of a satisfactory common denominator, she cannot even make objectively valid comparisons between the various gratifications which she may secure for ten dollars—attention to a child's teeth, a birthday present for her husband, two days at a sanatorium for herself. Only in the crudest way can subjective experiences of different orders occurring to different individuals be set against each other. Opinions regarding their relative importance change with the mood and flicker with the focus of attention. Decisions made one hour are often cause of regret the next. In fine, spending money cannot conceivably be reduced to such system as making money until someone invents a common denominator for money costs, and for all the different kinds and degrees of subjective gratifications which money can procure for people of unlike temperaments. Such household accounts as are kept doubtless have their value; but the most painstaking efforts to show the disposition of every cent spent still leave unanswered the vital question of what has been gained.

And what does the housewife seek to gain? The business man in quest of profits can answer such a question for himself in terms distinctly definite. To make money becomes an end in itself; to spend money involves some end beyond the spending. When the housewife pursues her problem to this final query she comes upon the most baffling of her difficulties. Doubtless she can tell herself that she seeks the happiness of her husband and herself, the fair development of their children. But before these vague statements can serve as guides in the intensely practical problem of spending money, she must decide what happiness and development mean in concrete terms for her particular husband and children. Of course our housewives are seldom philosophers, and if they were they could not let the dishes go unwashed while they wrestled with the question of what is best worth while in life. Most women, indeed, do their work in an empirical spirit, so busied with obvious difficulties of detail that they are saved from seeing the deepest perplexities of their position. It is commonly the very young wife whose conscience is worried about the ultimate aims of her spending; and she is more likely as the years go by to stop thinking about this problem than to think it out.

In accounting for the defects of the art of spending, as that art is currently practiced, there is little need to lay stress upon difficulties which are neglected by the great mass of practitioners. But there is one end which women assuredly do seek in spending, albeit unconsciously for the most part, which deserves attention because it is subversive of economical management.

Nassau Senior long ago pointed out the important role played by the desire for distinction in guiding conduct; and more recently Thorstein Veblen has developed the theme with much subtlety in his satirical *Theory of the Leisure Class.* We are all prone to draw invidious comparisons between ourselves and our neighbors. Such comparisons give us much edifying satisfaction when they can be twisted to our advantage, and produce a corresponding sense of discomfort when we cannot disguise our own inferiority. The subject matter of these invidious comparisons is drawn from the whole range of our experience, from appreciating Browning to catching trout, from observing the Sabbath to the weight of our babies. In the Money Economy of today, where so much of our attention is devoted to business, these comparisons turn with corresponding frequency upon our pecuniary standing. Money income is a crude, tangible criterion of worth which all of us can understand and apply. It needs a certain originality of character or a certain degree of culture to free us even in a measure from the prevailing concern with commerical standards. Most of us who are rich like to feel that the fact is known to all men; most of us who are poor strive to conceal the petty economies we are compelled to practice. Of course we see this unamiable trait of human nature more clearly in others than in ourselves; but in most of us that fact is but a subtle exercise of our inveterate habit of drawing biased comparisons between ourselves and others.

Now the simplest and most effective way of providing material for a soul-satisfying comparison with others on the basis of pecuniary competence is to show that we are better off by living in larger houses, wearing more stylish clothing, taking more leisure, and the like. Thus the Money Economy forms in us the habit of extravagant expenditure for the unacknowledged purpose of impressing both ourselves and our neighbors with an adequate sense of our standing. Of course, indiscriminate vulgarity in wasting money offends our taste. The ideal toward which we learn to strive is an ideal of refined elegance, such as is reputed to be the legitimate offspring of generations of wealth and leisure. But for working purposes, all classes of society exhibit the same species of impulse in a vast number of variants. The gaudy ribbons of the shopgirl are close kind to the paste jewels which the heiress wears to show that she keeps genuine jewels locked up in her safe-deposit box.

In their task of spending money the mass of housewives come under the sway of this paradoxical impulse. Not for themselves alone, but also for the sake of their husbands and their children, must they make it appear that the family stands well in a world where worth is commonly interpreted as dollars' worth. An appearance of poverty in comparison with their associates may disturb the husband's complacency and may handicap the children's chances of forming pleasant and profitable associations. Worldly wisdom, therefore, counsels the housewife to make as brave a show as may be with the income at her disposal. She must buy not only gratifications for the appetites and the aesthetic senses, but also social consideration and the pleasant consciousness of possessing it. The cost of the latter is an air of disregarding cost.

If this analysis of the reasons why the art of spending money is in so backward a state be sound, it follows that homilies upon the ignorance, foolish extravagance, and lack of system among our housewives are a vain exercise, productive of slight effect beyond the temporary indignation they arouse. However edifying such preachments may be made, they cannot remove the limits which family life sets to a more effective organization of expenditure, they cannot increase our knowledge of physiology and psychology, they cannot give us a common denominator for costs and gains in living, they cannot define our aims with definiteness, and they cannot cure us of seeking social consideration by living beyond our means.

What prospect of improvement can be seen lies in the slow modification of the broad social conditions which make woman's work so difficult at present. Despite certain relaxations of the family bond, we are seemingly inclined to maintain the essential features of the family group, with its large measure of privacy. Nevertheless, we are re-organizing certain forms of family expenditure on the basis of larger groups. Some among these tentative efforts may survive initial blunders and increase mightly in the years to come. The apartment building with its steam heat, janitor service, and common washtubs seems likely to increase in favor and perhaps will increase in the facilities it offers. The family hotel, which still seems to many of us the worst place for a family, may please a larger number of our children. Cooperative kitchens look promising on paper and may prove endurable in practice—particularly if wages of competent cooks continue to rise. Pure food laws, municipal certification of milk, and the like render easier the task of the housewife who is intelligent, though they doubtless disquiet her easy-going sisters by emphasizing dangers of which they had been but dimly conscious. Finally our cities are providing with a larger liberality playgrounds, parks, library stations, day nurseries—a socialized spending of money with a neighborhood instead of a family as the unit. In spite of the fact that all these forms of arranging expenditure for larger groups may be so managed as to increase the cost and diminish the benefit, they at least represent promising experiments which may result in solid gains. For one thing they give men a larger share in organizing expenditures, and men bring to the task a trained capacity for coöperation and the development of system—qualities to which the greater size of the unit allows free scope.

With greater confidence we may rely upon progress in physiology and psychology to make wider and more secure the scientific foundations of housekeeping. But such progress will have little practical effect unless the results of research are made available to far larger circles. This work of popularizing scientific knowledge, however, promises to become increasingly effective. Most of the magazines for women have departments devoted to matters of technical interest to housewives—channels through which trebly diluted applications of science may trickle to thousands of untrained readers. The ever increasing number of women's clubs, with their ever increasing membership, are other promising centers for the dissemination of knowledge concerning scientific cooking, domestic hygiene, sanitation and the like. Probably of more importance will be the growing attention to "domestic science" in the schools, and the efforts of colleges and universities to meet the popular demand for adequate instruction in the matters of gravest import to future wives and mothers. At best, however, a small percentage of women can secure this more elaborate training. And the more we learn about the sciences involved, the more prolonged, more difficult, and more expensive will such training become. Perhaps we may solve the problem by developing a professional class of Doctors of Domestic Science, who will be employed in organizing households, giving expert counsel to the newly wed, holding free dispensaries of advice for the indigent, assisting in divers municipal ventures in welfare work, and the like. Then the training of the mass of women may be confined to such an exhibit of the complexities and responsibilities of their work as will induce them to employ these elect as freely as they now employ physicians.

But even after many of the housewife's present cares have been reduced by the extension of business enterprise and municipal housekeeping, and after the housewife has received better training herself and can command the expert advice of a professional class, her task in spending money will still remain perplexing to one who takes it seriously. For the ultimate problem of what is worth while to strive for is not to be solved by sounder organization, by better training, or by the advance of science. Doubtless most women, like most men, will ever continue to accept uncritically the scale of conventional values which their day and generation provides ready-made. To such souls the only non-technical problems will be problems of reconciling minor inconsistencies, or striving to attain the more decorous standards of a higher social class. But to women of conscience and insight the ends of living will always be a part of the problem of spending money—the part which is most inspiring and most baffling. In this aspect the art of spending money differs from the technical pursuits of business and science, and is allied to philosophy and ethics. There is a scheme of values embodied in every housewife's work, whether she knows it or not, and this scheme affects for good or ill the health, the tastes, the character of those for whom she cares and those with whom she associates.

5

Consumers' Sovereignty Revisited and the Hospitability of Freedom of Choice

Jerome Rothenberg

The concept that the consumer is sovereign over the means to satisfy his wants and demands is questioned here, and a distinction is drawn between consumer sovereignty and freedom of choice. It is the author's contention that consumers' sovereignty is incomplete and highly ambiguous and is antipathetic to freedom of choice.

It is now twenty-five years since W. H. Hutt, in his book, *Economists and the Public*, coined the title, if not the substance, of the concept of "consumers' sovereignty." In the intervening period, developments have occurred which affect both the interpretation and the ethical persuasiveness of the concept. In this paper I shall first raise some issues connected with the scope of the concept; following this I shall consider how changes in products and tastes affect the ethical status of the concept. My conclusion is that consumers' sovereignty is incomplete and ambiguous. In order to make it operational, a series of highly controversial, partly normative decisions have to be made. Further, the extent to which consumers *can* be truly sovereign is questionable. In view of this, the concept loses attractiveness. By contrast, a principle which is distinguished from consumers' sovereignty but which has often been treated indistinguishably—freedom of choice—gains attractiveness. The analysis indicates that the two are likely to be competitive to some extent; so we must examine our preferences between them more closely than we have done.

Reprinted from *American Economic Review*, vol. 52, no. 2 (May 1962), pp. 260-268. Reprinted by permission.

Consumers' sovereignty was early used in two senses: one descriptive, the other normative. In its descriptive sense it simply signified that the consumer was in fact the ultimate king: production in a market economy is ultimately oriented toward meeting the wants of consumers. Production is the means, consumption the end. More particularly, market performance is responsive to consumer demands. If we should ask the more interesting question of how responsive this performance is, we move over to the normative sense. In its normative sense consumers' sovereignty asserted that the performance of an economy should be evaluated in terms of the degree to which it fulfills the wants of consumers. Different institutional systems, and even different market structures under a market system, fulfill these wants in different degree. Thus, despite the fact that consumers' sovereignty in this normative sense has from the beginning been intimately associated with a belief in the optimality of the free market, even Hutt finds the responsiveness of the market to consumer demands to be less than ideal where monopolistic elements are present. It is on the normative usage, as a keystone of welfare economics, that we shall focus in this paper.

I. THE SCOPE OF CONSUMERS' SOVEREIGNTY

The principle of consumers' sovereignty as presently employed is a value judgment which stipulates that we should take the degree of fulfillment of consumers' wants—or the degree to which performance accords with consumers' tastes—as a criterion for evaluating the social desirability of different social situations and, through these, the desirability of the various public policies or institutional structures which give rise to them. The form such a criterion should take is not obvious. For one thing, the central fact of scarcity means that no combination of social structure and public policy can lead to a satiation of all wants. The possible is limited by available resources and state of technological knowledge. Our criterion therefore becomes: how good is performance relative to the best it might conceivably be? Optimality consists in maximizing consumers' utilities subject to the constraints of available resources and techniques.

The first problem which must be faced in interpreting consumers' sovereignty has been recognized for some time. The criterion must be able to compare situations in which the well-being of a large number of individuals is involved. What does it mean to satisfy the potentially differing tastes of a numerous group? Does the principle itself determine a unique function of these tastes which is to be maximized? The answer is not clear. Indeed, even its epistemological status is not clear.

The principle surely requires at least that the first partial derivative of social welfare with respect to the welfare of any one individual be positive; that is, that any one person's improvement, everyone else's well-being being unchanged, is a sufficient condition for a social welfare improvement. Does it unambiguously imply any further restriction? In particular, does it require that the absence of opposite movements in the well-being of every pair of individuals be a necessary condition for such an improvement (so that in conjunction with the first requirement vector dominance in terms of the set of individual preference orders becomes the necessary and sufficient

condition for improvement—the criterion of Pareto optimality)? This second requirement defines the aggregate of tastes in a particular way—as a vector—and aggregate
taste comparisons in a correspondingly particular way—as vector comparisons. But
other definitions are possible: any one of the large family of functions of individual
orderings restricted only in that the first partial derivative of social welfare with
respect to every individual welfare argument is positive. The normative content of
consumers' sovereignty does not seem to me to imply or even to point decisively to
any one of these. Is it, for example, really in the spirit of consumers' sovereignty to
assert that no amount of improvement to 99 percent of the population can more than
offset a slight deterioration of well-being to the remaining 1 per cent in evaluating
social welfare?

Consumers' sovereignty has been thought to imply the Pareto optimality criterion. I
believe this to be largely because in its early treatments it was deemed equivalent to
allowing consumers to trade freely on purely competitive markets, pure competition
being taken as the institutional structure which permits the freest expression of tastes.
The set of outcomes of such trade, starting from each of the different logically
possible initial distributions of purchasing power, has been proved to be the Pareto
optimal set, given some qualifications originally thought to be minor. Two recent
emphases have diminished the association. One is the distinction stressed by Oskar
Lange and Abram Bergson between consumers' sovereignty and freedom of choice.
The first refers to consumer tastes as the goal (or end) of production and distribution.
The second refers to the administrative procedure of allowing consumers to use
purchasing power belonging to them to make whatever voluntary trades they wish on a
market. While the administrative procedure—or means—can be an end in itself, it is not
the same end as consumers' sovereignty. Consumers' sovereignty can exist without
freedom of choice, as where a central authority produces and distributes commodities
to the population on the basis of what he has discovered their tastes to be (by
questionnaires, etc.). Also, freedom of choice can exist without consumers'
sovereignty, as where the central authority decides on the basis of arbitrary reasons
not related to what it thinks consumers want what should be produced and then
allows this to be distributed by means of the market choice of the population, setting
relative prices so as to make all consumer markets clear. Thus, the Pareto optimality of
pure competition is a reflection not of consumers' sovereignty alone but of its
conjunction with freedom of choice. Consumers' sovereignty has an intimate link with
the Pareto criterion only by supplementing it with the value judgement that it be
realized through freedom of choice.

The second recent emphasis which weakens the association with the Pareto
criterion is that pure competition is Pareto optimal only if there are no external
effects. If external effects are present, pure competition is suboptimal (except through
"errors" being canceled out by extreme coincidence). Many economists, including
myself, believe external effects to be in fact widespread and important. If we are
correct, then to treat free competitive trade as most fully realizing consumers'
sovereignty is tantamount to employing a criterion which is inconsistent with Pareto

optimality. Thus, the Pareto criterion has no natural appositeness to consumers' sovereignty either in terms of logical implication or of the historically broader connotations of the latter concept.

I conclude that consumers' sovereignty does not logically imply a criterion restricted adequately to be at all useful. It is incomplete. To make it more complete requires deciding on a more precise treatment for aggregating tastes, thereby adding restrictions which will narrow down the family of acceptable social welfare functions. Such assumptions specify the relative compensatory effects of different individuals' tastes in welfare: they are normative judgments about distribution. Pareto optimality is one such restriction.

It has been thought that Pareto optimality is the least controversial value judgment that need be added to make the criterion useful. We know, however, that, however unexceptionable, it does not produce a complete criterion. We cannot use it to choose from within any set of nondominated situations—for example, from the Pareto optimal boundary. This is a serious limitation of scope. It is doubtful, for example, whether as many as 1 per cent of all economic changes and political acts in modern history would be evaluable under the principle. Societies have certainly been willing in the past to make changes which were not vector-dominance improvements; they give no indication of being less willing to do so in the future. Thus, the Pareto-optimum criterion could not judge the welfare impact of most of modern history and is not likely to do better in the foreseeable future.

The attempts of the New Welfare Economics to extend the scope of the Paretian criterion by means of the compensation principle involve adding still further normative assumptions. The version of the principle by which welfare judgments cannot be made unless compensation is actually paid can be interpreted either as going no whit beyond the original criterion (since it asserts that, except for equivalence, unless one outcome actually dominates another the two cannot be compared), or as recommending that the polity undertake actual compensation whenever possible so as to make more historical choices comparable. But the latter interpretation makes advocacy of the compensation principle a value judgment: the *status quo* distribution of well-being is made the normative frame of reference for welfare comparisons (whether because of an ethical content to the *status quo* or for the sheer convenience of the welfare evaluator). The version of the compensation principle whereby judgments about potential welfare can be rendered in terms of vector dominance resulting from hypothetical compensations, without actual compensation being necessary, clearly involves a value judgment supplementing Pareto optimality. This last argument, by the way, means that normative assumptions must be added to consumers' sovereignty to obtain a complete criterion—one that renders judgment in every choice situation even if one believes that the Pareto optimality criterion is actually implied by this concept. In sum, supplementing Pareto optimality with the compensation principle entails introducing additional value judgments considerably more controversial than Pareto optimality itself. If this is true of the Pareto optimality approach, the need to make controversial value judgments with other approaches can be *a fortiori* established.

The fact that consumers' sovereignty does not imply a unique complete criterion is serious. The family of functions possessing the property that the first partial derivative of social welfare with respect to every individual welfare argument is positive is very large. The leap from consumer's sovereignty to a complete criterion is accordingly substantial. The decision to use one particular function instead of another even only moderately different can make a bigger difference to social welfare evaluations than the most radical changes in the tastes of several individuals.

II. WHICH TASTES ARE RELEVANT?

The second problem in defining consumers' sovereignty as a criterion is that it is not obvious which tastes are the relevant ones to consult. Three dimensions of the problem can be distinguished: which tastes, whose tastes, and tastes for what. First, if an individual is obviously uninformed about certain kinds of commodities, are his expressed preferences the right ones to consider? Since he himself would change his preferences if he were better informed, should not his present evaluations be considered the wrong tastes—not really his—and be substituted for in the light of his "true" tastes?

How much information and experience concerning commodities is necessary to make an individual "correctly" informed? A conceivable empirical test would be to expose an individual to more and more information (experience) about the relevant consumption area so long as he keeps changing his preferences. Well-informedness would be the state of preference stability. Such a process *might* lead to a limit set of tastes.[1] But this cannot generally be expected. Accumulating exposure over time changes the individual; his expressed preferences may continue to change because his "true" tastes are changing. In these cases it is impossible in principle to distinguish "correctional" changes from "real" changes. Any judgment about well-informedness here would be a value judgment.

The second dimension involves a deeper problem. Psychologists believe in the existence of "erroneous preferences" which cannot be "corrected" by simply providing information or experience. Feeble-mindedness, psychosis, neurosis, dope addiction, immaturity, and perhaps criminality are such states where the individual wants what he does not "really" want. Does consumers' sovereignty require that individuals in these states be disenfranchised, or that an attempt be made to discover their "true preferences"? Psychiatrists claim to know what unconscious motives really impel some neurotics and psychotics; but these motives are often pathological and are unacceptable to the patients themselves. Also, the physician's concept of normality intervenes. It is felt that only when the patient is cured can his motives be said to be truly his. But while the practitioner can often understand existing unconscious complexes of motivation, he is likely to be far less capable of predicting what the person will—or would—be like when cured.

Thus, "correction" of the preferences of sick people is neither objectively straightforward nor ridiculous. Its possibilities rather depend on opinion which, given the empirical uncertainties and the emotive implications, are likely to be value-saturated. This conclusion is even stronger for children and, possibly, criminals. But what about the claim of psychologists that even most normal law-abiding adults do things they do not really want to? To be serious about sovereignty requires evaluating this claim and substituting corrected preferences in the criterion wherever it can be substantiated. Perhaps the enormity of the task and the controversiality of the objective grounds for correctly performing it would lead one to wish to confine it only to those cases where the existing distortion of tastes is substantial. But application of such a principle is likely to be at least as much value-laden as the decisions about the immature, the sick, the outlaw—and much more controversial.

The third dimension of the problem of defining relevant tastes concerns not which are the true preferences but rather what are the alternatives to which the preferences refer. This is probably the area where recent speculation differs most from the context evisaged by those who first proposed consumers' sovereignty. Welfare analysis has usually assumed that each individual's well-being, therefore his preferences, depends only on the commodities which he himself consumes. In this formulation, tastes are completely distinct from the function which joins them into a welfare criterion. But a number of economists have recently emphasized that an individual's well-being depends importantly on consumption by others as well as himself. There are three types of dependency. First, specific acts of consumption by others directly affect the individual; for example, the growing of roses by the neighbor of a man with a severe allergy. Second, the standard of living of specific other persons either angers him because of envy or pleases him because of empathy. Third, he has strong opinions about what should be the general shape of the frequency distribution about what should be the general shape of the frequency distribution of income. I have argued in the *Measurement of Social Welfare*[2] that the welfare impact on the individual of these external relations is psychologically of the same type as that of most of his own consumption, being a matter of social interaction. Thus, it seems reasonable to include them in spelling out the alternatives of choice to which tastes refer. Consumer sovereignty should concern consumer "values" rather than tastes, in Friedman's and Arrow's terms.

These external effects deserve consideration because they affect the individual's utility. Does any variable, therefore, deserve consideration if it affects utility? Individuals often have strong feelings about the kind of institutions they want to make social decisions about economic matters. Since these institutions reflect social rules or criteria for adjudicating among the various claims of the population, a concern about them can be treated as a concern about social welfare criteria. This is an external effect intimately related to attitudes about income distribution: it represents a concern about the principles which ought to govern that distribution. The allegiance to "free markets" or to "planning" is often considerably stronger than preferences about the exact composition of one's own consumption. Should these effects be included?

There is a difficulty. Suppose consumers' sovereignty is to be supplemented to construct a particular positive function of individual utility functions. Then the last inclusion would mean that these utility functions will themselves contain as an argument the set of possible functions of individual utilities that might serve as social welfare criteria, since each individual ranks not only commodity distributions but also welfare criteria. If our welfare criterion is designed to reflect tastes that include preferences about welfare criteria, our criterion should be in some sense "consistent" with these preferences. Other than unanimity, however, of what would such "consistency" consist? How could such a criterion be selected? Clearly, it would have to be selected by a "meta-decision," made outside the decision system which the criterion is to adjudicate. Consumer sovereignty should be defined on that level, too, but its definition will be subject to many of the same complexities we have met on the lower decision level. The criterion chosen to adjudicate on the two levels need not have the same structure. Indeed, it is not obvious how such a higher choice of criteria is to be made at all unless, by successive regression to higher and higher levels, unanimity is finally reached.

The analysis suggests that preferences about welfare criteria be excluded after all as arguments of the individual utility functions on our original decision level. But then perhaps general attitudes toward income distribution should also be excluded, since they are so initimately related to preferences about welfare criteria. Do such attitudes have relevance for resource allocation independently of their relevance for the choice of welfare criteria? If so, how could such independent influence be partitioned to the appropriate decision levels? I cannot answer these questions. Indeed, here too I am not even sure of the epistemological status of the answer. My conclusion is tentatively to suggest, as before, that controversial value judgments are probably involved. Consumers' sovereignty here too can only be defined by recourse to complex and controversial normative assumptions.

A final complication on this dimension. We have just questioned the inclusion of "impartial" judgments about the consumption of others on methodological grounds. What about "partial" judgments? If individual A begrudges high income to individual B because he dislikes B or is simply envious, does this have the same ethical status as his allergic complaint over B's roses? Personal experience suggests that many persons would wish to separate the two ethically. Some complaints about others' behavior seem justifiable, others do not. On what criterion should such a distinction rest: real versus unreal injury (or benefit)? The person feels just as "really" injured through envy as through asthma. Yet an outsider would often want to say that the first type of complaint, but not the second, is justified because it is just none of his business. Perhaps the implied desideratum is that individual A cannot help himself in regard to his asthma but can in regard to his envy. This too is a slender reed. Can an individual really help himself for his tastes—for his personality? The typical link in all these external effects is psychological, not physical. Again, any criterion in this area will be largely a normative one.

To summarize this section, we have indicated that consumers' sovereignty does not make clear exactly which structures of individual tastes are to be consulted, or which individuals, or even what are the appropriate types of alternatives to which these tastes are to refer. Each area involves thorny problems whose resolution requires making controversial normative assumptions. Consumers' sovereignty, even if unqualifiedly accepted, must be a variable patchwork of value judgments; it will therefore mean different things to different people.

III. ENDOGENOUS CHANGES IN COMMODITIES

The above complexities affect the ethical persuasiveness of consumers' sovereignty as we shall see, but indirectly. Now we shall consider problems which have a more direct effect. Up to now, tastes—however finally specified—have been implicitly held to furnish a criterion external to and autonomous of the situations being evaluated. Moreover, the conceivable alternatives of choice have been assumed to be clearly delineated. The resulting evaluational process has an "integrity" which is important to its attractiveness. I suggest that in fact both of these assumptions are at variance with the real world.

The problems stem from the economy's use of substantial resources deliberately to change products and consumer tastes. Product development and advertising, as representative of these uses, employ considerable resources which have been increasing both absolutely and as a percentage of total output in the postwar period.

Product development affects our criterion in two ways: first, through an impact on the set of feasible output alternatives; second, through an effect on tastes. We postpone consideration of the latter to the next section. The first has the effect of making less clear how the criterion can be used to evaluate the efficiency of resource allocation. If all commodities remain unchanged over time, the alternatives of choice are simply different output combinations of the given commodities. Efficiency can be evaluated by the criterion through traditional welfare analysis. Suppose, now, given known modifications can be produced in these commodities by specified known modifications of resource use. Call this the modification model. It is not now enough to compare all the different possible output combinations of the single pattern of product modifications chosen at a given time. One must be able to compare the whole set of different feasible product modifications. This still can be done in principle—by applying our criterion to traditional analysis—since each investment for modification is specific and its outcome is specific in terms of the modification achieved and its estimated effect on demand. Besides, external effects will be minimal since we have assumed that all modifications depend on known processes and not on the results of possible unforeseen developments elsewhere.

Let us now, however, admit true innovations. Call this the innovation model. Unlike predictable modifications, innovations typically result from unpredictable outcomes of investment policies. One commits resources to try to bring about a particular product change or develop new products without knowing beforehand what will occur. The cost and benefit categories of traditional analysis apply here, but with an important distinction: costs are for the project as a whole (justified by its expected returns) while the benefits are for the unpredictable successful outcomes only. In addition, innovations typically carry substantial external effects in production and consumption—also largely unpredictable. These properties substantially complicate the problem of comparing the desirability of all possible ways of using resources, both for producing commodities under existing technology and for changing that technology in various ways. To appeal to "expected values" for comparability of different projects is hampered by the lack of grounds for ascribing probabilities and pay-offs except in a small minority of possible investment directions, since most possible innovating directions have probably never been tried. The attempt to bypass this by confining comparisons to the actual outcome of a particular pattern of innovating investment on one hand and either a no-innovation situation or one with some alternative investment pattern calculated in terms of expected outcome on the other, would be extremely misleading.

The trouble is that the existence of investments for innovation makes unclear just what is the set of alternative feasible outcomes. This trouble affects the intergrity of many welfare criteria. But it especially affects consumers' sovereignty because, when applied to a free market system, performance is typically evaluated not directly by examining individual utilities but indirectly by looking at the degree of competitiveness of the system and the special provisions introduced in areas where external effects are significant. It is assumed that the market makes all feasible outcomes implicitly open to consumer choice and the degree of competitiveness determines the responsiveness of the market to these choices. The argument of this section is that the link between the resource implications of what the consumers think the alternatives are and those of what the producers think the alternatives are, becomes very loose. It becomes more hazardous to assume that actual market choices strictly "reveal" relevant preferences.

IV. ENDOGENOUS CHANGES IN TASTES

What causes most trouble is endogenous changes in tastes. Consider the most extreme case first. There is only one firm. It uses part of its resources to produce some output without considering consumers' tastes. Then it uses the remaining part successfully to persuade the consumers that this output is exactly what they want. Are consumers sovereign here when their tastes change accommodatingly to output, not because of some inner dynamic of personality, but at the influence of resources deliberately used by the producer to gain acceptance of his output? It is not taste changes per se, accommodating or otherwise, that damage the normative integrity of consumers' sovereignty. It is endogenous taste changes—changes induced by producer investments designed to effect just such changes.

Few would insist that the consumer in this case is sovereign in any useful sense. The real world diverges from this, however, in a variety of pertinent ways. First, persuasiveness is not invariably effective. While consumers can be easily persuaded to some things, it is much more difficult or impossible (within the relevant range of persuasive techniques) to persuade them to others. Second, the degree of persuasiveness is a function of the resources used for persuasion. Greater persuasiveness requires using more resources. Third, there exist many producers, whose combined persuasive efforts to some extent cancel, or to some extent complement, one another. Fourth, some portion of these efforts consists largely in giving information or making available a new product. In the former, their effect is to "correct" tastes. In the latter, they induce tastes to be realigned with a new set of consumption opportunities.

Given the incidence of attempted persuasion in the real world, how much damage is done to our criterion? The answer depands partly on how strongly tastes are actually influenced by producers' persuasive efforts. That we should expect to find some such influence is indicated by the large and increasing expenditures on product development and advertising. Most economists agree that advertising can shift market shares for different brands within a given commodity class. But this may not seriously damage consumers' sovereignty. In an opulent society with thousands of types of commodities available, preference changes among bands of a single type of commodity may have only trivial effects on individual welfare. The billions of dollars of annual resources spent to accomplish such changes may not so much discredit the welfare criterion as suggest considerable waste in terms of that criterion.

Are important taste changes brought about by producer persuasion? Product development *in toto* has radically changed some patterns of consumption. But much of this stems from the information content of substantial changes in consumption possibilities brought about by innovation. A large part of "informational" advertising is linked to such major product advances. For these the dominant effect on tastes is "correction," not change. Other product development, however, represents only slight modification and is amenable to linkage with the kind of persuasive differentiation which is believed to be the mainstream of modern advertising. For this highly persuasive area of development and advertising taste change is the battlefield—whether a firm's aim is to prevent already-attached customers from detaching or induce otherwise attached customers to become attached. There is no definitive evidence available as to the importance of changes here.[3] One may speculate; but it is easy to exaggerate in this area. Advertising is not the only, nor even the strongest, influence on tastes. Personality core, social role identifications, social mobility, and informal interpersonal relationships are important determinants. One should not expect advertising to do very radical things. Of course, some of the indirect effects of advertising—on market structure, technological changes—may have stronger influence on over-all consumption patterns.

While advertising is probably not accountable for drastic changes, it is reckless to assume only trivial impact. The complex of product development and advertising has produced more of the economy's atomistic product differentiation as well as the larger configurational swings known as fashion. Consumption has changed variously and frequently under their flailing. Critics and advocates of advertising alike claim that advertising changes tastes. To the extent that they are true, these claims damage the acceptability of consumers' sovereignty.

One attempt to salvage consumers' sovereignty, despite the presence of endogenous persuasion, emphasizes that the consumer is not passive but selective under the buffetings of the persuasive assaults aimed at him. Advertisers propose—and often in contradictory fashion—but the consumer disposes. Besides, when he allows himself to be persuaded it is because he is improving his tastes, not simply changing them.[4] Thus advertising is not at all destructive of consumers' sovereignty. Instead of making consumers less discriminating it makes them more so.

In evaluating this it is helpful to link some types of product development with advertising. Atomistic product differentiation probably does show instances of improved consumer discrimination, largely in areas where the desire for variety is important. In many other instances even in these areas, though, the differentiation is illusory, adding nothing to the consumers' sensorium. The fact that a consumer is pleased when he consumes a persuasively advertised brand does not imply that he would not be just as pleased if he were to consume other brands. Differentiation associated with fashion, on the other hand, is likely to boast far less development of tastes. Individuals here are not chiefly interested in variety but in social distinction.[5] Fashion leaders cast off the old and set the new fashions chiefly as a competitive search for prestige and status by appearing distinctive rather than because of taste elevation or need for variety. The content of new fashions is chosen to prevent easy emulation, not to display improvement of wants. This is especially clear where fashion content changes cyclically, the styles of, say, ten years ago reappearing as the latest. Fashion behavior of style followers has much the same competitive motivation. Prestige here is obtained by emulating the leaders, conforming rather than seeking variety.

Thus, correctional effects do not seem to bulk large enough to mitigate much of the damage to consumers' sovereignty. Ironically, in fact, the occurrence of any such effects raises a new question which may weaken the criterion from a different direction.

To say that tastes are "improved" implies there exists a criterion which can judge between better and worse tastes. To be consistent with consumers' sovereignty this criterion would have to be part of the consumers' own evaluative apparatus. It thus would enable them to criticise their own and possibly others' present preferences. This would raise more urgently the question whether present revealed tastes are the appropriate representatives for what the consumers want to want. But here the problem itself becomes fuzzy. Should "improvements" be envisaged as simply broadly defined corrections within stable tastes, in which case the criticism would not be criticism of tastes but only of uninformedness; or should they be considered true taste changes? Any appearance of taste criticism from within the tissue of consumer sovereignty strikes at the foundation of the doctrine that tastes shall be the final arbiter, not subject to scrutiny.

The discussion suggests a further problem, possibly the most basic of all. Why are an individual's tastes deemed worthy of serving as a criterion of his welfare? In an earlier era his tastes could be thought to be a unique representation of what was indissolubly his. The membrane distinguishing the individual from his environmrnt was deemed solid. Social science in the last thirty years has changed this view. Tastes, even personality itself, are now seen made and unmade by the social nexus. The bounding membrane is alarmingly porous. The tastes of an individual—even if we depreciate the effect of advertising—are not nearly so heroically his. They, and he himself, are "only" a relatively stable structure of organized interchanges with a social environment.

V. IMPLICATIONS AND PREJUDICES

As welfare criterion, consumers' sovereignty is incomplete, highly ambiguous, and lacks independence. In order to apply it with precision, a variety of decisions must be made which are extremely complicated and at least partly normative. These conclusions modify the attractiveness of the criterion for me.

If consumers knew more, knew better, were cured, were not as guillible, they would regret many of their present choices. So the preferences they reveal on the market are "wrong" in many respects. To give them what they "truly want, they would have to be diagnosed by authorized experts and prescribed for through a monopolization of persuasive information. The ability to accomplish this with any degree of accuracy depends on the capacities of the social sciences. It is far from clear that many individuals would entrust such a burden to the social sciences at anything like their current stage of underdevelopment.

The undesirability of the prospect stems from more than its questionable feasibility, however, As so conceived, consumers' sovereignty is antipathetic to freedom of choice. The presumed alienation of consumers' choices from their own true tastes makes it unlikely that sovereignty could be efficiently implemented by free choice. Central authoritative prescription and co-ordinated "correct" distribution is more efficient than a multiplicity of conflicting pleas for attention and idiosyncratic partly erroneous choices. Thus, one may have to choose between consumers' sovereignty and freedom of choice, or at least have to express the rate at which one would be willing to sacrifice degrees of attainment of one for the other.

Freedom of choice entails accepting the voluntary choices of consumers on whatever markets exist. Since freedom exists in degrees and is related to the range of alternatives available to choice, it will be largely illusory if the market has no responsiveness to consumer choices. A totalitarian state can reduce free choice to a triviality by presenting only a narrow and biased range of alternatives. Besides, it can resort to monopolized persuasion to change consumers' choices. Freedom of choice, no less than consumers' sovereignty, must bear up under analysis.

Yet our argument up to now lends attractiveness to it. Consumers' choices may not reflect their true tastes; but we have suggested that maybe these tastes cannot accurately be known; or that they are not really "owned" but only "loaned" tastes anyway, passed on from one person to another. What really can belong to the self and be accurately known is the experience of making and taking responsibility for choices, whether right or wrong, and seeking to know by this continuing dialogue across the permeable boundary of the self what if anything is worth preserving. It is possible that this quest, given any reasonable degree of responsiveness in the outside world, is what consumers want more than being given what they are told they really want. I suggest that when the doctrine of consumers' sovereignty was first presented, perhaps inadvertently attached to freedom of choice, an important part of its appeal rested really with freedom of choice. If forced to choose between them, our present visit may cause one to pause before automatically picking consumers' sovereignty. Might one not even actually prefer freedom of choice—the right to be often wrong, always wheedled and imperfectly hearkened to? It may be easier to hear the still small voice under the babble of TV hawkers than over the public address system.

REFERENCES

1. Indeed, I myself have argued that it sometimes would. "Welfare Comparisons and Changes in Tastes," *A.E.R.*, Dec., 1953, pp. 885-89.

2. Prentice-Hall, 1961, Chap 2.
3. My own attempt to rectify this lack led to a highly inconclusive empirical study.
4. Harry G. Johnson, "The Political Economy of Opulence" (unpublished paper).
5. This analysis owes much to Dwight E. Robinson, "The Economics of Fashion Demand," *Q.J.E.*, Aug., 1961, pp. 376-98.

6

Has
the Consumer
Really Lost
His Sovereignty?

G. William Trivoli

The author rejects the contention that the loss in consumer sovereignty can be attributed solely to the efforts of producers to create wants that never before existed.

John Kenneth Galbraith has eloquently stated in *The New Industrial State* [7], and other places, that the consumer has lost his sovereignty. Embarrassing? Yes, quite, for economists, anyway. This contention, if true, strikes at the very heart of the science of economics, which is based upon rational choice by a free and discerning consumer. This contention has obvious important implications for all the other social sciences as well. For, if true, all the study of man's behavior is irrelevant. What should be studied, then, are the institutions molding his wants, especially the large corporation.

According to Galbraith, so that the giant corporation may effectively plan its output it must be free from the whims of consumer sovereignty. This is supposed to be achieved by the corporation managing consumer demand largely through advertising and other subtle selling techniques.

This paper reviews briefly the theoretical arguments involved in the contention that consumers' wants are controlled by producers. An important implication is that if large firms are able to manipulate consumers' product desires, then most new products introduced by large firms should be successful. A further implication is that there

Reprinted from *Akron Business and Economic Review*, vol. 1, no. 4 (Winter 1970), pp. 33-39. Reprinted by permission.

should be a positive relationship between advertising and product acceptance by consumers.

Galbraith develops what he calls the "revised sequence" meaning that, instead of catering to the consumer's wishes, large firms attempt to eliminate uncertainties of the market by managing consumer demand. In Galbraith's own words:

> The mature corporation has readily at hand the means . . . for managing what the consumer buys at the prices which it controls. This control and management is required by its planning. [7]

Galbraith sees advertising in particular and salesmanship in general as the major methods by which the corporate behemoths manipulate consumers' wants. In fact, he seems to equate these tasks with controlling the consumer when he states "Advertising and salesmanship—the management of consumer demand—are vital for planning in the industrial system." [7]

This argument by Galbraith has been popular in one form or another for quite some time, not only in economics, but also in sociology and psychology. There has been a growing literature that has posited that advertisers are able to manipulate consumers. Recent developments in the science of psychology, and the publicity given some of its more sensational applications, such as subliminal advertising or brainwashing, have strengthened this belief [2]. Galbraith's argument thus falls upon receptive ears when he maintains that giant firms are now in a position to organize their research and marketing in such a way that they can impose upon the consumer the products they make. Yet, the hard evidence on this particular argument of the industrial system hypothesis is difficult to find.

The underlying theory of Galbraith's revised sequence is dealt with in greater detail in *The Affluent Society* [6] under the name of the dependence effect. Galbraith asserts that the marginal increments in consumer satisfaction from added production are low and declining. As the wealth of a society increases, the importance of economic goals is somehow lessened and private production consequently becomes less important.

The key contention of Galbraith's argument is that if the individual's wants are to be urgent they must be original with the individual. They cannot be urgent, he feels, if they must be contrived. Above all, wants must not be contrived by the process of production by which wants are satisfied. Thus, Galbraith maintains

> One cannot defend production as satisfying wants if that production creates the wants . . . . If production creates the wants, it seeks to satisfy, or if the wants emerge pari passu with the production, then the urgency of the wants can no longer be used to defend the urgency of production. Production only fills a void that it has itself created. [6]

Galbraith asserts that those wants of man that remain unsatisfied in modern society would not be experienced spontaneously by the individual if left to himself, leading to the conclusion that wants are increasingly created by the process by which they are satisfied.

Following the criticism of Friedrich Hayek [9], the revised sequence or dependence effect is found to be a non sequitur. Galbraith asserts that most consumer wants in a modern society would not be experienced by the individual in a primitive society; these acquired or learned wants, which are supposed to be generated by the producers themselves, are represented as not urgent and therefore unimportant. The first part of Galbraith's argument is probably true; that is, one would not desire any of the amenities of civilization if others in the economy did not provide them. The innate human wants are probably confined to a very few things such as food, shelter and sex [9]. The desire for food, for instance, may be satisfied crudely and simply or lavishly. Galbraith apparently would prefer that people choose the simpler satisfactions.

"To say a desire is not important," states Professor Hayek, "because it is not innate, is to say that the whole cultural achievement of man is not important." [9] In some contexts, Hayek states, it perhaps would be legitimate to say production generates wants. This clearly would not justify the contention that particular producers can determine the wants of individual consumers. The joint but uncorrelated efforts of producers create but a single element in the environment by which wants of consumers are shaped [9]. However, no producer can in any real sense determine the individual wants or desires of consumers. Yet this is the implication of such statements by Galbraith that wants are "both passively and deliberately the fruits of the process by which they are satisfied." [6]

Galbraith views the process of the revised sequence first from the production side, with the corporate form of business enterprise as an instrument for the accumulation of capital, the practical application of technical progress and the planning of future output. Next he views the consumption side, with the affluent consumer, whose standard of living is already above that which may be related to basic needs for food, clothing and shelter and is being raised continuously higher through the creation of new and more demanding wants. The link between the two sides, and the institutional manifestation of want creation driving the system to greater heights of production and consumption, is advertising [10].

GALBRAITH ON ADVERTISING

Galbraith's position on advertising may be interpreted as maintaining that advertising changes consumers' tastes. An opposing view is that consumers' changed behavior can be attributed not to a change in tastes but rather to a widened knowledge of choices available for the better satisfaction of wants [3]. Aligned with Galbraith are numerous sociologists and several economists, including Robin Marris. Although Marris claims that his theory places less emphasis on the effects of advertising as such, he still maintains that he sees

> ... the process by which consumer tastes develop as a complicated interaction of personal influence (meaning the influence of consumers on other consumers),
> greatly helped at critical points by advertising and marketing efforts generally. [12]

The contention raised by Galbraith is that, increasingly, the wants satisfied by additional production are themselves created by the production process itself; thus, the satisfaction of these wants cannot be regarded as a true increase in satisfaction. Harry G. Johnson has pointed out that Galbraith's contention, if correct, strikes at the heart of liberal economics, which is posited on the independence of consumer wants [10]. Galbraith is raising the fundamental question of the validity of economics science itself in both its positive and normative aspects.

For discussion, the above contention is separable into two parts: first, the observation that the growth of affluence is characterized by the creation and satisfaction of new wants by means of social and commercial pressures on consumers and second, the judgment that the wants so created are valueless or even contemptible.

The notion that progress essentially involves the creation of new wants is not new to economic literature. Alfred Marshall was drawing on a long tradition of economic thought when, in introducing his analysis of demand, he stated

> Speaking broadly therefore, although it is man's wants in the earliest stages of his development that give rise to his activities, yet afterwards each new step upwards is to be regarded as the development of new activities giving rise to new wants, rather than of new wants giving rise to new activities. [13]

Marshall fully recognized the desire for distinction as an influence on wants; thus he stressed the desire for excellence as a stronger motive than the inborn basic wants. Furthermore, Marshall left no doubt of his belief that the trend of wants was upward and not simply sideways.

To maintain a hierarchy of wants is to argue that changes in taste are governed ultimately by accepted standards of good and better taste, standards which are capable of being learned and applied by a consumer. The consumer learns standards of taste and applies them in response to both his own maximizing behavior and influences of fellow-consumers (the "Joneses"), advertising and the entire socio-economic environment [10]. It is toward influencing these standards as well as informing that advertising and marketing in general must ultimately appeal. Harry G. Johnson, in a discussion of this question of definable standards for recognizing improvements in the consumption function, states

> The notion of standards for recognizing improvements in the consumption function is admittedly much more hazy and imprecise than the notion of standards for recognizing improvements in the production function; nevertheless, their existence is I think, undeniable. [10]

Neil H. Borden, in a study of a number of products conducted to determine the economic effects of advertising, concluded that the basic trends of demand for products are determined mainly by underlying social and environmental conditions rather than by advertising [5]. In addition to demonstrating the inability of advertising alone to shape consumer demand, Borden found (1) that advertising is profitably used only when product demand in a particular area is comparatively new and hence demand is expandable and, conversely, (2) for certain products advertising over a period of years has tended to make new products more responsive to price competition [5].

To illustrate the first finding, Borden discusses dentifrices as a product for which advertising plays an important part in determining consumer values. Yet, following the Civil War there was a tremendous public education program to augment the basic desire for attractiveness in promoting awareness of the relationship of the teeth to health and the importance of care of the teeth in preventing oral ills. Borden concludes that although advertising was an important factor in stimulating the practice of brushing teeth, it had no appreciable effect on per capita consumption during the postwar decade; nor was advertising able to stem a marked decline in consumption during the Great Depression [5].

As an illustration of the second point, Borden cites the case of mechanical refrigerators as an example of a product whose elasticity of demand was increased by advertising and aggressive selling. The increased interest generated by advertising helped build public acceptance; thus the product became more responsive to lowered prices and price competition. Other products he mentions as having become more responsive to price competition as a result of advertising are automobiles, radios, oil burners and numerous electrical appliances.

An important distinction must be made regarding the meaning of the term "create." Whether the firm is considered to create the consumer demand, or respond to it, depends on the interpretation of the word create. Maurice Zinkin, in a discussion of Galbraith and consumer sovereignty, states that if, by create

> . . . one means produce a demand which was not there before in that form, then firms, big and small, very often do create demands. One could not want the latest style of the hairdresser round the corner before he had conceived it . . . . In that limited sense, the demand for any invention is a creation of its inventor . . . if it is implied that the new want is "created" in the sense of being artificial, then this is normally not true. The new want is nearly always an old want but satisfied in a new way. [16]

Galbraith would choose the latter definition; thus he sees giant producers somehow creating artificial wants, wants that would not be present if the consumer were left to his innate wants for food, shelter and clothing. This is brought out most clearly in Galbraith's famous quote:

> The fact that wants can be synthesized by advertising, catalyzed by salesmanship, and shaped by the discreet manipulation of the persuaders shows they are not very urgent. A man who is hungry need never be told of his need for food. [6]

The fact that consumers may occasionally be persuaded to spend some of their income unwisely, at least from Galbraith's point of view, does not prove that the dollars spent in this manner yield negative or zero utility. One may regard unwise expenditures as misguided effort, but it would not deny consumers sovereignty [9].

Galbraith, it seems, is confused by the fact that consumers willingly allow the manufacturer to take the risks of predicting their future demand and producing the commodities that possibly will satisfy that demand. Frank Knight reaches the core of the problem in his discussion of the uncertainty problem in economics. Knight points out that two elements of uncertainty are introduced in the process of production of goods over time, corresponding to two different kinds of foresight that must be exercised:

> First, the end of productive operations must be estimated from the beginning. It is . . . impossible to tell accurately when entering upon productive activity what will be its results in physical terms, what (a) quantities and (b) qualities of goods will result . . . . Second, the wants which the goods are to satisfy are also, of course, in the future to the same extent, and their prediction involves uncertainty in the same way. The producer, then, must *estimate* (1) the future demand which he is striving to satisfy and (2) the future results of his operations in attempting to satisfy that demand. [11]

The consumer is rationally and intelligently shifting these uncertainties of production and prediction of his future wants. The consumer willingly allows the producer to take the risks of choosing and estimating future consumer wants, but the consumer maintains his veto power if the resulting product in some manner fails to meet his tastes. In short, the important aspect neglected by Galbraith is the informational role advertising plays in a modern mass consumption economy. Thus, even the Soviets have discovered that production of vast amounts of goods and services requires huge amounts of information for factories to operate with efficiency and flexibility. George Stigler points out that

> Advertising plays a large role in providing this information, but Mr. Galbraith implies that most advertising is nonrational in method and persuasive in purpose. And he offers no support for this implicit measurement beyond caustic remarks on an evening at home with television.[15]

THE EMPIRICAL EVIDENCE OF THE SUCCESS OF NEW PRODUCTS

It is Galbraith's contention that failure of a new product introduced by a large firm is a rarity, thus establishing his supposition that corporations are able to control consumer wants. If it can be shown that new product failures are not a rare occurrence but instead quite common, the argument becomes suspect. An empirical test of new product success is suggested by Stephen A. Greyser, a leading authority in the field of marketing. He suggests

> New product introductions particularly represent a "test" of fit with consumers' wants. New product failures are very high; percentage estimates vary from 80% to 30% failures. [8]

Galbraith as much as concedes that such a test of his hypothesis may be proper when he states, regarding the failure of the Edsel, "Its notoriety owes much to its being exceptional." [7] His hypothesis concerning the ability of large corporations to control consumers' demand seems to imply the following: (1) new products of large corporations should not fail; in fact, most new products would be expected to succeed and (2) since advertising is the major device by which consumers' demand is manipulated, those who spend the most on advertising should have greatest success.

In a summary of extensive research and experience in the introduction of new products, Booz, Allen & Hamilton discusses the significant body of information on new product success gathered in over 800 client assignments conducted over the past several years. In addition, their management research department has made confidential studies of new product activities of 200 firms noted for their product development programs. The two basic conclusions of their experience are as follows:

> *Most manufacturers cannot live without new products.* It is commonplace for major companies to have 50% or more of current sales in products new in the past 10 years. In the next three years alone, about 75% of the nation's growth in sales volume can be expected to come from new products . . . .
>
> *Most new products are failures.* Even among the most important and effective United States companies, 1964 research shows that for about every three products emerging from research and development departments as technical successes, there is an average of only one commercial success. [4]

Management judgment in the new product development process meets its final test at the last state—commercialization. At that point, the firm must pronounce its product worthy and introduce it at great expense. Despite the lengthy screening process, analysis, development and testing, the ratio of successful to unsuccessful new products for prominent companies is two to one.

The failure rate of new products varies surprisingly little among the industries studied by Booz, Allen & Hamilton. There is, however, great variation in failure rates among individual firms, apparently as a reflection of differences in management effectiveness. The average product performance rate for several industries is shown in Table 1. The actual success rate for new product ideas for all industry groups studied was 1.7 percent. Successes for products once they reached the product development stage, which is turning the design into a product-in-hand, for all industry groups was 14.5 percent. Finally, the success of products actually introduced in the market (commercialization stage) rose to 62.5 percent for all industry groups studied, which is still only slightly better than half of all products marketed by leading corporations.

TABLE 1

RATE OF COMMERCIAL SUCCESS

	New product ideas	Product development projects	New products introduced
		Success percentages	
All industry groups	1.7	14.5	62.5
Chemical	2	18	59
Consumer packaged goods	2	11	63
Electrical machinery	1	13	63
Metal fabricators	3	11	71
Non-electrical machinery	2	21	59
Raw material processors	5	14	59

Source: Booz, Allen & Hamilton, *Management of New Products, 1968.*

Jules Backman reports a study made of the experiences of the 125 companies which were the largest advertisers in terms of dollars in 1964 and in 1965 [1]: *Advertising Age* published a list of 125 companies with the largest dollar expenditures for advertising, and, as part of this tabulation, the domestic sales for these companies and their expenditures as a percentage of these sales were reported. Profit data were available for 111 companies in 1965 and 114 in 1964. The advertising-to-sales ratios for these firms were related to their return on invested capital by Backman in order to determine to what extent more intensive advertising was accompanied by larger rates of profits. The average return on net assets for the 102 manufacturing companies included in this study was 14.7 percent in 1965 as compared with 13.8 percent for 2,298 leading manufacturers reported by the First National City Bank of New York. Even if the entire difference in profit returns were attributable to the effects of advertising, the most that could be said is that manufacturing companies with large dollar advertising expenditures reported profits that were 0.9 percent higher than the average of leading manufacturing companies. The relationship for 1964 gave the heavy advertisers a one percent margin over the average for leading manufacturers reported by the First National City Bank of New York. Backman concludes from this study that " . . . companies with large dollar expenditures for advertising have not earned much more on invested capital than leading manufacturing corporations generally."[1]

In the general range of manufactured goods, it is possible to find numerous cases of failures of products introduced by firms that Galbraith would consider large mature corporations. In an article describing several new product failures, Burt Schorr referred to studies of overall product performance. He mentions a study by Lippincott and Margulies, a New York industrial design firm, which indicates that of every 26 products introduced by industry, 23 fail. Also, McCann-Erickson, Inc., a large advertising agency, reported that of every 25 products test marketed, only one succeeds [14]. Some notable market failures discussed by Schorr in a survey of new product introductions by large firms include the following:

The Predicta line of television sets of advanced design was introduced in 1959 by Philco Corporation. Philco had exceeded development and retooling budgets by 25 percent as well as sponsored an extensive promotion and advertising campaign. Profits on the new Predicta line were negligible; it was regarded as a clear failure.

The Bristol-Myers Company introduced a new product called Analoze, a combination pain killer and antacid. The failure of Analoze indicates not only that a large producer was unable to shape consumers' wants, but in addition extensive consumer research could not even predict what the consumer wanted. The executives who conceived of the product were impressed by the fact that Americans were consuming record amounts of aspirin; thus they felt a combination analgesic and antacid that could be taken without water would have a ready market. Backed by heavy advertising outlays, Analoze moved into test markets: dealers were enthusiastic and prospects appeared bright. Then the sales figures indicated that, despite all the careful preparations, the public was buying only small quantities of the new product. After weeks of test marketing, Bristol-Myers finally withdrew Analoze [14].

Schorr goes on to list failures of such giants as General Mills, Inc. (a meringue mix in the fall of 1958) and General Foods (a line of gourmet foods that included imported biscuits and Swedish lingonberries) and, finally, to the failure of a heavily advertised cigarette by a leading cigarette manufacturer, the American Tobacco Company. The failure of American's Hit Parade cigarettes is significant since the cigarette manufacturers are regarded as the nation's most extensive advertisers. In his discussion about the American Tobacco Company's first entry in the filter tip cigarette market Burt Schorr states

According to a survey conducted by Brown & Williamson Tobacco Co., a competitor, American poured $40 million into Hit Parade advertising and promotion during the three years following the introduction of the cigarette in late 1956. While American labels this estimate "much too high," it's known the company paid over $17 million for air time and publication space alone during those three years.[14]

CONCLUDING REMARKS

The basic error of Galbraith and others in asserting the loss of consumer sovereignty is the assumption that producers somehow create wants that never before existed. The assumption is not warranted on the basis of existing evidence. One might legitimately question on normative grounds whether man should satisfy his wants in ever more affluent and ostentatious ways, but that man himself chooses, in a free market economy, from among a multitude of means to satisfy his wants is undeniable.

REFERENCES

1. Jules Backman, *Advertising and Competition*. New York 1967.
2. Raymond A. Bauer, "Limits of Persuasion." *Harvard Business Review*. XXXVI No. 5 (1958).
3. Robert L. Bishop, "Monopolistic Competition and Welfare Economics" in Robert E. Kuenne, ed., *Monopolistic Competition Theory: Studies in Impact*. New York 1967.
4. Booz, Allen & Hamilton, Management Consultants, *Management of New Products*. 1968.
5. Neil H. Borden, *Advertising in Our Economy*. Chicago 1945.
6. J. K. Galbraith, *The Affluent Society*. Boston 1958.
7. J. K. Galbraith, *The New Industrial State*. Boston 1967.
8. Stephen A. Greyser, Assistant Professor, Harvard University Graduate School of Business Administration, letter dated June 25, 1968.
9. Friedrich A. Hayek, "The Non Sequitur of the Dependence Effect." *Southern Economic Journal*. April 1961.
10. Harry G. Johnson, "The Consumer and Madison Avenue" in Lee E. Preston, ed., *Social Issues in Marketing: Readings for Analysis*. Glenview 1968.
11. Frank H. Knight, *Risk, Uncertainty and Profit*. New York 1965.
12. Robin Marris, "Galbraith, Solow, and the Truth about Corporations." *The Public Interest*. Spring 1968.
13. Alfred Marshall, *Principles of Economics*, 8th ed. New York 1948.
14. Burt Schorr, "Many New Products Fizzle Despite Careful Planning, Publicity." *Contemporary American Marketing: Readings on the Changing Market Structure*. Homewood 1962.
15. George Stigler, "Galbraith's New Book: A Few Problems." *Wall Street Journal*. June 26, 1967.
16. Maurice Zinkin, "Galbraith and Consumer Sovereignty." *Journal of Industrial Economics*. XV No. 1 (1967).

7

The
Muckraking
Era

Ralph M. Gaedeke

The consumer protection movement is not new, although
the extent of its fervor and the source of its strength may
be. The author points out that the early efforts at consumer
protection (some federal consumer protection legislation is
a century old) did not enjoy today's favor and were
generally branded as muckraking.

The movement for consumer protection began to crystallize as early as the late
nineteenth century. This was reflected in the formation of various local and regional
consumer groups,[1] in muckraking, and by concerted federal legislation.

In 1872, the first consumer protection law was passed, making it a federal crime to
defraud through the use of mails. The law revised, consolidated and amended the
statutes relating to the Post Office Department. Section 149 of the 1872 Act stated:

> It shall not be lawful to convey by mail, nor to deposit in a postoffice to be sent by
> mail, any letters or circulars concerning illegal lotteries, so-called gift concerts, or
> other similar enterprises offering prizes, or concerning schemes devised and in-
> tended to deceive and defraud the public for the purpose of obtaining money under
> false pretenses, and a penalty of not more than five hundred dollars nor less than
> one hundred dollars, with cost of prosecution, is hereby imposed upon conviction,
> in any federal court of the violation of this section.[2]

Adapted from: Ralph M. Gaedeke, *Consumerism in the 1960's: A Study of the Development of,
Underlying Reasons for, and Business Reaction to Today's Consumer Protection Movement*
(University of Washington Press, 1969), and Ralph M. Gaedeke, "The Movement for Consumer
Protection: A Century of Mixed Accomplishments," *University of Washington Business Review*,
vol. 29, no. 3 (Spring 1970), pp. 31-40. Reprinted by permission.

In 1883 the importation of unwholesome tea was prohibited, and in 1890 an act was passed preventing the importation of adulterated food and drink. These and certain other federal consumer protection laws were, however, merely piecemeal legislation establishing limited and superficial protection against impurities in foods, and were not aimed at the broad issues of general government regulation of the quality of products sold.

Between 1879 and 1905, more than 100 bills were introduced in Congress to regulate interstate production and sale of foods and drugs. But the Congress and public were largely apathetic, business opposition was strong, and no action was taken on any of the proposed measures.

Exposes of business corruption and avarice—e.g., muckraking—finally marked a substantive turning point in the movement for consumer protection. With Upton Sinclair's publication, THE JUNGLE,[3] Congress was at last jarred to action. The book focused on conditions in the Chicago meat packing industry which made the need for consumer protection apparent. It helped assure passage of the Food and Drug Act of 1906 which provided for "preventing the manufacture, sale, or transportation of adulterated or misbranded or poisonous or deleterious foods, drugs, medicines, and liquors, and for regulating traffic therein."[4]

Passage of the Food and Drug Act of 1906 was a substantial victory for consumers. It showed that consumer interests finally counted, at least in politics, and it "did a great deal to dissolve the old nineteenth-century American habit of viewing political issues solely from the standpoint of the producer."[5] It also demonstrated that the era of muckraking made the public and Congress more conscious of the need for consumer protection. Finally, it served as a stimulus for the formation of numerous private committees, clubs, and leagues which were organized to push for further protection of the consumer.

While these victories were indeed great achievements at the time, they were largely failures when viewed from a longer perspective. They were failures because the wave of strong pro-consumer public sentiment rapidly abated after 1906 and, with it, the political interest in consumer protection. Passage of the Act also failed to change the negative and indifferent posture of the business community toward consumer protection. *Caveat emptor* was very much the rule of the day.

In the years preceding and following World War I, consumer organizations[6] became largely concerned with sanitary conditions in food stores and retail prices which were considered excessive. Informal boycotts were arranged against merchants while housewives' leagues sold eggs (and later apples) at prices below those prevailing in retail stores. These activities, which were sporadic and confined to few cities—notably Chicago and Philadelphia—were generally inconsequential, having no measurable impact on retail prices.

The Food and Drug Act itself proved to have a number of serious weaknesses. It failed to eliminate practices which made the legislation necessary because the Act did not authorize inspection of food-processing plants. In addition, the Act was merely piecemeal legislation since it exempted foods sold under proprietary names and the sale of cosmetics and therapeutic devices, as well as the advertising thereof. The effectiveness of the Act was further weakened because it was administered by a small staff which had difficulty in obtaining convictions. Weaknesses inherent in the law provided, on the other hand, new exposes for consumer crusaders.

A new drive for consumer protection began to develop in the late 1920's and early 1930's with the publication of several popular books on the abuses of advertising and the sale of adulterated products. When Stuart Chase and F. J. Schlink published *Your Money's Worth* in 1927, it became an immediate best-seller.[7] It pictured the consumer as an "Alice in Wonderland" of conflicting product claims and bright promises and pleaded for impartial product-testing agencies.

Your Money's Worth was the first publication since *The Jungle* to arouse the public once again. This and subsequent protest literature helped crystallize a vaguely felt but widespread discontent among consumers, and succeeded in acquainting the public with the need for more protection than was provided by the Food and Drug Act of 1906. A period thus emerged which saw the rise of an articulate consumer consciousness, generally labeled as the "consumer movement."[8]

REFERENCES

1. The first national Consumers League was organized in 1899. See Helen Sorenson, THE CONSUMER MOVEMENT (New York: Harper and Brothers, 1941), p. 6.
2. George F. Sanger, editor, *The Statutes at Large and Proclamations of the United States of America*, from March 1871 to March 1873, and Treaties and Postal Conventions, Vol. XVII (Boston: Little, Brown and Company, 1872), p. 302.
3. Upton Sinclair, THE JUNGLE (New York: Doubleday, Page and Company, 1906), p. 345.
4. Gustavus A. Weber, *The Food, Drug and Insecticide Administration–Its History, Activities and Organization*, Service Monographs of the United States Government, No. 50 (Baltimore: The John Hopkins Press, 1928), p. 14.
5. Richard Hofstadter, THE AGE OF REFORM (New York: Random House, 1955), p. 172.
6. The American Home Economics Association was formed in 1908 and *Good Housekeeping* established its certification service in 1912. See, "What About the Consumer Movement?" *Advertising Age*, Vol. II, No. 2 (January 8, 1940), p. 25.
7. Stuart Chase and F. J. Schlink, *Your Money's Worth* (New York: The Macmillan Company, 1927). See also Arthur Kallet and F. J. Schlink, *100,000,000 Guinea Pigs* (New York: Grosset and Dunlap, 1933); M. C. Phillips, *Skin Deep–The Truth About Beauty Aids, Safe and Harmful* (New York: The Vanguard Press,1934); and Ruth de Forest Lamb, *American Chamber of Horrors–The Truth About Food and Drugs* (New York: Farrar and Rinehart, 1936).
8. One writer suggested that the consumer movement was in reality "a series of efforts having in common the feeling of dissatisfaction with goods and services and the marketing practices involved in their distribution." See Kenneth Dameron, "The Consumer Movement," *Harvard Business Review*, XVII (Spring 1939), pp. 276-277.

8
The Consumer Movement

Kenneth Dameron

This comprehensive analysis of the early history and the economic implications of the consumer movement was written over thirty years ago—long before there was widespread concern for and legislation on behalf of consumers' interests.

The "consumer movement" may be described as the organizations, activities, and attitudes of consumers[1] in their relation to the distribution of goods and services. It gives new emphasis to the consumer's right to full and correct information on prices, on quality of commodity, and on costs and efficiency of distribution. The movement displays the efforts of consumers themselves. Aware of their ignorance in buying, skeptical of the guardianship of private business, and doubtful as to whether or not they are getting their money's worth, they have become articulate. It is not a concerted movement; in reality it is a series of efforts having in common the feeling of dissatisfaction with goods and services and the marketing practices involved in their distribution. Coupled with this protest is a demand for information and for protection in the market.

The direction of the movement is not necessarily toward consumer cooperation. The history, objectives, and ideals of the cooperative movement are different from those of the consumer movement. The cooperative movement may perform a safety valve function to the extent that unless private distribution can meet the critical demands of consumers, they (the consumers) will turn to cooperative-owned distri-

Reprinted from *Harvard Business Review,* vol. 18, no. 3 (January 1939), pp. 271-289. Reprinted by permission.

butive organizations. This reflects a different attitude from those persons who, influenced by the ideal of cooperation, find in the cooperative movement the end in itself.

One of the chief objectives of the consumer movement is the demand for information—information concerning the qualities of goods, price, conditions of production and sale, use of goods—emphasizing the fact that the consumer is no longer content to know just where the goods may be secured and how much they cost. Consumers want lower prices and quality merchandise commensurate with the price they pay. To make certain of the attainment of these ends, they are turning to government protection and taking an active part in legislation designed to protect them and to promote the elimination of unfair business practices. They are also substituting collective action for individual action. Collective action has been common among labor and capital groups. It has never before had any sustained use by consumers.

One wing of the consumer movement is opposed to capitalism and the profit motive. Anything that discredits business is a gain for their viewpoint. They seize upon false advertising and similar practices to foster fear and suspicion in the minds of consumers.

THE ECONOMIC IMPLICATIONS OF THE CONSUMER MOVEMENT

The consumer movement is a product of economic evolution. It is an aspect of the transition from a producer's economy to a consumer's economy; from an economy of scarcity to one of plenty; and, with certain limitations, from a seller's market to a buyer's market. These changes have tended to make consumers more critical and to enhance their importance, notwithstanding the fact that much of our formal economic literature is fabricated around the producer viewpoint.

Our early economic problem was "how to get goods." Adam Smith pictured consumption as the goal of economic activities and labor as irksome exertion undergone for the sake of getting goods to consume. This view of economic behavior is a common one to many present-day economists. It suggests that economic theory should rest upon an analysis of consumption. Following Smith, most economists, after stating the importance of consumption, proceed to develop the major part of their work around production.

That economics is born of its own time and place is further exemplified by tests of some of the commonly accepted assumptions of our economic society. Amoung these assumptions are: the consumer guides production; consumption is the end and purpose of production; competition is an adequate safeguard of the consumer; retailers and other businessmen protect consumers; consumers are rational and awake and alive to their own interests.

In modern society, production for the most part, it is claimed, is guided by the choices of consumers. Does this mean that consumers have complete freedom of choice? Do they know enough about commodities to make intelligent selections? Or is it not true that industry is engaged not alone in making goods but in devising ways and means of manipulating consumers' demands? No doubt in the broadest sense of the term, consumers' choice guides production in that an industry cannot continue if consumers do not want the product or if the industry is unsuccessful in its attempts to make them want it.

> Paradoxically, the consumer has never been so free to choose as he is today and at the same time so little free, so completely bound as he is upon the wheel of an administered market and a commercially controlled standard of living. The consumer is free to take or leave under a system in which "free competition" is becoming increasingly unreal.[2]

Also, the consumer's choice is greatly handicapped by the fact that he knows so little about the products he uses that he is unable to make an intelligent choice. Furthermore, the economic processes have limited the consumer's relation with production until now he meets it only at the point of final or ultimate sale. As stated by Walton H. Hamilton: "The consumer must find a substitute for the direct action of the market place." The breakdown of market price as a protection to the consumer is accompanied by a lack of confidence on the part of the consumer.

Within certain limits, consumers do force changes in production. Students of fashion tell us that people become "bored" with a prevailing style and welcome a change despite the fact that the article in question is by no means worn out. Many of the changes originating with the producer are not what the consumer wants, and consumers find difficulty in gaining an audience with the manufacturer. The General Motors Customer Research Department is an example of the attempt of business to bridge this gap. Nevertheless, the introduction of the annual or seasonal model, induced by the dictum of progressive obsolescence, reflects the force of business competition and a commercially controlled standard of consumer buying.

It is true that "consumption should be the end and purpose of production" and that over a period of time only those articles which have consumer acceptance, and have stood the test of competitive salability, will be produced.

Under the present scheme, competition safeguards the consumer to the limited extent of giving him a choice between lower and higher prices. Those price differences mean little unless quality is defined. Consumers have made the mistake of identifying better quality with higher prices falling right in line with the sellers' claim that "you get just what you pay for." Again, one of the objectives of the consumer movement is to secure information which will reveal differences in quality and differences in prices. Some retailers are as ignorant as consumers of the essential qualities of many of the goods they sell. The consumer movement seeks to overcome this condition by asking for information at the point of sale. Many advertising assertions are confusing substitutes for facts.

It has been assumed that consumers are rational and awake and alive to their own interests. A man's desires can be developed so they will greatly overshadow his needs. Advertising and selling techniques have among their objectives the creation of a value in the mind of the consumer. Advertising men speak of a rationalized appeal as one giving an acceptable "reason" for an action, when the action really springs from an unacceptable cause.

As early as 1912, Wesley C. Mitchell gave an interesting analysis of the backward art of consumer spending[3] and the consumers' inability to make intelligent choices. In this article, Mitchell discusses consumer ignorance in spending, how the organization of family life contributes to inefficient and ineffective spending practices, and suggestions for improvement in spending.

In the scheme of modern life, making money and spending money are strictly correlative arts. Of the two, spending is rated as pleasanter and easier to practice. Certainly, for most of us it is not less important. A few, indeed, make so much money that they can slight the art of spending without suffering discomfort, but the vast majority would gain as much from wiser spending as from increased earning.

Many consumers scarcely know what becomes of their money, though well-schooled citizens of a money economy ought to plan for their outgoes no less carefully than for their incomes.

As a unit for consuming goods, the family has remained substantially as under simpler economic organizations, with the burden of household responsibilities resting with women.

A housewife can compare costs so long as they consist solely in the money prices she is charged for goods. She cannot make a precise comparison between the price of ready-to-wear frock and the price of the materials plus her work making it. She cannot make objective comparisons between the various gratifications which she may secure for $10.

In fine, spending money cannot conceivably be reduced to such a system as making money until someone invents a common denominator for money costs, and for all the different kinds and degrees of subjective gratifications which money can procure for people of unlike temperaments.

"The desire for distinction is one end which women do seek in spending," says Mitchell. "The Money Economy forms in us the habit of extravagant expenditure for the unacknowledged purpose of impressing both ourselves and our neighbors with an adequate sense of our standing." (This desire for distinction in spending was pointed out by Nassau Senior and developed by Thorstein Veblen.)

THE DEVELOPMENT OF THE CONSUMER MOVEMENT

Slichter states that most spending of money in modern economic society is done in spare moments by amateurs.

The consumer often doesn't know his or her own desires with sufficient definiteness to describe them to another person. Frequently he doesn't know what his wishes are until he has seen them for sale. . . . And finally . . . to most persons under most circumstances, spending money is itself a pleasure.[4]

The ignorance of the consumer makes it possible for him to be deceived as to quality, quantity, price, weight, measure, name, size, and any other factors involved in buying.

It remained for writers in the "protest" group to popularize and dramatize the weakness of the consumer in buying and to give impetus to the modern consumer movement. For at least a decade books of this type have been read by millions of consumers. One of the most influential of this group of books was *Your Money's Worth* by Stuart Chase and F. J. Schlink, published in 1927. In this book, the consumer is pictured as an Alice in a Wonderland "of conflicting claims, bright promises, fancy packages, soaring words, and almost impenetrable ignorance." In place of facts about the merchandise, the consumer was showered with meaningless phrases and victimized by the manipulation of demand through the channels of advertising, salesmanship, and sales promotion.

Paralleling in point of time the "protest" literature were books on the economics of consumption.[5] These books followed no set pattern. Some emphasized theories of consumption; others discussed practical problems of consumer buying, as for example, budgeting, commodity standards, administration of personal income, etc.[6] Another of these books (Nystrom) showed the dominance of the consumer and presented the other side of the argument developed in *Your Money's Worth.*

Concurrently, students in marketing and advertising exhibited an interest in the economics of these subjects. Their analyses revealed a critical viewpoint. They attacked the costs of distribution, the ethics of advertising, and similar problems which were offering opportunity for popular presentation by the "protest" writers.

In general, university courses in marketing and advertising do not neglect the viewpoint of the consumer. In some universities students of home economics are required to take these courses. The influence of this educational factor has been effective in creating an attitude which makes possible the growth of the consumer movement. The importance of fundamental educational factors must not be minimized in appraising the consumer movement.

Consumer Education

The consumer may be educated in a number of ways. She may receive formal training in schools and colleges; she may receive information from salespeople, through advertisements, government bulletins, and rating and advisory services. However, the more formal education of the consumer in high schools and colleges has been a formidable factor in the rise of the consumer movement.

Home economics courses are no longer the old-fashioned cooking and sewing courses. Emphasis is given to the term "Management"—household management—with the result that students gain a practical view of merchandise and an objective basis for criticizing retail stores, the goods they sell, and the services they offer. Through laboratory work, these courses instill the industrial purchasing agent viewpoint in consumer-buying. This results in a definite interest in quality and performance specifications and informative labels.

According to a survey of courses in consumer problems[7] in colleges and secondary schools by the Curriculum Laboratory of the Ohio State University, the college courses emphasize the following topics:

Government aid to consumer

Price

Distribution of wealth and income

Household accounting, budgeting

Standard of living

Consumers' education

Buying in general

Selling methods of retailer

Banking, saving, and investing

Problem of consumer

Consumption and culture

The secondary school courses emphasize:

Drugs and cosmetics

Banking, saving, and investing

Government aid to consumer

Clothing

Electrical appliances

Consumers' sources of information

Advertising

Household accounting, budgeting

Insurance

Standards, grading, informative labeling, and specification

The study of consumers' goods occurs most frequently in secondary school courses. This means that these courses are most likely to be practical and of permanent value. The college courses are organized around general purchasing subjects, such as price, advertising, and name branding. Financial problems are given about equal emphasis in college and secondary courses.

Approximately 25,000 secondary schools offer some form of consumer education to 6,557,940 pupils, of whom at least 4,000,000 are girls. Ideas gained from these courses reach the home, and, in turn, parents relay questions to the teacher or ask for tests of certain items. The specific courses embracing consumer education in the secondary schools are generally found under the following headings: consumers' goods course, domestic science, homemaking and home economics, hygiene, merchandising, sales, marketing, and advertising. It is stated that *100,000 Guinea Pigs* or some similar book is usually discussed in the hygiene courses.

In addition, a number of college courses in chemistry emphasize the study of consumers' goods, such as drugs, gasoline, soaps, and cleaning materials. The students determine the chemical nature of these commodities, the methods of adulterating them, and the hazards involved in using them. Courses in colleges of agriculture give attention to problems of grades, standards, meat buying, and other topics. Colleges of education are now setting up courses to offer teacher training in consumer economics.

A national consumer center set up at Stephens College, Columbia, Missouri, has the support of the Sloan Endowment Fund and the income from a million dollar trust. The activities of the Institute[8] fall under three main headings which may be designated as fact-organizing, fact-finding, and fact-using. The relations between and these main branches of the work and their subsidiary parts are indicated in the accompanying chart.

GENERAL ACTIVITIES

A		B		C	
Fact-finding (research)		*Fact-organizing (study)*		*Fact-using (education)*	
(1)	(2)	(1)	(2)	(1)	(2)
Economic research relating to consumer problems	Educational research contributing to the diffusion of consumer knowledge	Collecting and arranging material by library staff	Analysis and interpretation of material by economics staff	For Stephens College students	For other consumers

(a)	(b)	(c)
High school students	College students	Adults

The adult education programs of colleges and universities, extension programs, and radio courses have directed considerable effort toward the education of consumers.

Groups of consumers (women's clubs and similar organizations) are developing forums and conferences for the education of the consumer. Among the topics discussed in recent conferences of this type were: price legislation and the consumer; retailer and consumer relations; grading and labeling; advertising, the press, and the consumer; the manufacturers' place in the consumer movement; the radio and consumer education; what the consumer should expect of fabrics.

Women's organizations have supplied stimulus to the consumer movement, furnished leadership and direction, and provided local units for educational purposes. They are a potential "pressure" group whose action should prove highly effective. The household buying problems of the depression and the NRA provided these groups with tangible objectives

Consumer Guides and Commodity Rating Services

Consumer guides and commodity rating services[9] form an important part of the consumer movement. Indeed, to some they are the consumer movement. These services endeavor to inform the consumer in such a manner as to be of specific aid in buying. Underneath the objectives of some of them, one gains an impression of opposition to the capitalistic competitive system. Most certainly in some cases there is an anti-advertising bias.

In general, these consumer organizations perform one or more of the following services:

1. Test merchandise, give ratings, and advise consumers.

2. Aid in consumer education through performance of above service, plus preparation and distribution of materials to be used in consumer education programs.

3. Promote buying by grade and specification.

4. Lend support and lobby for legislation favorable to the consumer.

5. Provide films for use in consumer education.

6. In addition to commodity ratings, one service looks into conditions of production. If wage and hour conditions of production are not right, the product does not receive approval.

7. Another organization not only advises consumers what to buy, but serves as middlemen and supplies the item.

8. Some organizations perform a consumer news function; i.e., give news of consumer activities and suggest ways and means of improving the status of consumers.

9. The sale of books by members of the staff seems to be an important function of one of these organizations.

It is difficult to estimate the influence of these organizations. One estimate states that 100,000 families (1/3 of 1% of American consumers) have availed themselves of these services. However, Consumers Research alone is reported to have a membership of 60,000. The sphere of influence extends beyond membership, since members may loan reports to neighbors or discuss the contents of reports with other people.

We only guess to what extent subscribers to these services actually rely upon their guidance in making purchases. In shopping for a car, stove, or other durable consumers' goods, the salesman refers frequently to the status of his product in the eyes of one of these organizations. We cannot determine what the result would be if a majority of consumers followed the advice of such bureaus. Certainly a revenue of some 30 to 50 millions in subscription fees would tend to introduce some atmosphere of commercialism, and the power to decide the fate of various brands would offer temptations to the directors. On the hand, increased revenue should result in more effective merchandise tests. Doubtless, new groups would spring up to expose the weaknesses of all that preceded them. The consumer might be more bewildered in deciding which advisor to trust than in deciding which manufacturer or retailer or brand to trust.[10]

These guides and rating services have helped to educate the consumer to buy more rationally. They have contributed toward making advertising and selling more informative. They have accelerated the spread of the consumer movement. Through these services, consumers are given an organization which serves as a third-party influence in forcing a better consumer relations policy on private business. Their influence has been great in proportion to their numbers, as they have for members many school teachers and ministers who have some direction of public thinking. Their materials are used by consumer study groups as well as in schools and colleges. (It is not to be assumed that advertising and other information activities of provate business should have the right of way.)

These guides and rating services are by no means a solution to the consumer's problem. To rate all available merchandise in every commodity field would require reports of encyclopedic size. It has been necessary for them to revise their ratings, and they have found that their weighting of the various qualities an article may possess did not coincide with that of some of the consumers they advised. The ratings of commodities cannot possibly recognize the psychic and subjective valuations of consumers.

Government Protection and the Consumer Movement

The present Federal administration has acted on the assumption that in our highly industrialized society the consumer is in need of organized protection. This protection has taken two basic forms: (1) the furnishing of information, and (2) the establishment of certain legal privileges and prohibitions. It involves nothing new in kind, but in part because of the depression it has been accompanied by a new emphasis.

The Democratic party platform of 1936 states:

> We will act to secure to the consumer fair value, honest sales, and decreased spread between the price he pays and the price the producer receives

This new emphasis is a departure from the traditional postulate of government that inasmuch as consumption depends on industry, the government can best help the consumer by helping business. Invariably under this plan the businessman would gain, but wages would not keep pace with increasing retail prices. The New Deal government has not reversed this tendency, but it has taken active interest in consumers as such.

There are today a number of government bureaus[11] studying consumer problems and serving the interests of consumers. In general, these government divisions: (1) aid consumers in making prudent and economical purchases; (2) stimulate interest in the problems of consumers; (3) review public policy in so far as it relates to the consumer; (4) suggest ways and means to promote larger and more economical production of useful goods; (5) improve standard of living; (6) aid in planning household expenditures; (7) give information concerning the use and care of consumers' goods.

The government organizations furnishing consumer information have grown in numbers and activity during the New Deal Administration. Provision has also been made to give consumers representation in matters affecting them.[12]

Consumer representation gained recognition during early days of the New Deal through the Consumers' Counsel of AAA; the Consumers' Advisory Board of NRA, and the Consumers' Division of the National Emergency Council. More recently, the Bituminous Coal Act of 1937 provides for a Consumers' Council to appear in the interests of the consuming public in a proceeding before the Bituminous Coal Commission.

NRA's Consumers' Advisory Board had responsibility to "see that nothing is done to impair the interests of those whose daily living may be affected by these agreements." This board was at no time in a position "to see that nothing is done," as its powers were primarily advisory.

These consumer boards represented particular classes of consumers for particular codes. They are significant because they reflect government interest in the consumers and their problems. Codes dealing with retailing and the trade practice sections of consumers' goods codes were of most direct interest to the consumer movement.

The consumer division under NRA was relatively ineffective because of inability to present the case for the consumer, lack of facts, and a personnel which was either uninformed or of the sort called to Washington to serve for very short periods of time.

The *Consumers' Guide,* a publication of the Consumer's Council of the Agricultural Adjustment Administration, has stimulated great interest in the consumer movement. This publication contains articles and data designed to aid consumers both in understanding changes in prices and costs of food and farm commodities and in making wise and economical purchases, and moreover to acquaint consumers with efforts being made by individuals and groups of consumers to obtain the greatest possible value for their expenditures. A number of the articles published in the *Consumers' Guide* urge legislation for grade labeling. This publication has also given information and encouragement to cooperatives.

The New Deal Administration has been responsible for certain enactments which coincide with the objectives of the consumer movement. The consumer protection afforded by the Wheeler-Lea Act and the new Food and Drug Act is more definite and capable of swift and tangible results.

The Wheeler-Lea Act extends the powers of the Commission in three directions: First, it directs the Federal Trade Commission to prevent business practices injurious to consumers as well as those damaging to business competitors. Second, it makes cease and desist orders of the Commission more effective. Third, it gives the Commission specific powers to prevent false advertising[13] of foods, cosmetics, and healing devices.

The President's signature on the new Food and Drug Act enables the Administration to make use at once of some of its emergency provisions. Power is conferred to deal immediately with drugs which are dangerous to health when taken in accordance with the instructions on labels, with new drugs which have not been adequately tested for safety, and with cosmetics which may be harmful. A nefarious traffic is thus already under restraint.

Because it is more positive than the former law, it should have a salutary effect in raising the quality of foods, drugs, and cosmetics.

More effective control is now provided for poisonous or deleterious ingredients in food. No longer will it be possible to sell food which contains a "natural" poison. Especially stringent are the paragraphs that permit direct action when contaminated food causes outbreaks of disease.

Under this law it is impossible to sell a jam as a composition of pure fruit and sugar, small amounts of fruit acid, and pectin. Similarly, labels must indicate the contents of proprietary foods.

The government plays an important part in the formulation of standards of quality and in the promotion of the use of labels. The consumer movement in its demands for information and protection gives impetus to these activities of government.

Finally, there is the possibility of a Federal department headed by a cabinet officer with responsibilities on behalf of the consumer. This would doubtless have the effect of coordinating and consolidating the numerous government agencies interested in consumer problems. Some have argued for a separate consumer department. Others have argued for a consumer division under the Department of Agriculture or Commerce. The Reorganization of Government Act H.R. 4425, if passed, would enable the President to submit a plan whereby consumer activities could be consolidated under one head or division. A unified section would give attention to the establishment of grades and consumer information. It would provide a channel for consumer representation and advice in matters of legislation and procedure in which consumer interest is involved.

State Government and the Protection of Consumers

Federal legislation on consumer protection relates to interstate commerce. A number of state governments have legislative enactments designed to protect and inform the consumer.[14] (Consumer lobbies have been active in both Federal and state legislative bodies.) Several states including New York and New Jersey have established consumer information divisions. At least 16 other states have under consideration the formulation of similar divisions. The main purpose of these divisions is to inform consumers on the market supplies and prices of farm products, as well as on how to distinguish quality in such products.

Michigan has a Consumers' Bureau under the State Department of Agriculture, which was established January 3, 1938, by Executive Order of the Governor with the cooperation of the Commissioner of Agriculture. The bureau is the outgrowth of a four-year experimental program of the Wayne County Consumers' Council. The purpose of the Consumers' Bureau is to help the consumer buy intelligently and thereby to increase the value of his dollar. "It will gather and make available to the consumer factual information which will be helpful to him in achieving this end." This bureau seeks to bring together and make useful the services offered to the consumer by the state and Federal governments. The bureau encourages informative advertising, quality standards, and informative grade labeling.

Thirty-eight states have laws on their books which at least frown upon false advertising. Twenty-four states have truth in advertising laws modeled after Printers' Ink Statute, but only one, Wisconsin, has established a legal agency to enforce the law.

The State of Maine has a cosmetic law which provides for the refusal of registration to any product containing what are believed to be injurious ingredients. Some cosmetics bought freely elsewhere cannot be purchased in Maine. Louisiana has a law designed to keep some types of false and misleading advertising out of the state. North Dakota maintains a testing laboratory for certain consumers' goods and makes its findings available to the public. It sets up minimum standards for gasoline and requires paints and varnishes to be labeled to show their constituents.

All important cities have some regulations of their own. The commodity most generally supervised is milk, although standards set up for it vary greatly. Some cities have regulations as to the quality of butter, cheese, and ice cream which can be sold in their markets. Seattle and Schenectady lead in setting up special provisions for the quality of meat. Most cities have regulations for the cleanliness of markets.

Other Factors Contributing to the Development of the Consumer Movement

The depression played a threefold part. With household budgets reduced, it became imperative that household consumers secure their money's worth. That naturally caused a greater activity in the spread of information and formed a ready opening wedge for consumer organizations. The housewife also became more interested in local store prices and qualities of merchandise offered for sale. Business, in turn, was intensely competitive. It was increasingly difficult to maintain volume. A result of this intensified competition was an orgy of sales promotion and advertising which tended to shake the confidence of consumers. Special sales, contests, and extravagant claims created a situation of distrust. Quality standards were lowered—so much so, in fact, that the National Retail Dry Goods Association sponsored a drive for quality known as the Quality Movement. The very restrictions of consumer budgets tended to create irritations and dissatisfactions with merchandise distribution, and as has been indicated, depression augmented governmental interest in the consumer.

Certain psychological factors have exerted influence on consumer movements. The fear complex has been capitalized by some advertisers in copy stressing social disapproval because of odors, teeth, baldness, and a number of other personal flaws. The excessive use of the fear "appeal," which gives one the impression that America is a nation of gossips, has helped make it possible for the anti-advertising movement to "sell" to consumers the high social cost of advertising. The consumer movement is also marked by a rise of the consumer ego—a feeling of importance and of power on the part of the consumer.

It is estimated that about 10,750,000 women are gainfully employed, and of this number about 3,000,000 are married. These women are acquainted with the methods of business. Their economic viewpoint is changed by this experience. They want their money's worth. They have acquired more of a purchasing-agent viewpoint.

Several publications[15] maintain testing bureaus and one at least offers a seal of approval. The Crowell Publications have set up a Consumer Division to carry on research, educational, and consumer information services. In commenting on the organizations such as the Good Housekeeping Institute, Elizabeth Ellis Hoyt maintains:

> Relatively little protection is afforded to consumers by organizations such as Good Housekeeping Institute, which has one aim, the furtherance of advertising carried by the magazine. These organizations tell us that a certain product lives up to its claims, but they do not tell us how important these claims are or how good the product is compared to its competitors.[16]

Nevertheless, the consumer activities of publications have given impetus to consumer interest in the merchandising and advertising of goods and services and have called attention to the desirability of some agency of certification[17] and approval.

CONSUMERS' GOODS STANDARDS—INFORMATIVE LABELS

The development of commodity standards[18] and the use of labels[19] are devices whereby the consumer may gain protection in the market and secure information essential to intelligent buying. These are among the aims of the consumer movement. Consumers are especially interested in the standardization of measurement, characteristic, or performance of goods. When one considers the variety of goods stocked by a single department of the average store, the task of determining standards seems almost hopeless. However, there are certain key factors, such as color, permanence, shrinkage, etc., which affect whole lines and afford convenience to the customer. Furthermore, the effectiveness of grade and informative labels[20] must rest in many instances on the determination of standards. Specifications and standards at the present time mean little to the untutored consumer. Their meaning and importance must be amplified through labels, advertising, and personal selling.

Consumers have made definite demand for labels and especially informative labels. Stores sensing the value of the informative label in selling have demonstrated effective interest in informative labels. The label, within the limits of its kind and purpose, informs and protects the consumer. What should appear on it depends on the product. Consumers desire label information, giving washing and cleaning instructions, material content, size, special care, grade or quality, directions for use, construction or workmanship, measurement, guarantee, sensible warnings, as for example "not washable." Consumer surveys indicate interest in informative labels on dresses, aprons and house dresses, sweaters, corsets, linens and domestics, upholstered furniture, shoes, furs, cosmetics, women's neckwear, electric appliances, men's clothing, furniture (other than upholstered), luggage, floor coverings, pots and pans, garters and suspenders, kitchen tools and accessories, and canned foods.

Opinions differ as to the probable success of standardization and the use of labels. Hotchkiss[21] observes that "it is much easier to sell consumers the idea of government-standardized commodities than the goods themselves...." Consumers are, no doubt, in need of more education as to the significance of grades and standards. The Department of Agriculture in Canada has under way an advertising campaign to make consumers quality-grade conscious. The slogan is "Buy by grade—Buy with confidence."

It has also been contended that the consumer is *not* and never will be very much interested in buying to specifications. She is interested in buying satisfactions. Buying by specification should be the function of the retailer, and he must be held responsible for selecting the most desirable goods from those available.

It is also argued that the fixing of formulae for quality which would straight-jacket manufacturers and retailers would "freeze" quality standards.

There has been less argument against informative labels. Some retailers contend they are not significant in consumer buying and that they confuse the customer. Manufacturers claim that some stores remove the labels before placing the merchandise in stock. These viewpoints and actions fail to evaluate the present-day importance of consumer education and the economic factors inherent in the consumer movement.

RETAIL COOPERATION

The direct contact between consumers and retailers causes retailing to be the cutting edge of many of the demands of the consumer movement. The consumer movement asks of retailing quality merchandise at reasonable prices, commodity and price information, and protection from unfair trade practices.

Retailing is one of the most "consumer-minded" of all business activities. Individual store policies have been built around ideals of consumer satisfaction. The "customer is always right" slogan has formed the basis of many of these policies. For at least fifteen years, retailers, through their trade association activities, have asked for the consumer viewpoint and have made numerous gestures of cooperation.

Consumer Activities of Retail Trade Associations

For some time, the National Retail Dry Goods Association has been studying specific problems resulting from the consumer movement. Recently, the association went on record as officially sponsoring a program to advance the movement for consumers' goods standards and standardized description or terminology to characterize various aspects of goods as weight, size, thread count, etc. This program involves cooperation with manufacturers and with governmental bureaus and consumer organizations. It recommends that merchandise standards be submitted for the approval of the American Standards Association, and that in cases in which legal enforcement is desirable, the Federal Trade Commission be requested to recognize standards so approved. Labeling, publicizing facts about merchandise, and establishing a standard procedure for certifying commodities were endorsed.

Retail trade associations are taking an active interest in the National Consumer-Retailer Relations Council, which is made up of retailers and consumers with representatives of government, advertising, manufacturing, better business bureaus, and others as associate members. The objects of the Council, as announced in its by-laws, are:

a. To stimulate interest on the part of consumers, distributors, manufacturers, and the general public in the value of adequate standards for consumer goods.

b. To promote the general use of such standards.

c. To promote the general use of informative labeling.

d. To promote the use of uniform terminology in describing consumer goods and services.

e. To promote truthful and informative local and national advertising of all kinds.

f. To promote informative salesmanship.

g. To develop and promote the use of suggested codes of ethics for both retailers and consumers.

h. To encourage practices which will tend to reduce abuses of such privileges as customer accounts, returns, deliveries, and similar services.

i. To foster local cooperation between stores or groups of stores and local consumer groups.

In reviewing the first year's operation of the Consumer-Retailer Relations Council, Harold W. Brightman, its chairman, stated[22] that probably the most important accomplishment of the Council was the publication, June 1, 1938, of the pamphlet on informative labeling, which has been issued to consumers, retailers, and manufacturers.

The research committee of the Council believes that its activities should be limited to the encouragement of technical research for developing standards and testing methods on consumers' goods.

Retail trade associations are active in the Advisory Committee on Ultimate Consumers Goods of the American Standards Association. Several prominent retailers are on this committee as well as representatives of consumers and government. This affords a common meeting for those interested in commodity standards.

Activities of Individual Stores

One store has a three-way consumer program designed (1) to raise the standards of merchandise, (2) to educate the sales people, and (3) to educate the consumers. To carry out this program, this store analyzes and rates all basic lines stocked and endeavors to arrive at satisfactory standards of quality for each of these lines.

Several stores have pioneered in the use of informative tags and labels. One store states that its labels and tags will tell the consumer what the product is made of, how it is made, the service it will give, and the best care for longer use. Other programs of consumer education are found in the publication and distribution of Consumer Shopping Guides and "How to Buy" pamphlets.

Since 1911 the testing laboratory has been used in retail stores. More scientific store buying, protection to the consumer, and factual advertising and selling are some of the advantages claimed for the store testing laboratory. Consumer groups criticize the retailer's laboratory efforts because but few firms reveal quality specifications to consumers. Then, too, the phrase "laboratory tested" has been so misused in advertising as to minimize the value of the more serious efforts.

In some stores, buyers were directed to request the resource to describe correctly the fabric and content of the material and to enter this description on the order. Copywriters in the advertising department were required to insist in each case that the buyers write on their requests for advertising complete information regarding the fabric, wood, metal, or any other material of which the item is made. The copy writers were "urged" to write their copy so clearly that there could be no question in the reader's mind as to just what material was in the product. They were warned not to use an asterisk to qualify a word or phrase.

There has been a marked trend toward the use of consumer advisory boards and committees and the use of the consumers' counsel within the store. The consumers' counsel serves in a manner similar to the fashion advisor, interior decorator, household management adviser, and other services.

The advisory boards or committees may be set up as permanent boards or as temporary committees to present the consumer viewpoint to retailers.

Many of the "consumer" efforts of retailers are on trial. They are in the experimental stage. Merchandise testing, informative labeling, programs of consumer-retailer education, should become permanent features in the distribution of goods. The demands of the consumer movement should result in a redirection of retail activities.

Consumers are aware of their ignorance of retail prices. They can compare prices of like brands at different stores. Advertisements contain price information; but to secure adequate price information, it is necessary for the consumer to "shop" around. Lack of knowledge of prices has contributed to the success of special sales and to the presence of price differentials between stores of the same type. However, consumers are knowingly willing to pay a higher price for the privilege of trading at certain stores. Furthermore, they do not comprehend the costs of the many services involved in retail distribution nor do they always distinguish between the prices of stores offering many services with those of stores offering but few services. Therefore, an objective of the consumer movement is to secure definite information on the cost of retailing, of the detailed elements of the retailers' markup, and on the "why" of markdowns and special sales. Finally, the price policies of manufacturers, especially as they involve controlled or fixed prices, must come under the critical review of the consumer movement.

THE NEED FOR INFORMATIVE ADVERTISING

The advertising of any period mirrors the social character of business. This character grows out of the economic situation and reflects the changing attitudes of buyers and sellers. Consumers, better educated and better organized, have increased their criticisms of the methods employed by sellers. Because of their closeness to it, advertising has been a target for consumer criticism.

Among the more common consumer criticisms of advertising are the use of exaggeration, psuedo-scientific statements, the use of misleading names or terms, misleading labels, testimonial letters, comparative prices, and such use of premiums, prizes, and contests as to confuse the consumer as to the true value of the product. It is also claimed that advertising distorts the press, radio, and movies; that it draws consumers to rely on slogans and brand names instead of an education in impartially established quality standards; advertising contributes to false scales of social values by aiding haphazard competitive activity. Trade names and trademarks are criticized because they do not identify quality differences. Thus, advertising intensifies and magnifies the growing consumer distrust of private business and, as indicated in an earlier section, provides a ready selling point for the left wing of the consumer movement. A test of the function of advertising in terms of the consumer movement is: Does the consumer buy more wisely? With advertising, can the consumer become a wise buyer? Does advertising perform the information utility?

What does the buyer need to know that advertising may supply? Advertising should supplement the consumers' information through:

1. Telling what the market provides in commodities and services, when available, where obtainable, the form, season, and comparative costs in different markets;

2. Giving characteristics of goods, comparative values in relation to use, suitability to situations, durability and cost in operation and care;

3. Indicating, where desirable, the service record of the commodities, uses of them, and methods of using them.

For this information, the consumer-buyer is dependent in a large part upon the advertising function of business. Without this help, consumers would be decidedly handicapped in satisfying their wants. Other consumer education devices do not eliminate the necessity of securing help at the time, place, and upon the occasion of making the purchase. Advertising, thereby, becomes an essential service in marketing goods. The facts which consumers want in advertising are those which they need for buying in general.

Advertising men have apparently lacked a sense of public relations in meeting the consumer movement. Here and there, of course, have appeared the efforts of individuals to meet the situation through an active interest in informative advertising and clearcut statements of the role of advertising as a business-building force. More recently, there is the effort of one association in the advertising field to set up a consumer-advertising council.

According to one advertising association official:

Advertising is not supposed to give catalogue specification data about goods for sale; it is to sell the goods, not to label them. Facts should be provided, but not necessarily in advertising.

The growing familiarity of the public with the mechanics of advertising has tended to weaken somewhat the hold of advertising on the market. Naturally, consumers read books on sales and advertising and sometimes with growing indignation—forgetting perhaps that many of these books must necessarily be written from the viewpoint of the seller.

A difficulty with many group movements is the lack of a judicious viewpoint. We have a growing group of skeptical consumers who are critical of advertising whether it is honest or not. Furthermore, they are not aware of the importance of subjective values in buying. Consumers are generally unable to see the respective roles of national and local advertising in the demand creation process. On the other hand, advertising has an opportunity to function more effectively as a consumer education device. Advertising men would do well to assume leadership in meeting this opportunity rather then to be coerced into it by social pressure.

SERVICE INDUSTRIES AND PROFESSIONS AID
CONSUMER MOVEMENT

The service industries have been active in the protection of consumers. The American Institute of Laundering conducts a testing laboratory to which manufacturers may submit products for testing quality of cloth, color fastness (including trimming, thread, and buttons), shrinkage, construction of finished product, and satisfactory longevity. The National Association of Dyers and Cleaners also conducts a testing laboratory where improved methods of cleaning are developed for its members. Because of the need for facts on the cleanability of fabrics used in ready-to-wear, regular check tests are now offered to manufacturers to determine this factor before the fabric is sold to stores.

Consumer protection is afforded to some degree through the efforts of the National Board of Fire Underwriters, which examines and tests electrical, fire protection, gas and oil, automotive, burglary protection appliances, and others for insurance companies. Its stamp, "Underwriters Laboratories Inspected," is a safeguard to consumers. The laboratory seal of approval of the American Gas Company is given to appliances which conform to certain standards.

The Council of Pharmacy and Chemistry of the American Medical Association passes on the merits of proprietary medicine and therapeutic devices, both in themselves and in respect to the claims made in their advertising. It published the names of acceptable ones in its *New and Non-official Remedies*. Unacceptable remedies are often exposed in the *Journal of the American Medicine Association* and in publications pamphlets. It passes also on advertised foods and permits the use of a seal "Passed by the Committee on Foods of the American Medical Association" on acceptable products. The American Dental Association passes on quality of dentrifrices and advertising.

The cooperative self-regulation of industry offers many protective measures of value to the consumer. Of these efforts, the work of Better Business Bureaus in approximately fifty cities is outstanding. Most bureaus are distinctly consumer-minded; and their war on frauds, educational reports, shopping investigations, development of standards of advertising, and similar activities merit the consideration and support of consumer groups.

No attempt has been made to list all business activities of interest to the objectives of the consumer movement. However, an effort is made to reveal the nature of the efforts of business in order that leaders of the consumer movement will study business in its consumer interest role.

THE CONSUMERS' RESPONSIBILITY: CONCLUSIONS

If businessmen need to "clean house," so do consumers. Unfair practices are not a prerogative of private business. Under the policy of that nervous altruism, "the customer is always right," many customers have abused retail privileges and taken unfair advantages of the seller. Return goods and "on approval" sales are notable examples of this abuse. Retailers are, of course, in part to blame for this situation; but consumers must realize that these services add to the cost of distribution and to the price they must pay. Too often, consumers buy first and shop afterwards.

The thinking of the consumers shows some immaturity because of its failure to recognize the consumer protection efforts of business. Consumers have shown a tendency to respond to bally-hoo and the criticisms of professional defenders of the consumer. Many consumers have been alert to accept statements fostering suspicion between buyer and seller, without intelligent consideration of the accuracy of these statements or complete information as to their source. The consumer's interest in merchandising is all too often stimulated by propagandists or misinformed crusaders. The education of the consumer in distribution often comes through channels not primarily interested in whether the consumer gets an unbiased point of view. The consumer must endeavor to balance impressions she gets from reading advertisements and news items about distribution, information she gets through school systems, governmental agencies, clubs, and agencies promoting their own interests with her own experiences as a customer of a retail store.

There are numerous instances in which business thought has preceded and out-distanced consumer thought. Meantime, the consumer, not discriminating in her thinking, has been inclined to ascribe progress in "distribution—consumer" relations to the work of government or some consumer agency.

There is no simple formula for the solution of the consumers' problem. However, it is believed that consumers will gain from (1) cooperation with existing business channels, (2) securing unbiased useful facts on the kind or quality of things they buy, (3) securing facts behind the price they pay, (4) continuous study of consumer buying problems, and (5) support of efforts (government and business) which aid the consumer to buy quality goods at reasonable prices. Further, consumers must recognize the subjective values of goods and the numerous and often intangible factors in the consumer buying process. These efforts must be supplemented with more complete knowledge of marketing costs.

The economic and educational aspects of the consumer movement give it permanence. Because of its numerous and at some points disconnected elements, it is difficult to make any final conclusions. The limitations of the family as a spending unit and the inherent conflict between the individual's income-receiving and income-spending interests are factors limiting the effectiveness of the consumer movement.

The family is not an efficient spending unit, and individuals tend to be more producer-minded. The housewife is more likely to be concerned with the amount of her husband's income than in making savings in the grocery or clothing bill. These factors are offset to some extent by collective action on the part of consumers and the growth of consumer education. The income-receiving interest tends to give way to consumer spending interests when it is realized that "about three-fifths of the population of the United States are consumers whose productivity as measured by current income is less than current expenditures for the satisfaction of personal wants."[23]

It is contended that the consumer is a minority movement and hence cannot exert much influence in the market. In its numerous and varied elements, this is true. However, an intelligent minority can set the pace and cause changes which will affect all consumers. These minorities are active and aggressive in educating the mass of consumers.

It is claimed that much of the consumer movement propaganda rests upon the unproved assumption that the business groups, the risk takers, and especially those engaged in selling, are less honest than other economic groups. They are not less honest, but consumers have suffered from deceptive and stupid advertising and from the retailer's lack of knowledge of the goods he offered for sale.

It seems likely that the consumer movement will be marked by a consolidation of the many interests now comprising the movement, by a willingness to work with existing business channels and aid in the redirection of their effort, by continuing and improving present educational programs, and by adequate consumer representation wherever consumer interest is affected whether in relations with business, with proposed legislation, or in the administration of laws already passed. Consumers will also give more emphasis to their demand for price and cost of distribution information and will reflect greater interest in the various types of retail institutions. Consumer efforts should also aid in the elevation and maintenance of quality standards of merchandise.

REFERENCES

1. The consumer who buys for household or personal needs without object of making money out of the use of the goods purchased.
2. Robert S. Lynd, "Democracy's Third Estate: The Consumer," *Political Science Quarterly,* December, 1936, pp. 481-515.
3. Wesley C. Mitchell, "The Backward Art of Spending," *American Economic Review,* June, 1912, p. 269.
4. Sumner H. Slichter, *Modern Economic Society.* New York: Henry Holt & Company, 1931, chap. XXII, "The Position of the Consumer," pp. 539-591.
5. Chief among these are: Elizabeth Ellis Hoyt. *The Consumption of Wealth.* New York: The Macmillan Company, 1928, and *Consumption in our Society.* New York: McGraw-Hill Book Company, Inc., 1938; Hazel Kyrk, *A Theory of Consumption.* Boston: Houghton Mifflin Company, Inc., 1928; Paul H. Nystrom, *Economic Principles of Consumption.* New York: The Ronald Press Company, 1929.
6. As early as 1923, several universities were offering courses in "The Economics of Consumption."
7. See Bulletin 42, *Survey of Twenty-Eight Courses in Consumption* by Henry Harap, Curriculum Laboratory, Ohio State University, 1935.

8. *Bulletin of Institute for Consumer Education,* Stephens College, Columbia, Missouri, April, 1938.
9. These organizations include the following: Consumers' Research, Washington, N. J., Consumers' Union, New York City; Cooperative Distributors, New York City; Inter-Mountain Consumers' Service, Denver, Colorado; National Consumers League, New York City; The National Consumers News, New York City; The Consumers' Guild of America, New York City; and others.
10. See also George B. Hotchkiss, *Guardians of the Consumer,* Boston Conference on Distribution, 1936.
11. These include the Consumers' Counsel under the authority of the Agricultural Adjustment Administration, Bureau of Home Economics, Bureau of Agricultural Economics, Bureau of the Census, Bureau of Fisheries, Bureau of Foreign and Domestic Commerce, Bureau of Labor Statistics, Bureau of Public Health Service, Federal Power Commission, Federal Trade Commission, Food and Drug Administration, Office of Vocational Education (provides material on consumer education), United States Tariff Commission, and others, The Consumers' Project of the Department of Labor came to an end on June 30, 1938. On July 1, the Works Progress Administration created a Consumer Standards Project to continue and enlarge the research done by the Consumers' Project in the field of standards for consumer goods. The lifetime of the new project is fixed at eight months.

      Within its limitations of time and personnel, the new project will "(a) assemble and analyze technical data available on the standardization of consumer goods; (b) complete and bring up to date its survey of Federal, state, and municipal commodity specifications and standards, and of laws and regulations relating to these laws; (c) prepare analyses of standards for consumer groups participating in trade practice and other conferences where questions of consumer standards are involved."
12. In Great Britain consumer representation is given in the Food Council, set up by the Prime Minister in 1925, to investigate and report to the President of the Board of Trade, in the interest of consumers or traders, on matters relating to the supply or prices of articles of food; the Consumers Committee established by the Agricultural Marketing Act, 1931, to represent the interests of consumers of products marketed under approved schemes, and to report to the minister of agriculture and fisheries on the effect on consumers of any scheme. Coal Mines Act of 1930 provided for a committee to investigate complaints made with respect to operation of any coal schemes, and to report to Board of Trade. A consumers' board with an interesting combination of advisory and plenary powers is the Irish Free State Prices Commission set up by the Control of Prices Act of 1932.
13. "The term 'false advertisement' means an advertisement, other than labeling, which is misleading in a material respect; and in determining whether any advertisement is misleading there shall be taken into account (among other things) not only representations made or suggested by statement, word, design, device, sound, or any combination thereof, but also the extent to which the advertisement fails to reveal facts material in the light of such representations or material with respect to consequences which may result from the use of the commodity to which the advertisement relates under the conditions prescribed in said advertisement, or under such conditions as are customary or usual."
14. A bill establishing a department of the consumer in New York State has been proposed. The bill is sponsored by the American Labor Party and the City Affairs Committees.

      The major activities of the department as now prosed would be as follows:

      Supervision of business practice through an organization patterned after the Federal Trade Commission.

      Representation at hearings on price-fixing legislation, chain stores, etc.

      Maintenance of statistics on living costs and consumer income as well as on wholesale and distribution costs.

      Promotion of standards in labeling.

      Removal of abuses in instalment selling.

      A testing laboratory to test branded products and to issue reports to consumers at cost.

15. *Good Housekeeping: Better Homes and Gardens; The New York Herald-Tribune.*
16. Elizabeth Ellis Hoyt, *Consumption in Our Society.* New York: McGraw-Hill Book Company, Inc., 1938, p. 117.
17. There are three methods by which goods may be certified. The first is to set up standards by law which provide for checking quality at intervals. The second is through the work of a professional agency such as the "approved" certification of the American Medical Association. The body cannot enforce the standards, but it can withdraw the use of its name. The third method is through the work of certain private agencies which maintain testing laboratories and advertise only those goods which meet their standards.
18. *Standardization of consumers' goods* refers to the setting up of a quality standard which a good as a whole must attain and/or a standardized description, a standardized terminology, to characterize various aspects of a good, as its weight, size, threadcount, etc. (Hoyt, *op. cit.,* p. 121).
19. *Label*–as defined in Federal Food and Drug Act and Federal Insecticide and Fungicide Act as "including any legend and descriptive matter or design, printed, stenciled, stamped, seared, or impressed upon the article, or its container" and alos includes circulars, pamphlets, etc., which are packed with the articles.
20. The following definitions were developed by David Moser under the direction of Dr. R. S. Alexander of Columbia University:

    Informative labeling may be described as the practice of attaching to or imprinting upon an article offered for sale to consumers, or upon packages containing units of it, written material and/or illustrations descriptive of those properties and characteristics of the article which are, or purport to be, commonly regarded as measures or evidences of its quality and its usefulness to the consumer, or a grade designation based upon accepted standards or specifications prepared with reference to such properties and characteristics. The labeling is usually done by the manufacturer or wholesale distributor, less frequently by the retailer. There are two general types of informative labeling: (1) Descriptive labeling, which is currently gaining the attention and interest of retailers, manufacturers, and food canners; and (2) Grade labeling, which certain consumer organizations and governmental bodies have sponsored for several years as a proper means of classifying canned foods, domestics, and other consumers' articles. The major present application of grade labeling is confined to agricultural products.

    Descriptive labeling may be defined as the practice of attaching to or imprinting upon an article offered for sale to consumers, or upon packages containing units of it, written material and/or illustrations indicating the presence and extent of some or all of those properties and characteristics of the article which are, or purport to be, commonly regarded as measures or evidences of its quality and its usefulness to the consumer. There is a growing tendency for the descriptive label to include recommendations concerning the use and care of the labeled article.

    Grade labeling of consumers' goods may be defined as the practice of marking merchandise offered for sale to consumers, or the packages containing such merchandise, with a designation indicating that the articles so marked fall within one of a series of quality classes defined by specifications or standards set up by government agencies, trade representatives, and/or consumers' organizations, and usually accepted by the interested parties, with reference to the various properties and characteristics of the article which have been agreed upon as elements essential to a proper appraisal of its desirability.
21. George B. Hotchkiss, *Gardians of the Consumer,* Boston Conference on Distribution, 1936.
22. See *New York Times,* August 7, 1938, Business Section, p. 8 F, "Consumer-Store Unit Finishes First Year."
23. Charles S. Wyand, *The Economics of Consumption.* New York: The Macmillan Company, 1937, p. 106.

9

Consumerism — An Interpretation

Richard H. Buskirk and James T. Rothe

Forces underlying the present upsurge in consumer activity are analyzed, and some of the dangers of the remedies proposed by some consumer advocates that heretofore have remained unexamined are considered. Implications of the consumer movement for corporate policy are discussed and definite recommendations are made on what corporations should do in the current situation.

Consumerism has received much attention in recent business literature.[1] Most articles and editorials dealing with the topic have commented on its importance, its underlying causes, its implications or what interested parties (consumer, government, firms) should do, but most discussions have failed to deal with the topic in a total sense. This article attempts to (1) determine what consumerism is, (2) reveal what has caused it, (3) study its implications and potential dangers, and (4) develop guidelines for corporate policy in dealing with consumerism.

Peter Drucker offers the following definition of consumerism: "Consumerism means that the consumer looks upon the manufacturer as somebody who is interested but who really does not know what the consumers' realities are. He regards the manufacturer as somebody who has not made the effort to find out, who does not understand the world in which the consumer lives, and who expects the consumer to be able to make distinctions which the consumer is neither willing nor able to make."[2]

Another definition of consumerism has been developed by Mrs. Virginia H. Knauer, special assistant to the President for Consumer Affairs. She stated that the watchword for the new militant mood among American consumers is simply, "Let the seller beware," in comparison to the age-old *caveat emptor* or, "Let the buyer beware."[3]

Reprinted from *Journal of Marketing*, vol. 34 (October 1970), pp. 61-65. Reprinted by permission.

Both of these definitions provide some insight into this current phenomenon referred to as *consumerism*. Perhaps it would be most relevant to relate consumerism to what has been popularly accepted as the marketing concept for the past 20 years. The marketing concept, simply stated, suggests that the purpose of a business is to provide customer satisfaction. Thus, it is anticipated that the firm will maximize long-term profitability through customer orientation. The marketing concept is primarily a post-World War II development, produced largely by economic conditions which changed a seller's market to a buyer's market. The marketing concept was hailed as being the essential fulcrum with which business resources could be allocated to best enhance profitability for the firm in a buyer's market. Consequently, much has been written and said about the marketing concept—how it can be utilized and what it means. However, the marketing concept and the forces labeled *consumerism* are incompatible. If consumerism exists, the marketing concept has not worked. It may be that consumerism actually is the result of prostitution of the marketing concept, rather than a malfunction of it.

Examples of customer dissatisfaction are not difficult to find. For example, a recent article in *The Wall Street Journal* noted that roofs leak, shirts shrink, toys maim, mowers do not mow, kites do not fly, television sets burn up, service is difficult or impossible to obtain, and warranties are not honored.[4]

Certainly each of us, as a consumer, has experienced the cumulative frustration associated with products that do not conform to expectations. It is this sense of frustration and bitterness on the part of consumers who have been promised much and have realized less, that may properly be called the driving force behind consumerism. Accordingly, consumerism is defined as *the organized efforts of consumers seeking redress, restitution and remedy for dissatisfaction they have accumulated in the acquisition of their standard of living.*

CAUSE OF CONSUMERISM

There are two major opposing theories about the role of the consumer in the market place of a free enterprise system. One theory suggests that the consumer is "king." It is his dollar choice in the market which decides success or failure of producers; consequently, the consumer plays a decisive role in the entire process. This concept is referred to as "consumer sovereignty."

A completely opposite approach suggests that the consumer is a pawn in the entire process. The brilliance of Madison Avenue, sparked by research conducted by skilled behavioral scientists, has been used to deceive the consumer to the extent that he is incapable of intelligent selection. His dollar vote does not come across in any rational manner to decide who should be producing what; consequently, the consumer is not playing a decisive role in the process.

According to the marketing concept, the first of these two theoretical approaches would be correct: the consumer is viewed as the dominant force since his purchases determine market success for competing firms.

There is some truth in both theories. This can best be explained by relating purchase behavior to the type of product purchased. When consideration is given to the importance of the product purchased, the frequency of the purchase, and the information sources used, both theories are partially correct. For example, if a product is purchased frequently, the consumer has an outstanding information source—his previous experience with it. In such a situation he is capable of judging the product's effectiveness and how well it has lived up to his expectations, both physically and psychologically. Thus, the consumer is capable of exhibiting more rational behavior when buying frequently purchased products than when acquiring "once-in-a-lifetime" items. Collective consumer behavior of this type results in the market process being served appropriately. Competition for the consumer's choice is then the determinant which leads to congruity between perceived and received quality on the part of the buyers. This is, in essence, a fulfillment of the marketing concept and accurately reflects a situation in which the consumer plays a major role in deciding who is successful in the market place.

On the other hand, the situation in which the consumer purchases a product he has not bought before (or at best, infrequently) and which is of sufficient importance, often finds his attempt at rational behavior stymied by the lack of information. Since he has not previously purchased this product, his own experience is negligible. Another possible source of information is his peer group, but the limited accuracy of this type of information reduces its role in the transaction. Also, independent concerns' ratings of products are not widely used. This leaves the consumer with a basic information source—the company's marketing program. Evidently many marketing programs are not providing the information necessary for rational purchase behavior. This may be the result of short-term orientation on the part of management whose performance is judged on an annual basis. Top management's insistence on quarterly and annual budgeting performance may force operational management to make short-run decisions detrimental to the consumer because the impact of such decisions will not be reflected during operational management's tenure in that position. Consequently, when a product revision is needed, the response may be increased advertising and promotion expenditures rather than the more appropriate effort.

CATALYSTS IN CONSUMERISM MOVEMENT

The current wave of consumerism is not unprecedented in the history of business.[5] However, this time consumerism is enhanced by several major factors which were not evident in earlier expressions of consumerism. First, increased leisure time, rising incomes, higher educational levels, and general affluence have tended to magnify and intensify the forces of consumerism. The consumer's expectations with respect to the products he purchases are founded in a quest for individuality; yet, the market provides mass-consumption products with which the individual is not completely satisfied.

Second, inflation has made purchase behavior even more difficult. Rising prices have led consumers to increased quality expectations which are not achieved; thus, again contributing to the frustration of consumers.

Third, unemployment has been low. Therefore, the marginal laborer has been employed even though he has fewer skills. Such workers reduce output quality.

Fourth, demands for product improvement have led to increased product complexity. Further, this complexity has been stimulated by the emergence of new technology. This has led to increased service difficulties as well as performance and reliability problems. Moreover, society has been thoroughly conditioned to expect perfection from its technology. Moon landings, miracle drugs, organ transplants, and jet transportation make the housewife wonder why zipper manufacturers cannot make one that will not jam. The high degree of perfection that has been reached in recent years in a few fields only serves to disguise the higher *average* level of technical proficiency of present-day manufacturing. Yet, it is apparent that the consumer is demanding better products than those presently available, regardless of the economic and technical ability of the firm to provide it.

Finally, the popular success achieved by individuals such as Ralph Nader, in his crusade for consumerism, and the political support now developing for the forces of consumerism certainly reinforce the fact that this entire area must become a more important factor in business policy.

IMPLICATIONS OF CONSUMERISM

It seems apparent that consumerism will affect industries, firms, governments, and, if it is effective, the consuming public.

The consumerism movement will develop more power as its forces become more coordinated and as it develops more leadership and organization. This will be partly manifested in legal remedies, such as class suits, that the consumer will seek.

At present, it appears the success of consumerism will depend largely on governmental involvement, the beginnings of which are already evident. For example, truth in lending, truth in packaging, product safety standards, and other recent legislative efforts, as well as a great number of consumer protection and awareness bills, indicate that the role of government will be much greater. (Over 100 "consumer protection" bills have already been introduced in the 91st Congress since January, 1969.)[6]

The role of the federal government in consumerism was first set forth by President John F. Kennedy's directive to the Consumer Advisory Council in March of 1962. He said:

> Additional legislative and administrative action is required, however, if the federal government is to meet its responsibility to consumers in the exercise of their rights. These rights include: (1) the right to safety; (2) the right to be informed; (3) the right to choose; and (4) the right to be heard.[7]

It is apparent that the right to be informed, as well as the right to be heard, is of major importance. In fact, if all consumers were informed and were heard, this would then represent the fulfillment of the marketing concept as it was initially developed. The responsibility President Kennedy mentioned above should be industry's in a free society, not the government's. However, consumerism rightly claims industry has neglected its responsibility.

The relative role the government will play, and that which industry should play, is a critical aspect in the resolution of the consumerism issue. Given industry's traditional negative or complacent reaction to such issues, the result may be a coalition of consumer and government forces versus industry, which could lead to federal standards for industry. The resulting standardization and bureaucracy may stifle the economic process. It is imperative that industry recognize the message and seriousness of the consumer movement and take positive action *now* rather than having to live with legislation that may not be in the long-run best interest of society.

The basic premise is that consumerism is primarily the result of a lack of information on the part of consumers which hinders their ability to buy certain products. This reflects itself in an ever-increasing gap between product expectations and product performance. Moreover, consumers must be heard which indicates the need for an industry or company *ombudsman.* An excellent example of the *ombudsman* concept in action is that of the Whirlpool Corporation which has established a "cool line." The "cool line" enables owners to call the customer service director at all times.[8] A direct communication contact of this nature will greatly enhance consumer-company relationships; it represents the first step toward solution of oner problems.

The owner problem is not fraudulent or deceptive practices for the most part; rather, the problem is improper or nonexistent communication. This seems to be incongruous since communication efforts—primarily advertising—exist in great abundance. However, communications between the firm and the consumer emphasize *imagery* at the expense of *information.*

Consumerism is attempting to tell industry something their research has not found, or that management has rejected or ignored. Appropriate information flow from the firm to the market in the form of product performance characteristics, simple-language warranty specifications, and safety standards will improve the basic customer-firm relationship, particularly for the infrequently purchased item where long, low service life is a major objective of the consumer. Product performance characteristics must be improved for competitive success if communication is predicated on an information basis. Thus, the poor product quality problem will be largely eliminated.

The other link in this communication structure, that of the consumer to the firm, should be explored. It is imperative that some mechanism be developed which will enable the consumer to communicate more directly with management. The consumer *does* have something to say, but management must learn to listen and translate this information into action.

FALLOUT FROM CONSUMERISM—LOCUS OF LIABILITY

While it is easy for consumers' advocates to talk about "class suits" against manufacturers, it is not completely clear how these would work. If consumers as a group were damaged by an automobile made by General Motors, then General Motors would be the defendant in the class suit, and if it lost the case there would be some hope of collecting the resulting judgment.

But let us examine several other cases. Suppose consumers are damaged by an automobile produced by a small foreign automobile manufacturer. Who would be sued if the parent corporation did not do business in the United States, but rather operated through an independent agent, a corporate front set up to absorb such liabilities?

What about situations in which the manufacturer of a product is not apparent? Suppose a sales agency imports a product made by an unknown manufacturer. The sales agent takes the product and sells it. Later, a class suit is levied against the sales agent, who has taken care to have his corporate entity contain few assets.

It would seem that if class suits became a great risk businessmen would take steps to limit their personal liability and leave successful plaintiffs with judgments against nothing. Class suits strongly discriminate against the large, reputable American manufacturers to the benefit of the fly-by-night operator who is, from a practical standpoint, beyond the reach of such judgments. It is conceivable that a successful class suit against a significant U.S. corporation could bankrupt it. Who would benefit from such a development—competitors or consumers? Is this legal situation in the consumer's best interests? It is doubtful. Clearly, the class suit must be examined closely by all parties before being used.

WHO PAYS THE PRICE?

State and federal governments now pay more than half the cost of a class suit, because the defense costs and judgments are legitimate business expenses. The remainder comes from earnings. The economic facts of life indicate that if class suits and other costs of consumerism become a fact of corporate life, then management will have to budget for such costs because those costs must be covered by the price obtained for the products the company sells. The result of imposing more stringent legal and quality control regulations on industry will be to raise prices. This should not be underestimated. Evidence from the space industry indicates that the marginal costs of increased quality are high. The consumer has been conditioned to expect perfection from technology but not to the price this perfection costs.

A valid question can be asked concerning the economic wisdom of consumerism: Is it socially wiser to accept the present market-determined rate of consumer disatisfaction than to pay the marginal costs that will be incurred in reducing consumer dissatisfaction by government decree? Is the market willing to pay for these consumer recommendations? It may not be.

Only the well-established, reputable firm that fully intends to meet its costs and obligations under consumerism would be forced to raise its prices. Again, fly-by-night operators who are beyond the reach of the law from a practical standpoint would not have to include the costs of consumerism in their prices: therefore, such operators may become competitively stronger if consumers fail to discriminate between the reputable firm and the fly-by-night operation. Further, this problem will become increasingly acute in private label situations where the producing firm is unknown.

GUIDELINES FOR CORPORATE POLICY

Consumerism is here, and businesses should respond thoughtfully and rationally to the issues rather than react negatively or not at all. Several guidelines are developed below which businesses should follow in their response to consumerism.

Establish a separate corporate division for consumer affairs. This division would participate in all corporate decisions that have consumer implications. It would participate in research and design, advertising, credit, pricing, quality assurance, and other similar decisions.

It would respond to all consumer inquiries and complaints and would have the authority to make appropriate adjustments.

It would be responsible for the development and dissemination of factual product and service information.

It would work with industry or trade associations in the development of a consumer education program.

The division must be given the status and power necessary for it to fulfill its mission. It should not be placed in a position in which either marketing or production forces could dilute its effectiveness. Possibly the wisdom of placing all quality assurance programs in this division should be carefully examined.

Change corporate practices that are perceived as deceptive. The consumer affairs division should identify corporate practices that are perceived as deceptive and/or antagonistic by consumers. These practices should be reviewed and a viable resolution of the problem developed. Examples of such corporate practices include packaging, credit, advertising, warranties, and the like.

Educate channel members to the need for a consumerism effort throughout the channel system. Recognition of the need for a consumerism effort by all members of the channel will aid in the development of an industry consumerism program which will enhance performance of the channel system and provide better customer satisfaction. Moreover, a firm must be willing to eliminate an organization from its overall channel system if that organization is unwilling or unable to work within the constraints of corporate policy.

Incorporate the increased costs of consumerism efforts into the corporate operating budget. Unless the consumer affairs division is budgeted sufficient money to carry out its mission, it will be little more than a façade and its effectiveness will be hampered. These costs will be reflected either in higher prices or lower margins unless the consumer program affects sales sufficiently to lower costs commensurately. To date little or no research exists to document the market responses to such programs. However, it does seem apparent that substantial costs will be incurred by firms not meeting their responsibilities to the consumer because of both governmental and legal actions.

An analysis of the above guidelines suggests that an effective consumerism program will be directed primarily at the communications problem between firms and consumers. The main purpose of the consumerism program will be to enhance the quality of communications between the consumer and the firm and to incorporate valid complaints into corporate decisions.

The corporate leader has two basic options: He may take positive action in this matter, or he may ignore it. If he ignores it, he must be prepared for a government program. It would seem that the corporate decision maker should prefer to develop a consumerism program of his own. The alternative course of action, with its attendant governmental regulation and bureaucracy, would not be in the best interest of either the consumer or the firm because of its impact upon competition, prices, and consumer satisfaction.

REFERENCES

1. "Business Responds to Consumerism," *Business Week,* Vol. 2088 (September 6, 1969), pp. 94-108. "And Now, a Message From the Consumers," *Fortune,* Vol. 80 (November, 1969), p. 103. "Buckpassing Blues," *Wall Street Journal,* Vol. CLXXIV (November 3, 1969).
2. Peter Drucker, "Consumerism in Marketing,' a speech to the National Association of Manufacturers, New York, April, 1969.
3. "The Consumer Revolution," *U.S. News & World Report,* Vol. LXVII (August 25, 1969), pp. 43-46.
4. "Caveat Emptor," *The Wall Street Journal,* Vol. CLXXIII (June 26, 1969), p. 1.
5. Stuart Chase and F. J. Schlink, *Your Money's Worth* (New York: The Macmillan Company, 1934).
6. "The Rush to Help Consumers," *U.S. News & World Report,* Vol. LXVII (August 25, 1969), p. 47.
7. *Consumer Advisory Council, First Report,* Executive Officer of the President (Washington, D.C.: United States Government Printing Office, October, 1963), pp. 5-8.
8. "Appliance Maker Comes Clean," *Business Week,* Vol. 2088 (September 6, 1969), p. 100.

10

What Business, Government, and Consumer Spokesmen Think about Consumerism

Ralph M. Gaedeke

This article records the different perceptions of business, government, and consumer spokesmen as these perceptions pertain to the causes of consumerism and what might be done about it.

In spite of early predictions by industry that consumerism is but a political gambit that would quickly fizzle out, the phenomenon continues to widen its scope and support in almost geometric proportions as it enters the decade of the seventies. At local, state and national levels, it has already propelled the passage of numerous laws intended to protect the consumer's basic "rights" to product safety, product information, product choice and formal representation at the highest levels of government. With over a hundred additional consumer protection bills currently facing Congress, and more introduced every day, it is all but certain that consumerism is viable and here to stay.

While business, government and consumer spokesmen generally agree that consumerism will be here for years to come, there are differences in perceptions about the nature of consumerism, its underlying causes and the actions to be taken to protect and advance consumer interests. Both differences and similarities of perceptions pose significant implications to the respective groups and, more important, to the ultimate consumer. When perceptions are homogeneous, there are fertile grounds for coopera-

Reprinted from *The Journal of Consumer Affairs,* vol. 4, no. 1 (Summer 1970), pp. 7-18. Reprinted by permission.

tive efforts among business, government and consumers. When perceptions differ, however, avenues toward cooperation are impaired: and, consequently, maximum advancement and protection of consumer interests is difficult to attain. This article describes the results of a survey which attempted to ascertain the differences in perceptions among business, government and consumer spokesmen as they pertain to the nature and causes of consumerism and the choice of corrective measures.

THE SURVEY

A questionnaire of fixed alternative questions was assembled from a large number of frequently stated assertions about consumerism. Subjects were asked to respond to each statement in terms of several degrees of agreement or disagreement; namely: strongly agree, agree, uncertain, disagree or strongly disagree.

Potential business and consumer spokesmen were chosen from lists of individuals who testified or provided evidence for the record during recent Congressional hearings involving consumer issues. For the study, names were drawn from the following hearings:

1. *Traffic Safety,* Hearings before the Committee on Commerce, U.S. Senate, Eighty-Ninth Congress, Second Session, on S. 3005.

2. *Fair Packaging and Labeling,* Hearings before the Committee on Commerce, U.S. Senate, Eighty-Ninth Congress, First Session, on S. 985.

3. *Creating a Department of Consumers,* Hearings before the subcommittee of the Committee on Government Operations, House of Representatives, Eighty-Ninth Congress, Second Session, on H.R. 7179.

4. *National Commission on Product Safety,* Hearings before the Consumer Subcommittee of the Committee on Commerce, U.S. Senate, Ninetieth Congress, First Session, on S. J. Res. 33.

5. *Flammable Fabrics Act and Product Safety Commission,* Hearings before the Subcommittee on Commerce and Finance of the Committee on Interstate and Foreign Commerce, House of Representatives, Ninetieth Congress, First Session, on H.R. 5654.

6. *Truth in Lending—1967,* Hearings before the Subcommittee on Financial Institutions of the Committee on Banking and Currency, U.S. Senate, Ninetieth Congress, First Session, on S. 5.

These hearings were chosen because they involve interests representative of a broad spectrum of industries and consumer-oriented associations.

Of the individuals who testified or provided evidence during the above listed hearings, no more than one name was chosen per "business-oriented" or "consumer-oriented" association. Questionnaires were thus sent to 42 business spokesmen and 33 consumer spokesmen. The number of responses totaled 25 (60 per cent) for the former group and 17 (52 per cent) for the latter spokesmen.

TABLE 1

OPINIONS ABOUT SOME FREQUENTLY
STATED ASSERTIONS OF CONSUMERISM

(1) Consumerism is broadening to include man-made environmental hazards such as air and water pollution.

(a) Group I[*]	— agree	92%	disagree	4%	uncertain	4%
(b) Group II[*]	— agree	88%	disagree	6%	uncertain	6%
(c) Group III[*]	— agree	92%	disagree	8%	uncertain	0%

(2) Relations between the consumer-products industry and government are entering a new phase.

(a) Group I	— agree	72%	disagree	4%	uncertain	24%
(b) Group II	— agree	76%	disagree	0%	uncertain	24%
(c) Group III	— agree	100%	disagree	0%	uncertain	0%

(3) Consumerism is an attempt to preserve the free enterprise economy by making the market work better.

(a) Group I	— agree	12%	disagree	68%	uncertain	20%
(b) Group II	— agree	82%	disagree	6%	uncertain	12%
(c) Group III	— agree	76%	disagree	16%	uncertain	8%

(4) Consumer protectionism itself is a misnomer; we are talking about consumer information and how to improve it.

(a) Group I	— agree	64%	disagree	24%	uncertain	12%
(b) Group II	— agree	13%	disagree	81%	uncertain	6%
(c) Group III	— agree	8%	disagree	92%	uncertain	0%

(5) Consumerism is a natural and inevitable outgrowth of our increasingly sophisticated and affluent society.

(a) Group I	— agree	40%	disagree	40%	uncertain	20%
(b) Group II	— agree	82%	disagree	6%	uncertain	12%
(c) Group III	— agree	70%	disagree	15%	uncertain	15%

(6) Consumerism is simply a part of a larger subject, the new and broader dimensions of corporate social responsibility.

(a) Group I	— agree	40%	disagree	44%	uncertain	16%
(b) Group II	— agree	36%	disagree	40%	uncertain	24%
(c) Group III	— agree	50%	disagree	42%	uncertain	8%

*Group I   — Business spokesmen
 Group II — Consumer spokesmen
 Group III — Government spokesmen

Potential respondents from government were selected by Michael Pertschuk, General Counsel for the Committee on Commerce, and Norman K. Maleng, former Senate staff counsel. Both men have worked for several years on consumer affairs at the federal level of government, particularly on the Committee on Commerce; and were thus in a position to distribute the author's questionnaires to other colleagues working with consumer protection legislation, including members of the Consumer Adivsory Counsel and the President's Committee on Consumer Insterests. (It was decided not to distribute questionnaires to members of Congress since a personal response from the respective individuals would be unlikely.) The number of questionnaires distributed totaled 20. The number of responses totaled 13 (65 per cent).

TABLE 2

OPINIONS ABOUT THE NATURE OF CONSUMERISM

A.	*"Business-oriented" responses*	
	Consumerism is primarily:	
	1. Political in nature	67%
	2. Economic in nature	5
	3. Social in nature	14
	4. Psychological in nature	9
	5. Combination of all the above	5
		100%
B.	*"Consumer-oriented" responses*	
	Consumerism is primarily:	
	1. Political in nature	29%
	2. Economic in nature	29
	3. Social in nature	21
	4. Psychological in nature	0
	5. Other:	
	a. combination of all of them	14
	b. first economic, then it becomes political	7
		100%
C.	*Federal Government responses*	
	Consumerism is primarily:	
	1. Political in nature	47%
	2. Economic in nature	39%
	3. Social in nature	0
	4. Psychological in nature	0
	5. Combination of the above	14
		100%

THE FINDINGS

Nature of Consumerism

What is consumerism? Is it primarily a creature of vote-seeking politicians or is it perhaps a genuine attempt to preserve the free enterprise economy by making the market work better? Business, government and consumer spokesmen were asked their views about these and other statements listed in Table 1.

It is apparent from the responses that there was both agreement and disagreement among the spokesmen surveyed, as well as within the respective groups. All groups agreed that the scope of consumerism is broadening. Similarly, there was overwhelming agreement that relations between the consumer-products industry and government are entering a new phase.

On the other hand, businessmen did not agree with consumer and government spokesmen that consumerism is an attempt to preserve the free enterprise economy by making the market work better. Also, the majority of businessmen responding to the questionnaire did not share the views expressed by the other respondents concerning

TABLE 3

POSSIBLE UNDERLYING CAUSES OF CONSUMERISM'S GROWTH AND DEVELOPMENT

	Percent who agreed or strongly agreed			Percent who disagreed or strongly disagreed			Percent who were undecided		
	Business spokesmen	Consumer spokesmen	Government spokesmen	Business spokesmen	Consumer spokesmen	Government spokesmen	Business spokesmen	Consumer spokesmen	Government spokesmen
1. Greater public concern for social problems	55%	71%	92%	27%	0%	8%	18%	29%	0%
2. The affluency of today's consumers who demand better quality products	32	63	46	54	0	23	14	37	31
3. A feeling that business should assume greater "social responsibilities"	64	75	100	20	13	0	16	13	0
4. A sense of frustration on the part of shoppers	39	87	84	57	0	8	4	13	8
5. A bandwagon effect	68	54	50	16	13	10	16	33	40
6. A sudden awareness that many problems, particularly a lack of product safety, actually exist	20	93	66	60	0	17	20	7	17
7. The advance of science and technology which has resulted in highly sophisticated products	40	81	92	43	0	8	17	19	0
8. A recognition that voluntary business efforts don't work	25	88	55	71	6	15	4	6	30
9. Increased consumer expenditures for services	25	56	67	62	6	8	13	38	25
10. Price increases in essential food items	12	74	50	72	13	25	16	13	25
11. The obsolescence of *caveat emptor*	48	67	70	39	7	15	13	26	15
12. The mechanical and impersonal nature of the marketplace	50	79	92	29	7	8	21	14	0
13. Better educated consumers demanding more information	46	93	92	37	0	8	17	7	0
14. The language of advertising	76	87	82	12	0	9	12	13	9

15. The political appeal of consumer protection legislation	88	67	77	12	7	23	0	26	0
16. A widening consumer information gap	25	74	85	50	13	15	25	13	0
17. The nature of product guarantees and warranties	22	79	77	52	7	0	26	14	23
18. The spread of "big business"	8	57	40	71	7	30	21	36	30
19. More opportunities for consumer deception than ever before	17	87	77	70	0	15	13	13	8
20. A deterioration of business ethics	0	61	0	96	13	83	4	26	17
21. A lack of consumer protection at the state level	25	79	58	62	7	25	13	14	17
22. A change in national attitude	50	74	92	33	0	0	17	26	8
23. Lack of public awareness of the legislation which already exists	70	26	8	13	26	83	17	48	9
24. The "Great Society" and "war on poverty" programs	54	60	33	8	20	50	38	20	17
25. Failure of business to meet new and increasing needs of modern society	13	72	42	74	7	33	13	21	25
26. Lack of ability of consumers with the lowest income to spend their dollars wisely	48	74	92	40	13	0	12	13	8
27. An awareness by many individuals that they have rights and responsibilities as consumers just as they do as voters or wage earners or producers	29	93	92	50	7	0	21	0	8
28. Lack of governmental enforcement of current consumer protection laws	40	55	8	36	15	75	24	30	17

the statements "consumer protection is a misnomer; we are talking about consumer information and how to improve it" and "consumerism is a natural and inevitable out-growth of our increasingly sophisticated and affluent society."

Finally, the lack of consensus, either within or among the groups surveyed, was evident in response to the statement that consumerism is simply a part of a larger subject, namely the new and broader dimensions of corporate social responsibility.

Opinions about the general nature of consumerism are listed in Table 2 which shows that political overtones of consumerism were emphasized by a great majority of business spokesmen. Surprisingly, the greatest percentage of government spokesmen shared this view. On the other hand, only 29 per cent of consumer spokesmen felt that consumerism is primarily political in nature. A large percentage of the respondents of government and consumer spokesmen were also of the opinion, however, that consumerism is largely economic in nature; whereas relatively few respondents from any group felt that consumerism is of a social or psychological nature or a combination of political, economic, social and psychological phenomena.

It is thus evident that opinions about what consumerism is and represents differed among the groups included in the survey. But there also was some consensus of opinion which, as pointed out, was almost unanimous in the belief that the scope of consumerism is broadening.

Underlying Causes of Consumerism

Respondents to the questionnaire were asked their opinions about 28 statements (Table 3) which are repeatedly listed in the literature as being possible underlying causes of consumerism's growth and development.

As is evident from Table 3, just as business, consumer, and government spokesmen differed in their opinions about what consumerism is and represents, so do opinions differ about underlying causes of consumerism. To be sure, there was a general consensus of opinion only to the following statements as being underlying causes of consumerism:

1. the political appeal of consumer protection legislation;
2. the mechanical and impersonal nature of the marketplace;
3. the language of advertising.
4. a bandwagon effect;
5. greater public concern for social problems;
6. a feeling that business should assume greater "social responsibilities"; and
7. a change in national attitude.

Of the 28 listed underlying causes, a majority of business spokesmen agreed with only 9 of them; while most consumer spokesmen agreed with 27 of the statements and most government spokesmen with 21 of them. There is no statement to which all respondents either agreed or disagreed. On only one statement was there complete agreement among the respondents of a particular group: all government spokesmen

TABLE 4

POSSIBLE "SOLUTIONS" TO CONSUMERISM

	Percent who agreed Group			Percent who disagreed Group			Percent who were uncertain Group		
	I*	II*	III*	I	II	III	I	II	III
1. More cooperation among government, business and con-sumers	74%	64%	75%	13%	22%	8%	13%	14%	17%
2. New "consumer rela-tions" thinking	74	81	92	13	13	8	13	6	0
3. More voluntary business efforts	88	56	67	8	19	9	4	25	24
4. Additional legisla-tion at the federal level	17	94	92	58	0	0	25	6	8
5. Additional legisla-tion at the state level	21	88	92	62	0	0	17	12	8
6. Stricter enforcement of present laws	60	94	92	16	0	8	24	6	0
7. Broad consumer education program	87	100	100	9	0	0	4	0	0

*Group I   — Business Spokesmen
Group II   — Consumer Spokesmen
Group III — Government Spokesmen

agreed that an underlying cause of consumerism's growth and development was the feeling that business should assume greater "social responsibilities." It is interesting to note that not a single business or government spokesman agreed that a deterioration of business ethics is an underlying cause of consumerism, while the majority—61 per cent—of consumer spokesmen were of the opposite opinion.

Choice of Correctives

While it is generally agreed that there is no single or simple solution to the problems facing consumers today, there are notable differences of opinions about what correctives would best advance and protect consumer interests.[1]

Table 4 lists various broad courses of action frequently recommended by business, government and/or consumer spokesmen. The Table shows that there was general agreement among the respondents that most cooperation between government, business and consumers was necessary, as well as an enlightened "consumer relations" thinking, more voluntary efforts and stricter enforcement of present consumer pro-tection laws. (The consensus of opinion that more voluntary business efforts are needed appears contradictory since the majority of government and consumer spokes-men agreed with statement 8, Table 3, that voluntary business efforts are an underlying cause of consumerism.) All government and consumer spokesmen and 87 percent of business spokesmen perceived a broad consumer education program as desirable. However, the need for additional legislation, at either the state of federal level, was viewed differently. While it was the overwhelming opinion of both government and consumer spokesmen that additional consumer protection legislation is necessary, few businessmen subscribed to this course of action.

SUMMARY AND CONCLUSIONS

The differences in perception that emerge from the survey indicate that consumerism is a flueid and hard-to-define phenomenon. To be sure, consumerism is, as past consumer movements were, of a kaleidoscopic nature.

Differing perceptions prevail about certain possible underlying causes of consumerism. At the same time, however, there is congruency in the opinions of business, government and consumer spokesmen that the mechanical and impersonal nature of the marketplace, the political appeal of legislation and its accompanying bandwagon effect, the language of advertising, the increased public concern for social problems and the feeling that business should assume greater social responsibilities are basic factors contributing to consumerism's evolution.

Since there are differences in perceptions over the nature and specific causes of consumerism, it follows, as a practical matter, that there are also differences in perception over the choice of certain correctives. This is most evident with respect to consumer protection legislation.

Business spokesmen do not believe that additional legislation is the answer to consumerism; whereas consumer and government spokesmen view additional legislation as desirable. But there is also a consensus of opinion that the best interests of consumers can only be served through an effective cooperation among consumers, business and government and a broad consumer education program. If these correctives are actively pursued by all groups, it would indeed be a giant step for consumers and the appropriate response to the phenomenon labeled consumerism.

REFERENCES

1. The more visible correctives already undertaken are the many consumer protection bills which were passed by Congress during the 1960's. Voluntary business correctives, on the other hand, are still relatively invisible.

11

Consumer Action Programs of the Consumers Union of United States

Colston E. Warne

Here is traced the early turbulent history of the programs
of the Consumers Union of United States, once branded as
subversive and an attempt to undermine the American way
of life, and now a respected member of the Consumer
Federation of America with a monthly circulation of nearly
2 million for its *Consumer Reports.*

INTRODUCTION TO CONSUMERS UNION

Now that Consumers Union of United States has entered its thirty-fifth year, it seems
appropriate to pause to describe its role as a voluntary non-profit consumer organization. Consumers Union, chartered in 1936 by the State of New York to provide
information and counsel on consumer goods and services, was perhaps the only new
reform movement of the thirties to survive the Great Depression. Its effort to become
a forceful, discerning, and effective voice for the consumer may be of particular
interest to those interested in consumer protection programs. By January 1970,
Consumer Reports, its monthly publication, had attained a monthly circulation of
1,800,000, and, together with its other publications, furnished the organization with
its entire budget of about $10,000,000. At its headquarters in Mount Vernon, New
York, Consumers Union now employs a staff of 300.

The central emphasis of Consumers Union has long been that of product testing—of

Reprinted from *Economics of Consumer Protection* (Danville, Ill.: The Interstate, 1971), pp.
61-72. Reprinted by permission.

seeking to supply the consumer with an impartial assessment of the principal brands available on the American market. The organization's service to consumers has, however, been much broader in character. In keeping with the provisions of its charter, Consumers Union aims:

> to obtain and provide for consumers information and counsel on consumers' goods and services covering quality, price, and labor conditions under which such goods are produced and distributed; to give information and assistance on all matters relating to the expenditure of earnings and the family income; to initiate, to cooperate with, and to aid individual and group efforts of whatever nature and description seeking to create and maintain decent living standards for ultimate consumers; to maintain laboratories and to supervise and conduct research and tests for the better accomplishment of the objects of this corporation; to prepare and issue in all suitable forms material resulting from the work of the organization; . . .

Thus, Consumers Union has from its inception included a vigorous health and medicine section which passes critical comment on a wide variety of medical topics: from constipation, patent medicines, additives, preservatives, deodorants, and smoking and health to an assessment of dangers in "the Pill." Consumers Union has also felt a vital concern over problems of packaging, growth of consumer credit, values of tariffs and trade restraints, water pollution, the metric system, enforcement of weights and measures laws, and a host of other consumer issues. Consumers Union's conception of its social role has, from its beginning, gone far beyond affording a directory of best buys in television sets and toasters. It is now a member of the national Consumer Federation of America and is also affiliated with the International Organization of Consumers Unions in The Hague. The latter is an international consumer agency for the exchange of test techniques and test results and for the further development of international consumer protection through its consultative status with agencies of the United Nations.

In recent months, Consumers Union has testified before the National Commission on Product Safety, the National Advisory Committee on Flammable Fabrics, the National Motor Vehicle Safety Advisory Council, study committees of the National Academy of Sciences, as well as the Truth-in-Lending Advisory Committee of the Federal Reserve Board. Consumers Union also participated in the White House Conference on Food, Nutrition, and Health, and is represented in such technical organizations as the American Society for Testing and Materials and the Consumer Advisory Council of the Underwriters' Laboratories

GENESIS OF CONSUMER TESTING

The genesis of consumer testing may be traced directly to a book by Stuart Chase and F. J. Schlink, *Your Money's Worth,* which appeared in 1927.[1] It germinated the potent organization in the consumer testing field, Consumers Research of Washington and New Jersey.[2] Earlier glimpses of the potentiality of product standardization and product testing emerge in the report of Hoover's Federated American Engineering Societies on *Waste in Industry* in 1921,[3] in the early work of the American Home Economics Association, and in the World War I experience of the Federal Bureau of Standards. In part, the emergence of consumer testing is also related to the development of national markets for trademarked goods accompanied by extensive competitive advertising. Faced with a host of new products brought forth by an expanding technology, the consumer was confronted with the problem of sorting out those functionally well adapted to consumer needs and technical performance from those based more on advertising enthusiasm. The situation cried out for the emergence of an agency which was to do for the ultimate consumer what research departments of corporations were already doing for business—*the assessing of the performance characteristics of products through the employment of standard test techniques and rating systems.*

Those who formed Consumers Union in 1936 were, for the most part, staff and board members who had broken away from Consumers Research in the course of a bitter, protracted conflict. The new effort was initially most uncertain of its audience and equally uncertain as to effective ways of reaching that audience. Consumers Union offered a limited service for low-income consumers for $1.00. The full service sold for $3.00. The limited service proved unsuccessful and was abandoned.

In the formative period, probings were made with local and regional groups of consumers. Consequently, an experimental West Coast edition was issued in California for several years. In its initial stages, Consumers Union endorsed cooperatives and credit unions and made ratings of both product quality and the adequacy of the labor standards under which goods were made. Most newspapers and magazines of the time were bitterly antagonistic toward the new undertaking and refused to sell advertising space, claiming that consumer testing constituted an unfair attack upon legitimate advertising. The *Woman's Home Companion* called Consumers Union a "burrowing shrimp undermining the American way of life." The *Good Housekeeping* magazine assisted Martin Dies in proclaiming Consumers Union to be subversive. Nevertheless, by direct mail promotion and advertisements in liberal journals, a small but loyal band of supporters was assembled. Considerable assistance was given by academicians who introduced the consumer testing idea to their students in classroom discussions. Assistance was also furnished by advertisers whose intensity of opposition called attention to the effort and, unwittingly, helped to fill its empty coffers. After the lean years, the organization secured a firm footing following 1946.

THE OPERATION OF CONSUMERS UNION

Control over the operations of Consumers Union is lodged in a board of twenty-one members, each elected for three-year terms. Two candidates compete for each post on the board. "The directors shall be persons who have no such connections with commercial, business, manufacturing, or financial enterprises as are likely to affect their independent judgment as directors."

At present, the Board consists of seven economists, two engineers, one judge, one home economist, one agronomist, three lawyers, one medical doctor, one psychologist, one head of a state consumer movement, one educator, one social worker, and one journalist. In the last election, some 300,000 votes were cast by proxy at the Consumers Union meeting held at the University of Minnesota in September 1969.

The recruiting of members is largely by direct mail solicitation, employing lists classified by occupation. In recent years radio, magazine, and television advertising have also been employed. Word of mouth mention of Consumers Union has been an important source of support. Those subscribers who vote in the annual Consumers Union elections automatically become members of the organization.

Since its inception, Consumers Union has employed the technique of ascertaining the interests of its consumer audience through the employment of an annual questionnaire. These questionnaires have varied greatly from year to year. Their central focus has been that of identifying members, finding their experiences with particular products such as motorcars or washing machines, and ascertaining whether they are content with the existing "product mix" of testing. From time to time, supplementary surveys have also yielded information about reasons for failure to renew subscriptions or concerning the purchase expectations of our membership. A series of monographs was developed by the National Bureau of Economic Research in the latter area.

According to our latest count, the median income of our subscribers is $14,336; the median age is 40; 63 percent are in a professional or managerial occupation and 79 percent attended college. In terms of whether they felt we had placed sufficient emphasis upon a given field, the findings were:

	Too little	About enough	Too much
1. Medical and health information	42.0%	54.4%	3.6%
2. Clothing, footwear, etc.	38.7	58.0	3.3
3. Home furnishings	35.2	63.4	1.4
4. General consumer information	35.0	63.4	1.6
5. Every-day products	32.9	59.9	7.2
6. Leisure-time products	18.1	68.5	13.4
7. Small appliances	13.6	83.3	3.1
8. Major appliances	12.6	86.6	.8
9. Automobiles	11.1	76.4	12.5

From the beginning, one of the central interests of Consumers Union's membership has been the motorcar, an interest which has been well sustained over time. This interest has been so pervasive that few of our monthly issues fail to include some auto test.

The second leading interest has been in the field of household equipment—the standard package of the refrigerator, washing machine, and vacuum cleaner, followed by the deep freeze, air conditioner, clothes dryer, and dishwasher. A consistently high level of interest is also felt in Consumers Union's articles on health and medicine. Another most popular feature deals with articles on economic and social policies as these affect the consumer. While occasional members opt for a magazine dedicated to cold and impersonal test results, the dominant attitude has been that of balancing test results with attention to problems faced by the consumer in the market place—an attempt to sharpen consumer attitudes concerning market practices.

The scheduling of Consumers Union's projects is handled by an operations committee which seeks to keep a seasonal balance, a balance between leisure time and work-day items, and a balance between interests of men and women. Test samples are bought on the open market by shoppers scattered across the nation. These shoppers also secure market prices for Consumers Union of given brands and models. The brands chosen for tests are normally those which command a significant place in the national market or have a significant strength in a regional market. These test samples are channeled to one of the major departments of the organization—automotive, chemical, electronic, household equipment, textile, or special projects.

Test techniques employed by Consumers Union are often adapted from those in common use in the industry. Rating systems are used to balance the importance of given attributes. In the end, a composite judgment is reached and brands are ranked in order of over-all quality. A model which gives particularly advantageous performance is check-rated. A product which gives notably high value for the expenditure is designated as a "Best Buy."

Much of the value of Consumers Union's testing service lies not so much in its direct mention of brands, although this is important, but in the description of what to look for in the market. For example, Consumers Union's June 1970 issue considers the question of the purchase of a sailboat and indicates the types of boat and the problems one encounters with each type of boat. Much of the value of the article lies in the background information which accords the consumer at least some degree of product orientation. The annual *Buying Guide* which appears in December seeks to condense the product discussion into a compact handbook of some 400 pages.

LIMITATIONS OF CONSUMER TESTING

Consumers Union faces numerous problems in recommending products. The instability of brands in the American market place has long been notorious. Not a few models are withdrawn before Consumers Union even concludes its tests. If articles recommended by Consumers Union are to be of value to the member, companies must maintain careful workmanship and product inspection. The consumer must be able to procure something similar to the tested and recommended sample. This is not always the case.

Consumer test results have other marked limitations. Several months ensue between the planning of a project and its final execution in the form of a *Reports* article. Consumers Union's rankings may not fully reflect all of the articles on the contemporary market. Consumers Union also faces the difficult problem of sampling. Are Consumers Union's samples representative of the products in the actual market? Will the force-drafting of production of recommended articles on the market *after* the appearance of Consumers Union's report be accompanied by lowered quality?

Then, too, there are inevitable limitations of Consumers Union's own testing data. Has Consumers Union accurately weighted the attributes for any particular consumer? Will the price of recommended articles increase due to the extra demand generated by the test report that they may be underpriced for their value? Has Consumers Union adequately considered the warranties and guarantees afforded by a product? Will the servicing of a product be competently and expeditiously done in a given market?

Finally, how much light can Consumers Union really shed upon the durability of an article? In some fields it is possible to estimate, with reasonable accuracy, the longevity of a product. In other fields, such as the purchase of a motorcar, this is far more difficult. The pressure is to have tests appear rapidly. Sudden model changes limit Consumers Union's capacity to deal with this problem.

Yet these are not all of the problems of testing. Consider, for example, the choice of an automobile. Consumers Union may give the potential buyer some excellent general advice as he walks down "gasoline alley." Yet, we are here dealing with a complex product which manufacturers are tooled up to deliver with dozens of options. Indeed, with the Detroit *accent on style,* those cars which most nearly approach a rational, workmanlike design are not, uncommonly, laggards in market competition. Consumers Union is handicapped in passing comment on stylistic features such as pointed bumpers and designs shaped to catch the youthful eye. We are forced to deal with the market as it is, with its horsepower race, and its inadequate smog devices. For many years, "safety" has been a dirty, unmentionable word. Not until recently has the consumer-engendered wave of reform overtaken the industry. Even today, the results are not overwhelmingly reassuring.

In summarizing the imperfections of the consumer testing organization, it should be emphasized that Consumers Union's resources are deployed in a limited way over a vast market and that its efforts are subject to human error as well as to the many problems inhering in sampling and testing. It has attempted to span a substantial segment of the American market with total annual expenditures of less than those employed in advertising a single toothpaste. Consumer testing is by no means a perfected device, assuring maximization of consumer utility through rational choice. Small but meritorious brands may be omitted. Durability may be imperfectly measured. The values consumers seek in products may be imperfectly weighed. Recommended products may be unavailable. Consumers Union has, however, markedly improved in its technical work.

There remains an important residual benefit. Through the impartial orientation of the consumer testing organization, the buyer is often able to gain a new perspective. This quest is well shown in a 1970 survey which inquired of Consumers Union's subscribers the reasons for wanting the subscription. These were:

Wanted to know what to look for in order to tell a good product from a bad one	92.2%
Expected to save money on purchases	54.8
You can't rely on what the advertising or the salesman tells you	54.0
I wanted to become more aware of consumer affairs and issues	46.8
I was in the market for certain products at that time	29.4
To save time in shopping	24.4

Indeed over 99% of the respondents stated that, in their overall experience, Consumers Union recommendations were more often right than wrong. Before making a purchase during the previous year, two-thirds had bought the top-rated product among a list of items.

CONSUMERS UNION'S ACHIEVEMENTS

If Consumers Union has demonstrated many imperfections and limitations during its first third-of-a-century, it has also scored a number of significant gains.

In the first place, it has gained the allegiance of a substantial and highly influential segment of the American purchasing public. It reaches directly 1,800,000 families each month and, indirectly, a much larger total through library circulation, word of mouth communication, and borrowing of issues. Intense allegiance has been built by Consumers Union's policies of not accepting advertising, of not permitting competitive companies to use product ratings in their product promotion, and of reflecting an eagerness to learn the problems consumers confront in day-to-day purchasing. Consumer testing has proven itself as a viable idea which has now spread through all technically advanced countries of the world. These organizations operate sometimes with government subsidy, sometimes without. The presence of Consumers Union and its foreign counterparts has stimulated the development of governmental consumer protective endeavors.

The founding of a national consumer movement in the U.S., the Consumer Federation of America, and a recent drive of consumerism have been measurably influenced by the persistent campaigns Consumers Union has undertaken in the fields of consumer credit, packaging, fair trade laws, drug pricing, product warranties, cooling-off periods, auto insurance, product safety, food and drug inspection, and government release of scientific data.

Looking back over the years, many of Consumers Union's consumer crusades at the time met with little response. Whether Consumers Union was dealing with the Interstate Commerce Commission's handling of moving costs, the ineptitude of the Federal Communications Commission, or watered ham, we frequently seemed to meet with an unmovable bureaucracy bent on *avoiding* problems rather than *responding* to consumer wishes.

The action programs of Consumers Union have consistently been pragmatic in nature, reflecting the initiative of our staff in defining areas of high consumer priority. Because Consumers Union remains free from many of the restraints incident to government, the organization can link unethical practices to the brand name of offenders. Consumers Union can stir up those officials who had failed to enforce laws.[4]

Time permits only the quick mention of a few of these efforts mounted over the last decade.

1. *Weights and measures.* Here we have subsidized the able head of the Weights and Measures Research Center, Dr. Leland J. Gordon of Granville, Ohio, who is now completing his third study of state weights and measures laws and their imperfections. His studies have accented the uneven enforcement and somewhat chaotic condition of state enforcement.

2. *Packaging.* We first raised the question of deceptive packaging in the study of cornflakes in *Consumer Reports* in 1936 (Volume I, No. 1). Later we were among the first to note the erosion of product weight as a disguised price increase.

3. *Grade labelling.* From time to time we have stirred up the lethargic Department of Agriculture emphasizing the need of championing uniform grade nomenclature in the grade labelling of foodstuffs. Our success has been no greater than that of the National Commission on Food Marketing.

4. *Product safety.* The cumulative effect of our work here is well demonstrated in the product safety arena. A search of our non-acceptable ratings provided the basic evidence for the enactment of legislation establishing the National Committee on Product Safety. Incidentally, in its earliest days, Consumers Union kept pointing out the lethal hazards of nosedrops containing mineral oil. Eventually the government listened and acted. Whether in the field of electric toothbrushes, current leakage, flammable fabrics, strontium 90, tar and nicotine in cigarettes, filth in sausages, lawnmower safety, or standards for flotation materials in outboard boats, Consumers Union has lent emphasis to vital consumer issues.

5. *Quality control.* Consumers Union's data have demonstrated the shoddy condition in which new cars are delivered and the dissatisfaction with repair attempts under warranties.

6. *Unit Pricing.* Articles in the *Reports,* stemming from reader complaints, were instrumental in spurring the passage of the Truth in Packaging bill and have been the inspiration behind the present drive for unit pricing.

7. *Misleading advertising.* Since its inception, Consumers Union has been on the lookout for intrusive as well as deceptive advertising. The siren voices which punctuate radio and television programs on the quarter-hour have, by no means, been silenced by our efforts. I do think, however, we can take credit for the development of a more critical audience—one which wishes to substitute product standards for advertising hyperbole.

8. *Consumer education.* Consumers Union has been exceedingly active in fostering consumer education both at the high school and college levels. The current trend in this field is unmistakable. Several states have instituted marked curricula changes.

THE FUTURE IMPACT OF CONSUMER TESTING

In June 1966 Donald F. Turner, then Assistant Attorney General in charge of the Antitrust Division, spoke before the Federal Bar Association. He suggested the expansion of non-profit testing organizations, such as Consumers Union, through government subsidy or direct government product testing and evaluation. Mr. Turner, who was on leave from the Harvard Law School faculty, stated:

We all know that such consumer research organizations as Consumer Reports tend to promote informed consumer judgment, and we can reasonably surmise that reports of that kind, if generally circulated, would significantly limit the ability of advertising to enhance degrees of monopoly power, to say nothing of enabling consumers to spend their dollars more fruitfully. . . .

A major difficulty is that these publications are produced by non-profit organizations and that they frequently face difficulties in obtaining the funds required for adequate testing and evaluation. One prospective solution would be governmental evaluation and publication, or financial support for private organizations of this type. . . .

Mr. Turner was contending that excessive advertising outlays may well have a significant impact on the degree of market power exercised in many industries and that it may impair the functioning of a competitive economy. His idea, surprising as it was to Consumers Union, is based upon the theory that freedom of entry constitutes a pivotal factor in maintaining workable competition. The impact of extensive "brand-name" advertising competition, he affirmed, is far different from price rivalry between competitive brands. The excessive din created on behalf of established products tends to limit the salability of cheaper, but relatively unknown, brands. Either the new-comer has to incur heavy selling costs in penetrating a market, or, cut prices. Heavy advertising thus constitutes a barrier to entry and eliminates a major competitive price restraint. The considerable advantage already possessed by established products tends to be accentuated. Also, more messages per dollar can be provided by the larger firms through quantity discounts in the media.[6]

In essence, Professor Turner is suggesting that government policies be directed toward the broadening of the scope of test organizations in order to remove the uncertainty which surrounds the relative merit of products. It is this uncertainty which makes consumers peculiarly prone to accept the blandishments of established groups and, hence, enhances monopoly power. Once advertising expenditures have built up deeply entrenched consumer preferences, new competitors find market acceptance difficult. If new and accurate sources of consumer information are made available, rational choice may ensue and market shares would depend upon efficiency and superiority of a product rather than quantity of effective advertising.

Those of us who have been connected for some years with consumer testing groups are bound to be flattered by the pivotal role in antitrust enforcement suggested by Mr. Turner's thesis. We had long been accustomed to the use of extensive government subsidy for consumer testing in our world organization, the International Organization of Consumers Unions. In Norway, for example, half of the cost of consumer testing is carried by the government, partly with the idea of lowering the foreign exchange drain upon the country by stimulating economical expenditures for consumer products which are largely imported. Yet Mr. Turner has, perhaps, excessive faith in the power of consumer testing to search out and discover successful innovators in order to restore rationality and competition in the market place.

THE GOVERNMENT'S ROLE IN CONSUMER TESTING

This is perhaps the point to raise the question in regard to the appropriate role of government in consumer testing. The U.S. government has a vast storehouse of tests and test methods developed by its agencies in the course of government purchasing. A current episode in which Consumers Union is involved, a suit against the Veterans Administration, illustrates Consumers Union's attitudes in this field. The Veterans Administration has, for some years, been testing hearing aids before purchasing the models it supplies to veterans. It is only natural and perfectly proper that the Veterans Administration should employ the National Bureau of Standards to test hearing aids so that the right selection can be made. That is the *same principle* which is the backbone of Consumers Union. So what is the problem? It is simply that while the Veterans Administration spent the public dollars on conducting the tests, it would not release to the public the information that public money had bought. Then came the Freedom of Information Act of 1966 which was effective July 4, 1967.

Consumers Union has done testing of hearing aids in the past but *our* resources could not begin to approximate the government program. Under repeated requests in 1967 and a suit in 1968 by Consumers Union, the Veterans Administration has released data which are now approaching obsolescence. *If* similar data on 1971 hearing aid models are forthcoming, Consumers Union will print a comprehensive evaluation of hearing aids early next year. The key word is of course *if*. The Veterans Administration data were made available as a result of an administrative decision. Consumers Union cannot accept a result so based on the vagaries of politics and public pressure. Its current suit is aimed at the formal recognition, by the courts, that the Freedom of Information Act *requires* the government to release its consumer test data. In anticipation of success in this suit, Consumers Union is looking at the roster of tests of other government agencies which will benefit consumers—all of us who are footing this testing bill.

The rich resources of government testing agencies need to be tapped. While government agencies have been most cooperative in releasing test methods, little eagerness exists to release "brand-name" ratings. No basis exists for all the secretiveness concerning comparative tests. President Kennedy unavailingly admonished agencies in 1962 to release scientific results. Little however, seemed to happen until the Consumers Union suit against the Veterans Administration. As a result of this suit, it is hoped that product information stockpiles will be made generally available. As President Kennedy said:

> ... many departments and agencies are engaged ... in testing the performance of certain products, developing standards and specifications, and assembling a wide range of related information that would be of immense use to consumers and consumer organizations.[7]

CONCLUSION

Perhaps enough has been said to portray the consumer testing agency as a relatively unnoted and unfinished product of modern technology which has emerged in our midst. The Foundations have by-passed Consumers Union; it receives scant mention in economics texts or research monographs.

Thus far, it has reached a substantial band of eager and sophisticated consumers who could probably, in their own right, avoid most purchasing pitfalls, with an assist from technically trained neighbors and associates. The labor movement historically enlisted skilled workers first and then extended itself slowly and with immense difficulty to the ranks of the unskilled. So it is with the consumer testing movement which has thus far become a vehicle for product choice of the better educated members of the more affluent societies. They are destined to buy their ski equipment, high fidelity sets, automobiles electric self-cleaning ovens, and floor coverings on the basis of brand recommendations.

On the other hand, as David Caplovitz pointed out in his thesis, *The Poor Pay More*, low income groups are so heavily influenced by advertising, the quest to "keep up with the Joneses," and the influence of credit sellers, that *not a few* of the more costly models of household equipment come into the hands of those *least able* to afford such luxury items.[8] "Brand name loyalty" is high where income is low. Thus, low income consumers often become effective targets for much of our radio and television advertising. If advertising is not to be the educator and conditioner of the poor, new techniques are needed for extending consumer testing to the service of the whole community.

REFERENCES

1. Stuart Chase and F. J. Schlink, *Your Money's Worth* (New York: The Macmillan Company, 1927).
2. Consumers Research subsequently went into eclipse in the late 1930's through internal management problems and ideological difficulties.
3. Federated American Engineering Societies, *Waste in Industry* (New York: McGraw-Hill Book Company, 1921).
4. In retrospect, the Consumers Union approach has perhaps been too reasoned and too dignified to attain the impact of the more direct confrontation of a Ralph Nader.
5. Donald F. Turner, "Advertising and Competition." *The Federal Bar Journal*, Vol. 26 (Spring 1966), pp. 93-98.
6. *Ibid.*
7. Message from the President of the United States, *Congressional Record*, 87th Congress, second session, House of Representatives, March 15, 1962.
8. David Caplovitz, *The Poor Pay More* (London: The Free Press of Glancoe, 1963).

12

Protection of Consumer Rights

Consumer Advisory Council

The shift from *caveat emptor* to *caveat venditor* has increased the role of government in promoting the consumer's right to safety, the right to be informed, the right to choose, and the right to be heard.

THE RIGHT TO SAFETY

The Federal Government acts to assure the consumer's right to safety by limiting the sale of goods, e.g., narcotics and meat from diseased animals, that are potentially harmful to the user. It acts—e.g., in its programs to eradicate animal diseases—to eliminate conditions giving rise to unsafe products or services. And it also acts—in the cases of highway safety and the protection of air-navigation radio channels, for example—to regulate the use of goods by consumers themselves in a way that limits the hazards they create for other consumers.

In the long history of government policy as to the consumer's right to safety there has been a shift in emphasis away from consumer responsibility, under the doctrine of *caveat emptor,* to seller responsibility for damages arising out of negligence or implied breach of warranty, and to government responsibility for prevention of damage. In the case of food and drugs, for example, government now has authority to seize and prevent the sale of products that are potentially harmful, without waiting for damages to be shown. In some cases, as with immunizing serums, there is authority to prevent the sale if the product is not efficacious. The 1962 Drug Amendments extended this principal to the full range of drugs.

With the advance of science and technology, consumer products have become

Reprinted from *First Report of the Consumer Advisory Council,* (Washington: GPO, 1963), pp. 23-27.

highly complex, and the responsibility for the finished products has, in many instances, been widely dispersed among a range of producers and distributors. Consequently, it is difficult for the consumer to appraise his risk prospectively or fix responsibility for damages retrospectively. It is important, therefore, that he be shielded against hazards to his health and safety by alert and efficient administration of those laws that have followed upon the Pure Food and Drug Act of 1906 and the Meat Inspection Act of 1907. At the Federal level this responsibility is centered in the Department of Health, Education, and Welfare and the Department of Agriculture. But it also extends, for example, to the Department of Interior's voluntary inspection of fish products and to the Treasury Department's regulation of narcotics and alcoholic beverages. Likewise, the Interstate Commerce Commission, the Federal Aviation Agency, and other specialized agencies promote safety in transportation.

Plainly, of course, passage of a law is only a first step in achieving consumer protection. Equally important is vigorous and imaginative enforcement by adequately staffed agencies.

Enforcement must be adjusted to take account of the growing population and the changing nature of products. President Kennedy pointed to this in his Consumer Message, saying—

—Thousands of common household items now available to consumers contain potentially harmful substances. Hundreds of new uses for such products as food additives, food colorings and pesticides are found every year, adding new potential hazards.

—As Americans make more use of highway and air transportation than any other nation, increased speed and congestion have required us to take special safety measures.

THE RIGHT TO BE INFORMED

The right to be informed prompted the earliest Federal legislation concerned directly with the consumer, namely, the Mail Frauds Statute of 1872. Today implementation of this right extends from prevention of fraud and deception to government-sponsored and government-conducted research. Included within this range are the positive requirement of full disclosure (as in the case of issues of new securities), the establishment of standard weights and measures, performance testing (as in the case of drugs), grade labeling, standardization (a case of mandatory standards is that of bottle sizes for alcoholic beverages), and the provision of objective information on consumer problems.

The Wheeler-Lea Act of 1938 gave the Federal Trade Commission power to take action against false advertising, especially in the fields of foods, drugs, devices, and cosmetics. The commission's authority extends to requiring affirmative disclosure in advertising or labeling when necessary to prevent consumer deception. An advertisement is considered false if it is "misleading in any particular," thus giving the Federal Trade Commission a broad area for enforcement.

The positive requirement of full disclosure has also been extended through the years to the labeling of many products. Disclosure of identity, composition, and quality, or the presence of harmful ingredients was required in the case of drugs in 1906, insecticides and fungicides in 1910, seeds in 1912, animal viruses, serums, and toxins in 1913, horse meat in 1919, caustic poisons in 1919, substandard canned goods in 1930, and alcoholic beverages in 1935. Requirements were broadened in the case of foods in 1938, wool products in 1939 human viruses, serums, and toxins in 1944, fur products in 1951, and textile fiber products in 1958. Requirements with respect to labeling vary from commodity to commodity. The Federal Trade Commission has issued guides or rules relating to labeling practices, deceptive practices, and advertising for approximately 175 industries. A recent example of this is a Guide for Shoe Content Labeling and Advertising.

Action has been taken to protect the individual as a purchaser of securities. This was done primarily through the Securities Act of 1933 and the Securities Exchange Act of 1934, which, with certain exceptions, required the registration of new issues. The 1934 Act established the Securities and Exchange Commission, and in 1962 legislation was passed providing for reorganization of the Commission. The Commission has completed a major investigation of the securities markets, which has already provided the basis for pending legislation, the Securities Acts Amendments of 1963 (S. 1624 and H.R. 6789), and administrative changes.

The Congress has assigned primary responsibility for the establishment of standard weights and measures to the National Bureau of Standards. Certain acts have been passed establishing standard size packaging for some products. Fruits and vegetables are covered to some extent by the Standard Container Acts of 1916 and 1928. Alcoholic beverages are covered under the Alcoholic Beverages Administration Act of 1936. Quality of product is identified for the consumer in certain cases through government inspection and grading—especially of food products. For example, some meats and eggs are sold according to governmentally established grades.

The idea of the government's providing objective information directly to the consumer is not new. The Bureau of Home Economics of the Department of Agriculture, now incorporated in the Division of Nutrition, Consumer, and Industrial Use Research, was created in 1923. Information is provided by direct contact between consumers and government representatives—particularly, the Food and Drug Administration's consumer consultants and the Cooperative Extension Service's home demonstration agents. Information is also provided by government reports addressed to the consumer. Examples of the latter are listed in Appendix C.

The Federal Government also supports research of value to consumers in such agencies as the National Bureau of Standards, the Department of Agriculture, and the National Institutes of Health, as well as in universities and private nonprofit research organizations.

THE RIGHT TO CHOOSE

The direction of the American economy depends heavily, as we have seen, on consumers' choices among products and among producers. In asserting the consumer's "right to choose," President Kennedy has implicitly indicated the importance of there being a number of alternative producers and of there being effective freedom for producers to enter new fields and offer new products and services. Thus, the consumer's right to choose and the maintenance of competition are intimately related. Promotion of competition, however, is a complex undertaking. In pursuing it the Federal Government has employed a series of legislative acts, some general in scope, some specific with regard to a type of practice or a particular industry.

Government intervention to ensure competition is older than the legislation in this field. Common law courts would not consider a contract binding if it was a clear case of conspiring to monopolize. However, the Government itself did not initiate action against any conspiracy or on behalf of third parties injured by conspiracies until passage of the Sherman Act of 1890. This committed the Government to active prevention and limitation of monopoly, and declared every contract, combination, or conspiracy in restraint of trade, or attempts at such restraint, to be illegal. Later antitrust acts were designed to modify the Sherman Act's coverage and to define more precisely actions considered harmful to competition. The Federal Trade Commission Act and the Clayton Act in 1914, the Robinson-Patman Act in 1936, the Wheeler-Lea Act of 1938, the Trade Mark Act of 1946, the McCarran Insurance Act of 1948, and the Celler-Kefauver Anti-Merger Act of 1950 are among the leading statutes indicating Congressional intent with respect to competition. Responsibility for enforcing these laws is vested primarily with the Antitrust Division of the Department of Justice and the Federal Trade Commission.

In the administration of virtually every one of its economic programs the Government influences the structure and operation of commercial markets. In negotiating international trade agreements, in establishing agricultural labor, or transportation policy, in procuring defense supplies, in setting directions for housing finance, in regulating securities markets, in making loans to small businesses, in providing marketing services and technical information to farm and business firms—in all these and in many other ways—the Government affects the consumer's right to choose.

In some industries, however, technical considerations do not allow the consumer to have a choice among the varying products of numerous producers. In such cases the government may, while leaving the producing firms in private hands, act as agent for the consumers, regulating the number of firms in the industry, maximum or minimum price, quality and conditions of service. While the bulk of such detailed regulation is done at the State level in this country, the Federal Government has entered the field in a number of industries, beginning in railroading in 1887 with the establishment of the Interstate Commerce Commission, whose jurisdiction was extended to internal waterborne transport in 1920 and to interstate motor carriers in 1935. Other transportation rates and service are regulated by the Federal Maritime Commission and the Civil Aeronautics Board. Similarly, other specialized government agencies regulate interstate aspects of the telephone, telegraph, radio, and television industries; of banking and credit institutions; and of the electric power and natural gas industries.

In the case of electric power the Federal Government also serves the consumer directly through such public power suppliers as TVA and the Bonneville Power Administration. These have increased total power availability and afford "yardstick competition" to private suppliers.

In a dynamic economy not only do the problems facing regulators grow with the population and the size of business firms, but also they change with the demands of consumers and the technological frontiers within reach of the producers. Presently, for example, we face the mushrooming demands for improved urban transit, the exciting possibilities of transoceanic communication via satellites, and the economics promised by long-distance, extra-high-voltage transmission of electrical energy.

In order to play their intended role on behalf of consumers, the regulatory agencies must have clear rule-making authority, fair and efficient procedures, and adequate numbers of competent personnel.

THE RIGHT TO BE HEARD

Besides promoting the consumer interest, the Federal Government also promotes the interests of producers. It may be said to seek the public interest partly through balancing the separate private interests of producers and consumers. Consumers, however, are not organized to the same degree as are producers for the purpose of influencing government policy, nor are they likely to be so organized in view of their scattered and varied interests. While seeking to learn the views of voluntary associations of consumers, therefore, government must remember that these views are not always expressed effectively enough to achieve a balance automatically in the array of private opinion being brought to bear on public policy issues.

To some degree the regulatory agencies are charged with representing the consumer interest. But at various times in the past it has seemed appropriate to provide within government more direct means for assuring the expression of the consumer viewpoint. The history of such "consumer representation" includes experiments in assigning the function to government as well as private individuals to serve in a consultative relationship to the government.

13

Unsafe at Any Speed: Preface

Ralph Nader

For over half a century the automobile has brought death, injury, and the most inestimable sorrow and deprivation to millions of people. With Medea-like intensity, this mass trauma began rising sharply four years ago reflecting new and unexpected ravages by the motor vehicle. A 1959 Department of Commerce report projected that 51,000 persons would be killed by automobiles in 1975. That figure will probably be reached in 1965, a decade ahead of schedule.

A transportation specialist, Wilfred Owen, wrote in 1946, "There is little question that the public will not tolerate for long an annual traffic toll of forty to fifty thousand fatalities." Time has shown Owen to be wrong. Unlike aviation, marine, or rail transportation, the highway transport system can inflict tremendous casualties and property damage without in the least affecting the viability of the system. Plane crashes, for example, jeopardize the attraction of flying for potential passengers and therefore strike at the heart of the air transport economy. They motivate preventative efforts. The situation is different on the roads.

Highway accidents were estimated to have cost this country in 1964, $8.3 billion in property damage, medical expenses, lost wages, and insurance overhead expenses. Add an equivalent sum to comprise roughly the indirect costs and the total amounts to over two per cent of the gross national product. But these are not the kind of costs which fall on the builders of motor vehicles (excepting a few successful law suits for negligent construction of the vehicle) and thus do not pinch the proper foot. Instead, the costs fall to users of vehicles, who are in no position to dictate safer automobile designs.

In fact, the gigantic costs of the highway carnage in this country support a service industry. A vast array of services—medical, police, administrative, legal, insurance, automotive repair, and funeral—stand equipped to handle the direct and indirect consequences of accident injuries. Traffic accidents create economic demands for these services running into billions of dollars. It is in the post-accident response that lawyers and physicians and other specialists labor. This is where the remuneration lies and this is where the talent and energies go. Working in the area of prevention of these casualties earns few fees. Consequently our society has an intricate organization to handle direct and indirect aftermaths of collisions. But the true mark of a humane society must be what it does about *prevention* of accident injuries, not the cleaning up of them afterward.

Unfortunately, there is little in the dynamics of the automobile industry that works for its reduction. Doctors, lawyers, engineers and other specialists have failed in their primary professional ethic: to dedicate themselves to the prevention of accident-injuries. The roots of the unsafe vehicle problem are so entrenched that the situation can be improved only by the forging of new instruments of citizen action. When thirty practicing physicians picketed for safe auto design at the New York International Automobile Show on April 7, 1965, their unprecedented action was the measure of their desperation over the inaction of the men and institutions in government and industry who have failed to provide the public with the vehicle safety to which it is entitled. The picketing surgeons, orthopedists, pediatricians and general practitioners marched in protest because the existing medical, legal and engineering organizations have defaulted.

A great problem of contemporary life is how to control the power of economic interests which ignore the harmful effects of their applied science and technology. The automobile tragedy is one of the most serious of these man-made assaults on the human body. The history of that tragedy reveals many obstacles which must be overcome in the taming of any mechanical or biological hazard which is a by-product of industry or commerce. Our society's obligation to protect the "body rights" of its citizens with vigorous resolve and ample resources requires the precise, authoritative articulation and front-rank support which is being devoted to civil rights.

This country has not been entirely laggard in defining values relevant to new contexts of a technology laden with risks. The post war years have witnessed a historic broadening, at least in the courts, of the procedural and substantive rights of the injured and the duties of manufacturers to produce a safe product. Judicial decisions throughout the fifty states have given living meaning to Walt Whitman's dictum, "If anything is sacred, the human body is sacred." Mr. Justice Jackson in 1953 defined the duty of the manufacturers by saying, "Where experiment or research is necessary to determine the presence or the degree of danger, the product must not be tried out on the public, nor must the public be expected to possess the facilities or the technical knowledge to learn for itself of inherent but latent dangers. The claim that a hazard was not foreseen is not available to one who did not use foresight appropriate to his enterprise."

It is a lag of almost paralytic proportions that these values of safety concerning consumers and economic enterprises, reiterated many times by the judicial branch of government, have not found their way into legislative policy-making for safer automobiles. Decades ago legislation was passed, changing the pattern of private business investments to accommodate more fully the safety value on railroads, in factories, and more recently on ships and aircraft. In transport, apart from the motor vehicle, considerable progress has been made in recognizing the physical integrity of the individual. There was the period when railroad workers were killed by the thousands and the editor of *Harper's* could say late in the last century: "So long as brakes cost more than trainmen, we may expect the present sacrificial method of car-coupling to be continued." But injured trainmen did cause the railroads some operating dislocations; highway victims cost the automobile companies next to nothing and the companies are not obliged to make use of developments in science-technology that have demonstrably opened up opportunities for far greater safety than any existing safety features lying unused on the automobile companies' shelves.

A principal reason why the automobile has remained the only transportation vehicle to escape being called to meaningful public account is that the public has never been supplied the information nor offered the quality of competition to enable it to make effective demands through the marketplace and through government for a safe, nonpolluting and efficient automobile that can be produced economically. The consumer's expectations regarding automotive innovations have been deliberately held low and mostly oriented to very gradual annual style changes. The specialists and researchers outside the industry who could have provided the leadership to stimulate this flow of information by and large chose to remain silent, as did government officials.

The persistence of the automobile's immunity over the years has nourished the continuance of that immunity, recalling Francis Bacon's insight: "He that will not apply new remedies must expect new evils, for time is the greatest innovator."

The accumulated power of decades of effort by the automobile industry to strengthen its control over car design is reflected today in the difficulty of even beginning to bring it to justice. The time has not come to discipline the automobile for safety; that time came over four decades ago. But that is not cause to delay any longer what should have been accomplished in the nineteen-twenties.

14

Perspective on Product Safety

National Commission on Product Safety

This report of the National Commission on Product Safety measures the exposure of consumers to product hazards, identifies product categories where hazards are most often found, comments on the efficacy of industry self-regulation, and reviews the extent to which regulatory agencies and common law protect the consumer against such hazards.

SUMMARY FINDINGS

This Commission has now, within the resources and time allotted, carried out the direction of the President and the Congress to "conduct a comprehensive study and investigation of the scope and adequacy of measures now employed to protect consumers against unreasonable risks of injuries which may be caused by hazardous household products."

Congress requested our answers to several critical questions:

(1) What is the measure of exposure of American consumers to unreasonable product hazards?

(2) Which specific categories of products were found to present such hazards?

(3) To what extent does self-regulation by industry afford adequate protection against such hazards?

(4) To what extent do Federal, State, local authorities, and

Reprinted from *Final Report of the National Commission on Product Safety,* National Commission on Product Safety (June 30, 1970), pp. 1-8.

(5) to what extent does the common law protect the consumer against such hazards?

Our answers to these questions in summary are as follows:

Measure of Exposure

Americans—20 million of them—are injured each year in the home as a result of incidents connected with consumer products.[1] Of the total, 110,000 are permanently disabled and 30,000 are killed. A significant number could have been spared if more attention had been paid to hazard reduction. The annual cost to the Nation of product-related injuries may exceed $5.5 billion.

The exposure of consumers to unreasonable consumer product hazards is excessive by any standard of measurement.

Unreasonable Hazards

Within the following categories of products, we found a number of makes, models, or types harboring unreasonable hazards to the American consumer: architectural glass, color television sets, fireworks, floor furnaces, glass bottles, high-rise bicycles, hot-water vaporizers, household chemicals, infant furniture, ladders, power tools, protective headgear, rotary lawnmowers, toys, unvented gas heaters, and wringer washers. Not all products in each category are unreasonably hazardous. Still other categories which may harbor unreasonable hazards were not investigated in sufficient depth by us to warrant a specific finding that unreasonable hazards exist.

Self-Recognition

As related to product safety, self-regulation by trade associations and standards groups, drawing upon the resources of professional associations and independent testing laboratories, is legally unenforceable and patently inadequate.

Competitive forces may require management to subordinate safety factors to cost considerations, styling, and other marketing imperatives.

There is a dearth of factors motivating producers toward safety. Only a few of the largest manufacturers have coherent, articulated safety engineering programs. Manufacturers' efforts to obtain data on injuries and on the costs and benefits of design changes that will reduce unreasonable hazards can be charitably described as sketchy and sporadic.

Industry activities to develop safety standards can provide an important forum for marshaling the technical competence necessary for this work, but their voluntary nature inherently inhibits the development of optimal standards.

The consensus principle, which is at the heart of all voluntary standards making, is not effective for elevating safety standards. It permits the least responsible segment of an industry to retard progress in reducing hazards.

The measure of voluntary consumer protection provided by the certification programs of independent laboratories is substantial, but is theoretically flawed by the laboratory's economic dependence on the goodwill of the manufacturer even if the laboratory is nonprofit.

The protection afforded by various seals of approval is no better than the technical competence, product-testing protocols, and independence of the certifier. When an industry association awards the seal, or when it is awarded in return for paid advertising, the seal may convey a deceptive implication of third-party independence. Consumers appear to attribute to such endorsements a significance beyond their specific meaning.

Protection by Law

Federal Law. Consumers assume that the Federal Government exercises broad regulatory authority in the interest of their safety. And yet the short answer to this question is that Federal authority to curb hazards in consumer products is virtually nonexistent.

Federal product safety legislation consists of a series of isolated acts treating specific hazards in narrow product categories. No Government agency possesses general authority to ban products which harbor unreasonable risks or to require that consumer products conform to minimum safety standards.

Such limited Federal authority as does exist is scattered among many agencies. Jurisdiction over a single category of products may be shared by as many as four different departments or agencies. Moreover, where it exists, Federal product safety regulation is burdened by unnecessary procedural obstacles, circumscribed investigative powers, inadequate and ill-fitting sanctions, bureaucratic lassitude, timid administration, bargain-basement budgets, distorted priorities, and misdirected technical resources.

Nevertheless, where there is adequate authority and administrative support, Federal safety standards programs have demonstrated a capacity for substantially upgrading industry safety practices.

The Federal Government operates no injury data center charged with responsibility for the systematic collection, evaluation, and dissemination of data related to product safety. It has no early-warning system to alert responsible officials in business and Government of suspected areas of latent product risk. Data on the number and nature of injuries from consumer products remain far from satisfactory, despite several revealing probes in the data collection field conducted by us.

Federal law now provides no machinery to enjoin a manufacturer from marketing consumer products that are unreasonably dangerous. There is no way to compel the recall of such products for repair or replacement.

No Federal law provides meaningful criminal penalties for manufacturers who knowingly or willfully market consumer products that create an unreasonable danger to life and health.

No Federal agency has authority to order studies or hearings to determine the presence of an unreasonable hazard in most consumer products; to order the development of standards or to issue regulations to reduce the hazard; to enforce such orders; to evaluate safety standards, tests, and standards-making procedures; to monitor compliance with safety standards; to accredit independent laboratories to check compliance; to require that information on product safety be collected and freely exchanged; to support voluntary or State programs to reduce product hazards; or to conduct programs of training and research in product safety.

State and Local Law. Our studies of State and local laws show a hodgepodge of tragedy-inspired responses to challenges that cannot be met by restricted geographical entities. Local prohibitions against sale of hazardous items cannot be enforced against the retailer across the city line. Manufacturers of hazardous products can make and ship out items that cannot be sold at retail in their own community. Without central leadership, States and municipalities are unable to chart broad spectrum product safety programs. Balkanized jurisdiction plagues some manufacturers with diverse manufacturing specifications that interfere with distribution of their products.

Common Law. The common law has not been primarily concerned with prospective enforcement of product safety but with postinjury remedies. There are no reports of consumers successfully restraining the marketing of potentially hazardous products. The costs of such litigation would be beyond the means of citizens or concerned groups.

In the absence of the contingent fee, the injured consumer most often would be unable to seek compensation for damages caused by product-related injuries. He must first be aware of his legal right to sue the producers of the defective product and, second, he must have sustained sufficient damage so that an attorney will find in his cause the promise of an adequate fee. Then, after intolerable delays, the consumer finally has a day in court in which he may be faced with overcoming an array of practical and legal hurdles.

Despite its humanitarian adaptations to meet the challenge of product-caused injuries, the common law puts no reliable restraint upon product hazards.

Conclusion

Because of the inadequacy of existing controls on product hazards, we find a need for a major Federal role in the development and execution of methods to protect the American consumer.

PATHS TO SAFETY

In formulating our recommendations, we elected not to choose between describing general policies, on the one hand, and prescribing specific action, on the other. Since we do not presume to anticipate the wishes of Congress, we determined to state both our general policies and their specific implications. The proposed Consumer Product Safety Act which we respectfully submit with this report is the concrete expression of our recommendations.

Injury Factors

There are those who believe that safety, like charity, begins at home in the behavior of the family—steadying ladders, storing knives, supervising children. Others believe that safety begins with the home itself, the environment where hazardous products find their uses—good lighting, well-insulated wiring, slipproof bath tubs and rugs, latched cabinets for medicine and household chemicals. A third view is that safety begins in the factory and involves design, construction, hazard analysis, and quality control.

None of these views is wholly right or wrong. The classical concept of epidemiology counts all three factors: host, environment, and agent. Close examination of the three uncovers many subsidiary factors: hosts of different capacities and habits; differing social, political, and psychological as well as physical environments; and agents acting in combination, additively, or serially.

With due regard for the multiple factors affecting household safety, sound strategy for a safety program is to seek the weak link in a chain of events leading to injury and to break the chain at that point.

After considering the many forces contributing to the toll of injuries in and around the American home, we have concluded that the greatest promise for reducing risks resides in energizing the manufacturer's ingenuity.

We do not mean that manufacturers by themselves can do all that is needed to achieve an optimal safety record. We mean that with Government stimulation they can accomplish more for safety with less effort and expense than any other body—more than educators, the courts, regulatory agencies, or individual consumers.

Manufacturers have it in their power to design, build, and market products in ways that will reduce if not eliminate most unreasonable and unnecessary hazards. Manufacturers are best able to take the longest strides to safety in the least time. The capacity of individual manufacturers to devise safety programs, without undue extra cost, has been demonstrated repeatedly in the course of our short history: in safety glass, double-insulated power tools, baffles on rotary mowers, noncombustible TV transformers, and releases on wringer washers.

Energy Factors. We do not imagine that, even without regard to cost, safety programs on the manufacturer's level can eliminate all household hazards. A society which uses energy in the volume and variety of forms prevalent in ours is certain to see traces of that energy go astray. Instead of doing the work intended, the energy can damage property and person. In whatever form—chemical, mechanical, thermal, electrical, nuclear, acoustic—energy which is misdirected cuts, strangles, burns, bruises, fractures, suffocates, poisons, shocks, and ruptures.

Behavioral Factors. Danger is a regrettable but unavoidable facet of life. Many persons who like to fly, surf, dive, or speed are proud of their ability to cope with it. Usually, they are keenly conscious of the hazards and take pains to control them.

But everyone, at one time or another, suffers from complacency, a certainty that everything is under control, that injuries happen only to the other fellow. Then, in that moment of carefree confidence, disaster strikes. The mower goes over a grade, slips out of control, and the blades chop at the feet. Many, with utmost care, commit themselves to handling dangerous instruments which, for lack of experience, knowledge, or skill, they cannot manage. An ineradicable minority is careless; they will wear a flammable garment near an open fire; use a power saw without a guard; work a lathe without safety glasses.

Environmental Factors. In addition to such behavioral factors, a hazardous environment aggravates the frequency and severity of injuries. Some environmental hazards are sporadic: power surges, extremes of temperature or humidity. The worst hazards are common and chronic.

The majority of American homes contain potential electrical fire and shock hazards: worn or defective wiring, overloaded circuits, or an absence of grounding. Injuries result from dim lighting, uneven floors, irregular steps, slippery surfaces, obstacles, steep inclines, poor drainage, or faulty ventilation. Broken glass and rusty cans litter yards and alleys. Much of a child's play amounts to running a gantlet of environmental hazards.

Manufacturers' Responsibility

Prospects for measurable reform of human behavior are distant. Similarly, there is little hope for an early improvement of the home environment. The limited power of conventional educational methods has been described by our witnesses.

Consequently, while continuing to educate and seeking even better ways, there seems little choice but to concentrate on reducing unreasonable hazards by encouraging additional care in the design and manufacture of products.

The law has tended in recent years to place full responsibility for injuries attributable to defective products upon the manufacturer.

But beyond his liability for damages, a producer owes society-at-large the duty to assure that unnecessary risks of injury are eliminated. He is in the best position to know what are the safest designs, materials, construction methods, and modes of use. Before anyone else, he must explore the boundaries of potential danger from the use of his product. He must be in a position to advise the buyer competently how to use and how to maintain and repair the product.

Technical problems of assuring the quality of a product can be difficult to manage, particularly when demands are high and labor in short supply. When the will to make a product safe is weak, protection for the consumer is even weaker. Among many manufacturers, fortunately, the will to reduce hazards is not weak, but it may be frustrated by competitive forces.

The Government Role

Paradoxically, the processes of Government share the onus for our lagging product safety efforts. Rightly or wrongly, antitrust considerations are broadly construed to outlaw agreements by competitors to expunge particular hazards from the marketplace. While exemption from the antitrust laws would create more problems than it would solve, the sincere efforts of many producers to achieve uniform optimum safety for their products can be frustrated without positive governmental involvement.

For the following reasons, we conclude that the Federal Government, both to protect consumers and to strengthen manufacturers' efforts, should enact comprehensive legal measures to reduce hazards:

In the absence of compulsion to reduce risks in consumer products, manufacturers who cut corners on safety have an unfair competitive advantage over responsible manufacturers.

Manufacturers have advised us that they seek Government aid in gathering data which will help to explain injuries and their causes and to suggest priorities for preventing injuries.

Potentially, the cost of meeting safety requirements may require sellers to raise prices above a desirable level or may impose an unwarranted and unacceptable design on a product; accordingly, Government must participate, in behalf of the consumer, in making the quasi-political decision of determining how much risk to safety the public should tolerate under the circumstances.

Voluntary safety standards decided upon by an industry may unfairly penalize some manufacturers, small businessmen particularly, to the advantage of others.

Although safety standards must be written with the assistance of technical personnel who know most about the product, Government can best determine impartially whether a safety standard is sufficient.

When some manufacturers ignore safety standards, only Government can assure compliance. To implement compliance, only Government can require that authorized laboratories certify that products meet safety requirements. Government can assure that programs to inspect products and report injuries will be effectively financed. Government should enjoin actions which carelessly put the consumer in jeopardy. And, when voluntary safety standards are absent or insufficient, Government should insist that industry devise a sufficient standard or develop and issue its own.

CRITICAL QUESTIONS

Having concluded that remedial action was essential to reduce product hazards to consumers, we faced certain critical questions:

1. Should Federal authority be extended to new programs to reduce unreasonable hazards in consumer products and, if so, what form should such authority take?

2. In view of the frustrations and disappointments characterizing some Federal efforts in behalf of the consumer, what could be done to strengthen such efforts and bolster the position of the consumer in the sometimes intricate regulatory processes?

3. What role should mandatory safety standards play in reducing product hazards?

We approached these questions without prejudice. In framing judgments, we relied on our own hearings and inquiries as well as the literature of administrative law and Government regulation. On the whole, our approach was pragmatic. We looked at what had been done and at a variety of critiques and proposals as indications of what might be done. And we concluded, with virtual unanimity, that—

Broad responsibility for the safety of consumer products should be vested in a conspicuously independent Federal regulatory agency, a Consumer Product Safety Commission (CPSC), appointed by the President and confirmed by the Senate.

There should be one official appointed by the President as a Consumer Safety Advocate to the Commission's staff, whose primary responsibility is to serve as the consumer's spokesman before the CPSC on all issues within its jurisdiction.

Extensive authority to issue regulations and develop mandatory safety standards should be granted to the CPSC to anticipate or reduce unreasonable hazards in a wide range of consumer products.

Independent Federal Authority

Statutory regulatory programs buried in agencies with broad and diverse missions have, with few exceptions, rarely fulfilled their mission. The specific experience of safety programs relating to hazardous substances, pesticides, and flammable fabrics is discussed later in some detail.

The reasons for their weaknesses include lack of adequate funding and staffing because of competition with other deserving programs within an agency; lack of vigor in enforcing the law caused by an absence of authority and independence in some Federal administrators; and a low priority assigned to programs of low visibility.

Of course, not all Federal safety programs which are part of larger agencies exhibit these symptoms. The broad-based Federal Trade Commission displayed admirable vigor in proceeding against health hazards of cigarettes. The Federal Highway Administration of the Department of Transportation, though lightly staffed and funded, is working effectively to reduce the toll of injuries from automobile accidents.

Notwithstanding these efforts, when a Federal agency must take up substantial and controversial issues of consumer safety and economics, we believe it needs independent status.

Independence can be furthered by appointment of commissioners on a nonpartisan basis, for staggered fixed terms subject to removal only for cause, and by designation of a permanent chairman to serve an entire term in that capacity.

Another reason for our recommendation of an independent commission stems from our own experience over the past 2 years. Elsewhere in this report, we describe some of the significant safety innovations which have been adopted by industry after issues were raised by this Commission. As a result of our hearings and public exposure, industry took important steps for safety.

Visibility has aided us in communicating public needs to business. We believe that a highly visible Consumer Product Safety Commission will have the potential to deal firmly and at arm's length with the industries it must regulate in behalf of the public.

The high visibility of a vigorous independent commission would also be a constant reminder of the Federal presence and would itself stimulate voluntary improvement of safety practices. The issues before the CPSC should be publicly aired; they are less likely to be smothered in the competition of Federal agencies for public notice. Similarly, CPSC's needs for staff and funds will receive more public attention and consideration by the Congress and by the Bureau of the Budget than those of a section of a branch of a division of a bureau of a service of an office of a department.

Finally, in developing acceptable safety standards for consumer products, it is important that manufacturers confront Government officials who, like themselves, are in command of resources and authority and able to make firm commitments and decisions.

The preference of at least some in the business community for an independent agency over one of the existing agencies in the product safety area was indicated in an informal poll of more than 50 industry officials taken by Underwriters' Laboratories in August 1969. The poll listed 14 proposed governmental safety functions; the group preferred that an independent agency—about which they knew nothing—administer 12, in preference to the Department of Health, Education, and Welfare and the Commerce Department's National Bureau of Standards.

A Consumer Advocate

Contrary to the common concept that "we are all consumers" and the simple assumption that a public agency always defends the public interest, in reality most if not all public decisions represent a compromise among contending factions.

Recognition of the consumer's need for representation in Government decision-making was the motivating force in the creation of the President's Special Assistant for Consumer Affairs in 1963 and for the continuance of that function in the President's Committee on Consumer Interests.

On day-to-day matters of product safety, however, the consumer has no official champion. The assumption that Federal officials represent the general public interest breaks down when, in a bargaining situation, no one bargains for the consumer. Frequently, instead of serving the consumer, the Federal agency merely provides the forum where the consumer is an affected but helpless bystander.

We believe that the highly complex issues which will face the Consumer Product Safety Commission require a specialized Consumer Safety Advocate to make the voice of the consumer heard. When the agency serves as an arbiter, seeking to reconcile contending interests, the Advocate will defend the consumer. By institutionalizing a focus of consumer representation, it may no longer be said that "everybody's business is nobody's business."

The relationship between the President's Special Assistant for Consumer Affairs and the Consumer Safety Advocate of the Commission can be expected to be complementary. The role of the Advocate will, however, be quite different from that of the proposed Consumer Protection Division in the Department of Justice, which has a potential for filing suits to enjoin deceptive practices and intervening in agency proceedings.

In the past, the legal doctrine that participants in adversary proceedings must have a direct economic interest has deprived consumers of "standing" before courts and agencies. This "standing" doctrine, admitting only parties with substantial economic interest, has been broadened recently by several court decisions.

A Consumer Safety Advocate in Commission proceedings will assure consumers of the representation now authorized by the courts and supplement the efforts of non-governmental advocates, if granted authority and staff sufficient to draw upon the technical resources of other Federal agencies.

We do not propose that he have any jurisdictional authority over the Commission or other Federal regulatory agencies. We propose that, through him, the consumer will be assured the same rights as any other interested group: access to information and the resources for asserting and defending his rights. There is clear justification for an office which will defend public interests against bureaucratic excess or private indifference.

Mandatory Standards

In the absence of unreasonable risks, Federal action is unnecessary. Government should avoid needless intervention in private enterprise and the expense of developing redundant standards. At the same time, the existence of Federal authority to set mandatory safety standards may well stimulate improvements in, and compliance with, adequate voluntary standards. We have designed proposed standard-setting provisions to operate only when an identified product hazard is found and then only after a reasonable opportunity has been given to private individuals and consumer and industry groups to develop a draft standard for submission to the CPSC.

When the Commission determines that a product presents an identified hazard to life or health, the task of forming safety standards must be performed promptly but with sure-handed judgment. Because informal rule-making is best suited for the determination of the kinds of issues in the development of standards and to prevent obstruction, the informal procedure rather than a formal hearing is preferable, with judicial review for all interested persons.

In any event, the Commission must be selective, limiting its development and updating of safety standards to categories of consumer goods which contain an unreasonable risk or the threat thereof.

When the need for action is apparent, the writing of safety standards must not drag on for months. A standard must be completed as quickly as governmental and private resources permit. We have provided in the proposed system that the Commission may make an interim product safety standard effective immediately where it finds an imminent risk to safety.

In the event that private sources fail to frame a needed and adequate standard, the CPSC must have its own technical resources and authority to tap personnel and facilities of the Federal Government and private sources to develop mandatory safety standards. Safety standards cannot be deferred until all makers of a product are satisfied; dissatisfied manufacturers will be able to appeal what they consider unjustifiably stringent standards to the CPSC or, ultimately, to the courts.

DIGEST OF RECOMMENDATIONS

It is not the number or kinds of injuries but the fact of injury—the chronic disability, the mental anguish, the burden of medical costs, and the economic waste—that demands remedial action to reduce unreasonable product hazards by the most direct and efficient means.

By way of remedy, our recommendations, stated in full at the conclusion of this report, provide:

1. That the Congress of the United States enact an omnibus Consumer Product Safety Act committing the authority and resources of the Federal government to the elimination of unreasonable product hazards.

2. That an independent Consumer Product Safety Commission be established as a Federal agency concerned exclusively with the safety of consumer products.

3. That the Consumer Product Safety Commission be directed to secure voluntary cooperation of consumers and industry in advancing its programs and that, when necessary to protect consumers from unreasonable risks of death or injury, the Commission be empowered to—

- Develop and set mandatory consumer product safety standards;
- Enforce compliance with consumer product safety standards through a broad range of civil and criminal sanctions;
- Enjoin distribution or sale of consumer products which violate Federal safety standards or which are unreasonably hazardous.
- Require notice to consumers of substantially defective products, and recall of products which violate consumer product safety standards or which are unreasonably dangerous.
- Make reasonable inspections of manufacturing facilities to implement compliance with safety standards and regulations; and
- Conduct public hearings and subpoena witnesses and documents.

4. That the Consumer Product Safety Commission be given the further responsibility to—

- Establish an Injury Information Clearing-house to collect and analyze data on deaths and injuries associated with consumer products;
- Disseminate information to the public about hazardous consumer products and practicable means of reducing hazards; and
- Cooperate with and assist States and localities in programs germane to consumer product safety.

5. That a consumer Safety Advocate to the Commission be appointed by the President, with specific responsibility to represent consumer interests before the Commission.

6. That the Consumer Product Safety Commission, in cooperation with the Secretary of Commerce, be authorized to accredit private testing laboratories which are qualified to test and certify compliance with specific product safety standards,

and that the Commission be empowered to require independent testing of consumer products which may present an unreasonable risk.

7. That the Federal Trade Commission promulgate trade regulation rules for those who certify or endorse the safety of consumer products.

8. That Federal agencies provide industry and standards-setting groups with relevant technological information which may be utilized to reduce product hazards and that, where proprietary, such information be ruled in the public domain with provision for adequate compensation.

9. That upon enactment of a comprehensive Consumer Product Safety Act a method be developed to permit Federal technical experts other than those with responsibility for evaluating the adequacy of industry standards and testing programs to participate in voluntary safety standard activities.

10. That the Consumer Product Safety Commission be authorized and afforded funds for the construction and operation of a facility suitable for research, development of test methods, and analysis of consumer products for safety considerations.

11. That existing programs of the Small Business Administration be expanded to authorize low interest loans to assist small businesses in meeting requirements of product safety standards.

12. That the Federal Government, through its purchasing and insuring agents, look to established safety standards and, wherever practicable, new safety designs in selecting products for use, and that Federal agencies publicize acquired information about hazards in consumer products.

13. That injured consumers be permitted to file claims for treble damages in the District Courts of the the United States against manufacturers who intentionally violate Federal safety standards; that Federal class action procedures be made applicable; and that the principles of strict tort liability be adopted by State and Federal courts to assure fair compensation for injury to consumers in suits at common law.

14. That consumer products for import into the United States be denied entry if they violate Federal safety standards and that export of consumer products which do not meet Federal safety standards be prohibited unless waiver is obtained from a responsible official of the country of destination.

15. That the United States support the development of international consumer product safety standards, and assure fair representation of consumer interests in such proceedings

REFERENCES

1. *We use the term "consumer products" (instead of "household products" as referred to in our enabling law) because that term best describes our statutory mandate and most products which are not now subject to adequate Federal safety regulation. Consumer products include all retail products used by consumers in or around the household, except foods, drugs, cosmetics, motor vehicles, insecticides, firearms, cigarettes, radiological hazards, and certain flammable fabrics.

15

New Pressures for Consumer Information—Will "Uncle" Talk?

Sales Management

Interior tests frozen fish products, Agriculture the effectiveness of insecticides. FTC the inflammability of furs and fabrics, FDA anything from skin preparations to clinical thermometers. What happens to this wealth of information? That's what militant consumers and now Congress want to know.

Ever since consumerism came into vogue, there have been demands that the federal government open its valuable storehouse of product performance test data to a supposedly information-starved buying public. Locked therein, say the consumer crusaders, are government-held secrets that could help consumers buy more intelligently, more economically, and with greater assurance of safety. So far, federal agencies have remained both silent and reluctant, tending to view their storehouse as a Pandora's box whose sudden opening might unleash a plague of misunderstandings, injuries to manufacturers, and possible lawsuits against the government.

But now the consumer crusaders are joined by a three-man study panel of the House Government Operations Committee, which calls itself the "Special Consumer Inquiry." Headed by vocal Rep. Benjamin S. Rosenthal, a Queens, N.Y., democrat long identified with consumerism, the special unit has been holding sporadic hearings this spring and summer, summoning federal agencies one by one to ask why they

Reprinted from *Sales Management,* vol. 94, no. 7 (September 20, 1967), pp. 41-43. Reprinted by permission.

aren't sharing more of their product test data and brand-name comparison studies with the general public.

If nothing else, the hearings have revealed that there is indeed a wealth of product information, which if released might upset a lot of corporate apple carts. Perhaps the richest lode of extractable data is located within the General Services Administration (GSA), which maintains federal purchasing specifications for some 5,000 items plus a "Qualified Products List" showing those manufacturers rated as acceptable to bid on about 90 categories of more complex equipment. In order to establish the specifications and standards, products of each classification must be tested by government technicians or contracting research organizations. About 40% of the items on GSA purchasing lists are tested by its own staff, with the rest done on assignment by Commerce Dept.'s National Bureau of Standards, the Dept. of Defense, and other agencies. (Sometimes, would-be sellers to government are allowed to arrange for independent tests of their own products.)

In addition, many government agencies are constantly making product evaluations entirely apart from any connection with federal purchasing. The most active is the National Bureau of Standards (NBS), which, besides testing for other government agencies, helps set some 300 voluntary standards for private industry and (infrequently) conducts calibrations at the request of individual companies. Other executive agencies are actively testing in their own respective fields. Interior Dept.'s Bureau of Commercial Fisheries regularly analyzes frozen fish products in consumer packages (but conceals manufacturers' identities in its reports). The Agriculture Dept., perhaps government's most consumer-oriented agency, makes product comparisons that range from the efficacy of insecticides to the performance of home freezers. The Federal Trade Commission evaluates flammability of certain furs and fabrics, and the new Dept. of Transportation has been given responsibility for testing such automotive products as tires, seat belts, and brake fluids. Testing at the Food and Drug Administration ranges from skin preparations to antibiotics to clinical thermometers. FDA's sister agency, the Public Health Service, has just opened a large laboratory in Cincinnati to conduct safety studies on aerosol containers, radiation-producing appliances, and other products that may cause injuries in the home.

The confidential reports that emerge initially from such tests sometimes identify manufacturers and brand name products—but seldom, if ever, after they've been refined and published for public consumption. Often, a test evaluation, such as a report on acoustical and fire-resistant properties of building materials by the Bureau of Standards, will list individual manufacturers by code numbers. But more frequently, the basic product evaluations are used to develop general instructions for government agencies or the consuming public on how to buy and use a certain class of product more efficiently.

Consumer crusaders don't feel it's enough. What they want now is the basic product-by-product data behind the buying specifications, voluntary standards, and how-to-do-it consumer booklets. "Let's take hearing aids," says Peter S. Barash, chief investigator for the House study unit. "Tests have shown that some products on the market are simply no good. The government [the Veterans Administration for one] knows exactly which ones they are." Barash adds that government-held data need not involve brand comparisons to prove helpful to consumers. "For example," he says, "GSA specifications tell when to use rubber asbestos tile and when to use vinyl. They tell what types of scouring pads shouldn't be used on glass products and what kind of lawn mowers will tip over on a 30° slope. All of these bits of information can be used by consumers to get a better buy."

Armed with similar convictions, an increasingly impatient consumer lobby is badgering the federal establishment to tell all. The most persistent argument is that a data bank built with the dollars of taxpayers has an obligation to reward the people on their investment. A more pragmatic reason, perhaps, is advanced by Morris Kaplan, technical director of the Consumers Union, who states that "if consumers purchased products on the basis of objectively determined values, savings of as much as 50% could be realized." Still another appeal—safety—is typified by an outburst from Rep. Rosenthal at one of his panel's recent hearings. "Look at the area of safety electrical cords," he exclaimed. "Thirty-five thousand kids are injured each year by pulling cords of electrical appliances. Now you [the government witness] don't buy items with retractable cords and yet you look aside and say, 'We won't tell anybody about it.' Or let's take wringer-type washing machines, which GSA doesn't permit the government to buy. Last year, 100,000 children were hurt in wringer washing machines. It seems to me that mothers of those 100,000 children would be happy to know that their government doesn't think wringer washing machines are safe, and that maybe they ought to think twice before buying one."

Despite strong pleas like these, many government officials remain both skeptical and reluctant. Those at the Bureau of Standards, for example, want to avoid any stigma of telling customers what to buy. Nor do they want any part of making comparison evaluations between brands. Others fret that release of such information might subject the government to a deluge of lawsuits. Example: What if the government said Brand X was safe and it wasn't? Perhaps the greatest reason for skepticism stems from doubts as to its practical benefits. Heinz A. Abersfeller, commissioner of GSA's Federal Supply Service, raised a question during the House hearings as to how valuable a shopper would find federal buying specifications when looking over a product in a store. "After all," said Abersfeller, "she can't buy a product simply to test it. And she can't test it when she's in the store, either." Another GSA spokesman added, "It wouldn't do much good for a housewife to know what mops we think are top quality because we buy them for institutional use, not household use. The smallest of our mops weighs three pounds dry. When loaded with water, it would be much too heavy for a housewife."

But consumer spokesmen are quick to pooh-pooh Abersfeller's doubts. Says the Consumers Union's Morris Kaplan: "It would be relatively simple to convert the various purchasing specifications and highly technical test results into meaningful consumer information, and at little expense." At least one federal official agrees. Asked by Rep. Rosenthal if such a project would entail a "major increase in personnel requirements," Malcolm W. Jensen, the Standards Bureau's manager of engineering standards, replied, "Negative." According to Jensen, "We would only need a few general engineers in chemistry, physics, and engineering, and a few technical writers and clerks. With the assistance of the President's Committee on Consumer Interests, we could then set up an order of priority for gathering information from all agencies concerned and convert it." He envisions nickle and dime pamphlets being made easily accessible to all consumers. "We could have just one small office to handle both inflow from the agencies and output to the consumer." Jensen adds quickly, however, that, "We couldn't have just one agency doing the job. It would have to be made the over-all policy of the government."

Right now, it's not too clear just what the "over-all policy of the government" really is. On one hand, it appears that there is nothing at all to impede a greater flow of "how-to-do-it" material and technical translations relating to general product categories. As GSA's Heinz Abersfeller replied when asked by Rosenthal why he couldn't release an internal booklet on *Cleaning, Waxing, and Maintenance of Soft Floors,* "We'd be pleased to make it available if someone would pick up the tab for printing." On the other hand, a stiff down-the-line resistance appears to exist on the subject of brand name comparisons. Initially, consumer spokesmen hailed the newly enacted "Freedom of Information" law as the wedge that would break open government's lock on brand name data. But if anything, it's worked the other way. "Before the law was passed," says a top NBS official, "our policy against releasing data on individual company products was negative and, admittedly, a little fuzzy around the edges. Now we've been required to sort out all of our files and determine just what can and can't be opened up. As a result, we now have a clear-cut policy on not releasing brand name comparisons. This goes not only for consumers but for any company that may be after competitive secrets." The statement was pretty much echoed by the public affairs chiefs of five other consumer-oriented agencies contacted by SM, as by several spokesmen for three regulatory agencies (FTC, CAB, FCC) whose files hold confidential marketing data.

Despite budget barriers on the release of "general" consumer information and the rigid policies against sharing brand name data, Rep. Rosenthal intends to keep up the pressure on both fronts. If persuasion eventually won't work, he sees three possible alternatives. One might be to prevail on the President to issue an Executive Order that would lower the federal drawbridge to consumers throughout the nation. A second would be enabling legislation on an agency-by-agency basis. A third would be to persuade Congress to create an agency charged with pulling together for publication all the consumer information now held by individual government agencies. Rosenthal, in fact, has long sponsored a bill calling for creation of a "national consumer service foundation" to do not only that but to act as the "consumer's voice in government." A similar measure is being promoted in the Senate by Michigan democrat Philip Hart and 21 co-sponsors.

Which route? Rosenthal, who points out that his hearings aren't finished yet, insists he'll continue his policy of friendly persuasion first. "We aren't going to bring in the heavy artillery," he says, "until we've at least fired our rifles."

16

Consumer Class Action: Selected Statements

The following three statements before the Senate Judiciary
Committee regarding class action proposals present the
contrasting views of the business community (National
Association of Manufacturers), an administrative officer of
a regulatory agency (FTC Commissioner Mary Gardiner
Jones), and consumers (Ralph Nader).

National Association of Manufacturers

The following statement is submitted on behalf of the National Association of Manufacturers, a voluntary Association of business and industrial firms, large and small,
located in every state, and producing a major part of the nation's manufactured goods.

In considering S. 3201, the Consumers Protection Act of 1970, already reported
favorably by the Senate Commerce Committee, we are confident that the Judiciary
Committee will examine fully its provisions and make assessment of its potential
impact on the business community as well as upon consumers. Where amendments are
needed, we trust these will be offered.

We are particularly distressed that many changes in this proposed legislation were
made by the Commerce Committee after the close of hearings and without sufficient
opportunity for comment. In the paragraphs which follow we deal with these aspects
of the bill, plus those other provisions we deem to be of paramount importance.

At section 103 provision is made for civil penalties—up to $10,000 for each unfair
consumer practice as spelled out under section 201 of the Act—where the Federal

Reprinted from *Consumer Protection Act of 1970* (Hearings before the Committee on the Judiciary, United States Senate, 91st Cong., 2d Sess., on S. 3201, 1970), pp. 376-378.

Trade Commission can demonstrate in federal district court that the act or practice was knowingly engaged in. At the outset, this might appear to be the creation of a reasonable preventative measure. However, certain difficulties are inherent in this procedure.

It was clearly recognized by the Commerce Committee that any attempt to categorize the acts or practices which are unfair or deceptive to consumers is impractical since any listing said to be complete today would be incomplete at the time of enactment into law. The device hit upon to solve this dilemma was to add the following to the list of enumerated "unfair consumer practices" at section 201 of the Act:

"Sec. 201(1)(P). Any other unfair or deceptive act or practice prohibited by rule or regulation promulgated by the Federal Trade Commission in accordance with section 6(g) of the Federal Trade Commission Act, as amended by this Act."

Amended section 6(g) referred to in the quote above gives the Commission the power to promulgate trade regulation rules defining unfair or deceptive acts or practices. Hence the list of prohibited practices is essentially open-ended since at any time the Commission may decide to exercise its substantive rule making power and thus create additional unfair consumer practices. Under settled legal doctrine, a trade regulation rule issued under these circumstances would have the force and effect of law.

We take serious exception to these procedures on a number of grounds.

As originally created, the Federal Trade Commission was empowered to restrain the continuation of unfair and deceptive practices through cease and desist orders. It was not designed to punish those who had engaged in such practices. Since one would be put directly on notice concerning those facets of his business conduct to be thereafter proscribed, the Commission was given broad powers to determine what was unfair or deceptive. The Commission may also make findings on the basis of substantial evidence—as opposed to a preponderance of evidence—and need not observe strictly the rules of evidence or be concerned about retroactivity since its orders operate prospectively.

In this context, a broadly worded prohibition, coupled with loose procedural methods, at least maintains an essential fairness if, on being found guilty of a violation, one's future conduct is restrained. The result becomes grossly unfair, however, where harsh consequences such as heavy civil penalties may flow from such a finding. In this instance specificity is particularly called for in order that one may make sound judgments concerning proposed business conduct.

The difficulties here outlined are further complicated by other important factors: not only will an unfair consumer practice give rise to civil penalties, but under this legislation it may also generate a whole range of actions for redress of injuries to consumers by the FTC (section 103) and the Justice Department (section 205). Coupled with this, section 206 of the Act would create the right of consumers to bring suit singly or in a representative capacity. And still one additional consequence might flow: willful commission of an unfair consumer practice which endangers the health or safety of consumers would constitute a misdemeanor under section 203 and could result in a $10,000 fine for each such act plus imprisonment for a year, or both.

We urge in particular that neither the Federal Trade Comission, nor any other administrative agency, is properly suited to formulate criminal law. To preserve constitutionally guaranteed rights, such conduct must be spelled out in great detail and in advance if there is to be fair warning provided concerning proscribed conduct. Neither the Commission's current procedures nor those which would be added by this legislation are sufficient to guarantee that this need will be met.

Since these are the circumstances which could attend promulgation of each new rule by the FTC designating an unfair consumer practice, there seems pressing reason for Congress to reserve this area for its own action. Added to its current authority to investigate, prosecute and judge, S. 3201 would empower the Commission, in effect, to legislate. And each addition to the list of unfair consumer practices would expand the jurisdiction of the federal courts by giving rise to new causes of action and would spawn both public and private suits.

In our view, this would be a dangerous, if not unauthorized, delegation of authority on the part of Congress to be avoided.

Section 206(b) of the Act would give rise to consumer class actions. Notwithstanding the fact that actions for redress of consumer injuries initiated by the Federal Trade Commission or the Justice Department would operate to stay and consolidate private class actions relating to the same subject matter and the same consumers, it is obvious that government action cannot and should not take place in every instance where complaints of unfair consumer practices are noted. As a result, passage of this legislation will open the federal court system to a flood of privately initiated consumer class actions. Chief Justice Burger has already noted his concern over this aspect in an August 10, 1970, speech to the American Bar Association. President Nixon, in his October 30, 1969, Consumer Message to Congress cited the need to prevent "harassment of legitimate businessmen by unlimited nuisance law suits" and thereafter the Administration proposed legislation calling for the successful completion of actions brought by FTC or the Justice Department charging unfair consumer practices as a prerequisite for the institution of private class action suits. This "trigger mechanism" would at least provide a prior screening of the merits of the case and would allow those with most significance and far-reaching effect to be selected for pursuit in court or with the Commission. Consumers seeking redress thereafter would benefit from the assistance of government investigative and prosecutorial efforts. The important point is suits without merit could be weeded out by those charged with guarding the public interest.

Something unfortunate has occurred, however, since the Administration's proposals were sent to Congress. Class action has become a popular cry and one begins to see this "remedy" appearing in a variety of legislation. Seemingly little or no thought is given to serious reservations expressed by responsible members of the business community, the Bar, Congress itself, and the Chief Justice of the United States. There is an inevitable price for legislating now and "sorting out" the difficulties later. In this instance, legitimate business, faced with frivolous, harassing actions or those based more upon defendant's ability to pay rather than the seriousness of any offense, seems most likely to be injured. But others could be injured too, and we believe there are implications for the Bar to consider. A highly damaging situation might come about which could find lawyers competing to represent a class or filing conflicting class actions. Also, there is the possibility of solicitation of class members and funds, and of misrepresentation of the purpose of the suit and of the possible effect of court orders.

Two aspects of the provisions made for payment of attorneys at section 206(d) are troublesome. In addition to damages, a successful plaintiff may be awarded the costs of suit, including attorney's fees. In determining the reasonableness of the latter, the court is to consider among other factors the actual time spent by attorneys in preparation and prosecution of the action. This seems a dis-incentive to the timely solution of controversies and could easily lead to dilatory tactics rather than honest efforts at settlement or compromise.

We are similarly disturbed by other provisions of section 206(d) which seem to make it more difficult for defendant to be awarded attorney's fees in the event of plaintiff's unsuccessful suit. In such instance, defendant must show that suit was brought "frivolously, with knowledge that the claim lacks probable cause and with intent to harassment or intimidate the defendant." We submit that such a strict measure of proof is excessive.

We would note finally that under section 206(e) class actions may be brought three years after claim arose. This seems an unnecessarily long time and, in the event there is legislation, this should be shortened by at least two years.

For a more detailed explanation of the views of this Association with regard to the general subject matter of consumer protection as covered by S. 3201, we refer you to the NAM statement of March 11, 1970, filed with the Subcommittee on the Consumer, Senate Commerce Committee, a copy of which is attached for your convenience.

Mary Gardiner Jones

The real freedom of any individual is measured by the alternatives available to him for making choices within our democratic system. As Robert McNamara said recently:

"The enhancement of human dignity and the consequent capacity to lead a fuller, freer, more thoroughly human life is the ultimate objective of human development" (Robert McNamara, address to World Bank, 9/29/69).

Today, with the increasing complexity of our technological society and the sheer increase in the numbers of people who live together in our urban areas, the citizen's opportunity to develop his capacities and sense of individual dignity is too often thwarted by his day-to-day experiences.

The marketplace is one area in our lives where our own intelligence is adequate for the job at hand—making sensible purchases and choices between things and values. It is the one area in our lives when no one disputes—at least in theory—the fact that the individual's wants and needs are the touchstone and, indeed, the sole objective, of our production and marketing system. The system may pressure us into excess purchases but it is basically geared to serve at least our material needs. Further, group action should not be necessary in order for consumers to be effective.

Yet today, consumers are confronting a marketplace in which the persons responsible for many of the problems of concern to them are too often unknown or unreachable. Consumers are concerned about package sizes, ingredient labelling and generally, with a need for more information about the products. They are increasingly frustrated in their attempts to obtain prompt and satisfactory service for the products which are being offered to them. Yet, it does them little good to voice their complaints about these matters to the retailers from whom they purchase these goods. Too frequently, they are met with the statement that the manufacturer is responsible for the packaging or labelling, that the retailer is as much at sea as respects the functional nature of the product as the consumer. In the case of service or repair, too often the delay or difficulty is attributed to the need to obtain critical parts from the factory or to the product's design or to a defect in its manufacture which the serviceman can do little about.

Consumers are also troubled today about the proliferation of goods which create such serious problems of disposal. They are worried about the potential health and environmental hazards of many of the products now on the market. They are concerned about the congestion of their highways and streets, the noise and ugliness of their communities and the increasing pollution of the air which they breathe, the rivers and lakes in which they swim and the foods which they eat. Health care has grown so astronomical in cost and skilled medical personnel so scarce a commodity that the sick and elderly can no longer be assured that they can receive care of any kind—adequate or inadequate.

Consumers cannot look to nor rely on the normal functioning of the market system

Reprinted from *Consumer Protection Act of 1970* (Hearings before the committee on the Judiciary, United States Senate, 91st Cong., 2d Sess., on S. 3201, 1970), pp. 392-396.

for any immediate and personalized response to their individual needs and grievances. Consumer sovereignty has very little practical meaning for consumers who feel themselves aggrieved.

The right not to purchase a product which is desired and needed is an ineffective way at best of expressing one's dissatisfaction with its quality or performance when no real options to purchase what would be a more desirable or satisfactory product exists. If consumers prefer smaller American cars or cars which do not pollute the atmosphere and only large cars which do pollute the atmosphere are on the market, their sovereign right not to purchase is meaningless. The list of such non-options is, of course, endless.

If consumers feel themselves "had" in the market, if they are the victims of frauds and deceptions, if unfair sales practices are used against them. If they dislike and resent particular advertising messages which are thrust upon them in the course of their TV-watching, their freedom to turn off their set, to search for a more honest merchant or to guard against being taken a second time in no way provides them with the redress to which they believe themselves to be entitled.

Yet unfortunately, the ordinary political and legal mechanisms established by society in order to enable citizens to express their views, seek change and secure redress for any injuries which they have suffered are as ineffective as the short-range functioning of the market system in enabling consumers to deal with the day-to-day problems which they typically encounter in the marketplace.

We have created government agencies for the specific purpose of protecting consumers from frauds and deceptions in the marketplace. We have also created government agencies with specific responsibility for the nation's health and education, for overseeing its transportation needs, for regulation of essential communications, travel and moving services. All of the problems served by these agencies are of direct and immediate concern to consumers. Yet today, consumers are increasingly of the belief that the regulatory policies and programs developed by these agencies do not sufficiently respond to their real needs and concerns as they perceive them. And they can find no direct means of influencing or shaping these policies.

The consumer's powers to compel action either by his government or by the business community are only of the most tenuous kind. His right to vote or to seek the assistance of his Congressman is too indirect a leverage to influence the immediate form of governmental policy. Moreover, it is of no use at all when his need is to make his retailer or serviceman respond to his immediate problem. Too often the marketplace grievances of consumers do not involve legally recognizable injury and hence our legal system offers him no means of redress for these grievances. But even where his legal rights may be violated, the consumer's right to go into court is of little value to him when the expense of bringing the suit in most instances is greater than any possible damages he might recover.

Consumers are demanding that the institutions of society—both private and governmental—created ostensibly to serve their needs operate in fact and not just in theory for their benefit and in their basic interests. This, to me, is the essential thrust and challenge of the consumer movement today.

It is vital for those of us who are individually and professionally concerned with the need to promote consumer interests to identify and work for the establishment of new mechanisms which will enable consumers to grapple more effectively with all of their various problems which confront them in today's marketplace.

In the last analysis, it is the business community which must make the changes necessary to respond to consumers' needs in the marketplace. But it is society's obligation to see to it that the changes are made and to this end it is essential to ensure that consumers' needs are known and responded to. Our challenge, therefore, is to identify and promote the changes which are necessary in a peaceful orderly manner under democratic procedures we understand. For this, we need a strong effective consumer program. It is in this area that the work of consumers' organizations is so vital.

I believe that the consumer legislation currently pending before Congress represents the most important and constructive step yet taken to provide consumers with the mechanisms which they need in order to participate intelligently and effectively in the marketplace decisions affecting their lives. I am speaking of S. 3201 recently reported out by the Senate Commerce Committee and now before the Judiciary Committee: and of H.R. 18214 now before the House Rules Committee. Together these two bills, if enacted into law, would provide a governmental and legal structure which I believe will enable consumers to ensure that the institutions of society—both private and public—which most directly affect their lives will in fact be responsive to their needs.

The House Government Operations Committee reported out a bill (H.R. 18214), now before the House Rules Committee, which would create an independent consumer protection agency and an Office of Consumer Affairs in the Executive Office of the President. The bill also establishes a Consumer Advisory Council. The independent consumer agency is empowered to protect consumer interests in government programs, conduct investigations, refer consumer complaints to appropriate agencies, and publish a consumer register containing such information as product testing results. It is also authorized to intervene in federal agency proceedings affecting consumer interests. The Office of Consumer Affairs is enpowered to coordinate the programs of all federal agencies relating to the interest of consumers. The Advisory Council is established to advise the office and the agency in matters relating to consumer interests including specifically the consumer problems of the poor. At the present time, no one can be certain of the support that exists for this bill.

Many of you undoubtedly feel strongly about the particular structure which a statutory consumer office should take. But I believe today we can all agree on one point and that is the need now to create a specific office whose sole responsibility is to represent the interests of consumers. There is no doubt in my mind that the consumer interest must be specifically represented in our governmental system. I am convinced that such an office, irrespective of whether it is a cabinet department or an independent executive agency or a statutory office within the Executive Office of the President, will be able to pinpoint the problems confronting consumers, it will be able to make the necessary investigations to determine the dimensions of their problems and point the way towards their solution. Most important, it will provide the consumer interest in our society with a much needed visibility, and it will give to consumers a vitally needed voice in the determination of all of the many national policies which so vitally affect consumers. Therefore, I believe that it is essential for those of us concerned with consumer problems to put our weight behind the establishment of a Consumer Affairs Office, however structured and even though its particular form may not represent the solution which we would prefer. What is important now, I am convinced, its to establish a statutorily defined consumer office. Once that office is functioning, experience will point the way towards changes in its structure and its powers.

The Senate bill (S. 3201, 91st Cong. 2d Sess.) which has also just been voted out of the Commerce Committee (Committee Print No. 4, July 29, 1970) is also of crucial importance to consumers because it provides consumers with essential weapons with which to combat unfair and deceptive practices which may be visited upon them in the marketplace.

One of the major handicaps under which the Federal Trade Commission has operated in the past has been its lack of effective sanctions which it could impose on merchants engaged in unfair and deceptive practices. As you know, the Commission's only power has been to impose a cease and desist order on those companies and individuals whom it has found to have violated the law. It has no broad powers to direct redress for injuries suffered by individual consumers and it has been powerless even to enforce its own orders in the event of their violation. Such toothless enforcement powers are an open invitation to law violations and in no way arms the Commission with the type of potential deterrent powers which any law enforcement agency needs in order to perform effectively its statutory responsibilities.

S. 3201, as now approved by the Senate Commerce Committee, goes a long way towards rectifying these deficiencies in the Commission's enforcement powers. Sections 102 and 103 of the bill authorize the Commission to go into the United States District Court to obtain preliminary injunctions against alleged law violators, to seek civil penalties against those companies or individuals which it has found to have engaged in certain enumerated law violations or which have violated its orders, and, most important, to initiate actions for the direct relief of injuries suffered by consumers in the form of payment of damages or of refunds or the cancellation or rescission of contracts.

In addition to providing the Commission with these essential enforcement tools, Title II of the bill confers additional consumer protection powers on the Attorney General and also deals with the vitally important question of consumers' access to the courts in order to bring their own actions to obtain redress on their own against merchants engaged in unfair and deceptive practices.

Section 201 delineates fifteen specific unfair consumer acts or practices to which Title II applies and provides that the Commission may expand this list through the promulgation of trade regulation rules. While limiting Title II to enumerated unfair practices has certain obvious disadvantages in a world where change or innovation is the rule, nevertheless, the provision enabling the Commission to expand this list of practices gives the Section some much needed flexibility and meets some of the Commission's original misgivings about this provision.

Sections 203 and 205 of the bill direct the Attorney General to enforce Title II and empower him to seek both civil and criminal penalties up to $10,000 for each unlawful practice, and, in the case of a criminal proceeding to ask in addition for a possible jail sentence. The bill also authorizes the Attorney General to seek appropriate remedies for the aggrieved party such as damages, refunds, restitution, reformation or rescission of sales agreements, repair or replacement of faulty goods, etc. These and other remedies are in addition to the liability for civil penalty. Additionally, Section 205(b) provides that the court may also order the defendant to pay money into, or otherwise secure a fund for aggrieved consumers thus insuring payment of established losses. In certain instances where there is a determination to be made of the amount due each consumer, the Federal Trade Commission as a master in chancery, may be ordered to ascertain and propose a finding of the awards to be made to the court.

I am very much in favor of this portion of the bill which authorizes the Department of Justice to act in preventing consumer frauds. In my judgment, these provisions are extremely important because they provide valuable additional resources with which to protect consumers, and thus, strengthen the enforcement tools of the government to move against law violators.

But perhaps the most crucial part of Title II is Section 206 which sets out the Senate Subcommittee's plan for consumer class actions. The Section represents a compromise between the Administration's original triggering device to precondition a consumer class action on prior governmental proceedings and the broader unrestricted Tydings-Eckhardt approach.

Under the bill as it is now approved, Section 206(a) provides that consumers may bring individual or class actions against suppliers who have been found either after final adjudication or by consent decree by either the Attorney General or the Federal Trade commission to have engaged in any of the enumerated unfair consumer practices. Subsection (b), however, empowers consumers injured by an unfair practice as defined in Title II to bring an independent class action ninety days after the Federal Trade Commission has been notified of the unfair practice. Such actions must be maintainable as a class action under the Federal Rules of Civil Procedure and consumers, to be eligible as a member of the class, must have lost or stand to lose more than $10 in such transaction. The ninety day notification provision is designed to avoid a multiplicity of actions seeking relief for the same consumers and to enable either the Attorney General or the Federal Trade Commission to give notice within that ninety day period of their intention to bring action against the challenged practice. If in fact such action is brought and is commenced within six months of such notice the independent action by the consumer must be stayed and consolidated as provided in Federal Rules of Civil Procedure 42(a). Again, the provision is a compromise between those persons who fear the abuse of a class action provision and those who have urged this right as an essential step to enable consumers to obtain justice in the marketplace. I think the compromise represents a fair and good solution. It does not place unreasonable obstacles in the government to take leadership in proceeding against a law violator where circumstances indicate the desirability or necessity of such a course.

These two bills, of course, will not satisfy everyone. Legislation of necessity is an act of the possible rather than a reflection of the millenium. Nevertheless, I am convinced that in their essential features these bills do in fact provide the protection which consumers need now in order to have their interests effectively represented on a national level and to be able to defend their rights and be protected from fraud and chicanery in the marketplace.

The Chamber of Commerce is reported to have already sent "urgent" messages to its members to defeat the proposed statutory Office of Consumer Affairs. The business community has consistently opposed the class action proposal and so far I have not seen any indication that they are willing to accept the current proposals with respect to class actions even though they go a long way towards meeting their objections to the earlier versions of this bill.

It is vital that consumers mobilize themselves in support of these two bills. You cannot expect your Congressman to support this bill unless he is convinced first, that the bill is necessary and second, that consumers care about the bill being passed. I urge you, there, to get busy. It is most important that you exert every effort to get these bills enacted into law by *this* Congress. If this does not happen, it will be necessary to start all over again for, as you know, pending legislation does not survive the final adjournment of a Congress.

John Gardner has voiced concern over the relationship between the individual's growing sense of powerlessness and impotence to affect his own destiny and the rise of civil tumult in our society. He said:

"[Civil tumult] stems, at least in part, from people who want to have their say and feel that they have not been listened to, who feel that they have suffered injustice and have been denied redress, and who feel that in matters of self-government they have been lulled with rhetoric and denied effective power. The solution lies in giving them outlets *within the system,* that is, in providing them constructive paths of action." (John Gardner in his undelivered address to the Illinois Constitutional Convention, May 1970).

H.R. 18214 and S. 3201 provide just the type of constructive paths of action which I believe consumers need today in order to participate effectively in the marketplace, to be able to ensure the responsiveness of that marketplace to their needs and to be able to interact with their suppliers on a basis of equality and self-respect.

If our nation is to have the type of creative and imaginative citizenry on which its future and our own happiness ultimately depends, we must make sure that our system is in fact responsive to citizen demands. In the consumer area, the operations of the marketplace offer consumers an important potential for developing their self-confidence, self-respect and sense of self-mastery and self-achievement. It is up to us to see to it that the marketplace fulfills this potential. This is the ultimate challenge to which consumer organizations must respond. H.R. 18214 and S. 3201 provide the mechanism and the framework through which consumers can achieve recognition of their interests and solutions to their problems. We must act now to make sure that these bills become law.

Ralph Nader

Mr. Nader. Mr. Chairman, distinguished members of the Senate Judiciary Committee, I am grateful for the invitation to comment on section 206 (the consumer class action provisions) of S. 3201 and its impact on the Federal courts.

For the past 6 years, Congress has been conducting hearings and studies which document a truly immense amount of fraud, deception and hazard arising out of market exchanges between manufacturers, retailers and consumers. One can use the word "immense" even without accepting Senator Philip Hart's estimate of approximately $200 billion spent by consumers last year (out of about $750 billion) which received no value. I accept his estimate and add that the human tragedy and anguish proceeding out of hazardous products deserves inclusion even though it cannot be quantified other than to cite the tens of thousands of fatalities and millions of injuries and afflictions annually.

Out of these phenomena must arise the frame of reference for considering procedural improvements in class-action rights. For on closer scrutiny, vast portions of the consumer fraud and hazard problem involve thousands of little claims in the $10, $50, $100 or $500 categories. These grievances are conflicts which can be resolved in a variety of ways within and without the legal system or not resolved at all. Whether they are resolved informally between buyer and seller or whether they are not resolved at all depends on the climate of expectation proceeding from the likelihood of access and remedy within the formal legal system—namely the courts.

The reality of our court system is that it is structured by formidable price and time mechanisms that effectively shut out the large majority of consumer grievances from any prospect of consideration. Too expensive, too time-consuming, too esoteric for self-help without a lawyer, is the way to sum up the situation.

Large dollar amounts are what receive legal representation in this country and such amounts are needed to weather the attrition of judicial expense and delay. Without access to the judicial system, tremendous injustice and waste occur pursuant to a loss of faith in the courts to resolve disputes that affect millions of people in small ways or expose them to risks and hazards not part of the market exchange, as they bargain for or as they understood the seller's representations.

National, volume selling with ready counsel to use the courts has not been balanced by the ability of consumers, commonly abused, to join together in order to leap over the hurdle of expense and inadequate or nonexistent counsel. While collection techniques and remedies have been refined to a spectacular degree by sellers against buyers, the same has not been true on the other side of the aisle.

Shocking imbalance, therefore, has been the shameful mark of injustice. It is sobering to read the thousands of consumer complaint letters that flow into Government agencies to note a very common absence of any feeling by the complainants that the law or the courts can help them. For to them, the law and the courts are remote

Reprinted from *Consumer Protection Act of 1970* (Hearings before the Committee on the Judiciary, United States Senate, 91st Cong., 2d Sess., on S. 3201, 1970), pp. 212-217.

and priced out of their expectations. The door to the courtroom says to them, in effect, "No Admittance." The radiating effect of such difficult access tells unscrupulous manufacturers and sellers that it is easier to be more unscrupulous until, indeed, such behavior becomes institutionalized for an industry or trade and any contrary, better behavior becomes a competitive disadvantage.

Why the frantic and determined opposition to this class action proposal? Because and precisely because it would open the doors to the courtroom to bring high volume, small dollar abuses to justice.

I am not speaking of various wrinkles in the wording of the act because the issue really here is much more basic. The issue is access to the courts, not the manner of access and the various subsidiary points that reasonable men can differ on. It is basically the access to the Federal court system for national class action abuses that are at issue. If you hear the mummblings during today and other days among business representatives in this room, you will see that that is basically what is at issue. They are not much worried about the wrinkles here. They want to defeat the entire concept of opening the doors to aggrieved consumers here.

The deterrent effect of several consumer class actions brings something rare to the business world—an order enforceable to pay back ill-gotten gains. This repay is much more effective than the FTC-type power over the years of issuing cease and desist orders which can be designed around or easily violated and at any rate are entirely prospective in whatever impact they may have on the defendant. Judicial deterrence by way of repay of ill-gotten gains is the most effective way for the judiciary to reduce the number of disputes that should be adjudicated.

The hearings in Congress are filled with decades long abuses whereby there never was a repay. The odometer rigging that went over three decades, cheating people right and left, not just in rental cars, the odometer overrigging which as exposed about 5 years ago slightly attenuated in its fraudulent impact on the motorists, never involved a repay of the millions of dollars that were consciously stolen from the motorists by calculating motor vehicles corporations and their minion-type engineers who should have known better.

The abuse of a brake measurement device is probably the most crass and crude form of consumer deception in the country.

Consumer class actions are also a way of decentralizing regulatory impacts from Government to citizens and of providing current and necessary information for developing more pertinent standards for more deterrence or prevention of abuses. It is a self-help type of operation quite simply. It is a remarkable testament to the flexibility of those who want to avoid the extension of Federal power as an ideological matter, to hear their opposition to giving citizens practical remedies to help themselves or more equitable procedures to achieve the same purpose.

Indeed, before Mrs. Virginia Knauer became integrated in the administration's anticonsumer stance, she, too, recognized that this was a way to protect the consumer without adding more regulation and more budgets.

The Justice Department's position to require completed government action or consent decrees before consumers could initiate class actions is about as outrageous a Federal interference in a citizen's legal rights as can be espoused in a statute purporting to protect that citizen. It is also a rather ambitious prediction of the longevity of many consumers who wait out the Federal Trade Commission's tenor 12-year initiatives that have been going on.

A number of objections have been raised against the provision in S. 3201 which are so insupportable as empirical or normative propositions as to reflect a deeper animus against exposing mass business fraud to the adjudicatory processes of Federal courts. Let a brief discussion of them ensue:

1. It is claimed that the major portion of consumer injustices are local in origin and should be handled by local or State courts. I would comment the following:

There is a certain uniformity of factual abuse that is required for class actions that is correlative with national, large volume manufacturers or sellers such as automobile producers, mail-order houses, insurance companies, drug companies and the like. Increasingly, the ambit of intrastate deceptive or harmful practices is receding in significance in terms of sheer volume of sales and customers affected. What is left of the "Ma and Pa" grocery, to take an example, from the most enduring type of local store? Moreover, with the decline of privity and other obstacles to legal accountability between consumer and distant producer, the national scope of consumer abuses is ever more dominant.

Moreover, consumer class actions regarding national abuses in local courts are inherently limited and productive of immense duplication and less competent or dedicated counsel. Attorney Jay Dushoff in testimony before this committee last week elaborated the reasons why such a course cannot suffice at all. National abuses are Federal matters in the courts as well as for Congress, which is also illustrative. If anything is new about the consumer movement jurisdictionally it is its relentless shift from local and State concern to Federal concern because of the overlapping jurisdiction, the fact that these abuses are national in spread and most accessible to national policy, although concurrent jurisdiction would be something well worth consideration.

Second, there will be a flood of litigation that will tie up the Federal courts and overburden them.

My comment to that objection is that this is not only nonsense, it is historic nonsense. Every move forward for citizens as any law student knows, whether in the common law or statutory law, has been opposed with this tired shout, the flood of litigation. The flood of litigation argument has never materialized not just because there are hosts of other obstacles for citizens of modest means to overcome but because lawyers and judges screen out or stand ready to screen out the frivolous and baseless claims.

Summary judgment always stands in the wings as we all know.

An additional note about overburdening the Federal courts is in order. Any society that presumes to be a society under law must develop the operational ethic that the courts exist and expand to serve the people's need for justice. What has never been decided as national policy is the necessity to develop criteria for growth of the Federal judiciary to respond to such indexes as population growth, gross national product growth, social crises levels (e.g., narcotics, civil rights, and other areas of predictable litigation) the complexity and velocity of exchanges between individuals in the marketplace and service areas and other similar standards. Before the brows of Chief Justices wrinkle with worry over the overburdened Federal courts and consumer legislation pending let a little perspective emerge.

The current budget for the current fiscal year to operate the entire Federal judicial system is $126 million. As Chief Justice Burger noted in his speech, this is less than the cost of a single C-5A airplane which now goes for $200 million apiece. It is not sufficient to stop here and expect people's needs for justice to adjust to the courts. It is crucial that this committee take the lead to expand the Federal judiciary to adjust to the needs of the people for justice. The United States of America have sufficient claim on Federal justice to warrant the equivalent of at least one nuclear carrier's cost or $450 million.

There is, however, no indication that there will be a burdening of existing Federal courts. I might add here it is touching to see one corporate lawyer after another come before committees of Congress on this provision and indicate his solicitude for unburdening the Federal courts. If anything has burdened the Federal courts, it has been the ingenious misuse of civil procedure by corporate lawyers to delay and make prohibitive any challenge to their clients by other aggrieved parties.

I have just gone through a case, for example, where General Motors with corporate clients took 3½ years to dispose of a motion to dismiss, just a motion to dismiss, 3½ years. One can only imagine the outcome of a full trial that appears as a challenge to attorneys. There are far more trivial and insignificant cases burdening the courts presently which cannot be used as an excuse to block consumer class actions. In Arizona, Minnesota, and a few other States where consumer class actions can proceed relatively smoothly, there has been no flood of burdensome cases in the State courts.

Incidentally, the same argument has always been made against developing design liability for defective products, like automobiles. The flood of litigation arguments has been used for years and has never materialized.

A third objection to the bill is that national consumer class actions are impossible for the courts to administer and adjudicate.

The comment to that is as follows:

Even in the past under inadequate procedures, class actions have been administered. Certainly, the large ones are complex and raise many questions but the flexibility of the courts in ascertaining the best way to distribute the damages can lead to creative use of trust funds and other community wide uses where the class is too impossible to contact entirely or where members do not put in their claims.

The reason why, for example, Attorneys General and other States which have received a good portion of the settlement proceeds in the tetracycline cases is because the court accepted a theory of trust whereby these institutions held in trust for public hospitals and other public needs the proceeds. The tetracycline cases illustrate further some of this judicial flexibility in fact and in proposed consideration.

Many of the objections raised by previous business witnesses are simply the usual alarums about notice, costs, and the like which can be handled by judicial discretion or by added procedural assists such as preliminary hearings for probable cause, which would tend to dispose rather quickly of frivolous or worthless class action claims.

The national consumer class action reduces multiplicity of litigation, discovery, and other judicial processess. This is something which many of the witnesses seem to overlook.

It has the requisite repay impact that generates deterrence and encourages lawyers, corporate lawyers, to advise their business clients to be more responsive to consumer justice, given the legal consequences to the contrary.

When there is a judicially imposed sanction like class action waiting in the wings, lawyers tend to counsel their business clients more seriously about what they cannot do and what they should not do. It is that kind of class action that allows lawyers to extend such counsel and such restraints on the parameters of finality or negligence.

In many ways the consumer class action provision of S. 3201 is telling us a great deal about the business establishment and their legal and governmental satellites. While prating about the need for the young and the minority groups and now more of the working bluecollar people to work within the system, when it gets down to real decisions, the dominant groups choose to defend the blocking of access to that part of the system which should be the most nondiscriminatory as to who has what—namely the Federal courts.

When the dominant forces of a society block substantive rights of people, the situation is bad enough. When these same forces begin to close out or block procedural rights of people, the situation assumes even worse proportions, I think. It is time to recognize that the true test of presumed believers in law is when the challenge is clear and near. Today that is the case.

17

Establish a Department of Consumer Affairs

Betty Furness

A former Special Assistant to the President for Consumer Affairs recommends a Department of Consumer Affairs in the Executive Office of the President. Miss Furness presents her reasons before the Senate Subcommittee on Executive Reorganization.

I greatly appreciate the opportunity to appear before this subcommittee to testify on the need for consumer protection in the Federal Government. This matter certainly concerns me as much now that I'm special assistant to only my family as it did when I was special assistant to President Johnson.

CONSUMER REVOLUTION

In recent months I've talked a great deal about the consumer revolution afoot in this country. I meant what I said. I truly believe it, but I'm sure there were listeners who felt that I was preaching the self-interested gospel of my office, or my own personal prejudice. I'm sure there were people in and out of the Government who thought if only I'd go away so would all the talk of consumer interest and protection; and certainly the exaggerated claims of a consumer revolution.

Abridged from *Establish a Department of Consumer Affairs* (Hearings before the Subcommittee on Executive Reorganization, Committee on Government Operations, United States Senate, 1st Sess., on S. 860 and S. 2045, March 19, 1969), pp. 343-346.

Well, it didn't turn out that way. The full force of the consumer revolution was brought home, even to me, through the reaction of the press and individuals to what the present administration must have thought of as a relatively minor appointment. The mere whisper of conflict of interest in the guardian of consumer affairs, justified or unjustified, reaped the whirlwind.

There was a time when the consumer issue in America could hardly be described as sexy. It got scant notice from the press, little support from the Government, and very limited interest from the public.

All that has changed now, not because the consumer has become a crank, but because the size of our marketplace and its tremendous technological growth has outstripped our ability to understand and evaluate the products we buy. We now have a growing public clamor for improvement in our marketplace, and I think the Government must respond to that cry.

These hearings are very important because there is no question in my mind but that Congress should carefully reexamine the Governments' consumer apparatus and come up with a better way of doing business.

VOLUNTARY APPROACH INADEQUATE

Of course, not everyone agrees that the Federal Government should take on protection of the consumer. Industry continues to cry, "Please Mother, I'd rather do it myself." But after my experience in this area I've concluded that industry, even with the best of intentions, cannot do it all, itself.

When industry sets out to establish voluntary standards and practices there are severe limitations to what they can actually accomplish. The very word "voluntary" tells the story. Even if the largest and most powerful trade associations advocate voluntary standards they can be ineffective. A trade association cannot force even its own members to comply, and obviously nonmembers don't even have an obligation to consider complying.

Let's say, for example, that three-quarters of an industry decides to comply to some voluntary regulation that will be a solid benefit to the consumer.

If the other one-quarter finds itself in a better competitive position, what happens to the regulation? My guess is it won't last long. Even organizations devoted solely to establishing industry standards have no power to enforce them, once established. Already in instances where voluntary standards were inadequate the Government has established compulsory standards.

Safety is a primary area of consideration. There have, of course, been instances of recalls of merchandise on a voluntary basis. But too often some catastrophe or lawsuit has triggered the recall. A major retailer recently recalled a dangerous defective gas heater and widely applauded itself for such a noble gesture. It developed that several years earlier the company had settled out of court with the estate a man who had died of brain damage caused by leaking fumes from the same defective appliance.

Even more recently a major automobile manufacturer recalled 5 million cars because of two possible defects. Some of the cars were 3 years old and one of the companies own inspectors had warned them in 1966 that one of the defects could cause death to passengers. Three years and four deaths later the recall came.

If business can be so cavalier about the very lives of consumers, what voluntary action can be expected in telling them more about products and how to use them, in writing clearer and stronger warranties, in improving services and repairs and all the things the consumer needs if he's going to gain an equal and honest exchange in the marketplace for his hard-earned dollar?

In establishing the National Commission on Product Safety the Congress has taken a first step toward looking into the safety of household products. When the Commission completes its report in 1970 we may have a better idea of what standards and regulations are necessary and whether or not they can be accomplished voluntarily.

I think it is probably true that business thinks it is moving in the direction of voluntary action and there is some slight movement in that direction. But sometimes it seems that business is taking its cue from the Red Queen of Alice in Wonderland; moving faster and faster just to stay where it is.

I feel that Government has an obligation to take action where business fails to protect the consumer and that action should be able, vigorous, and well coordinated. I don't consider this harassment of industry any more than I think traffic laws harass the driver of an automobile.

The question then is, How can the Government best do its part of the job of consumer protection?

Should the responsibility be left to the various agencies and departments, some 33 in number, who are already concerned with the consumer?

Should the President's Committee on Consumer Interests be left as it is, having been established by Executive order, and running the constant risk of being disestablished by another Executive order?

Should there be a statutory office within the Executive Office of the President?

FAVORS SINGLE CONSUMER OFFICE

Or, should there, as has been suggested, be a Cabinet post?

I am distinctly in favor of one office, permanently established and given the authority to coordinate the efforts and programs of all the interested Government agencies.

As it is now, Federal consumer protection is a hydraheaded creature with no single head to tell each of the heads what the other heads are thinking.

The need for coordination is greater now than ever before since consumer issues have become so popular that all kinds of agencies are climbing into the grocery cart.

For example, in late 1968, the Department of Health, Education, and Welfare, set up an excellent consumer affairs office without consultation with, or knowledge of, the White House consumer office. Their plans and programs were highly commendable, but in some instances were duplications of efforts of the White House office.

This concern is splendid, but coordination is essential.

CONFLICTING RESPONSIBILITIES OF DEPARTMENTS

I am also concerned about leaving consumer protection in various departments whose primary interest may lie elsewhere.

Given the opportunity to protect commerce or the consumer but not both at the same time, who do you think the Department of Commerce will protect?

Given the same opportunity with the farmer and the consumer, who will the Department of Agriculture protect?

These agencies, and the others involved in consumer affairs, do have their own special constituencies after all.

What we need is an agency whose special constituency is the consumer, all 200 million of them.

WHITE HOUSE OFFICE RECOMMENDED

I would suggest that the next step be a permanent office, one that is mandated by Congress, and I should like to see it function within the Executive Office of the President.

I would like to see it have a congressional mandate simply because I believe it should be a continuing office and not subject to the winds of political change.

Such an office would function as a window through which the administration might look at the consumer; the consumer could look at the administration and industry would be able to view both. Such three-way accommodation is essential if the consumer is going to be given the protection he needs and demands.

Let me emphasize that we are not talking about a bureaucratic boondoggle or a vote-getting gimmick. We are not suggesting scratching the consumer's back to make him feel good. That is a very serious issue.

18

Exploitation of Disadvantaged Consumers by Retail Merchants

*National Advisory Commission on
Civil Disorders*

This report is another item in the conflicting evidence regarding whether the disadvantaged pay more and are exploited. Often a practice may not be exploitative, but if there is a lack of understanding of price and quality relationships the practice will be exploitative in the consumer's perception.

Much of the violence in recent disorders has been directed at stores and other commercial establishments in disadvantaged Negro areas. In some cases, rioters focused on stores operated by white merchants who, they apparently believed, had been charging exorbitant prices or selling inferior goods. Not all the violence against these stores can be attributed to "revenge" for such practices. Yet it is clear that many residents of disadvantaged Negro neighborhoods believe they suffer constant abuses by local merchants.

Significant grievances concerning unfair commercial practices affecting Negro consumers were found in 11 of the 20 cities studies by the Commission. The fact that most of the merchants who operate stores in almost every Negro area are white undoubtedly contributes to the conclusion among Negroes that they are exploited by white society.

Reprinted from *Reports of the National Advisory Commission on Civil Disorders* (Washington: GPO, 1968), pp. 139-141.

153

It is difficult to assess the precise degree and extent of exploitation. No systematic and reliable survey comparing consumer pricing and credit practices in all-Negro and other neighborhoods has ever been conducted on a nationwide basis. Differences in prices and credit practices between white middle-income areas and Negro low-income areas to some extent reflect differences in the real costs of serving these two markets (such as differential losses from pilferage in supermarkets), but the exact extent of these differential real costs has never been estimated accurately. Finally, an examination of exploitative consumer practices must consider the particular structure and functions of the low-income consumer durables market.

INSTALLMENT BUYING

This complex situation can best be understood by first considering certain basic facts:

Various cultural factors generate constant pressure on low income families to buy many relatively expensive durable goods and display them in their homes. This pressure comes in part from continuous exposure to commercial advertising, especially on television. In January 1967, over 88 percent of all Negro households had TV sets. A 1961 study of 464 low-income families in New York City showed that 95 percent of these relatively poor families had TV sets.

Many poor families have extremely low incomes, bad previous credit records, unstable sources of income, or other attributes which make it virtually impossible for them to buy merchandise from established large national or local retail firms. These families lack enough savings to pay cash, and they cannot meet the standard credit requirements of established general merchants because they are too likely to fall behind in their payments.

Poor families in urban areas are far less mobile than others. A 1967 Chicago study of low-income Negro households indicated their low automobile ownership compelled them to patronize primarily local neighborhood merchants. These merchants typically provided smaller selection, poorer services, and higher prices than big national outlets. The 1961 New York study also indicated that families who shopped outside their own neighborhoods were far less likely to pay exorbitant prices.

Most low-income families are uneducated concerning the nature of credit purchase contracts, the legal rights and obligations of both buyers and sellers, sources of advice for consumers who are having difficulties with merchants, and the operation of the courts concerned with these matters. In contrast, merchants engaged in selling goods to them are very well informed.

In most states, the laws governing relations between consumers and merchants in effect offer protection only to informed, sophisticated parties with understanding of each other's rights and obligations. Consequently, these laws are little suited to protect the rights of most low-income consumers.

In this situation, exploitative practices flourish. Ghetto residents who want to buy relatively expensive goods cannot do so from standard retail outlets and are thus restricted to local stores. Forced to use credit, they have little understanding of the pitfalls of credit buying. But because they have unstable income and frequently fail to make payments, the cost to the merchants of serving them is significantly above that of serving middle-income consumers. Consequently, a special kind of merchant appears to sell them goods on terms designed to cover the high cost of doing business in ghetto neighborhoods.

Whether they actually gain higher profits, these merchants charge higher prices than those in other parts of the city to cover the greater credit risks and other higher operating costs inherent in neighborhood outlets. A recent study conducted by the Federal Trade Commission in Washington, D.C., illustrates this conclusion dramatically. The FTC identified a number of stores specializing in selling furniture and appliances to low-income households. About 92 percent of the sales of these stores were credit sales involving installment purchases, as compared to 27 percent of the sales in general retail outlets handling the same merchandise.

The median income annually of a sample of 486 customers of these stores was about $4,200, but one-third had annual incomes below $3,600, about 6 percent were receiving welfare payments, and another 76 percent were employed in the lowest paying occupations (service workers, operatives, laborers, and domestics)—as compared to 36 percent of the total labor force in Washington in those occupations.

Definitely catering to a low-income group, these stores charged significantly higher prices than general merchandise outlets in the Washington area. According to testimony by Paul Rand Dixon, Chairman of the FTC, an item selling wholesale at $100 would retail on the average for $165 in a general merchandise store, and for $250 in a low-income specialty store. Thus, the customers of these outlets were paying an average price premium of about 52 percent.

While higher prices are not necessarily exploitative in themselves, many merchants in ghetto neighborhoods take advantage of their superior knowledge of credit buying by engaging in various exploitative tactics—high-pressure salesmanship, bait advertising, misrepresentation of prices, substitution of used goods for promised new ones, failure to notify consumers of legal actions against them, refusal to repair or replace substandard goods, exorbitant prices or credit charges, and use of shoddy merchandise. Such tactics affect a great many low-income consumers. In the New York study, 60 percent of all households had suffered from consumer problems (some of which were purely their own fault), about 43 percent had experienced serious exploitation, and 20 percent had experienced repossession, garnishment, or threat of garnishment.

GARNISHMENT

Garnishment practices in many states allow creditors to deprive individuals of their wages through court action without hearing or trial. In about 20 states, the wages of an employee can be diverted to a creditor merely upon the latter's deposition, with no advance hearing where the employee can defend himself. He often receives no prior notice of such action and is usually unaware of the law's operation and too poor to hire legal defense. Moreover, consumers may find themselves still owing money on a sales contract even after the creditor has repossessed the goods. The New York study cited earlier in this chapter indicated that 20 percent of a sample of low-income families had been subject to legal action regarding consumer purchases. And the Federal Trade Commission study in Washington, D.C., showed that retailers specializing in credit sales of furniture and appliances to low-income consumers resorted to court action on the average for every $2,200 of sales. Since their average sale was for $207, this amounted to using the courts to collect from one of every 11 customers. In contrast, department stores in the same area used court action against approximately one of every 14,500 customers. [1]

VARIATIONS IN FOOD PRICES

Residents of low-income Negro neighborhoods frequently claim that they pay higher prices for food in local markets than wealthier white suburbanites and receive inferior quality meat and produce. Statistically reliable information comparing prices and quality in these two kinds of areas is generally unavailable. The U.S. Bureau of Labor Statistics, studying food prices in six cities in 1966, compared prices of a standard list of 18 items in low-income areas and higher-income areas in each city. In a total of 180 stores, including independent and chain stores, and for items of the same type sold in the same types of stores, there were no significant differences in prices between low-income and high-income areas. However, stores in low-income areas were more likely to be small independents (which had somewhat higher prices), to sell low-quality produce and meat at any given price, and to be patronized by people who typically bought smaller-sized packages which are more expensive per unit of measure. In other words, many low-income consumers in fact pay higher prices, although the situation varies greatly from place to place.

Although these findings must be considered inconclusive, there are significant reasons to believe that poor households generally pay higher prices for the food they buy and receive lower quality food. Low-income consumers buy more food at local groceries because they are less mobile. Prices in these small stores are significantly higher than in major supermarkets because they cannot achieve economics of scale, and because real operating costs are higher in low-income Negro areas than in outlying suburbs. For instance, inventory "shrinkage" from pilfering and other causes is normally under 2 percent of sales, but can run twice as much in high-crime areas. Managers seek to make up for these added costs by charging higher prices for good quality food, or by substituting lower grades.

These practices do not necessarily involve "exploitation," but they are often perceived as exploitative and unfair by those who are aware of the price and quality differences involved, but unaware of operating costs. In addition it is probable that genuinely exploitative pricing practices exist in some areas. In either case, differential food prices constitute another factor convincing urban Negroes in low-income neighborhoods that whites discriminate against them.

REFERENCES

1. Assuming their sales also averaged $207 per customer.

Part Three

Government and the Consumer

The readings in this part review and assess the many activities of government dealing with the protection and advancement of consumer interests. The first section focuses on existing consumer protection programs; whereas the second section reviews consumer protection legislation. Consumer representation is the subject matter of the third section. In the concluding section of Part Three, the role of government and the consumer interest is appraised.

The section on existing consumer protection programs opens with an article in which Richard J. Barber, Special Counsel, Senate Subcommittee on Antitrust and Monopoly, examines the federal government's response to consumer difficulties in the marketplace during the past thirty years. In his assessment of governmental activities, Barber focuses on numerous consumer-related protection actions at both the federal and state level. The second selection, Chapter V of the "Report of the ABA Commission to Study the Federal Trade Commission," examines the Federal Trade Commission's consumer protection programs that account for the majority of total FTC consumer protection work, namely: deceptive labeling, false advertising, wool and textiles, and localized marketing schemes.

In the second section, three articles survey consumer protection laws. The article by James R. Withrow, Jr., points to the inadequacies of consumer protection by administrative action during the past eighty years. "Truth-in-Packaging" and "Truth-in-Lending"

legislation are the subjects of the other selections. H. E. Dunkelberger, Jr., reviews the mandatory and discretionary regulations of
the 1966 Fair Packaging and Labeling Act two years after enactment. The Board of Governors of the Federal Reserve System
assess consumer awareness of finance charges and interest rates and
the extent of compliance with the requirements of the 1968
Consumer Credit Protection Act for the year 1970.

　　Included in the section on consumer representation are contri-
butions by Frank E. McLaughlin, Director for Industry Relations,
President's Committee on Consumer Interests (PCCI) and Virginia
H. Knauer, Special Assistant to the President for Consumer Affairs.
From the perspective of Director for Industry Relations, PCCI,
McLaughlin reviews some of the difficulties encountered in the
government-business dialogue regarding consumer issues. He points
specifically to problems encountered by the Office of the Special
Assistant for Consumer Affairs. Mrs. Knauer stresses the need for
stronger consumer representation at the federal level and compares
various legislative proposals which seek to assure "the right to be
heard."

　　Dean Richard H. Holton and Prof. Dorothy Cohen appraise
government activities and the consumer interest in the concluding
section of Part Three. Dean Holton argues that due to a lack of
understanding of the issues involved, both government and business
may miss the point in proposing or opposing consumer protection
legislation. In the article, "The Federal Trade Commission and the
Regulation of Advertising in the Consumer Interest," Dr. Cohen
reviews and assesses the present means by which the FTC regulates
advertising for the protection of the consumer. She suggests that
the FTC. consider the behavioral characteristics of the consumer
and amend its regulatory framework accordingly.

PART THREE, CONTENTS

Existing Consumer Protection Programs

Consumer Protection Legislation

Consumer Representation

An Appraisal

19

Government and the Consumer

Richard J. Barber

I believe we are on the threshold of a fundamental change
in our popular economic thought, that in the future we are
going to think less about the producer and more about the
consumer.—Governor Franklin D. Roosevelt (May 1932)[1]
In Washington, consumer legislation is still a
dream.—Senator Philip A. Hart (December 1963)[2]

The consumer has long been a subject of political concern, yet his problems as a purchaser are now probably greater in number and more serious than ever before. The failure of public policy to respond adequately to consumer needs must certainly be one of the most perplexing chapters in any examination of our federal government's response to the challenges of an increasingly complex economy. What is particularly intriguing is that the consumer's difficulties in the marketplace have long been recognized, both by the public in general and by political spokesmen. Indeed, it seems that more ink has been spilled, more speeches delivered, and more presidential and congressional documents issued on the subject of consumer problems—all with less effect—than in any other area of public concern, except, perhaps, for issues of war and peace.

Adam Smith, that shrewd Scot who recognized the need for government involve-

Abridged from the original in *Michigan Law Review*, vol. 64, no. 7 (May 1966), pp. 1203-1217. Reprinted by permission.

ment in a private economy more often than many of his twentieth-century "conservative" followers like to admit, emphasized nearly two centuries ago that "consumption is the sole end and purpose of all production" and that "the interest of the producer ought to be attended to only so far as it may be necessary for promoting that of the consumer."[3] Smith was quite right to emphasize the importance of the consumer's role. In fact, consumer expenditures today account for almost two thirds of the $700 billion in goods and services produced annually in the United States.[4] Yet if the consumer is as important as the producer, government has been concerned far more with the interests of producers. Although competition is essential to a free enterprise economy (disregarding Schumpeter, and his assumptions about the necessity of monopoly for technological progress[5] have been seriously challenged[6]), the businessman has eagerly (and understandably, from his standpoint) sought to secure a monopolistic shelter from its unmitigated and often harsh winds. Moreover, government has done at least as much to help sellers gain a monopoly as it has to delimit or destroy their protected positions.

As a result of the attention accorded to producers, the consumer's problems have been considered only erratically, haphazardly, and sporadically. In contrast to producers (and the Government itself), who are armed with information and who are otherwise able to make informed, rational decisions, the individual buyer, who is besieged by advertising, deceived by packages, confronted with an expanding range of highly complex goods, limited in time, and exhausted by a trek along the aisles of a supermarket, is simply not qualified to buy discriminately and wisely. The "art of spending money" remains as backward as the distinguished economist, Wesley C. Mitchell, depicted it in his classic article published more than a half century ago.[7] Government, in spite of the quantitatively large number of steps taken with the declared objective of aiding the consumer, has not helped significantly to correct this imbalance between producers and consumers.

One major reason for the lack of positive governmental action in this area is that the problems of the consumer have never been defined in any systematic fashion and thus have not been comprehensively confronted. Consumers' problems have almost always been viewed on an *ad hoc* basis—as isolated cases to be resolved individually. Seldom have they been placed in a more general framework or seen as symptoms of a fundamental economic disorder that must itself be diagnosed and treated.

This article takes up four major topics. First, the principal characteristics of governmental action with respect to consumer protection are reviewed, with emphasis on developments during the past thirty years. Second, the traditional pleas for consumer protection are examined with a view toward determining the inadequacies in governmental action. Third, the problems of the consumer are studied in the context of oligopolistic industrial markets in which nonprice competition accentuates the place of advertising and severely restricts the dissemination of factual information that is essential to enlightened purchase decisions. Fourth, the ingredients of a meaningful consumer protection program are outlined and the probabilities for their political implementation appraised.

I. GOVERNMENT AND THE CONSUMER:
A SURVEY OF THE EXPERIENCE

The question of the protection of the consumers is one of protracted historical interest.[8] For at least seven hundred years the hand of authority—church, guild, or state—has played a role in regulating the affairs of the market, often, but not always, with the aim of assisting the consumer. The Scholastics insisted upon a "just price." The Tudors took various steps in the sixteenth century to regulate what they regarded as improper conduct in the evolving medieval markets. Legislation which condemned forestalling, engrossing, and regrating was in part designed to protect buyers from monopolists.[9] In the eighteenth and nineteenth centuries laws were passed to control prices which were thought to be "too high." More recently, state and federal antitrust laws adopted in the United States during the latter decades of the nineteenth century had their origin as much in a broad feeling of pricing abuses as in any other single factor.[10]

To acknowledge past governmental efforts to deal with problems of consumer interest is not to indicate that those activities significantly helped the individual buyer. Twelfth century laws banning engrossing and related practices protected the exclusive market rights granted by the Crown. Moreover, the enactment of the Statute of Monopolies in 1623 did not terminate the exclusive powers conferred on chartered trading companies, cities, and boroughs. Other laws that might appear to have aided the consumer were just as much designed to bolster the trade-restraining practices of the guilds. Thus, it can be seen that the consumer's market position remained nearly as limited as ever.[11]

Concern for the consumer over the centuries has not been confined to prices and the price mechanism. At least as early as the fifteenth century, authoritative proclamations were issued that closely regulated the content and quality of food products. For example, in 1450 the Munich Brewers Guild specified the contents for beer.[12] Similarly, weights and measures have been controlled for hundreds of years, and it is interesting to note that this is the subject of one of the few specific provisions in the United States Constitution that is of immediate concern to citizens in their role as consumers.[13] Even the conditions of retail trade have long been subject to governmental control, as indicated by an early English decree which forbade merchants "to set up red or black cloths or shields whereby the eyes of the buyers were deceived in the choice of a good cloth."[14] Moreover, governments have always been concerned with fraud and deceit.

A. The Consumer's Need for Information

While extensive government intervention in the economy, partly designed to aid the consumer, has been apparent for about seven centuries, the *caveat emptor* philosophy has dominated both the legislatures and the courts since the nineteenth century.[15] The ascendance of this philosophy should not be regarded as an indication that public authority has shown no real concern for consumer problems in this period; it has, however, helped create a widening gulf between the realities of the contemporary retail market and judicial and legislative action. The changing character of retail markets, both in terms of the range and type of products available for sale and the conditions of trade, has generated new problems for the individual consumer, to which government has only tardily and haphazardly responded.

Even though the *caveat emptor* doctrine has recently become less rigid, existing consumer policy fails to meet the central issues presented by the marketplace of the 1960's. The law of fraud and misrepresentation is a good example. Courts and legislatures have gradually expanded their definition of fraud to include statements or representations that, although literally true in themselves, are misleading due to the failure to state additional relevant facts. This approach has helped curtail some advertising abuses. For example, in 1965 the Supreme Court upheld a Federal Trade Commission decision that an advertisement which purported to offer two cans of paint for the price of one ("buy one, get one free"–"every second can free") was unfair and deceptive when the product had never been sold at the stated single-can price.[16] While recent enlargements of the fraud doctrine have helped contribute greatly to consumer protection, the fact is that most advertisements and related promotional techniques still are not regarded as deceptive.[17]

The factor that most frequently renders an advertisement misleading is not the character of the statements that it contains, but rather the information that is omitted. To make wise purchase decisions, the consumer needs more factual information about products than he now is given. At present, sellers of consumer goods deliberately refrain from providing many essential facts, since such information often would run counter to advertising claims that their products are distinctive. For instance, a producer finds substantial economic advantage in conveying the message that a product like Clorox is considerably more effective than Purex or other brands of liquid bleach when, in fact, they are chemically indistinguishable. However, producers will not disclose the fact that the chemical composition of such products is identical, and this type of deliberate omission tends to confuse and mislead consumers. The law of fraud and deceit, even though enlarged by the courts, legislatures, and administrative agencies, is simply out of touch with market realities. This situation is evident from the fact that the concepts of fraud and deceit focus on statements actually made in advertisements, whereas the consumer needs information which sellers now fail to disclose.

A related problem exists with respect to several other governmental policies that are often said to benefit the consumer. For example, weights and measures are rigorously controlled by governments, but if a seller of a consumer product is not required to state the weight of his goods, the ability of the National Bureau of Standards to define and measure a "pound" with scientific precision is irrelevant. Even if a manufacturer states the weight of his product on the containers but does so in fractional terms (such as 13-3/8 ounces in a small box, 19-7/16 ounces in a medium size box, and 28-17/32 ounces in a large box), the purchaser, trying to make a judgment as to the "best buy" on a cents-per-ounce basis, is effectively frustrated.

Similarly, the ineffectiveness of current governmental controls is evident in regulations dealing with the adulteration of foods and other products. While existing law prohibits certain additives, it does not always require the manufacturer to state the ingredients in an intelligible way. In fact, contents frequently do not have to be revealed at all. And when they are, manufacturers may reveal only part of their story; it can be very important to consumers whether the amount of water in a particular food mixture is one per cent or fifteen per cent of the total. Again, the law is out of touch with market realities, largely because it is essentially negative rather than affirmative in its appraoch—it forbids rather than requires.

When physical injury is sustained through use of a dangerous product (sometimes, one that seems not so dangerous), the courts in recent years have been increasingly willing to impose liability on the manufacturer. The scope of implied warranties has been markedly expanded, and for this reason, as well as the curtailment or outright abolition of the privity element, sellers have been held liable for harm sustained in the use of a growing list of goods.[18] Moreover, the strict liability doctrine has been expanded to provide relief in tort for injury caused by unreasonably dangerous products.[19] However, while the much-discussed evolution of doctrine in these areas has afforded consumers (and others) additional relief for physical injuries they have sustained, related economic losses have been given practically no attention. It seems fair to say that consumers "lose" far more each year through the deception inherent in the sophisticated means of modern merchandising and by being effectively denied the information needed to make wise purchases than they do as the result of physical harm. Surveys show, for instance, that buyers pay about ten per cent more for most goods purchased in supermarkets than they would if they bought only the most economical (price adjusted for quantity) packages of such products.[20] Even more striking, if consumers disregarded trade names and purchased products on the basis of objectively determined values, without regard to trade name, savings of as much as fifty per cent could be realized.[21] Since American consumers are currently spending about $100 billion annually for retail food purchases alone,[22] the size of their loss is considerable. If provided meaningful information that would permit informed purchase decisions, consumers would save a considerable sum of money, and yet the Government has shown very little concern for this economically vital aspect of consumer protection.

B. Governmental Activities

To appreciate more fully the inadequate and haphazard character of current consumer protection activities calls for a review of existing programs at the federal and state levels. The following assessment will reveal the large number of consumer-related activities and will also disclose their disorderliness.

The most complete available tabulation of federal consumer programs, compiled in 1961, showed that thirty-three of the thirty-five principal departments and agencies of the federal government were involved in some activity that protected or promoted consumer interests.[23] Several of the agencies were responsible for only a single activity, but others were engaged in a sizable number of consumer programs—ranging from twenty in the Department of Commerce to fifty in the Department of Agriculture.[24] In the performance of those activities which the departments and agencies regarded as "directly" protecting and promoting consumer interests (118 of the 296 activities identified), the Government spent less than a billion dollars in 1961.[25] Even though this figure amounted to only about one per cent of the federal budget and to less than one third of one per cent of total personal consumption expenditures, it is seriously overstated, since it includes the compensation of workers who devoted some of their time to other job assignments.[26]

More important than their number is the diffuse nature of federal consumer activities. The great bulk of these governmental programs deal with classical forms of fraud and deception and with the enforcement of laws banning the sale of adulterated, unsafe, or untested products, almost exclusively foods and drugs. As in the case of court-made doctrine, there is a marked emphasis on activities with a negative quality— the prohibition of certain practices and the suppression of conduct which could inflict bodily harm. Few programs call for the affirmative disclosure of information essential to informed purchase decisions.

Nevertheless, some federal laws and programs have the effect of providing a consumer with facts that can be useful in buying products at retail. Food and drug labels must disclose the net weight, contents, and manufacturer's identity,[27] and under the 1962 Drug Act Amendments,[28] drugs must bear their generic names as well as their trade names. The labels of textile,[29] wool,[30] and fur[31] products must also specify content, and disclosure requirements for the sale of securities are now common.[32] Prices for new automobiles must be displayed in accordance with the Automobile Information Disclosure Act of 1958.[33] Although it is not mandatory, most meat packers avail themselves of the grade-labeling service provided by the Department of Agriculture. Finally, standards of identity are prescribed for some food products, and standards have occasionally been established to control the size and shape of packages in which such products as bread and milk may be sold.[34]

Thus it can be seen that certain specific problems have been identified, and occasionally specific remedies have been devised for their resolution. Federal meat inspection was required only after the shocking conditions in the country's meat packing plants were so starkly revealed by Upton Sinclair in *The Jungle*. Deaths and horrible injuries attributable to drugs brought about enactment of the first federal drug act in 1906 and the subsequent amendments in 1938 and, following the thalidomide catastrophe, in 1962.[35] Similarly, scandal in the securities industry resulted in the pervasive scheme of federal legislation, which is designed to provide investors with more information and to permit them to sue for losses incurred through issuers' misstatements.[36]

Several pages could be filled with a recitation of the specific situations which gave rise to each of the federal consumer-related activities, but for present purposes it is enough to emphasize that governmental policy as it relates to the consumer is random, being responsive to narrowly-defined needs rather than the product of any comprehensive effort to assess the situation and develop appropriate, generalized corrective programs. This aimless policy is reflected in—and in some respects caused by—the absence of any administrative apparatus in the federal government designed to view the consumer problem as a whole.

When the National Recovery Administration was created in the summer of 1933, a Consumers Advisory Board was appointed to assert the interests of the consuming public in the industry code-making process. Similarly, at the behest of the Secretary of Agriculture, a Consumers Counsel was appointed in 1935 by the Agricultural Adjustment Administration. Likewise, in both the Bituminous Coal Conservation Act of 1935 and its successor, the National Bituminous Coal Act of 1937, specific statutory provision was made for an Office of the Consumers Counsel. The Counsel was charged with the responsibility of protecting the interest of the consuming public in all proceedings of the National Bituminous Coal Commission.[37]

Although the establishment of consumer spokesmen in the NRA, AAA, and the Bituminous Coal Commission was an unequivocal attempt to fill the need for assertion of the consumer interest, this effort failed to achieve its purpose. The reason for this failure is quite apparent. The three agencies to which these spokesmen were attached were principally engaged in carrying out programs that were designed to assist defined producer groups by artificially raising prices that the consumer was expected to pay. While consumer spokesmen may have helped somewhat in curtailing the excesses of specific agency programs, the facts are that the NRA "codes of fair competition" usually called for or brought about price increases; that the AAA curtailed farm production with the goal of boosting farm income by raising commodity prices; and that the principal means of dealing with the bituminous coal industry called for a complicated system of price-fixing. As a result of these circumstances, the consumer view was generally provided no more than a polite audience, and sometimes not even that. Indeed, by the time of the outbreak of World War II, formal representation of the consumer within the federal government was all but nonexistent, just as it had been before the 1930's.

Since 1962 there has been renewed governmental interest in the consumer's plight. Steps have been taken by both Presidents Kennedy and Johnson to give the consumer a spokesman. In 1962 President Kennedy, declaring that consumers have a "right to be heard" and to have their interests given "full and sympathetic consideration in the formulation of Government policy," created a Consumers' Advisory Council as an adjunct to the Council of Economic Advisers "to examine and provide advice to the Government on issues of broad economic policy, on governmental programs protecting consumer needs, and on needed improvements in the flow of consumer research material to the public."[38] The Council was given somewhat more formal status by an Executive Order issued by President Johnson on January 3, 1964.[39] In addition to the Council, which is composed of twelve private citizens, President Johnson has also established a Committee on Consumer Interests.[40] The Committee is composed of the private citizens who serve on the Advisory Council and representatives of ten governmental agencies. A Special Assistant for Consumer Affairs was appointed by the President early in 1964.[41] The holder of this position, currently Esther Peterson (who is also an Assistant Secretary of Labor), is the principal spokesman for the consumer in the federal government and serves as chairman of the Committee on Consumer Interests.

This conglomeration of councils, committees, and special assistants that supposedly represent consumers at the federal goverment's highest policy-making levels resembles the disorganized and random assortment of activities that are carried out by the thirty-five principal departments and agencies. Groups and individuals have been hurriedly assembled to meet a vaguely felt need, but there is no clear sense of purpose. Although both a Committee on Consumer Interests and a Consumer Advisory Council exist, it is difficult to determine the separate functions which they serve. The Committee's responsibility is to "consider" federal "policies and programs of primary importance to consumers," while the Council has been directed to "advise the Government on issues of broad economic policy of immediate concern to consumers." Both groups are served by the same staff, which in turn reports directly to the Special Assistant, and the holder of that office is chairman of the Committee and an ex officio member of the Advisory Council. If the Committee implemented programs developed by the Council and approved by the President, its function would be understandable. However, the Committee's job is not to implement, but rather to advise, and that is a responsibility also of the Advisory Council. The point at which one ends and the other begins is a puzzle, like so much governmental activity in the consumer area.

Perhaps the single most important weakness in the entire scheme is the lack of authority noticeable in both the Council and the Commission, as well as in the Special Assistant. Each organization is charged with the responsibility of "advising," "reviewing," or "consulting," but none has the power to modify, execute, or instigate any program of its own. Existing programs designed to aid the consumer are in a state of disarray and reveal many deficiencies, but the Advisory Council and the Committee can do no more than hope that their recommendations will induce the President and Congress to take corrective action.

Occasional proposals have been made to create a central consumer agency to implement and coordinate the numerous federal programs, but they have not been seriously considered. Moreover, past proposals have not really promised to meet the need for better organization. Creation of a Department of Consumers was urged by Senator Kefauver, but this bill was accorded only a single day of hearings and then promptly forgotten.[42] A group of eighteen senators is currently supporting a bill that would establish an independent agency to be known as the Office of Consumers.[43] This proposed agency would be under the direction of a Consumers Counsel, and the Office's principal function would be "to protect and promote the interests of the people of the United States as consumers." However, as in the case of the current Advisory Council and the Committee on Consumer Interests, the proposed Office of Consumers would lack the authority to plan and carry out programs on behalf of consumers and would not encompass any of the nearly three hundred separate consumer activities now carried out in many governmental departments and agencies. If such an office is to play a meaningful role, it must have the power to act on its own and to coordinate existing consumer activities.

C. The Inadequacy of State Regulation

At the state level, consumer representation presents a pattern of activity which resembles that at the federal level. Most states have some sort of program that protects or promotes the consumer interest; as is true at the federal level, however, the focus is almost entirely on the suppression of fraud and on the inspection of food and other products for human consumption. Even in these respects, the states' programs are considerably less effective than the corresponding activities of the federal government. For example, only eighteen states have meat inspection laws which are similar to the federal regulations for meat shipped in interstate commerce.[44] Drugs are subjected to some sort of inspection and control in most states, but the level of effort is generally so limited as to suggest that the programs are extemely inadequate. A survey completed in 1963 showed that the states at that time were spending approximately $1.7 million a year for the regulation of drugs. [45] However, nearly a third of this amount was spent in California and New York, and, as a group, the states spent only about one cent per capita per year in this effort. It is also interesting to note that while various industry practices specifically aimed at consumers are recognized as a serious problem, only fourteen states have established a special enforcement unit to deal with the diverse problems of consumer protection.[46]

A few states, though, have been alert to the merchandising atmosphere in which we now live and to the resulting needs of consumers. South Carolina, for example, has attempted to regulate some packaging practices that may be deceptive or misleading by imposing standards governing size, shape, and label contents. Unfortunately this initiative has not been generally followed, and South Carolina officials acknowledge that there must be a broader-based effort if the problem is to be dealt with adequately.[47]

Once, therefore, we lay aside questions of outright fraud and adulteration, governmental policy is a maze of specific requirements. At both federal and state levels there is no uniformity with respect to such important matters as standards of identity, disclosure of weight and content, quality grading, or packaging requirements. Nevertheless, each of these subjects is of material significance to the consumer who wishes to make purchases on a rational basis rather than by a combination of luck and guesswork.

The failure to provide an organizational apparatus that can deal with consumer matters deliberately and comprehensively is itself compelling evidence of the weakness in the entire effort to secure government recognition of consumer problems. However, the lack of effective organization is not so much a cause as it is a symptom of other deficiencies. The arguments advanced in support of pleas for the consumer are themselves typically disorganized and random, stemming from a variety of divergent assumptions and philosophic positions that are generally unsystematic in their analysis and conclusions.

REFERENCES

1. *The Public Papers and Addresses of Franklin D. Roosevelt* 639, 645 (1938).
2. Address to the Association of California Consumers Convention, Dec. 7, 1963, p. 1 (mimeo.). Speaking more recently, Senator Hart—who has become a hero among consumers because of his sponsorship of the Truth-in-Packaging Bill (see note 74 *infra*)—assessed the situation again: "The fact is that Congress has [still] not passed one piece of legislation tailored specifically for the economic interests of consumers." Testimony before the Michigan House of Representatives Judiciary Subcommittee on Consumer Protection, Nov. 30, 1965, p. 2 (mimeo.). The Senate passed a Truth-in-Packaging bill June 9; House action is still uncertain as this article goes to press.
3. Smith, *An Inquiry Into the Nature and Causes of the Wealth of Nations* 625 (Modern Library ed. 1937). Smith also asserted that "the point is so perfectly self-evident, that it would be absurd to attempt to disprove it." *Ibid.* However, Smith recognized that consumers were not

accorded equal consideration vis-à-vis producers. See note 58 *infra*. An analogy can be drawn to the elementary Keynesian point that "effective demand" is a product of consumption and investment expenditure, with what is not consumed being regarded as "invested." Keynes, *The General Theory of Employment, Interest, and Money* (1936).

4. In the fourth quarter of 1965 the country's gross national product, seasonally adjusted at an annual rate, totaled $695 billion. Personal consumption expenditures amounted to $440 billion (if interest paid by consumers were included, the figure would exceed $452 billion). *Economic Report of the President* 209 (table C-1), 226 (table C-14) (Jan. 1966).

5. Schumpeter, *Capitalism, Socialism, and Democracy* (1942). In Schumpeter's view, innovation is critical for "the competition that counts" is, "the competition from the new commodity, the new technology, the new source of supply . . . ." *Id.* at 84. Schumpeter regarded monopoly as an essential precondition for innovation.

6. Recent empirical studies tend to rebut the notion that large business firms are more innovative than smaller organizations. In fact, most basic inventions made during this century have come from individuals or small firms. See Jewkes, *The Sources of Invention* ch. IV (1958); Schmookler, "Inventors Past and Present," 39 *Rev. Econ. & Stat.* 321 (1957). One analyst concluded that "there are inherent incompatibilities between the large industrial laboratories and high-level invention achievement." Hamberg, "Invention in the Industrial Research Laboratory, 71 *J. Pol. Economy* 95, 115 (1963). For additional material on this subject, see *Hearings on Economic Concentration Before the Senate Subcommittee on Antitrust and Monopoly*, 89th Cong., 1st Sess., pt. 4 (1965).

7. Mitchell, "The Backward Art of Spending Money," 2 *Am. Econ. Rev.* 269 (1912). "Important as the art of spending money is, we have developed less skill in its practice than in the practice of making money." *Ibid.*

8. For a brief, well-written study of the historical aspects of consumer protection, see Levett, *The Consumer in History* (1929).

9. See Letwin, "The English Common Law Concerning Monopolies," 21 *U. Chi. L. Rev.* 355 (1954).

10. For a general review of state regulatory efforts, particularly during the past century, see Jones, "Historical Development of the Law of Business Competition" (pts. 1-4), 35 *Yale L. J.* 905 (1926), 36 *id.* 42, 207, 351 (1927). The considerable distaste for business trusts among buyers who felt they were being exploited was a significant factor, and perhaps the major consideration, leading to the passage of state and federal antitrust laws during the late nineteenth century. See Letwin, "Congress and the Sherman Antitrust Law: 1887-1890," 23 *U. Chi. L. Rev.* 221 (1956). This sentiment—a form of consumer discontent—ran especially strong in the farm community. See Hicks, *The Populist Revolt* (1931).

11. See Letwin, note 9 *supra*.

12. N.Y. Times, Oct. 17, 1965, § 1, p. 13, col. 1 (city ed.).

13. "The congress shall have the power to . . . fix the standard of weights and measures." U.S. Const. art. I, § 8.

14. 1 Bland, Brown & Tawney, *English Economic History* 155 (1920).

15. "Not until the nineteenth century did judges discover that *caveat emptor* sharpened wits, taught self-reliance, made a man—an economic man—out of the buyer, and served well its two masters, business and justice." Hamilton, "The Ancient Maxim Caveat Emptor," 40 *Yale L.J.* 1133, 1186 (1931).

16. FTC v. Mary Carter Paint Co., 1965 Trade Cas. ¶ 71194. The Commission reasoned that since the seller had no history of selling single cans of paint, its practice of allocating the price of two cans to one can and calling the other "free" amounted to misrepresentation. A majority of the Court found that there was substantial evidence to support the Commission finding.

17. Occasionally a court will impose liability for economic harm sustained as the result of deceptive advertising. For example, in one recent case a court awarded damages to the buyer of a new car who claimed that the manufacturer has breached its warranty as defined by advertisements that represented its cars to be trouble-free, economical, and of high quality. The court felt that "the protection of the defenseless consumer has proved its value as a

cornerstone in the structure of our national administration of justice." Inglis v. American Motors Corp., 3 Ohio St. 2d 132, 141, 209 N.E.2d 583, 588 (1965).

18. The recent developments are surveyed in Ray, "Products Liability—A Symposium: Introduction," 19 *Sw. L.J.* 1 (1965). As an instance of the expansion in the law's coverage, see Piercefield v. Remington Arms Co., 375 Mich. 85, 133 N.W.2d 129 (1965) (bystander allowed recovery for an injury caused by defective shotgun ammunition). For general comments, see Kessler. "The Protection of the Consumer Under Modern Sales Law: A Comparative Study," 74 *Yale L.J.* 262 (1964); Southwick, "The Disenchanted Consumer—Liability for Harmful Products" 18 *Mich. Bus. Rev.* 5 (Jan. 1966); Wall Street Journal, Sept. 9, 1965, p. 1, col. 6.

19. For a discussion of the developments, see Prosser, "Assault Upon the Citadel," 69 *Yale L.J.* 1099 (1960); Wade, "Strict Tort Liability of Manufacturers," 19 *Sw. L.J.* 5 (1965).

20. This was the conclusion drawn from a carefully administered test in which thirty-three young married women were instructed to select the most economical package for each of twenty products on sale at a supermarket. Based on the results of this survey, it appears that the typical economy-minded shopper would spend between nine and ten per cent more than one who was in fact consistently able to select the most economical packages. See Friedman, Truth in Packaging in an American Supermarket (mimeo. 1965). (A brief version of this paper was presented at the 1965 annual meeting of the American Psychological Association.)

21. Oxenfeldt, "Consumer Knowledge: Its Measurement and Extent," 32 *Rev. Econ. & Stat.* 300 (1950).

22. The nation's families spend an average of slightly less than 20% of their after-tax income for "food prepared at home." Murphy, "Spending and Saving in Urban and Rural Areas," 88 *Monthly Labor Rev.* 1169, 1171-72 (table 1) (1965). Consumer expenditures in 1965 reached the $450 billion mark (see note 4 *supra*) and will climb close to $500 billion in 1966.

23. House Comm. on Government Operations, "Consumer Protection Activities of Federal Departments and Agencies," *H.R. Rep.* No. 1241, 87 Cong., 1st Sess. (1961). The committee's survey was based on questionnaires sent to thirty-five departments and agencies. Their detailed responses are contained in the House report. *Id.* at 63-338.

24. *Id.* at 23 (table 1).

25. *Id.* at 24 (table 2).

26. Moreover, it is clear that some of the activities which the sponsoring departments and agencies feel protect or promote consumer interests do not do so. Indeed quite the opposite. For example, the Department of Agriculture asserted that its regulation of milk supply and control of sugar production—both of which have the effect of raising prices—help the consumer! *Id.* at 93-95.

27. See 52 Stat. 1047 (1938), 21 U.S.C. § 343 (1964) (food); 52 Stat. 1050 (1938), 21 U.S.C. § 352 (1964) (drugs).

28. 76 Stat. 785 (1962), 21 U.S.C. §§ 301-60 (1964).

29. Textile Fiber Products Identification Act, 72 Stat. 1717 (1958), 15 U.S.C. §§ 70-70k (1964).

30. Wool Products Labeling Act of 1939, 54 Stat. 1128, 15 U.S.C. §§ 68-68j (1964).

31. Fur Products Labeling Act, 65 Stat. 175 (1951), 15 U.S.C. §§ 69-69j (1964).

32. See Securities Act of 1933, 48 Stat. 74, 15 U.S.C. §§ 77a-aa (1964).

33. See 72 Stat. 325, 15 U.S.C. §§ 1231-33 (1964).

34. For a description of the Department of Agriculture's various activities dealing with the marketing of food products see *H.R. Rep.* No. 1241, *op. cit. supra* note 23, at 63-114. For a more general discussion of the Government's current role in the marketplace, see Massel, *Competition and Monopoly* 51-54 (Anchor Book ed. 1964); Wilcox, *Public Policies Toward Business* ch. 8 (rev. ed. 1960).

35. The widespread use by women during early pregnancy of a sleeping pill, generally known as thalidomide, resulted in the birth of more than seven thousand deformed babies. This disaster and its role in the passage of drug legislation is considered in Harris *The Real Voice* 154, 181-93 (1964).

36. For a discussion of the background to the adoption of federal securities legislation, see 1 Loss, *Securities Regulation* 119-28 (1961).

37. The New Deal experience is thoroughly considered in Campbell, *Consumer Representation in the New Deal* (1940).
38. *Message on Consumers' Protection and Interest Program,* H.R. Doc. No. 364, 87th Cong., 2d Sess. (March 15, 1962).
39. Exec. Order No. 11136, 29 Fed. Reg. 129 (1964).
40. *Ibid.*
41. In taking steps to appoint consumer representatives in the executive branch of the Government, President Johnson, in a message delivered to the Congress on February 5, 1964, noted that "for far too long, the consumer has had too little voice and too little weight in government. As a worker, as a businessman, as a farmer, as a lawyer or doctor, the citizen has been well represented. But as a consumer, he has had to take a back seat." H.R. Doc. No. 220, 88th Cong., 2d Sess. 1 (1964). More recently, in both his 1966 State of the Union Address and in his Economic Report, the President has endorsed legislation designed to assist the consumer. 112 *Cong. Rec.* 129, 131 (daily ed. Jan. 12. 1966); *economic Report of the President* 19 (Jan. 1966).
42. For a brief history of congressional efforts to establish a special consumer agency, see 111 *Cong. Rec.* 2254 (Feb. 9, 1965).
43. See S. 1952, 89th Cong., 1st Sess. (1965). Senator Hart. chief sponsor of S. 1052, has also urged the creation of a national commission to anticipate the problems consumers will face in the future. Testimony, *supra* note 2, at 5-6. Another proposal, embodied in a resolution offered by Senator Javits and supported by eighteen other senators would establish a Select Senate Committee on Consumers "to conduct a continuing comprehensive study and investigation with respect to the nature and extent of economic problems of consumers within the United States." S. Res. 84, 89th Cong., 1st Sess. (1965). In 1966 a bill (H.R. 7179) was introduced in the House that would create a Department of Consumers.
44. Although all the states have some legal requirements concerning the sanitation of slaughtering and processing facilities and the adulteration and misbranding of meat products, in only 30 is there legal authority for ante and post mortem inspection and in only 18 is such inspection mandatory." House Comm. on Government Operations, "Consumer Protection Activities of State Governments," *H.R. Rep.* No. 921, 88th Cong.. 1st Sess., pt. 2, at 17 (1963). About 20% of the commercially slaughtered meat in the United States is not subject to existing federal meat inspection regulation because it moves only in intrastate commerce.
45. House Comm. on Government Operations. "Consumer Protection Activities of State Governments," *H.R. Rep.* No. 921, 88th Cong., 1st Sess., pt. 1, at 12 (table 2-A) (1963).
46. In 1965 special consumer protection officials were provided for by statute in Hawaii and North Dakota. Such offices also exist in California, Michigan, New York, Ohio, Pennsylvania, and several other states. See State Government News, Oct. 1965.
47. The South Carolina experience is discussed in *Hearings on Packaging and Labeling Legislation Before the Senate Subcommittee on Antitrust and Monopoly,* 88th Cong., 1st Sess., pt. 1, at 220-28 (1963).

20

FTC Performance: Evaluations and Recommendations

ABA Commission to Study the Federal Trade Commission

The American Bar Association Commission to Study the Federal Trade Commission concludes that the FTC's efforts to investigate the basis in fact and respond to the public outcry regarding marketing frauds against consumers have been inadequate. An evaluation of existing FTC programs is presented here.

A. CONSUMER PROTECTION

There is a general conviction that marketing frauds against consumers are wide-spread in this country and constitute a problem of major national concern.[1] The feeling is not that business practices have changed significantly but rather that the public is increasingly unwilling to tolerate exploitation. To a large extent, the publicity spotlight has fallen upon deceptive schemes practiced against the poor, uneducated and elderly, particularly in the urban ghettos of the United States, although, of course, these are not the only victims of such abuses.

Our study has led us to the conclusion that the FTC's efforts to investigate the basis in fact for this public outcry and to find ways of coping with whatever underlying problems exist have been inadequate. It is true that the FTC's resources may not match the scope of the problem, and we do not fault the FTC for failing to still all complaints of consumer fraud. Indeed, much of the responsibility for action in this area, particularly with regard to the local types of misconduct rests with state and

Reprinted from *Report of the ABA Commission to Study the Federal Trade Commission* (Washington: The Bureau of National Affairs, 1969), pp. 36-54. Reprinted by permission.

municipal authorities. However, the FTC has fallen far short of what it could have done. It has failed to instill a sense of mission either in its own personnel or in the states and municipalities which are so badly in need of the information and expertise which should be at the FTC's disposal. Its efforts have been piecemeal, and have lacked the study and planning which are essential to identify the most pressing problems faced by consumers, and to create a unified approach toward their solution. Often the agency has seemed more concerned with protecting competitors of an enterprise practicing deception rather than consumers.

In the succeeding sections, we will examine the FTC's existing programs in the areas of deceptive labeling, false advertising, wool and textiles, and localized marketing schemes, and will evaluate the agency's performance in each area.[2] Following that evaluation, we will indicate the areas where the FTC, although it has not been entirely inactive, should show new initiatives in the commitment of its resources.

1. EXISTING PROGRAMS

a. Deceptive Labeling

(1) The FTC Effort. The FTC has committed a substantial portion of its total resources available for direct consumer protection to prevention of "unfair or deceptive acts or practices" in the labeling area.[3] Of the more than 200 formal proceedings initiated in the consumer protection field over the last three fiscal years, roughly 20% concerned deceptive labeling practices; the vast majority of the respondents were manufacturers. In addition, a substantial number of assurances of voluntary compliance were negotiated and advisory opinions issued in connection with labeling problems—particularly in the foreign origin area. Finally, a major commitment of resources to labeling problems was made in the Bureau of Industry Guidance; most of the guides and virtually all of the trade regulation rules promulgated by that bureau dealt, in whole or in part, with labeling problems.[4]

(2) Evaluation. The FTC has made some vigorous efforts in the deceptive labeling field. The Commission required health warnings on cigarette packages in the face of determined Congressional and industry opposition.[5] Guides promulgated by the FTC which seem to us particularly useful include those relating to automobile tire labeling and deceptive labeling of dry-cell batteries.[6]

Notwithstanding these achievements, the FTC's deceptive labeling program does not seem to us to be designed to enforce Section 5 in a way that will protect important consumer interests or serve other sensible enforcement goals. For lack of adequate planning, the FTC has tended to select relatively trivial practices for staunch enforcement measures. While simultaneously asserting the lack of manpower and funds to initiate programs to combat ghetto frauds, monitor advertising, and secure effective compliance with orders, the FTC has issued complaints attacking the failure to disclose on labels that "Navy shoes" were not made by the Navy, that flies were imported, that Indian trinkets were not manufactured by American Indians, and that "Havana" cigars were not made entirely of Cuban tobacco. The record in relation to rules and guides also displays a preoccupation with projects of marginal importance. Thus the Commission announced that the use of the word "automatic" is deceptive when used in relation to sewing machines because "sewing machines, unlike 'automatic' washing machines or dishwashers, cannot be turned on and left, to operate by themselves."[7]

There are a number of reasons for the preponderance of trivia in the FTC's deceptive labeling activities. The range of matters which may be chosen for enforcement action is severely limited by the FTC's almost exclusive reliance on applications for complaint received through the mails. There has been an almost complete failure to identify areas of high consumer concern, affirmatively to seek out labeling deceptions or otherwise to generate investigations and projects from within the agency. In addition, the vagaries of the passive mailbag approach have been compounded by the FTC's failure to set priorities within the deceptive labeling field or within the broader context of the FTC's overall consumer protection program.

Beyond the problems of input and planning, the involvement of the FTC in matters having a minor impact on consumers may be explained by the fact that the agency often acts at the behest of one group of industry members against another group. Sometimes these complaints of competitors deal with matters of concern to consumers, but often they do not. Also, there appears to be a great deal of effort spent on protecting industry members from product imitation by competitors.[8]

If the FTC had unlimited resources, we would be hard put to demonstrate any affirmative harm resulting from its preoccupation with trivial deceptive labeling practices. But where the FTC points to shortages in allocations as one reason for its inability to combat serious consumer frauds, it becomes clear that the consequence of the commitment of resources to these marginal projects is that more significant projects are left undone.

b. False and Deceptive Advertising

When considerations of health or safety are not directly involved, and the fraud is not so blatant that criminal sanctions can be sought, the FTC is virtually the sole effective protector of defrauded consumers in this area of the law. Section 5 of the FTC Act, conferring jurisdiction over "unfair or deceptive acts or practices in commerce . . . ," and Section 12, dealing with the false advertisement of food, drugs, devices, and cosmetics, constitute an exceptionally broad grant of power in the FTC to deal with deceptive advertising. State advertising laws, private damage actions, and competition among advertisers in which they might publicize deceptions in a rival's advertising campaign are not now practical alternatives. Although the FTC has not been inactive in this area, lack of planning has led the agency to commit insufficient resources to the area, and to deploy them badly.

(1) The FTC Effort. The FTC has been active in recent years in promulgating trade regulation rules and industry guides relating to false advertising, and some of its most effective administrative action has occurred in this area. There are guides dealing with deceptive advertising of guarantees[9] and tire advertising,[10] and it now has pending a proposed guide and trade regulation rule for advertising non-prescription analgesics.[11]

(2) Evaluation. The FTC has done some innovative work in the field of false advertising, particularly with regard to cigarettes,[12] and its successes should not be ignored. Unfortunately, however, commendable initiatives in conception often have been undermined by failures in implementation. The recurrent flaws of FTC enforcement—failures of detection, undercommitment of resources to important projects, timidity in instituting formal proceedings and failure to engage in an effective compliance program—tend to outweigh its occasional successes. To some extent, this is because Congress has refused funds to support enforcement activities. On the other hand, until very recently the FTC did not press Congress for additional funds to mount a more energetic campaign against false advertising, and, in any event, the FTC with present resources reallocated ought to be able to do a better job in this area.

Deficiencies in the FTC's current program are most pronounced in the following respects:

(a) Detection. The FTC's monitoring program is limited almost exclusively to examination of commercial advertising on national television. This monitoring consists of a review by attorneys and scientists of commercial scripts broadcast during the first week of each month, which are submitted to the FTC by the three major networks. Although vast amounts of material are accumulated dealing with national and local magazine advertising, national and regional radio scripts regional television, and local newspaper advertising, no personnel have been assigned to screen this material.[13] FTC employees have been requested, however, to report any questionable advertising that they may have seen personally. National TV does affect a great number of consumers. However, the ghetto frauds which the FTC believes numerous—such as fictitious pricing, home improvement frauds, and bait-and-switch schemes—usually appear in those local media that the FTC entirely ignores. We believe the FTC cannot mount an effective campaign against false and misleading advertising unless it monitors all interstate media with adequate personnel.

(b) Undercommitment of Enforcement Resources. The FTC has undertaken in recent years a broad range of investigations of questionable advertising, but it simply has not made the commitment of personnel necessary to carry out these investigations expeditiously and efficiently.

To take one example that came to our attention, the Division of Special Projects of the Bureau of Deceptive Practices is now responsible for conducting the following investigations which principally involve false advertising but also include other consumer fraud problems: misbranding of softwood lumber, cigarette advertising and labeling, fair packaging and labeling, encyclopedia and magazine subscription frauds, failure to publish or deceptive publication of gasoline octane ratings, advertising campaigns dealing with gasoline additives, promulgation of product safety standards, automobile warranty claims, and several other matters that are still confidential and cannot be listed at this time. A total of 12 attorneys have been assigned to handle all of these investigations, and six of those work exclusively on fair packaging and labeling. The predictable result is that investigations, once initiated, disappear from public view and surface, if at all, many years later. For example, in one way or another, the FTC has been investigating and dealing with the problem of false advertising of analgesic drugs since 1955. In March 1962, the Commission announced that it was initiating a study of the advertising of cold remedies to determine whether manufacturers of these products were overstating their effectiveness, but the results of that study remain unpublished and unimplemented. It is true that the agency has called for increased allocations, partly to expand the staff of attorneys available for false advertising work, only to see Congress cut the requested appropriations, and some of the responsibility for delay must be attributed to legal maneuvers by attorneys for the firms being investigated. Nevertheless, the fundamental determination to commit a large number of important investigations to a staff of 12 lawyers in the Division of Special Projects, while almost 100 employees (lawyers, investigators, and others) staff the Bureau of Textiles and Furs, represents, in our view, an erroneous evaluation of enforcement priorities.[14]

(c) Enforcement Procedures. In the past few years, the FTC has resorted to formal enforcement procedures on the average less than 7 times per year in cases primarily involving false advertising charges. Most of these cases were terminated by negotiated consent arrangements so that rarely were the resources of the Commission devoted to the litigation process.

We recognize that in the false advertising area much can be accomplished by advising and consulting with advertisers, and encouraging voluntary compliance. On the other hand, if advertisers believe the FTC is reluctant to enforce the law vigorously where flagrant false advertising is uncovered, we fear they will not take the FTC seriously.

This failure to put some bite into enforcement is illustrated by the long history of the FTC's dealings with the J. B. Williams Company over advertising campaigns for Geritol. After more than three years of investigation, the FTC, in December, 1962, directed the issuance of a complaint in which it alleged, among other things, that respondents had misrepresented the efficacy of Geritol in the treatment of tiredness, nervousness, loss of strength and irritability. No preliminary injunction was sought. About three years later a cease and desist order was entered which was eventually affirmed with slight modification by the Court of Appeals.[15]

Early in 1968 respondents submitted their first compliance report. The new advertising campaign for Geritol was aired and, on November 14, 1968, the FTC held a public hearing for the purpose of determining whether the new Geritol commercials conformed with the Commission's order. The FTC found that the new Geritol commercials *still* violated the cease and desist order, but instead of seeking civil penalties the FTC merely ordered respondent to submit a second compliance report. In March, 1969, almost 10 years to the day after the beginning of the investigation, the FTC found that certain of Geritol's commercials *still* violated the cease and desist order, but again it did not seek civil enforcement penalties. No further action has been taken. Whatever the merits of the Commission's original complaint against the Geritol ads, we believe the Commission should have taken more effective action in the full decade since its investigation was initiated.

(d) Ineffective Compliance Program. Responsibility for securing compliance with cease-and-desist orders issued against respondents engaged in false and misleading advertising lies with the Compliance Division of the Bureau of Deceptive Practices. Eleven attorneys are assigned to this work, which consists largely of a review of compliance reports submitted by respondents, and the investigation of complaints received from the public alleging violations of orders.

According to the FTC's own personnel, this limited compliance program is falling further and further behind, and there is no program to institute a systematic check of compliance with orders or assurances of voluntary compliance after compliance reports have been approved. The last time such a survey was attempted was more than 15 years ago, and it resulted in penalty investigations in 25% of the cases surveyed, and civil penalty proceedings in 50% of the cases investigated.

The FTC recognizes the shortcomings of its compliance program in this area, and plans have been proposed within the agency to strengthen this area of its operations in the future. Such plans are long overdue.

(e) Studies and Reports. Little or no work has been done in recent years with respect to such questions as the evolving rule of new techniques of advertising on buying patterns, the incidence and effectiveness of subliminal or motivational advertising, or the extent to which advertising has been directed toward establishing artificial product differentiation in the minds of consumers. Moreover, the FTC determines the "meaning" of advertisements and their impact on consumers without the benefit of empirical surveys conducted by advertising and marketing experts. In short, the FTC has made little use of its powers to investigate, study and report on problems in this area. In the future, hopefully, resources will be made available to undertake these activities.

(f) Consumer Education. Another area in which the FTC has been passive relates to possible programs of consumer education designed to make purchasers aware of flagrant deceptions and schemes to defraud. The Kerner Report indicated that 88% of all Negro households and 95% of poor families in New York City have television sets.[16] Thus, an aggressive informational program on national and local television holds out the prospect of disseminating knowledge among low income groups who can ill afford to be victimized by deceptive practices.

We understand that the FTC is now considering establishing a Consumer Education Office to replace its present sporadic efforts. We commend this initiative, and propose that the office make efforts to secure, without charge, television and radio time by seeking the cooperation of the Federal Communications Commission, the national networks, local stations, and the Corporation for Public Broadcasting.

c. Bureau of Textiles and Furs

(1) The FTC Effort. In terms of total dollars and the proportion of resources allocated, enforcement operations of the Bureau of Textiles and Furs have been and continue to be among the most preferred in the FTC over the last 8 or 10 years. In our view, this commitment represents poor planning and a misallocation of resources.

The Bureau of Textiles and Furs is engaged exclusively in the enforcement of four statutes: the Wool Products Labeling Act ("Wool Act"),[17] the Textile Fiber Products Identification Act ("Textile Act"),[18] the Fur Products Labeling Act ("Fur Act")[19] and the Flammable Fabrics Act.[20] Of these, the first three are primarily aimed at protecting producers rather than consumers.[21] We do not fault the FTC for enforcing these protectionist statutes. It is the judgment of Congress that these industries deserve some protection from competition, and it is neither our province, nor that of the FTC, to repeal the statutes. We believe, however, that in allocating its resources along the whole spectrum of social problems which the agency could attempt to ameliorate, the FTC has given inordinate attention to these areas. Moreover, the FTC's enforcement effort again has focused on trivial matters which bear little or no functional relationship either to the protection of competitors, or the protection of consumers.

For example, in *Marcus* v. *FTC*,[22] the FTC found a violation of the Act because of mislabeling on 4 wool blankets. One was labeled 70% wool and 30% rayon when it actually contained 79% wool, 5.9% nylon and various other fabrics, and a second was labeled 90% wool and 10% nylon, when it in fact had 93.7% wool. The FTC complained because the blanket labels understated the amount of wool, but the Court of Appeals found that understatement of wool content was not a violation. Another blanket was labeled 90% wool, but in fact had 89.9% and that label was held valid by the Court as an "unavoidable variation in manufacture." The fourth blanket was labeled 100% wool when in fact it contained 14.3% residue other than wool, and this was held to be a meaningful variation. Since the respondent had sold over one million blankets during the period under investigation, the Court concluded that the variations found did not constitute substantial evidence of misbranding.

Typical cases enforcing the Textile Act involve sleeping bags that were labeled "all acetate" but were found to contain "substantially less",[23] or men's trousers that were labeled 75% dacron-polyester and 25% cotton whereas "substantially less dacron" was present.[24] There are probably some consumer protection advantages that result from enforcement of the Textile Act. Most consumers cannot tell by sight or touch whether a textile is, for example, 60% cotton and 40% dacron, or contains other fibers, and the Act requires that the label disclose that information. For a sophisticated shopper, such information is relevant. On the other hand, the consumer interested in more practical considerations, such as durability, shrinkage, launderability, and warmth, needs to be told how these qualities relate to fiber content.

In enforcing the Fur Act, the FTC has adopted rules which provide that all information on the label must be in English, forbid the use of abbreviations on the label, and limit the minimum size of labels and the size of type that may be used on the label. Other rules prevent fictitious price comparisons, fraudulent claims of value, and bogus going-out-of-business sales. The following list of violations, taken from a report of a case that eventually reached the Court of Appeals, is some indication of the kind of infractions that may occur:

A few hand written labels containing (in addition to the required data) non-required words "fur name" on the same side; one garment with no fur identification; a hand written label which omitted the information that the fur was dyed and which contained the non-required words "romance flank muskrat"; more than thirty labels containing non-required words, e.g., "romance" and "fur name"; several labels omitting the information that the fur was dyed; about ten labels omitting the name or registered number of the marketer; several labels omitting the name of the mink trimming used on the garment of another fur; more than a dozen labels having the words "Southwest Africa" abbreviated as "S.W. Africa"; and several labels or garments of Persian Lamb in which the word "lamb" was omitted.[25]

It is difficult to justify such literal-minded enforcement of this statute by the Bureau of Textiles and Furs. Many of the trivial violations found in the literal text of labels, invoices and advertising are hardly relevant to any serious consumer interest. Indeed, if the misleading information were deceptive in a significant way—for example, if rabbit were labeled as Persian Lamb—Section 5 would be available to prevent continuation of such practices.

The fourth statute enforced by the Bureau of Textiles and Furs is the Flammable Fabrics Act, passed in 1953 and amended in 1967. It is not a labeling or disclosure statute, but directly prohibits the manufacture and marketing of any wearing apparel that does not conform to standards promulgated by the Secretary of Commerce. The Act resulted from a number of highly publicized incidents in the early 1950's involving severe burning of children by highly flammable children's cowboy playsuits and so-called "torch-sweaters", and was amended in 1967 to allow for more flexibility in standards and to broaden the coverage of the Act to include household furnishings, draperies and blankets.

Time and effort devoted by the Bureau of Textiles and Furs to enforcement of this statute has been relatively minor compared to enforcement of the three labeling statutes. Of all Textile and Fur Bureau cases on the FTC docket in July 1962, 13.3% involved violations of the Flammable Fabrics Act. The percentage rose to 30% in 1964 and dropped to 5.6% in 1966 and 5.8% in 1967. By 1968 it was up to 16%. Budget allocations for Flammable Fabrics Act enforcement have run at about 10% of total textile and fur allocations over the last five years—compared to about 40% per year for Textile Act enforcement during the same period. In budget requests for fiscal 1970, the FTC has put substantially more emphasis on Flammable Fabrics Act enforcement. Thus, of 70 additional employees requested for fiscal 1970, 54 are to work in this area of enforcement.

(2) Evaluation. Operations of the Bureau of Textiles and Furs (other than in Flammable Fabrics Act enforcement) represent a glaring example of misallocation of resources and a misguided enforcement policy. Each year larger allocations are requested and increasing amounts spent on an energetic program to achieve results of highly dubious value to anyone. Moreover, the examples of concern with trivial labeling errors, mentioned above, came up in enforcement actions that were appealed to the Courts of Appeals; we suspect—and several of the present Commissioners in the FTC support us in this view—that even more trivial violations are involved in enforcement through voluntary compliance procedures.

Time and again, the FTC has defended itself against charges of inadequate consumer protection programs on the ground that a sufficient allocation to support these programs had not been made available. Keeping in mind that money saved by cutting the allocation to the Bureau of Textiles and Furs could be used for serious consumer protection work, we conclude that:

a. The Flammable Fabrics Act is a legitimate and important aspect of consumer protection which, accordingly, should be rigorously enforced.

b. Present efforts of the Bureau of Textiles and Furs to inspect 20% of all mills and manufacturers in the United States each year, and 10% to 15% of all retail outlets, are out of proportion to the contribution that such an ambitious program can make to consumer protection. We believe a carefully devised sampling program—cutting present expenditures on enforcement of the Wool, Textile, and Fur Acts by one-half to two-thirds—would be entirely adequate.

c. The tendency of the Bureau to insist on literal compliance not only with the statutes but with the FTC's regulations under the statutes must cease. In other words, the Commission should devise a set of criteria for actionable violations that distinguishes between trivial, nitpicking deviations as opposed to potentially serious deceptions of consumers.

d. Retail Frauds

(1) The FTC Effort—A Limited War. Despite findings in its own studies that retail fraud against consumers is practiced on a vast scale, and findings by many others that it is a problem of major national concern, the FTC has devoted very limited resources to coping with these problems. The only comprehensive and organized effort to deal with retail marketing frauds was its consumer protection project begun in late 1966 in the District of Columbia. This program represents an embryonic effort at the type of study which the FTC needs in order to produce a unified plan of attack on consumer problems, but it was conducted on too small a scale, and for too short a period of time, to accomplish a sufficiently broad result.

As a result of this single program, however, 108 investigations of sellers in the District of Columbia were opened and 42 formal complaints issued. Several important FTC opinions were eventually handed down in connection with these complaints, including a few that broke important new ground in the development of consumer rights.[26] The knowledge gained as a result of the project influenced the drafting of the FTC's guides on retail installment credit sales, and is said by FTC personnel to have influenced the enactment by Congress of truth-in-lending legislation. These are extraordinary results from a program which, at the height of its activities, involved an average of five full-time lawyers. Nevertheless, the project itself has been allowed to dwindle to a skeleton operation, and no other similar project has been attempted. Several of the guides published in recent years touch upon consumer fraud problems,[27] and the FTC also has issued some complaints in this area. For example, we found that in the last three years the FTC had filed an average of about 15 complaints per year alleging fraudulent bait-and-switch practices or other fraudulent pricing tactics, about 12 complaints per year charging misrepresentations of potential earnings of franchises and dealerships (mostly involving chinchilla breeding franchises), about 7 complaints per year against home improvement frauds (e.g. bogus contests, phony commissions for "model home" displays, and fictitious pricing) and about 4 per year dealing with misrepresentations as to potential earnings upon graduation from various types of schools. With the exception of cases emerging from the D.C. Program, we are advised that every one of these actions developed from complaints received in the mail by the FTC. Determination whether to react to a letter of complaint alleging retail fraud is made on a case-by-case basis, and we are advised that no effort has been made to distinguish any trends in the approximately 12,000 letters of complaint now received each year. The planning failure is evident.

Another FTC program to combat localized consumer abuse has been its "federal-state coordination" program. This program involves referral of complaints received at the FTC to local enforcement officials when they involve essentially intrastate problems, solicitation of complaints from state and local officials where interstate problems are involved, responding to requests from state legislators and other state officials for advice or assistance in drafting legislation, preparing drafts of model legislation for consideration by states, and appearing and participating in conferences and meetings of local enforcement officials. We commend all of these efforts, but we also note that from the time the program was started in October, 1965, until a few months ago, the entire operation consisted of one lawyer and one secretary.[28] As a result of this undercommitment of resources, described as "miniscule" by the FTC's present General Counsel, this one-man operation has been unable to keep up with current responsibilities, much less expand the office's operations into new and promising areas.

Finally the FTC, in order to be more fully informed on consumer fraud problems in the nation and to receive advice as to the role it could best play in dealing with these problems, held extensive hearings in November and December of 1968. No action has yet been taken on the basis of these hearings.

(2) Evaluation of Reasons for the FTC's Cautious Approach. It is the view of the majority of the present Commissioners of the FTC that the agency should not become deeply involved in ghetto fraud and other retail consumer abuses. Three reasons have been offered in support of this judgment: (a) retail fraud principally involves criminal conduct, and the FTC, with the power to do nothing more than enter a cease-and-desist order, cannot play an effective role in this area; even where noncriminal conduct is involved, the sellers tend to be fly-by-night operators who are not likely to be deterred by injunctive remedies; (b) local consumer problems are best dealt with by state and local officials, and cannot be dealt with effectively by a federal administrative agency in Washington; and (c) the language of Section 5 making it applicable to unfair or deceptive acts or practices "in commerce" rather than "affecting commerce" creates a jurisdictional bar to the FTC dealing with most localized consumer fraud practices.

It is interesting that no single reason attracts the support of a majority of the present Commissioners. In any event, we suggest that these problems and difficulties have been exaggerated and that none of these reasons justifies the FTC's position that it should exclude itself from playing an effective role in this important area.

(a) Inadequacy of FTC Remedies. While many of the most flagrant consumer fraud

schemes deserve to be prosecuted criminally, it by no means follows that there is no role to be played by an enforcement agency with solely civil sanctions. The President's Commission on Law Enforcement and Administration of Justice noted that the line between criminal and civil fraud often is unclear, and concluded that "the amount of civil fraud probably far exceeds that of criminal fraud."[29] Our interviews with FTC staff personnel who had experience in the consumer fraud area, and written submissions to our Commission by others active in the field, support this conclusion. For example, the head of the criminal fraud unit in the U. S. Attorney's office in New York advised us that he frequently had been placed in the awkward position either of seeking an indictment and criminal enforcement, or abandoning efforts to cope with consumer fraud violations because his office has no civil remedy. His view was that exclusively criminal sanctions were not adequate, and that there were important areas in which an aggressive FTC program could be effective. It was suggested that, at a minimum, FTC orders could be entered against interstate sources of credit or supplies who often appear to be tied closely to local sales outlets.[30]

(b) Preferred Enforcement by Local Agencies. In an ideal world, a solution to consumer fraud problems might well be that U. S. Attorneys' offices, using available criminal sanctions, would proceed against the more flagrant consumer fraud schemes, and state and local government units would cope effectively with civil fraud problems. We grant the force of the argument that many consumer fraud schemes are local in origin and effect and preferably should be dealt with by local enforcement units rather than a Washington-based federal bureaucracy. Our proposals for new FTC initiatives, described below, take these considerations into account.

The fact is that resources now devoted to protection of consumers against widespread fraud and deception are inadequate; some municipalities and states have no consumer protection program, and others have consumer fraud programs in name only. As a result, the present coordination and referral system often consists of the FTC referring local complaints to state enforcement offices which have inadequate legislative power and resources to do anything effective about the complaint; meanwhile, state and local officials are urged to forward complaints concerning "interstate" problems to the FTC, where problems of delay, unwillingness to resort to formal proceedings, and the relatively small allocation of resources to consumer protection activities mean that little or nothing is done.

The FTC has some advantages in dealing with consumer fraud that are not duplicated in any other sector of federal or local government. Many defrauding sellers operate across state lines and cannot be dealt with effectively by local law enforcement agencies. Also, the FTC has an extraordinarily flexible statutory grant in Section 5 to deal with unfair or deceptive acts or practices, broad investigatory powers under Section 6, a large staff of lawyers and other professionals trained to deal with economic problems, and rule-making and other administrative enforcement devices which would allow the FTC to deal with a wide range of consumer problems in a single proceeding. If existing powers of the FTC are deficient in some respect—for example, because of the lack of power to enter a preliminary injunction against fraudulent schemes or to assess sufficient damages to deter wrongdoers—the FTC can seek additional authority from Congress.

At a bare minimum, it seems to us that the FTC has a responsibility under its legislative mandate to engage in a sufficiently active program of detection, enforcement and study of consumer fraud problems to report to Congress on the exact nature and dimensions of the problem, the economic conditions that permit these fraudulent schemes to flourish (including, if it is so determined, inadequate competition), and the needs, in terms of appropriations and new legislation, to cope effectively with this important problem area.

(c) Alleged Jurisdictional Limitations. The reason most frequently cited by Commissioners and FTC staff members for avoiding an active program of detection and enforcement against ghetto and other localized frauds is that the jurisdiction of the FTC under Section 5 of the FTCA is inadequate to permit effective enforcement. Section 5 provides for the issuance of a cease-and-desist order when firms have engaged in an "unfair method of competition . . . [or] unfair or deceptive acts or practices in commerce", and it has been argued that the "in commerce" language furnishes enforcement jurisdiction substantially narrower than the "affecting commerce" language of the Sherman Act and other regulatory statutes.[31]

The FTC's cautious approach in this area depends almost entirely on deference to a single 1941 Supreme Court decision, *FTC* v *Bunte Brothers*[32] in which a 6-3 majority of the Court held that the FTC did not have jurisdiction to enforce Section 5 against a localized fraud. Bunte Brothers, a candy manufacturer, allegedly had been using an unfair sales promotion to sell candy to children in Illinois. There were no interstate aspects to Bunte Brothers' sales activities, but the FTC argued that its fraudulent sales practices were "in commerce" because they adversely affected the competitive success of interstate rivals selling into the Illinois market. The Supreme Court majority rejected that contention.

We believe that the Commission has exaggerated the jurisdictional problems that might arise if it pursued a more active program against localized marketing frauds. In most consumer frauds of sufficient importance to justify commitment of the FTC's enforcement resources—i.e., the kinds of cases we propose the FTC deal with—we believe evidence could be introduced to circumvent any problems generated by the *Bunte Brothers* decision. For example, one line of evidence sufficient to distinguish *Bunte Brothers* would be that the fraudulent seller could foresee that some customers coming into its establishment would cross state lines.[33] In that connection, it is noteworthy that *de minimis* principles have been almost completely disregarded in interpretations of comparable jurisdictional limitations.[34] If the sales unit engaging in the alleged fraud or deception is a subsidiary or division of a multi-state seller, that also is likely to be sufficient to establish jurisdiction under Section 5.[35] In addition, if the fraud relies in any way on systematic use of interstate mails (for example, requesting information in connection with Credit reporting)[36] or if the seller advertises on TV, radio or any interstate media,[37] that is a sufficient basis to challenge fraudulent and deceptive statements included in the advertising, and also may provide a basis for challenging any and all fraudulent and deceptive conduct by the seller whether or not it is directly related to the advertising.[38]

If the *Bunte Brothers* decision cannot be avoided, we suggest a direct effort to test its continuing validity in the courts. We note that some of the theories used by the lower courts to distinguish *Bunte Brothers* since 1941—for example, finding interstate commerce where a subsidiary of a multi-state seller engages in purely localized frauds—are scarcely compatible with the theory underlying the decision that the "in commerce" provision be interpreted solely by looking at the geographic area directly affected by the fraudulent scheme.[39] Moreover, an expansionist reading of Section 5, whereby the "in commerce" provision is interpreted to have a jurisdictional reach approaching or coextensive with "affecting commerce" statutes, would be consistent with post-1941 Supreme Court interpretations of similar statutory provisions in several other regulatory areas.[40]

REFERENCES

1. This has been the conclusion reached by Congressional committees that have conducted investigations in this area in recent years. *See Hearings on S. J. Res.* 130-S. 3066 *Before the Senate Commerce Comm.,* 90th Cong. 2d Sess. (1968) [hereinafter cited as *Home Improvement Fraud Hearings]; Hearings on S. 1599 Before a Subcomm. of the Senate Comm. on Commerce,* 90th Cong., 2d Sess. (1968). *See also,* among research studies, D. Caplovitz, *The Poor Pay More.* (1967); W. Magnuson & J. Carper, *The Dark Side of the Marketplace* (1968); *President's Comm'n on Law Enforcement and Administration of Justice, The Challenge of Crime in a Free Society* 127 (1968) [hereinafter cited as *President's Comm'n on Law Enforcement]; Kripke, Consumer Credit Regulation: A Creditor-Oriented Viewpoint,* 68 Column, L. Rev. 445, 450 (1968). The FTC itself drew this conclusion in FTC, *Report on District of Columbia Consumer Protection Program* 16 (1968). This was also the unanimous testimony of the more than 90 witnesses who appeared before the FTC in its public hearings into the problem of consumer fraud, held in November and December, 1968. (A transcript of these hearings, not yet published, was made available to the staff of our Commission).

   The Kerner Commission found that 43% of ghetto families in New York "had experienced serious exploitation." *Report of the National Advisory Commission on Civil Disorders* 276 (1968), and that two of the major grievances producing conditions conducive to riots were "unfair commercial practices affecting Negro consumers" and the belief that "Negroes are sold inferior quality goods . . .at higher prices and are subjected to excessive interest rates and fraudulent commercial practices." *Id.* at 144-45.

2. These categories do not cover all FTC consumer protection work, but account for over 90% of the total. Some of the matters that do not easily fit into these categories include investigations of games-of-chance, fraudulent warranties and misuse of audience rating claims by broadcasters, and the recently proposed trade regulation rule concerning the mailing of unsolicited credit cards.

   In general, our comments concerning the strengths and weaknesses of FTC performance with respect to false advertising, deceptive labeling and localized marketing abuses apply equally to this miscellaneous category of projects.

3. In areas other than labeling of hazardous substances and food, drugs, and cosmetics, the FTC is the principal federal agency charged with dealing with deceptive labeling problems. *See* 15 U. S. C. §§1261 et seq. (1964) *as amended* 1261-73 (Supp. III, 1965-1967), 21 U. S. C. §§301-92 (1964), conferring jurisdiction on the Department of Health, Education and Welfare.

   The present discussion excludes FTC labeling activities in the fur, wool, and textile areas; for a discussion of enforcement in those areas, see pp. 45 to 49, *infra.* Further, it should be borne in mind that the distinction drawn between labeling and advertising often is tenuous. While it may be said that labels convey information, whereas advertising primarily is an attempt at persuasion, many advertisements have an informational purpose, and most labels, by the manner in which the contents are described, attempt to persuade the consumer to purchase the product. *See generally*, 80 *Harv. L. Rev.* 1005, 1117 (1967)

4. *See, e.g.*, Guides for the Dog and Cat Food Industry, 16 CFR §241 (1969); Guides for the Decorative Wall Paneling Industry (proposed), 16 CFR §243 (1969); Guides for the Watch Industry, 16 CFR §245 (1968); Tire Advertising and Labeling Guides, 16 CFR §228 (1967); Guides for Shoe Content Labeling and Advertising, 16 CFR §231 (1963); Trade Regulation Rule on Deceptive Advertising and Labeling as to Length of Extension Ladders, 16 CFR §418 (1969) Trade Regulation Rule on Unfair or Deceptive Labeling of Cigarettes in Relation to the Health Hazards of Smoking (proposed), 16 CFR §408 (1969); Trade Regulation Rule on Advertising and Labeling of Sleeping Bag Sizes, 16 CFR §400 (1963).

5. Trade Regulation Rule on Unfair or Deceptive Labeling of Cigarettes in Relation to the Health Hazards of Smoking, (proposed) 16 CFR §408 (1969).

6. Tire Advertising and Labeling Guides, 16 CFR §228 (1966); Trade Regulation Rule on Deceptive Use of "Leakproof," "Guaranteed Leakproof," etc. as Descriptive of Dry Cell Batteries 16 CFR §403 (1964).

7. Trade Regulation Rule on Misuse of "Automatic" or Terms of Similar Import as Descriptive of Household Electric Sewing Machines, 16 CFR §401 (1965). In a similar vein, the FTC has looked into the question of deceptive labeling of extension ladders since "the maximum working or useful length of an extension ladder is invariably less than the total length of the component sections." Trade Regulation Rule on Deceptive Advertising and Labeling as to Length of Extension Ladders, 16 CFR §418 (1969). Other guides and rules deal with such topics as the size of sleeping bags and tablecloths, nonprismatic binoculars, mislabeling of the leather content of waist belts, mislabeling of adhesive compositions, and deceptive labeling of watchcases and watch bands. *See* Guides for the Watch Industry, 16 CFR §245 (1968); Guides Against Deceptive Labeling and Advertising of Adhesive Compositions, 16 CFR §235 (1967); Trade Regulation Rule on Deception as to Nonprismatic and Partially Prismatic Instruments Being Prismatic Binoculars, 16 CFR §402 (1964); Trade Regulation Rule on Deceptive Advertising and Labeling as to Size of Tablecloths and Related Products, 16 CFR §404 (1964); Trade Regulation Rule on Misbranding and Deception as to Leather Content of Waist Belts, 16 CFR §405 (1964); Trade Regulation Rule on Advertising and Labeling as to Size of Sleeping Bags, 16 CFR §400 (1963).

8. *See, e.g.*, Guides for the Decorative Wall Paneling Industry (proposed) 16 CFR §243 (1969); Trade Regulation Rule on Deception as to Nonprismatic and Partially Prismatic Instruments Being Prismatic Binoculars, 16 CFR §402 (1964); Trade Regulation Rule on Misbranding and Deception as to Leather Content of Waist Belts, 16 CFR §405 (1964).

9. See Guides Against Deceptive Advertising of Guarantees, 16 CFR §239 (1960).

10. Tire Advertising and Labeling Guides, 16 CFR §228 (1967).

11. Proposed Guides for Advertising Over-the-Counter Drugs. 16 CFR §249 (1969); Trade Regulation Rule on the Advertising of Nonprescription Systemic Analgesic Drugs (proposed), 16 CFR §415 (1967).

12. *See* Trade Regulation Rule on Cigarettes in Relation to the Health Hazards of Smoking (proposed), 16 CFR §408 (1969). Of course no views as to the merits of issues underlying this controversy are intended.

13. There is a procedure whereby attorneys in the FTC, investigating advertising with respect to a particular product, can ask two or three part-time undergraduate law students hired for the purpose to clip advertisements for that product from written materials submitted to the FTC by TV and radio stations, magazines and newspapers. This obviously does not qualify as a monitoring program.

14. *See* p. 15, *supra.*

15. J. B. Williams Co. v. FTC., 381 F. 2d 884 (6th Cir. 1967).

16. *Report of the National Advisory Commission on Civil Disorders* 274 (1968).

17. 15 U. S. C. §68 (1964).
18. 15 U. S. C. §70 (1964).
19. 15 U. S. C. §69 (1964).
20. 15 U. S. C. §1191-1204 (1964), *as amended* (Supp. III 1965-1967).
21. *See Hearings on H. R. 944 Before a Subcomm. of the Comm. on Interstate and Foreign Commerce,* 76th Cong., 1st Sess. 17 (1939) (Wool Act); *Hearings on H. R. 469, 5606 and 6524 Before a Subcomm. of the Comm. on Interstate and Foreign Commerce,* 85th Cong., 1st Sess. 22, 38, 42 (1957) (Textile Act); *Hearings on H. R. 2321 Before the Comm. on Foreign and Interstate Commerce,* 82d Cong., 1st Sess. 8 (1951) (Fur Act).
22. 354 F. 2d 85 (2d Cir. 1965).
23. Geotrade Industrial Group., 62 FTC 102 (1963).
24. Brash & Sons, Inc., 58 FTC 1033 (1961).
25. The Fair v. FTC, 272 F. 2d 609, 611 (7th Cir. 1959); *see also* Mannis v. FTC, 293 F. 2d 774 (9th Cir. 1961), affirming a Commission order although one of the violations was "far fetched" (the word "muskrat" was spelled "mustrak") and other asserted violations were "hypertechnical."
26. *See, e.g.,* In re Leon Tashof, CCH Trade Reg. Rep. ¶ 18,606 (FTC 1968); Empico Corp. [1965-1967 Transfer Binder] CCH Trade Reg. Rep. ¶ 17,859 (FTC 1967).
27. *See, e.g.,* Guides Against Deceptive Pricing, 16 CFR §233 (1967); Guides Against Bait Advertising, 16 CFR §238 (1967); Guides Against Deceptive Advertising of Guarantees, 16 CFR §238 (1967).
28. The staff for the office of Federal-State Cooperation was doubled a few months ago; it now consists of 2 lawyers and 2 secretaries.
29. *President's Comm'n on Law Enforcement* 127.
30. For a similar view, *see Home Improvement Fraud Hearings.*
31. *See Id.* at 89-90 (testimony of Paul Rand Dixon)); Address by James Nicholson before the ABA Admin. Law Section, Phila., Aug. 5, 1968.
32. 312 U. S. 349 (1941).
33. Standard Oil Co. v. FTC, 340 U. S. 231 (1951); Bankers Securities Corp. v. FTC, 297 F. 2d 403 (3rd Cir. 1961).
34. Safeway Stores, Inc. v. FTC, 366 F. 2d 795 (9th Cir. 1966), *cert. denied,* 386 U. S. 932 (1967); Guziak v. FTC, 361 F. 2d 700, 703 (8th Cir. 1966), *cert. denied,* 385 U. S. 1007 (1967).
35. Holland Furnace Co. v. FTC, 269 F. 2d 203 (7th Cir. 1959), *cert. denied,* 361 U. S. 932 (1965).
36. National Clearance Bureau v. FTC, 255 F. 2d 102 (3rd Cir. 1958); Rothschild v. FTC, 200 F. 2d 39 (7th Cir. 1952), *cert. denied,* 345 U. S. 941 (1953).
37. *See* Guziak v. FTC, 361 F. 2d 700 (8th Cir. 1966), *cert. denied,* 395 U. S. 1007 (1967); Bankers Securities Corp. v. FTC, 297 F. 2d 403 (3rd Cir. 1961); Morton's Inc. v. FTC, 286 F. 2d 158 (1st Cir. 1961). *See also,* First Buckingham Community, Inc., *3 CCH Trade Reg. Rep.* ¶ 18,357 (FTC 1968) (FTC charged real estate brokers and apartment owners with false advertising because of failure to disclose that they would not sell or rent to Negroes; interstate commerce requirement based on advertising in interstate media).
38. *Cf.* Shreveport Macaroni Mfg. Co. v. FTC, 321 F. 2d 404 (5th Cir. 1963); *cert. denied,* 375 U. S. 971 (1964) (jurisdiction over discriminatory advertising allowances, based, *inter alia,* on advertisements in interstate media).
39. Note, *Jurisdictional Fetter on the FTC,* 76 Yale L. J. 1688, 1693 (1967).
40. *See, e.g.,* Fair Labor Standards Act: Wolling v. Jacksonville Paper Co.. 317 U. S. 564 (1943); Natural Gas Act: California v. Lo-Vaca Gathering Co., 379 U. S. 366 (1965); Federal Power Act: FPC v. Southern California Edison Co., 376 U. S. 205 (1964); Fur Labeling Act: FTC v. Mandel Bros., 359 U. S. 385 (1959); Morton's Inc. v. FTC, 286 F. 2d 158 (1st Cir. 1961).

21

The Inadequacies of Consumer Protection

James R. Withrow, Jr.

Antitrust policy and the consumer's interest are often contradictory and the author feels the sympathies of enforcement agencies are with preserving competition, often to the
detriment of the consumer. He proposes a set of programs
to change this condition.

Were I to take a biblical text for my comments it would be the oft-quoted parable
from *Luke,* Chapter 5, verses 37 and 38.

And no man putteth new wine into old bottles; else the new wine will burst the
bottles, and be spilled, and the bottles shall perish.

But new wine must be put into new bottles, and both are preserved.

The new wine of protecting consumers should not be allowed to jeopardize the
basic antitrust approach of protecting competition and removing restraints and unfairness from the competitive race.

During the past 80 years, from birth if we look to our common law heritage, the
United States has invested more time, energy and just plain faith in the concept of
Competition than any other nation in the history of the world. It has been the taproot
of our democracy, serving as the parent of our economic system, umpire of disputes in
the market place and protector of the consumer. Competition has been the great

Reprinted from *1967 New York State Bar Association Antitrust Law Symposium* (New York:
Commerce Clearing House. 1967), pp. 58-73. Reprinted by permission.

equalizer in our society and, in Thorelli's words, the "mainspring of what we have labeled economic egalitarianism."[1]

Congress, in 1890, first codified this country's dedication to the principle of competition by passing the Sherman Act.[2] Since then, a host of additional acts have appeared on the Statute books, all tracing their genesis to the Sherman Act and each in its own way demonstrating a nexus to the overriding concern for competition. Best known of the Sherman Act's progeny are:

The Clayton Act[3] —an effort to stop monopoly "in its incipiency" (a) by forbidding certain practices so far as they were likely to impair competition—price discrimination, exclusive dealing and buying—and (b) by forbidding certain methods of increasing business concentration—interlocking directorates and acquisitions.

The Federal Trade Commission Act[4] —an effort both to preserve competition and to regulate its quality with unfair methods of competition forbidden, partly as practices by which competitors were deprived access to markets or of freedom of action therein and partly as practices otherwise undesirable—exclusionary, coercive and collusive activities and also misrepresentation, bribery, and inequitable conduct that was damaging to competitors or unfair to consumers.

The Robinson-Patman Act[5] —amending the price discrimination provisions of the Clayton Act in an effort to prevent discriminatory practices not only when market competition was likely to be impaired thereby but also when inequitable treatment was likely to impair the opportunities of certain enterprises.

In addition to these, numerous other statutes have been enacted which, though usually relating to specific industries or products, similarly expound the controlling concept of competition. To mention only some of these, we might cite: The Packers and Stockyards Act of 1921[6]; The Federal Power Act of 1920[7]; The Atomic Energy Act of 1954.[8]

The aggregate of this congressional concern about competition in the market place has developed a name of its own—antitrust policy.

Unquestionably antitrust policy has been America's faithful navigator for at least 50 years and has piloted this country to full economic maturity. Figuratively, antitrust policy has been at the helm of the ship of state as we traversed the five stages noted by Rostow in his impressionistic view of national growth:

Stage 1 —*Traditional* A society developing within limited production functions and generally based upon pre-Newtonian Science, technology and attitude toward the physical world;

Stage 2 —*Ready for Takeoff*
Where emerging insights into science begin to be translated into new production functions in both agriculture and industry;

Stage 3 —*Takeoff*
When old impediments to steady growth are finally overcome;

Stage 4 —*Maturity*
Signified by a long interval of sustained, if fluctuating, progress with a regularly growing economy driving to extend modern technology over its entire front. [9]

Rostow further tells us that on his chart of economic growth America is in, but about to depart what he refers to as Stage 5 or "The Age of High Mass-Consumption"—where the leading sectors of the economy shift towards durable consumers' goods and services. As he says:

> As societies achieved maturity in the twentieth century two things happened: real income per head rose to a point where a large number of persons gained a command over consumption which transcended basic food, shelter, and clothing; and the structure of the working force changed in ways which increased not only the proportion of urban to total population, but also the proportion of the population working in offices or in skilled factory jobs—aware of and anxious to acquire the consumption fruits of a mature economy.

> In addition to these economic changes, the society ceased to accept further extension of modern technology as an overriding objective. It is in this post-maturity stage, for example, that, through the political process, Western societies have chosen to allocate increased resources to social welfare and security. The emergence of the welfare state is one manifestation of a society's moving beyond technical maturity; but it is also at this stage that resources tend increasingly to be directed to the production of consumers' durables and to the diffusion of services on a mass basis, if consumers' sovereignty reigns. The sewing-machine, the bicycle, and then the various electric-powered household gadgets were gradually diffused. Historically, however, the decisive element has been the cheap mass automobile with its quite revolutionary effects—social as well as economic—on the life and expectations of society.

> For the United States, the turning point was, perhaps, Henry Ford's moving assembly line of 1913-14; but it was in the 1920's and again in the post-war decade, 1946-56, that this stage of growth was pressed to, virtually, its logical conclusion.[10]

In this age of high mass consumption we have begun to hear significant rumbling that competition—or antitrust policy—falls far short of serving the consumers' interest. Responsible critics are pointing out failings in competition's role as protector of the consumer. Under attack is basic, although somewhat ritualistic, antitrust doctrine that competition is "the dispenser of justice to consumer and producer alike,"[11] that the consumer has an ultimate interest in antitrust enforcement because if government suits, or private ones between competing businessmen, enable competition to be furthered then, according to the theory of free competition, prices will be reduced, quality enhanced and choices increased.[12]

Of a part with this upheaval in what we can call the "benefit" factor in antitrust policy, is the change being witnessed in some seemingly sacrosanct theories of government *per se*. For example, and as alluded to in Rostow's description of America's current economic plateau, it has usually been reliable political doctrine that Americans favor as little government as possible.[13] Not so any longer. In recent years, Americans, regardless of party stripe or political philosophy, have increasingly embraced government involvement in a multitude of economic and social problems, including full employment, growth, monetary stability and business subsidies, to name but a few.[14]

Also, it has been said, and I believe wisely so, that the relationship between competition and personal freedom has changed with the times.

At one time personal freedom meant absence of government interference. Currently, it has a much broader connotation. It has taken on elements of economic and political freedom. It relates to immunity from private as well as governmental interference. It is recognized that the various freedoms do require some governmental restrictions which lay down the general rules of the game. Therefore there is little support today for the contention that the government should not interfere with the liberty of the individual businessmen to enter contracts which will restrict competition. Instead there is a feeling that such restrictions may affect the freedom of others who want to enter a market and of consumers who would like to make their own choices.[15]

We are told no man can keep up with the times for more than seventy years since after that, his frantic efforts to do so look silly forever.[16] This is surely the age of the consumer sovereignty and it does appear that our old friend of four score years —antitrust policy—is beginning to look a little tremulous in the face of the new king's problems.

Probably for the first time in history it is true, in the words of Adam Smith, that—

Consumption is the sole end and purpose of all production; and the interests of the producer ought to be attended to only so far as it may be necessary for promoting that of the consumer.[17]

These few comments are not meant to imply some recent "discovery" of the consumer[18] by the government since it is certainly true that he has long been the subject of political concern. We are pointing out, however, that his problems as a purchaser are probably greater in number, more complex and far more serious now than ever before. As one scholar rather bleakly summarizes the consumers' plight:

The failure of public policy to respond adequately to consumer needs must certainly be one of the most perplexing chapters in an examination of our federal government's response to the challenges of an increasingly complex economy. What is particularly intriguing is that the consumers difficulties in the market place have long been recognized, both by the public in general and by political spokesmen. Indeed it seems that more ink has been spilled, more speeches delivered, and more presidential and congressional documents issued on the subject of consumer problems—all with less effect—than in any other area of public concern, except for issues of war and peace.[19]

The difficulties being faced by the consumer today are best understood in terms of the new "impersonality" of the market place. The massive changes in retailing—supermarkets, discount houses—have meant that retailing has become intensely impersonal and modern consumer markets are far removed from those that classical economics presupposed. Sellers are few and confine their rivalry to non-price factors. Products, though fungible, are differentiated thru advertising—packaging and other tricks of contemporary merchandising. Price data are often vague or misleading.[20]

Antitrust policy as we know it and have watched it develop has created this impersonality—maybe not entirely but certainly the goal of competition has had a major share in its evolution. And here we see the basic conflict between antitrust policy and consumer protection, spelling the demise of the old "benefit" factor in antitrust enforcement.

The traditional premise supporting competition as the prime principle of economic democracy has been that the consumer should be the first arbiter in the market. It has been assumed that he makes his selection on the basis of price and quality and that the rewards go to the more able producers and distributors.

As Judge Learned Hand said so long ago:

It (Antitrust Policy) recognizes that with the consumer in the end must lie the decision between producers, and that those who fail to secure the market by the quality and cost of their services must pass out of the field.[21]

A host of critics are now attacking this assumption, and rightly so, since price and quality are being constantly undermined in the impersonal market of today. These critics are contending that effective quality and price comparisons are becoming more and more difficult while, concomitantly, a producer's gains are becoming more conditioned on his ability to mislead and less on his productive performance.[22]

We can perhaps better visualize the potential magnitude of this problem when we realize that disposable personal income in the United States has skyrocketed year after year, until in 1965 it reached $431.8 billion.[23] Equally impressive is the great leap in outstanding consumer credit the lifeblood of the retail market: from $8,338 million in 1940 to $76,085 million in 1965.[24]

Lest I mislead anyone into thinking that I am on the verge of heresy—I hasten to state that I do not advocate scrapping the antitrust laws. Nor do I believe that the solution to this very real problem merits anything close to such drastic surgery. It is my thought that the problem can be solved by focusing not on the policy but rather upon that physical superstructure which government has created as its guardian—the antitrust enforcement agencies. And my premise is relatively simple—that these enforcement agencies, because of time's incrustation, when forced to choose between the consumer's interest and antitrust policy—producer competition—will opt for the policy decision. Not every time certainly, nor probably most times—but sometimes and that, in our supposedly ordered universe, entitles an observer to claim that consumer protection by administrative agencies is inadequate.

The Robinson-Patman Act,[25] which in quantitative terms probably accounts for 25% of formal or statutory antitrust policy, highlights the short shrift paid consumer's interest by administrative agencies when they opt for policy in the employment of their resources.

Time does not permit and personal inclination militates against any detailed analysis of Robinson-Patman's 30 years of enforcement history. Suffice it to say that even in the most generous view of this statute, it must be conceded that its enforcement results in a uniformity of treatment of customers by suppliers to the literal detriment of the consumers choice in the market place. For instance, the price discrimination prohibitions of Section 2(a) cast such a burden on suppliers should they be called on to "justify" different prices to different customers, one wonders how any price competition among sellers survives in the market place today. Another facet of the Act's non-consumer orientation is the artificiality it breeds into the competitive arena by obviously "propping up" the inefficient and yes, oftentimes small enterprise in requiring that it receive the same price and terms of sale consideration as its more efficient competitors.[26]

Probably John McGee at Duke said it all, in his recent article dealing with existing Robinson-Patman issues when he concluded:

Using standards of allocative efficiency, with consumer benefit the goal, I have argued that the Robinson-Patman Act has suffered both from inadequate economic theory and explicit anti-economic biases, has been enforced with no socially rational system of priority; and has produced a core of scientific information that is relatively meagre and sometimes wrong and implicit definitions of competition and efficiency that are confusing to the body politic. Competition is not handicap trapshooting, and I do not think it pays to force the better performers to stand farther from the targets.[27]

There are other situations, besides those found in the enforcement of the price discrimination law, where antitrust agencies abandon consumer interest to the altar of antitrust policy. Take for instance the so-called "single shot" approach to enforcement, where we find the agency prosecuting only one company for an act or practice which permeates an entire industry. Admittedly, during Mr. Dixon's tenure as Chairman, this has occurred less frequently than was observed in past operations of the Federal Trade Commission.[28] Nevertheless, significant situations of "whipping boy" litigation by the FTC continue to exist. The Seventh Circuit found and overturned one just recently. In that case the Commission sued Universal Rundle Corp., manufacturing a line of vitreous china and having only six (6%) per cent of this market, for violations of the Robinson-Patman Act based upon its quantity of truckload discounts averaging ten (10%) per cent, thus discriminating against less than truckload purchasers. During the FTC hearing it was evidenced that the practice of quantity truckload discounts was industry-wide, with Universal's competitors usually granting discounts between 13 and 18%. The Court of Appeals set aside the Commission's order and remanded the case with the following caustic commentary on the FTC's judgment in bringing the case:

This inequitable approach to the solution of an antitrust problem, submitted to us because of the action of the Federal Trade Commission in centering this proceeding solely on petitioner, was unjustified. Its contrary determination was a patent abuse of discretion and must be overturned [citation omitted]. We cannot, in the name of antitrust prosecution, lend our support to the sacrifice of a comparatively small manufacturer, when its larger and more guilty competitors are not prosecuted. We are not convinced that the Clayton Act requires us to approve the imposition of sanctions upon only one of the smallest of a group of law violators. If we did, the giants in the field would be the real benefactors—not the public.[29]

However, the inadequacy of the antitrust agencies in their efforts to protect the consumer is most often apparent in their efforts to deal with problems involving advertising.

Advertising has become the hobgoblin of the market place. Few people can find a good word for it. Robert Hutchins, for instance, has said:

Advertising causes us to buy goods we don't want at prices we cannot pay and on terms we cannot meet.[30]

And in tones of abject resignation we must all have shared at one time or another, Marya Mannes laments,

As a housewife I buy what is sold to me. It is packaged. I buy it on faith. This is why these days, the word consumer is spelled 's u c k e r'[31]

Granted, the administrative agencies appear to be waging a highly commendable campaign, in light of the resources available to them, against advertisements detrimental to the consumers health and safety. Parenthetically though, we should note that there may be a consumer protection problem extant here, not relating to conflicts with antitrust policy but still worth mentioning, and that is the multitude of federal programs and the abundance of overlapping jurisdiction among the agencies in this field.

At last count, 33 of the 35 federal agencies were administering a total of 296 health and safety programs, most of which relate in some way to product advertisement [32] Aside from questions of possible dilution of the effectiveness of such programs, one wonders how the consumer with a complaint determines which program covers it and what agency has jurisdiction over that program.

Antitrust policy seems to impede or distract adequate consumer protection in relation to advertising in two principal ways. *First:* Agency rules of practice preclude any immediate consumer protection from questionable ads.

To paraphrase the old adage: Protection delayed is protection denied. As to the Federal Trade Commission for example, it has been said—

The regulatory scheme envisioned in the FTC Act for the slower-paced antitrust problems was not ideally suited for the faster moving advertising field, in which speed in enforcement might become of the essence.[33]

True the Wheeler-Lea Amendment of Section 5[34] did remove the necessity for alleging competition in Section 5 actions, thereby focusing attention on the detriment to the consumer occasioned by advertising misrepresentations.

As Senator Wheeler said—

. . . this legislation is designed to give the Federal Trade Commission jurisdiction over unfair acts and practices for consumer protection to the same extent that it now has jurisdiction over unfair methods of competition for the protection of competitors.[35]

But no matter how noble the goal—the approach was antitrust policy oriented. This shiny 1938 "consumer" law was dumped into a 1915 horse and buggy as far as procedure was concerned and there it rides today.

Recently, a congressional committee took an experimental jab at studying delay in administrative agency proceedings and the evaluation charts which it prepared dealing with 61 typical proceedings conducted by federal agencies show the Section 5 proceedings conducted by the Federal Trade Commission are second place in the amount of delay between filing and determination.[36]

This might well be an unfair indictment of FTC practice and is not offered to vilify Chairman Dixon's conscientious and hardworking staff. It is offered for the limited purpose of showing that present agency practice is probably ill-equipped when it comes to questionable advertisements which daily if not hourly, beat on the consumers eardrums. Simply stated—if it takes three years or 1,080 litigation days to put a stop to an ad that is eventually ruled false and/or misleading, then by no standard is the consumer's interest being served during that period.

Second: Administrative agencies emphasize the negative—not the positive—in advertising.

By and large, the agencies, like the courts, have been preoccupied with the question whether the laws were violated.[37] It often seems, the protestation of their spokesmen to the contrary notwithstanding, that the agencies with enforcement responsibilities play the "numbers game" and strive for many proceedings and a large number of victories.[38]

In sum, the agencies are caught up in the enforcement of "thou shalt nots" and we outsiders are left with a task not unlike stringing popcorn—the review of numerous cases to locate the "shall" areas.

That the agencies perform in the manner described is consistent with their antitrust heritage and, again, responsive to their god of antitrust policy. In this dynamic and affluent age when concepts of fraud and deceit are constantly changing, such agency performance is just unsatisfactory.[39]

Probably the major area of potential action by the agencies in this field is the failure of advertisers to fully inform the consumer about the product. As was recognized as far back as the days of Rome:

> A wrongdoer is often a man that has left something undone; not always he that has done something.[40] More recently, Earl Kintner has counseled us that

> The success of an economic democracy, no less than that of a political democracy, depends on informed, intelligent choice.[41]

The point for emphasis here is not that the agencies are not doing their jobs. They are—as they see them. Rather, we question whether the job that is being done on violators truly serves as an adequate measure of protection for the consumer. As we read newspapers and cock an eye to the commercials on TV and an ear to those on radio, in honesty we have to say no. The work of the agencies is constricted by a policy and an approach devised for a different economic plane—competition. It ill serves the day-to-day decision of the housewife and homeowner in this year of 1967. As long as the consumer's problem remains with these agencies for a solution—there will be no solution save the warmed over theorems, statistics and approach of the 1930's. And no amount of increased concern and dedication among the personnel of these agencies can change this unfortunate fact.

As aptly described by Professor Harry G. Johnson in his book *The Canadian Quandary*—

> The really difficult problem is the omission or concealment of relevant information, such as that though it tastes good it will kill you several years before your time, or that it makes no noise because it is designed to use considerably more electricity and wears out faster than rival models. Problems of this sort have become especially acute in modern times, in consequence of advancing medical knowledge and the

increasing technical complexity of consumer goods, especially those containing machinery, which make it difficult for the consumer even to know what characteristics of a product are important to his welfare.[42]

We may have been losing battles in attempting to protect the consumer but we have not lost the war. Some hard thinking on the part of the Congress and the rest of government remains to be done. Some of the thoughts which have come to mind in preparing this paper will be mentioned briefly.

1. An Officer of Consumer Affairs as an Executive Department is certainly required. We have been moving in this direction for years.[43] In 1965 Senator Hart submitted a bill along these lines which unfortunately was not acted upon.[44] Quoting Victor Hugo, Senator Hart said at that time: "There is one thing stronger than all the armies in the world and that is an idea whose time has come."[45]

That sentiment is as true today and I believe we can look forward to renewed interest in such legislation.

2. Immediate and effective action against questionable ads, consistent with constitutional guarantees, is certainly required. Since the Federal Trade Commission has successfully invoked the All Writs Statute[46] in seeking preliminary injunctive relief in a merger case,[47] similar application might be considered in the advertising field. However, some form of indemnification not unlike that required by the Federal Rules[48] when private plaintiffs seek injunctions, should be required of the government in such cases. Consequently, amendment of either the All Writs Statute, but preferably Section 5 of the Federal Trade Commission Act[49] along these lines might be considered.

3. Finally, provision must be made for the promulgation of a definitive advertising code which sets out the dos and dont's which should control, to be followed by an effective and coordinated program of supervision particularly in those industries most strategically related to the consumers interests.

Our great problem is: How can *we protect consumers* from themselves or from being misled (not just in matters affecting health and safety) and *yet continue to obtain the benefits* of the producing power of our flourishing economy.

The FTC is bound by law and custom to adhere to the *American Philosophy of industrial freedom and the promotion* of competition. It must continue to do so as long as that is its mandate—as a result it *can never really be the spearhead for customer protection.*

Some new authority (I hesitate to say agency) which would collect all the pieces and control this entire area seems called for. It would not emasculate the Sherman Act, the Clayton Act, the Robinson-Patman Act or the Federal Trade Commission Act, and should be able to provide tests which the honest businessman could regard with confidence.

The antitrust laws are intended to equalize conditions of competition and to insure that industry shall play the competitive game according to the accepted rules of social justice.

Consumer protection programs are based on a different philosophy and, no doubt, will result in developing new rules and obligations. To do so will be a test of American skill in government.

REFERENCES

1. Hans Thorelli, *The Federal Antitrust Policy,* 571 (1955).
2. 26 Stat. 209 (1890), as amended, 15 U.S.C. §§1-7 (1964).
3. 38 Stat. 730 (1914), as amended, 15 U. S. C. §§22-27 (1964).
4. 38 Stat. 717 (1914), as amended, 15 U. S. C. §§41-46, 47-58 (1964).
5. 49 Stat. 1526 (1936), 15 U. S. C. §§13-13b, 21a (1964).
6. 42 Stat. 159 (1921), as amended, 7 U. S. C. §§181-231 (1964).
7. 41 Stat. 1063 (1920), as amended, 16 U. S. C. §§791-828 (1964).
8. 60 Stat. 755 (1946); as amended, 42 U. S. C. §§2011-2296 (1964).
9. W. W. Rostow, *The Stages of Economic Growth: A Non-Communist Manifesto* (1960).
10. *Id.* at pp. 10, 11.
11. Thorelli, *The Federal Antitrust Policy,* 571 (1955).
12. Forkosch, *Antitrust and the Consumer,* 2 (1965).
13. The less government we have the better—the fewer laws and the less confided power. Ralph Waldo Emerson, *Politics* in Essays.
14. Massel, *Competition and Monopoly: Legal and Economic Issues,* 317 (1962).
15. *Id.* at p. 17.
16. Eastman, *The Enjoyment of Laughter.*
17. *The Wealth of Nations,* 625 (Modern Library Ed., 1937).
18. It is probably well to identify this fellow as being a retail purchaser who retains for personal or family use the commodity obtained. See Forkosch. *Antitrust and the Consumer,* 18 (1956).
19. Barber. "Government and the Consumer," 64 *Mich. L. Rev.* 1203 (1966).
20. *Id.* at p. 1226.
21. *United States v. Corn Products Refining Co.,* 234 Fed. 964, 1012 (S. D. N. Y. 1916); app. dism. 249 U. S. C. 621 (1919).
22. Massel, *op. cit. supra,* note 14 at 22.
23. The Nation's Income, Expenditures and Savings, U. S. Bureau of Census Statistical Abstract of United States. p. 325 (86 Ed. 1965).
24. *Id.* at p. 469.
25. 49 Stat. 1526 (1936), 15 U. S. C. §13-13b, 21a (1964).
26. See, Levi. "The Robinson-Patman Act—Is It in the Public Interest?" 1 *A. B. A. Antitrust Section,* 60, 62 (1952).
27. McGee, "Some Economic Issues in Robinson-Patman Land," 30 *Law and Contemporary Problems* 531, 551 (1965).
28. Address by Paul Rand Dixon, 63rd Annual Convention. Advertising Association of the West (6/28/66).
29. *Universal-Rundle Corp. v. FTC,* 1965 *CCH Trade Cases* ¶ 71, 578, 352 F. 2d 831, 834 (1965) cert. granted 385 U. S. 809 (1966).
30. Statement by Robert Hutchins, quoted in *Masters, The Intelligent Buyers Guide to Sellers,* 87 (1965).
31. Hearings on Packaging and Labeling Practices before the Senate Subcommittee on Antitrust and Monopoly, 87th Cong., 1st Sess., Pt. 1 at 24 (1961).
32. House Committee on Government Operations. Consumer Protection Activities of Federal Departments and Agencies, H. Rept. No. 1241, 87th Cong.. 1st Sess., 2, 23 (1961).
33. Millstein, "The Federal Trade Commission and False Advertising," 64 *Col. L. Rev.* 439, 451 (1964).
34. 52 Stat. 111 (1938), 15 U. S. C. §45 (1964).
35. 83 *Cong. Rec.* 3256 (1938).

36. Evaluation Charts on Delay in Administrative Proceedings, Senate Judiciary Comm., Subcom. on Admin. Practice and Procedure, 89th. Cong., 2nd Sess. (1966).

37. Massel, *op. cit. supra* note 14 at p. 321.

38. McGee, *op. cit. supra* note 27 at p. 534.

39. Barber, "Consumer and the Government," 64 *Mich. L. Rev.* 1203, 1211 (1966).

40. Antoninus, IX *Meditations* 5.

41. Kintner, "Federal Trade Commission Regulation of Advertising," 64 *Mich. L. Rev.* 1269 (1966).

42. At pp. 283-284, quoted in Turner, "Advertising and Competition," 26 *Fed. Bar. J.* 93, 96-97 (1966).

43. See Petersen, "Representing the Consumer Interest in the Federal Government," 64 *Mich. L. Rev.* 1323 (1966) for a summary of the history of consumer representation in Washington since the 1930's

44. S. 1052, 111 *Cong. Rec.* 2254 (Daily ed., Feb. 9, 1965).

45. *Ibid.*

46. 23 U. S. C. §1651(a) (1964).

47. *FTC v. Dean Foods Co.,* 1966 *CCH Trade Cases* ¶ 71, 788, 384 U. S. 597 (1966).

48. Fed. R. Civ. P. 65

49. 52 Stat. 111 (1938), 15 U. S. C. §45 (1964).

22

The Fair Packaging and Labeling Act — Some Unanswered Questions

H. E. Dunkelberger, Jr.

The author sees slow progress by both industry and govern-ment in adopting packaging regulations under the Fair Packaging and Labeling Act. He identifies causes of the delay and hints at the dilemma presented by the coopera-tion required of industry in setting packaging standards possibly constituting an antitrust violation.

As all of you well know, the three major aspects of the Fair Packaging and Labeling Act (FPLA) are the industry-wide mandatory labeling regulations promulgated by the Food and Drug Administration (FDA) and the Federal Trade Commission (FTC), the commodity-line discretionary regulations to be issued by these same two agencies, and the encouragement of voluntary package size standards by the Department of Commerce.

THE MANDATORY REGULATIONS

Turning first to the mandatory regulations, the food regulations have of course been adopted in final form and most manufacturers are well on their way toward

Reprinted from *Food, Drug, and Cosmetic Law Journal*, vol. 24, no. 1 (January 1969), pp. 17-36. Reprinted by permission.

bringing all of their labels into compliance. The FDA regulations for drugs and cosmetics were published in final form in June of this year to become fully effective on July 1 of next year, but as of this date the FDA has not announced whether objections were filed that will necessitate the holding of a hearing on some aspects of these regulations.

It is by now almost ancient history that the FDA virtually stared down the industry when it refused to schedule a hearing on any of the numerous objections that food companies had filed to the final food regulations. Many food industry lawyers, and indeed a number of trade associations and companies, felt that the FDA was not acting in accordance with the procedural requirements of Section 701(e), (f), and (g) of the Federal Food, Drug and Cosmetic Act, which are incorporated by reference in the FPLA.[1] But that question has not become academic, for none was sufficiently outraged or concerned to take the FDA to court to test its right to refuse to hold a hearing on what many industry representatives considered to be valid objection to the regulations raising substantial issues of fact.

Presumably, the FDA is now facing a similar decision under the drug and cosmetic regulations, and almost certainly the agency will be criticized for whatever course it takes. If it grants a hearing of objections on some of the drug and cosmetic regulations, then undoubtedly many people in the food industry will feel they have been discriminated against and that there is no rational basis for denying procedural regularity for one segment of industry and observing it for another. If no hearing is granted, then many may conclude that this merely confirms their belief that the FDA has sought to rewrite the requirements of Section 701 without the inconvenience of Congressional action.

The FTC published its final regulations for other consumer commodities three months before the drug and cosmetic regulations were published in final form, and it too has yet to indicate publicly whether it will further modify its regulations, hold a public hearing on some of its provisions, or merely decide that the March 19 regulations will go into effect as published.

The question common to all consumer commodity manufacturers with respect to the mandatory regulations is whether state authorities will follow the letter and spirit of the federal FPLA regulations and give substance to the universally stated goal of uniformity in regulation among federal and state jurisdictions. At the June meeting of the National Conference on Weights and Measures, sponsored by the United States Department of Commerce, the Conference rejected industry's proposals (1) that the Model State Packaging and Labeling Regulation reflect without variation the FPLA Regulations and interpretations of the FDA and the FTC, and (2) that the exemptions under the Federal Act and Regulations be automatically incorporated by reference in the Model Law or Regulation.

Although most of the revisions that the Conference adopted for the Model Regulation faithfully follow the requirements under the Federal Act, there are a few notable departures. For example, Section 5.3.3 of the Model Regulation would require that multi-unit packages of the same commodity declare not only the number of individual units and the quantity of each individual unit, but also the total quantity of the contents of the multi-unit package. The FDA regulations are not explicit on this point, but they have generally been interpreted not to require declaration of the total quantity of all the packages in the multi-unit container. Indeed, the FTC regulations contain an example in Section 500.7 that makes it clear that total quantity is not required:

> The net quantity of contents shall be expressed in terms of weight, measure, numerical count, or a combination of numerical count and weight, size, or measure (for example numerical count and sheet dimensions of writing paper, *numerical count and net weight per bar of multiunit packages of bar soap, etc.*) . . . . (Emphasis added.)

A second difference between the federal requirements and the Model Regulation is that Section 5.8.1 of the latter purports to prohibit a supplemental or combination declaration in larger type than the required declaration. The federal regulations contain no such prohibition (see, for example, Section 1.8(o) of the FDA Food Regulations).

Of even greater significance is the refusal of the Conference to provide for automatic adoption of federal exemptions, which prescribe particularized labeling requirements for a large number of products. Instead, the Conference or its Executive Committee will review each federal exemption and decide whether it should be added to the Model Regulation. It is not at all clear how each state will so conveniently consider and adopt—or reject—each exemption promulgated by the FDA and the FTC.

This disparity between federal and state regulation is particularly disappointing—and puzzling—in view of the major role of the Department of Commerce in providing administration and leadership for the National Conference, and the directives of Congress to the Secretary of Commerce that he work to achieve uniformity in federal and state weights and measures regulations.[2] At the Conference Department officials maintained that states were permitted under the FPLA to adopt labeling regulations imposing more stringent requirements and supported this conclusion with an opinion from the Department's General Counsel's office. There can be no doubt that the expression of these views and the announcement of this opinion were major factors in persuading the states to reject industry's arguments in favor of complete federal-state uniformity.

Very frankly, I do not see how these events at the National Conference can be squared with Congress's directives to the Secretary of Commerce. The basic statutory authority for the Department of Commerce's sponsorship of the National Conference is found in Section 272 of Title 15 of the United States Code. That section authorizes the Secretary of Commerce to undertake a number of specific functions, one of which is: "(d) Cooperation with other governmental agencies and with private organizations in the establishment of standard practices, incorporated in codes and specifications."

In carrying out these functions the Secretary is authorized to undertake certain listed activities "and similar ones for which need may arise in the operations of government agencies, scientific institutions, and industrial enterprises . . ." One of the listed activities is: "(5) cooperation with the states in securing uniformity in weights and measures laws and methods of inspection . . ."

Congress has thus made it clear that the Secretary is to cooperate with the states in securing uniformity in weights and measures laws. One of the stated goals of the National Conference has been to work for the achievement of such uniformity, and the development of the Model Law and Regulation has been consistent with that goal.

In addition to this general directive to the Secretary of Commerce to work for uniformity in federal and state weights and measures regulation, the FPLA contains an even more explicit directive:

> Section 9(a). A copy of each regulation promulgated under this Act shall be transmitted promptly to the Secretary of Commerce, who shall (1) transmit copies thereof to all appropriate State officers and agencies, and (2) furnish to such State officers and agencies information and assistance to promote to the greatest practicable extent uniformity in State and Federal regulation of the labeling of consumer commodities.

The Congressional purpose could hardly have been more clear. What is not clear is why the General Counsel's office of the Department of Commerce should announce an interpretation of the preemption clause in the FPLA that could only have the effect of discouraging, rather than encouraging, uniformity in federal and state regulation.

The federal preemption clause of the FPLA varied in content during the five years of Congressional consideration of the bill. During the first few years the bill made clear Congress's intent *not* to supersede or preempt any state law unless absolutely necessary because of a direct and positive conflict. The provision read in relevant part:

> Nothing contained in this Act shall be construed to repeal, invalidate, supersede, or otherwise adversely affect . . .
>
> (d) any provision of State law which would be valid in the absence of this Act unless there is a direct and positive conflict between this Act in its application to interstate or foreign commerce and such provision of State law.

Clearly what the sponsors had in mind at this stage was to give the state a completely free hand in adopting their own labeling requirements, except in those instances when compliance with a state regulation would require violation of a federal regulation.

When the bill was under consideration by the Senate Commerce Committee in the spring of 1966, this approach was turned completely around, and a new preemption section was added, which read:

> Section 12. It is hereby expressly declared that it is the intent of the Congress to supersede any and all laws of the States and political subdivisions thereof insofar as they may now or hereafter provide for the labeling of the net quantity of contents of the package of any consumer commodity covered by this Act which differs from the requirements of section 4 of this Act or regulations promulgated pursuant thereto.

The Senate Report made no effort to explain the significance of this about-face except to state that the regulations under the Act "shall supersede state law only to the extent that the states impose net quantity of contents labeling requirements which differ from requirements imposed under the terms of the Act." The Report went on to make clear that it was not intended to affect the regulation of intrastate commerce, as distinguished from interstate commerce, saying that the "bill is not intended to limit the authority of the states to establish such packaging and labeling standards as they deem necessary in response to state and local needs."

Apparently the Senate Committee, and in turn the Senate, felt that its intent was clear. If a state regulation imposed a labeling requirement for a consumer commodity that was different from a requirement that was imposed under the federal requirement, then the federal provision would take precedence, and the state provision would be inapplicable to commodities covered by the Federal Act.

This interpretation of Section 12 is supported by the House Commerce Committee's explanation of virtually identical language in the Child Protection Act of 1966, adopting amendments to the Federal Hazardous Substances Labeling Act.[3] which explained the "differs from" language as:

a limited preemption amendment which would encourage and permit States to adopt requirements identical to the Federal requirements for substances subject to the Federal Act, and to enforce them to complement Federal enforcement, but at the same time would free marketers of products sold interstate from varying or added labeling requirements for such substances now existing or which States and cities might otherwise adopt in the future.

There was thus no doubt that the "differs from" language was intended to prevent the adoption of "varying or added" requirements by the states. This Congressional interpretation of language in one bill under consideration in 1966 can fairly be applied to the virtually identical language in another labeling bill under consideration at the same time.

When the FPLA was considered by the House of Representatives, the House Commerce Committee accepted the Senate language verbatim, except to change "which differs from" to "which are less stringent or require information different from." The "different from" language was retained, and the "less stringent" language was added. The logical interpretation of this change is that the Senate's understanding of the "different from" language would remain—that is, that a state could not oppose *varying* or *added* labeling requirements. But the House Committee wished to make it clear that if a State proposed to require *less* information than the federal regulations, the federal regulations would still take precedence. In other words, compliance with less stringent state regulations could not be claimed as a justification for ignoring more stringent federal regulations.

The House Commerce Committee Report stated that preemption was intended for state laws that "impose inconsistent or less stringent" net quantity labeling requirements. No explanation was given for the use of the word "inconsistent" in the Report, when the Act contained the words "different from." The Conference Report makes it clear that it was the House version that was accepted by the Conferees, but sheds no further light on the meaning of either the statutory or Report language.

On the basis of this somewhat ambiguous legislative history, a representative of the

General Counsel's office of the Department of Commerce stated publicly at the 1968 National Conference of Weights and Measures that the effect of Section 12 was to permit states to impose labeling requirements going beyond those imposed under the federal regulations. Apparently he relied on the "inconsistent" wording of the House and Conference Reports, and totally ignored the clear language of the Act itself and the Senate's understanding of that language.

If a federal regulation imposes labeling requirements A and B, and a state regulation requires A, B and C, then it seems clear that the state requires information that is "different from" the federal requirement. And the added state requirement C can be said to be inconsistent with the more limited federal requirements.

But the Commerce Department attorney apparently concluded that the House Committee Report use of "inconsistent" transformed the statutory language of "different from" into nothing more than an intent to preempt only state requirements that were in direct and positive conflict with federal requirements.[4] This approach had, of course, been totally repudiated by the sponsors of the bill when they discarded the original language of the preemption section. Such an interpretation makes the "different from" language totally unnecessary, for the supremacy clause of the Constitution has repeatedly been held to invalidate state law that directly conflicts with federal law.

My purpose in going into the detail of this preemption quagmire is two-fold:

1. If uniformity between federal and state requirements is to be achieved, then a proper understanding of Section 12 of the FPLA can contribute significantly to this goal; and

2. The Department of Commerce has failed to carry out its statutory directive of encouraging uniformity in weights and measures laws, and uniformity in state and federal regulation of the labeling of consumer commodities, by adopting a questionable interpretation of Section 12.

I personally feel that the language of Section 12 is clear on its face. States may not impose *additional* or *varying* or *less stringent* requirements than those imposed by the federal regulations. A federal exemption excusing a commodity from a particular labeling requirement cannot be nullified by a state regulation. That understanding is reflected in the explanation of the similar preemption provision in the Child Protection Act of 1966.

At the very least, this is a logical and reasonable interpretation of the Act and the legislative history. Why, then, did the Department of Commerce feel obliged to reject an interpretation that would most effectively carry out Congress's directive to achieve uniformity, and instead publicly to espouse an interpretation that could only encourage states to adopt requirements in addition to those imposed under the federal regulations?

It is my hope that the Department of Commerce will recognize its clear statutory responsibility to encourage uniformity, not diversity, in labeling requirements, and will emphasize the overwhelming need for one set of labeling requirements for products shipped in interstate commerce.

DISCRETIONARY REGULATIONS UNDER SECTION 5 (c)

In recent months there have been a number of indications that the FDA and FTC are considering the promulgation of regulations under Section 5(c) of the Act, although nothing has yet appeared in the *Federal Register*. These so-called discretionary regulations differ from the mandatory regulations in several respects.

The mandatory regulations are based on a Congressional finding of general need for prominent disclosure of certain information on all labels, and the only question at issue in their promulgation was the appropriateness of the detail of the regulations to carry out the Congressional directive. Under section 5(c), however, the agencies have the burden of establishing that additional regulations are necessary for particular commodities in order to prevent deception or to facilitate value comparisons.

The Section 4(a) regulations apply across-the-board to whole categories of consumer commodities: all foods, all cosmetics, all proprietary drugs, and all other covered commodities. But Section 5(c) is worded differently. It refers to deception or value comparisons "as to any commodity," and the promulgation of regulations "with respect to that commodity." Apparently Congress intended that these regulations would not apply across-the-board to all or many different commodities, but instead would be applicable on a product-by-product or commodity-line basis.

The legislative history supports this clear meaning of the statutory language. The Antitrust and Monopoly Subcommittee, for example, stated in its Report on one of the first revisions of the bill that these regulations would be adopted on a "product-by-product basis" and "only on a product-line basis."[5] Similarly, the Senate Commerce Committee Report on S. 985 stated that regulations under Section 5(c) would be adopted "on a commodity line basis " and that this section "authorizes the promulgating authority to issue commodity-by-commodity regulations."[6] And the House Commerce Committee Report stated that this section authorized the agencies "to promulgate regulations with regard to particular consumer commodities."[7]

There is nothing in the Act or Reports, however, that authoritatively spells out what would constitute a "product," a "product-line," or a "commodity-line." The most logical explanation is that a Section 5(c) regulation can be made applicable only to those commodities for which a finding is made—and can be justified on the facts—that deception has been fostered or value comparisons have been rendered difficult by existing industry practices that will be corrected by the regulation. A finding that manufacturers and distributors of commodities A and B have fostered deception of consumers by their misuse of "cents-off" labeling could thus be relied upon as a basis for promulgating a regulation regulating that practice for commodities A and B, but it could not be used to justify a regulation of broader applicability—to products C, D and E, or to all foods. This interpretation squares both with the "product-by-product" language, and with the explicit requirement of a finding of deception or difficulty of value comparisons.

A related question under Section 5(c) is what type of showing will have to be made by the FDA or the FTC to support a finding that a regulation is "necessary to prevent the deception of consumers or to facilitate value comparisons as to any consumer commodity." There was some discussion of the term "deception of consumers" during the course of the House hearings, but it was at best inconclusive, and the legislative history in total provides no clear picture of Congress' intent as to the content of this term.

It may be expected that the FTC will seek to rely on its experience and precedents under Section 5 of the Federal Trade Commission Act, which declares unlawful "unfair or deceptive acts or practices in commerce," and that the FDA will look to its practice under Section 403(a) of the Federal Food, Drug and Cosmetic Act, which defines misbranding to include "false or misleading" labeling. But there may be a significant difference between a determination of deception in an adjudicatory proceeding and a determination of whether a particular regulation is necessary to prevent deception under Section 5(c) of the new Act.

The question of what constitutes deception under section 5(c) may well become academic, however, if the agencies decide to rely on the determination that a regulation is necessary "to facilitate value comparisons as to any consumer commodity." The first version of Senator Hart's bill—S. 3745 in the Eighty-Seventh Congress—authorized additional regulations for particular commodities upon a determination that they were necessary "to establish or preserve fair competition between or among competing products by enabling consumers to make rational comparisons with respect to price and other qualities, or to prevent the deception of consumers as to such products." This language was retained in S. 387 in the Eighty-Eighth Congress, except that the Antitrust and Monopoly Subcommittee changed the word "qualities" to "factors." The Subcommittee Report does not explain this change, nor does it throw any light on meaning of the "comparison" and "deception" criteria.

S. 985 as introduced in the Eighty-Ninth Congress repeated the language as revised by the Antitrust and Monopoly Subcommitee. The Senate Commerce Committee further changed this language to provide for additional regulations when the agencies determine they are necessary "to prevent the deception of consumers or to facilitate price comparisons as to any consumer commodity." The Committee Report contains no explanation of this language or the reasons for the change from previous versions.

The House Commerce Committee substituted the word "value" for the word "price" and reported out the bill in that form, again with no explanation of the change, or of the language. The House passed the bill as reported, and the Conferees recommended the House version. The Statement of the Managers on the part of the House in the House Conference Report explained the change by saying that "'value comparison is broader than the concept of 'price comparison.'"[8] but did not otherwise throw light on the intended meaning.

Senator Hart sought to explain this change of wording on the floor of the Senate prior to the Senate adoption of the Conference Report:

What this means is that the U.S. Congress has now assumed responsibility for assisting consumers by facilitating "value comparisons." This declaration is significant because it enlarges Congressional policy to include quality comparison—a component of value. This quality element has vastly greater implications than the more limited concept of price. For instance, it opens the door to consideration of legislation such as grade labeling and Government testing of consumer products.[9]

Congressman Gilligan, a member of the House Commerce Committee, took exception to Senator Hart's interpretation of the Committee's change from "price" to "value." He stated that he was responsible for proposing the change, and that the Committee intended only to emphasize that price is just one aspect of value.[10]

In practice, the term "value comparison" may become equated with "price comparison," for it is difficult to see how most of the Section 5(c) regulations could bear upon other factors of "value," whatever that may be understood to mean. The trouble may come when an attempt is made to specify which commodities are subject to a particular 5(c) regulation—similar products differing significantly in quality or "value" should perhaps not be subject to the same regulation.

At any rate, the agencies will be obliged to justify a regulation under this provision on the basis of one of the two criteria. The burden of establishing the justification will be on the agency, for until it makes the necessary determination—on the basis of the evidence before it—no regulation may be promulgated.

Four different types of regulations may be adopted under Section 5(c), and the legislative history throws at least a little helpful light on each.

Package Size Descriptions

The first type of regulation authorized by section 5(c) is that described in section 5(c)(1), under which the regulation would:

establish and define standards for characterization of the size of a package enclosing any consumer commodity, which may be used to supplement the label statement of net quantity of contents of packages containing such commodity, but this paragraph shall not be construed as authorizing any limitation on the size, shape, weight, dimensions, or number of packages which may be used to enclose any commodity.

This provision was retained virtually without change throughout the entire history of the bill, from S. 3745 as introduced in the Eighty-Seventh Congress, through final enactment, except that the Senate Commerce Committee added to S. 985 the proviso to make it clear that regulations under this provision could not authorize any limitation on the packages themselves.

The Antitrust and Monopoly Subcommittee Report explained:

[Subsection] (e) (3) provides for the defining of size nomenclature relating to quantity such as "small," "medium" and "large." . . .
The purpose of this section is to make size nomenclature meaningful as between competing products in the same product line so that one manufacturer's "king size" does not represent less product than another manufacturer's "large." Should such standards be established on a product line basis, there is no commpulsion for the manufacturer to use them if he chooses to use no size designation whatsoever. If, however, he wishes to use size designations, they would have to be those established for the range of quantity into which the amount within his package falls.[11]

The House Commerce Committee in its Report stated that regulations under this provision may establish "specific weights and measures, or ranges of weights or measures, for such designations." A regulation under 5(c)(1) might thus specify that the term "small" may be used only on packages of a particular consumer commodity ranging from two to four ounces. Or it might specify that the term "small" may be used only for packages containing three ounces.

The statement in the Subcommittee Report quoted above suggests that once a regulation was adopted specifying size designations for a particular commodity, packages of that commodity could not use any size designations unless they were those specified in the regulation. Thus if the regulation specified "small," "medium" and "large" for certain sizes, but no others, apparently no other terms could be used to describe the size of any package containing that commodity.

In the case of Section 5(c)(1), as in the case of all 5(c) regulations, the burden will be on the agency to establish that the specific regulation proposed is necessary either to prevent deception or to facilitate value comparisons. If manufacturers during the course of the hearing can establish that there is in fact no consumer deception with respect to the use of size designations for the commodity in question, or that no such standardize terms would facilitate value comparison, then no regulation could be adopted.

Cents-Off and Economy Size

Under Section 5(c)(2) regulations would be adopted by the promulgating agency with respect to a particular consumer commodity to

> regulate the placement upon any package containing any commodity, or upon any label affixed to such commodity, of any printed matter stating or representing by implication that such commodity is offered for retail sale at a price lower than the ordinary and customary retail sale price or that a retail sale price advantage is accorded to purchasers thereof by reason of the size of that package or the quantity of its contents.

In the earlier versions of the packaging and labeling bill introduced by Senator Hart the agencies were directed to adopt regulations to *prohibit* "cents-off" and "economy size" label statement practices for *all* consumer commodities.[12] In response to strong objections by industry witnesses that the "cents-off" promoting practice was highly regarded by consumers and afforded them substantial savings. Senator Hart himself proposed an amendment to the bill in March 1966 (see Committee Print, March 15, 1966) to transfer this provision from Section 4(a) to Section 5(c), so that such a regulation could be adopted only on a commodity-by-commodity basis, and only upon the finding required by Section 5(c).

This provision was modified further by the Senate Commerce Committee, which substituted the word "regulate" for the word "prohibit" at the beginning of the subsection. The provision as thus changed was explained in the Senate Committee Report as follows:

> This provision is primarily directed at "cents off" label representations placed on the package by the manufacturer and at such label designations as "economy" size. While the committee was of the opinion that these practices should be prohibited where abused, the agencies are granted a measure of flexibility in establishing regu-

lations for the utilization of such promotional techniques in a nondeceptive manner. Nothing in this subsection would inhibit the retailer's right to set retail prices or to make sale offers.[13]

The House Commerce Committee considered a further modification of this provision, to add the words "but not prohibit" after the word "regulate" at the beginning of the subsection. (See H. R. 15440' Committee Print of September 13, 1966) But as reported by the House Committee the provision was left unchanged, and these words were not added. Nevertheless, the Committee sought to achieve the same effect by indicating in its Report that this provision was intended to authorize regulations "to regulate (but not prohibit) the use of such promotions as 'cents off' or 'economy size' on any package."[14]

The Committee's intent was further expressed when it stated that regulations under Section 5(c)(2) would be for the purpose:

> To regulate, but not prohibit, the use of such promotions as "cents off" or "economy size" on any packages in order to assure that insofar as practicable any sprice reductions claimed on the package will be passed on to the consumer. Such regulations, for example, may require a showing on the part of manufacturers that the wholesale price has been reduced in an amount sufficient to enable retailers to pass on the appropriate "cents off" to the consumer; or they may limit the duration of, and the intervals between such promotions; or the percentage of the output annually which may be marketed under "cents off" promotion.[15]

The Senate and House Committee Reports thus reflect a slightly different interpretation of this provision. The Senate Committee felt "that these practices should be prohibited where abused," whereas the House Committee felt that regulations under this provision should regulate "but not prohibit" the practice. In view of the fact that the Senate and House Conferees recommended enactment of the House bill, with only two changes, and the Senate acquiesced in this recommendation, it may reasonably be concluded that the House interpretation of Section 5(c)(2) should prevail over that stated in the earlier Senate Committee Report and that cents-off labeling may not be prohibited altogether for any commodity.

Another question that comes up in connection with a cents-off regulation is whether the FDA or the FTC could require a retailer to reduce the retail price by the amount of the stated cents-off reduction on the label. For example, if a product labeled to be sold at five cents off the regular price in fact was regularly sold by a retailer at $.40, could the FDA require in a regulation that the retailer sell the product for $.35?

Several provisions in the FPLA are relevant to the resolution of this question. Section 3(b) provides that regulations under the Act shall not apply to wholesale or retail distributors except to the extent that they are engaged in the packaging or labeling of a commodity, or prescribed or specify the manner in which the product is packaged or labeled. Since a manufacturer's cents-off label statement is not prescribed by the retailer (except for private labeled products), it might be argued that this exemption wholly protects the retailer from coverage under a cents-off regulation.

But a label is defined in Section 10(c) to mean any written, printed or graphic matter appearing on a package containing a consumer commodity. Because the retailer marks the package with the selling price of the commodity, that marking would appear to consitute labeling under the Act. If so, the retailer has engaged in the labeling of the commodity and would thus not be covered by the exemption contained in Section 3(b).

There is another limitation in the Act, however, that would appear to prevent the application of any FPLA regulation to the marking or labeling of a commodity after it has reached the retail store. Section 3(a) makes it unlawful for any person to distribute or to cause to be distributed in commerce any packaged commodity which does not conform to the provisions of the Act and regulations. Thus, regulations adopted under the Act apply only to the commodity as it is labeled when shipped in interstate commerce. If the product is lawful when shipped in interstate commerce, then any labeling that takes place after it has come to rest within a state is not subject to the reach of the Act.

This conclusion is supported by a letter from the Department of Health, Education and Welfare (HEW) to Senator Magnuson, reprinted in the Senate Commerce Committee Report at pages 14-18. HEW suggested that the bill should be amended to make it clear that the Act was coextensive with the Federal Food. Drug and Cosmetic Act "including violations that occur after an article has been shipped in interstate commerce, for example, by alteration of the label while the article is held for sale after such shipment." No such amendment was adopted, and it thus seems clear that unlike the Food, Drug and Cosmetic Act the FPLA does not apply to labeling that takes place after shipment in interstate commerce.

It is entirely conceivable, however, that the FDA may take the position that the failure of a retailer to pass along the savings promised on the label would constitute false or misleading labeling under Section 403(a) of the Federal Food, Drug and Cosmetic Act. Many provisions of the FDA's mandatory labeling regulations are based on both the FPLA and the Food, Drug and Cosmetic Act. If this same approach is taken, then conceivably the FDA could regulate retailer practices in a cents-off regulation.

Ingredient Information

Regulations under Section 5(c)(3) would:

require that the label on each package of a consumer commodity (other than one which is a food within the meaning of section 201(f) of the Federal Food, Drug and Cosmetic Act) bear (A) the common or usual name of such consumer commodity, if any, and (B) in case such consumer commodity consists of two or more ingredients, the common or usual name of each such ingredient listed in order of decreasing predominance, but nothing in this paragraph shall be deemed to require that any trade secret be divulged.

This wording was added by the House Committee as a substitute for a provision in the Senate bill that would have authorized the adoption of regulations to require that "information with respect to the ingredients and composition of any consumer commodity . . . be placed upon packages."

Nothing can be found in the legislative history to explain the significance of subparagraph (A), which would require that all commodities bear a label specifying the identity of the commodity, which in most cases is the same as the "common or usual name" of the commodity.

A regulation under subparagraph (B) would require the listing of ingredients in decreasing order of predominance. The exclusion for foods is explained in the House Committee Report on the ground that the Food, Drug and Cosmetic Act requires that all nonstandardized food labels include a list of ingredients.

The only legislative history which throws any further light on the meaning of this provision occurred during the floor debate in the House. In an exchange between Congressman Kornegay and Chairman Staggers, the former pointed out that many drugs and cosmetics contain literally dozens and dozens of nonactive ingredients, and asked whether these ingredients which have no value so far as price comparison is concerned need be declared on the label under such a regulation. Chairman Staggers answered. "Not unless the listing is necessary in order to make the value comparison possible."[16]

Thus, although the language of this section might conceivably be read to provide that a regulation under Section 5(c)(3) must require that every ingredient in a commodity be declared on the label, it can very well be argued that in the light of the legislative history, the intent of Section 5(c), and the statutory purposes, ingredients need not be declared if they are not relevant to a value comparison or to the prevention of deception. Such a conclusion can be justified further on the ground that the discretionary authority in Section 5(c)(3) to require the listing of every ingredient must include the lesser authority to require the listing of only those ingredients relevant to the question of value comparison and deception. Quite obviously a narrow interpretation of the language to require the listing of fifty or a hundred ingredients on the label would tend to defeat one of the basic purposes of the Act to enable consumers readily to obtain accurate information as to consumer commodities.

Nonfunctional Slack-Fill

Section 5(c)(4) authorizes regulations effective to "prevent the nonfunctional slack-fill of packages containing consumer commodities." The final sentence in Section 5(c) provides that "a package shall be deemed to be nonfunctionally slack-filled if it is filled to substantially less than its capacity for reasons other than (A) protection of the contents of such package or (b) the requirements of machines used for enclosing the contents in such package."

This provision was added to the bill by the House Commerce Committee. The only explanation found in the legislative history is in the House Committee Report, which states:

When a consumer buys a nontransparent package containing a consumer commodity, he expects it to be as full as can be reasonably expected. He makes his purchase in many instances on the basis of the size of the box. There are practical justifications for less than a complete fill in many instances. A container has to be large enough to protect the contents and it is necessary to recognize that many consumer packages are prepared by machine operations. Therefore, to the extent that the safety of the product requires additional wrapping and a somewhat larger box and to the extent that machine packaging requires that the box be somewhat larger to accommodate the machine closing, slack-fill is necessary and justifiable. However, nonfunctional slack-fill which involves, for example, the use of false bottoms and/or unnecessary bulky packaging is not justified. The bill would allow the Department of Health, Education and Welfare and the Federal Trade Commission to prevent abuses of that kind.[17]

The definition of nonfunctional slack-fill in Section 5(c)—a package filled to substantially less than its capacity for reasons other than protection of the contents or the requirements of machines used for enclosing the contents in the package—was thus apparently intended to include all legitimate technological reasons for less than a complete fill.[18]

As for the content of these regulations, a logical approach would be for the agencies to adopt standards of fill similar to those that have been adopted by the FDA under Section 401 of the Food, Drug and Cosmetic Act, which authorizes regulations to establish for any food a reasonable standard of fill of container. The FDA has adopted standards of fill under Section 401 based on at least four standards of measurement:

1. A percentage of the total capacity of the container *(for example,* the standard of fill of container for canned tomatoes is a fill of not less than 90% of the total capacity of the container);

2. Volumetric determinations *(for example,* the standard of fill of container for canned peas is a fill such that, when the peas and liquid are removed from the container and returned thereto the level peas, irrespective of the quantity of the liquid, 15 seconds after they are so returned completely fill the container);

3. The drained weight of the food product measured against the water capacity of the can by weight *(for example,* the total weight of drained fruit cocktail must be not less than 65% of the water capacity of the container); and

4. The maximum quantity which can be sealed in the container and processed without crushing or breaking *(for example,* canned fruits).

VOLUNTARY PACKAGING STANDARDS

The third major area of coverage in the FPLA concerns the encouragement of voluntary packaging standards designed to reduce the number of weights or quantities in which a particular commodity is packed. I will not try to rehearse here the legislative history that most of you are familiar with during which the compulsory standard provisions of the earlier versions of the bill were finally converted to voluntary standards provisions by the House Commerce Committee. It is enough for present purposes to emphasize that the House Committee—and subsequently Congress—concluded that there were indeed some significant drawbacks to compulsory packaging standards and that industry should be given an opportunity to work through voluntary means to reduce the number of package sizes in those instances where "undue proliferation" exists.

There have been a number of developments in this area in the two years since enactment, but many questions remain. Let us look briefly at what has happened and at some of the most obvious questions that most companies and associations in the consumer commodity industries are now facing.

Many of your companies and associations are working on or have completed a program to reduce or stabilize the number of package sizes. The Department of Commerce has on several occasions announced those products for which standards have been developed or are in process. Some industries have been working through the voluntary standards procedure of the Department of Commerce, but most have chosen to work through their industry trade associations.

To date, there have been no formal proposed determinations by the Department of Commerce that undue proliferation exists in the package sizes for any commodity. Apparently the Department has decided that the best approach for all concerned is to encourage industry segments to move voluntarily to reduce or stabilize package sizes without the necessity of a formal finding of undue proliferation.

The Department's regulations do not define "undue proliferation" and do not spell out what constitutes the impairment of the reasonable ability of consumers to make value comparisons with respect to a consumer commodity or commodities. The substantive content of these terms will remain to be determined on a case-by-case basis. Until that time, industries will have no clear guidance in trying to decide whether a voluntary reduction in package sizes is desirable, or necessary, in order to preclude a charge of undue proliferation.

A second question concerns the degree of industry adherence to a voluntary standard. Obviously, if the bulk of the industry disregards a voluntary standard, then its existence would have little or no relevance for purposes of an undue proliferation inquiry. But is a finding of undue proliferation justified if there are only regional aberrations, or if a single manufacturer feels he must market a size that is not included in the standard?

The Department's voluntary standards procedures contain the proviso that:

A standard published by the Department under these procedures is a voluntary standard and thus by itself has no mandatory or legally binding effect. A person may choose to use or not to use such a standard.

Although I have not seen the documentation of most of the industry voluntary standards that have been developed over the past year or so, I assume that this same noncompulsory concept is included in most of them. Nevertheless, failure of an industry to observe a standard might well raise the question of undue proliferation and trigger the Section 5(d) and 5(e) procedures of the FPLA.

Under those procedures, if the Department finds undue proliferation, it must then request the industry to cooperate in the development of a voluntary packaging standard under the Department's procedures. Subsequent failure to develop such a standard or to observe a standard that is developed must be reported by the Secretary of Commerce to Congress, with his recommendation as to whether Congress should enact legislation providing regulatory authority to deal with the situation in question.

Thus, the third major unanswered question in this area is whether conditions will arise in 1969 or thereafter that would lead the Secretary of Commerce, or others, to propose once again that compulsory packaging standards be authorized by Congress. Undoubtedly it is this possibility that has prompted many segments of industry to make the voluntary approach an effective and workable one.

CONCLUSION

Finally, a brooding specter over all voluntary standard efforts is the question of compliance with the federal antitrust laws. Some of you may have seen reports in the trade press that the Department of Justice has been in communication with the Department of Commerce concerning the procedures that should be observed by an industry that is developing a voluntary standard. I am confident that many industry groups will be very interested in seeing the outcome of these inter-Departmental discussions.

I have talked to more than a few industry-representatives who believe they are caught between the pressure of the FPLA toward voluntary package size reduction on the one hand, and the threat of antitrust prosecution on the other. In the meantime they must continue to compete effectively, and meet the changing tastes and demands of customers and ultimate consumers.

I doubt whether any of these questions will be finally resolved in 1969. Indeed, the prospect is that at least some of these questions will become rather acute for many segments of industry over the next few years.

REFERENCES

1. *See,* for example, Forte, *Fair Hearing in Administrative Rule-Making,* 1968. Duke L. J. 1 (1968). 23 *Food Drug Cosmetic Law Journal* 366 (July 1968).
2. There can be no doubt that the activities of the Department of Commerce, through the National Bureau of Standards and the National Conference on Weights and Measures—augmented by such industry efforts as the Industry Committee on Packaging and Labeling—have been the major factor in bringing about uniformity in federal and State labeling regulation. Indeed, it is precisely because of the excellent past record of the Department in this regard that the few disparities between the FPLA regulations and the Model Regulation, and the Department's interpretation of section 12 of the FPLA that is discussed below in the text, stand out as such glaring exceptions.
3. The provision in the 1966 amendments to the HSLA reads: "It is hereby expressly declared that it is the intent of the Congress to supersede any and all laws of the States and political subdivisions thereof insofar as they may now or hereafter provide for the precautionary labeling of any substance or article intended or suitable for household use . . . which differs from the requirements or exemptions of this Act or the regulations or interpretations promulgated pursuant thereto. Any law, regulation, or ordinance purporting to exempt such a labelling requirement shall be null and void." in U. S. C. §1261, note.

4. This preference of the General Counsel's office for the legislative history over the language of the Act brings to mind the statement by Mr. Justice Frankfurter that "Spurious use of legislative history must not swallow the legislation so as to give point to the quip that only when legislative history is doubtful do you go to the statute." Frankfurter, "Some Reflections on the Reading of Statutes," 47 *Columbia Law Review* 527 (1947).

5. Report on Truth in Packaging of the Subcommittee on Antitrust and Monopoly of the Senate Committee on the Judiciary, 88th Cong., 2d Sess. 5 (1964).

6. S. Rep. No. 1186. 89th Cong., 2d Sess. 2, 6 (1966).

7. H. Rep. No. 2076, 89th Cong. 2d Sess. 11 (1966).

8. The conferees wish to make it clear that the concept of 'value comparison is broader than the concept of price comparison' and includes the latter within the former as a very important factor in making a value comparison." H. R. Rep. No. 2286, 89th Cong., 2d Sess., Conference Report to Accompany S. 985 on the Fair Packaging and Labeling Act 9 (1966).

9. 112 Cong. Rec. 26564 (Daily ed. Oct. 19, 1966).

10. "I am the author of this amendment in the House Committee on Interstate and Foreign Commerce. It is designed to insure that the government agencies and officials charged with enforcing the law and issuing regulations thereunder do not exercise the powers conferred upon them, particularly by section 5, for the sole purpose of facilitating a mathematical computation: that is, a price comparison, in the supermarket aisle. Price is only one element in a consumer value decision: other factors of equal or greater importance are product performance, the convenience of the package, and the suitability of the size or quantity of the product in satisfying a consumer's personal desire or need. Obviously what constitutes value is highly subjective.

It is a decision that must be made by each individual and is a personal judgment of the kind the Federal Government is ill-equipped and should not be asked to make for the consumer. In sponsoring the change from price comparison to value comparison it was never my intention to include the Federal Government into quality determinations or grade labeling and Government testing of a consumer products, as Senator Hart has suggested.

In short, the amendment was conceived to avoid having this new statute mislead consumers by over accentuating price at the expense of other and often more important elements of true value, rather than opening broad new areas of regulatory control or experimentation. I am sure I can fairly say that all members of the House Committee had this understanding when I offered the amendment and obtained its approval." 112 Cong. Rec. 27536 (Daily ed. Oct. 21, 1966).

11. Report on Truth in Packaging of the Subcommittee on Antitrust and Monopoly of the Senate Committee on the Judiciary, 88th Cong., 2d Sess. (1964).

12. See §3(A)(b)(4) of S. 3745 in the Eighty-Seventh Congress; §3(A)(c)(4) of S. 387 in the Eighty-Eighth Congress: and §3(a)(5) of S. 985 as introduced in the Eighty-Ninth Congress.

13. S. Rep. No. 1186, 89th Cong., 2d Sess. 6 (1966).

14. House Report at 7.

15. See footnote 12.

16. 112 Cong. Rec. 23865 (Daily ed. Oct. 3, 1966).

17. House Committee Report at 8.

18. For discussions of the technological reasons for less than a complete fill, see 72 Yale Law Journal 788, 794-95 (1963); Forte, "The FDA, the FTC and the Deceptive Packaging of Foods," 40 *New York University Law Review* 860, 874-75 (1965). 21 *Food Drug Cosmetic Law Journal* 205 (April 1966).

23

The 1970 Survey of Consumer Awareness of Finance Charges and Interest Rates

Board of Governors of the Federal Reserve System

Federal Reserve System surveys following passage of the Truth in Lending Act indicate that consumers are becoming increasingly aware of the finance charges and interest rates they are paying for credit transactions

During 1970, the Board of Governors of the Federal Reserve System conducted the Second Survey of Consumer Awareness of Finance Charges and Interest Rates. The purpose of the 1970 Survey is to determine the changes in consumer knowledge relating to finance charges and interest rates since July 1, 1969, the effective date of the Truth in Lending Act. The results of the 1970 Survey are compared with the results of the first Survey, which was conducted in June 1969 and serves as a benchmark of consumer awareness prior to the advent of Truth in Lending. The results of the 1969 Survey were reported in the 1969 Annual Report to Congress.

Both the 1970 and the 1969 Surveys asked consumer borrowers about their knowledge of the finance charges and interest rates they were paying on their credit transactions. These questions were asked with respect to each of the major types of consumer credit contracts, including first mortgages, debt for home improvements,

Reprinted from *Annual Report to Congress on Truth in Leading for the year 1970* (Board of Governors of the Federal Reserve System, January 4, 1971), pp. 7-13 and pp. 20-22.

credit purchases of automobiles and of household appliances and furniture, personal cash loans, retail charge accounts and credit cards. Consumers covered in these Surveys were also asked about their general knowledge of Truth in Lending.

SURVEY RESULTS

Comparison of the results of the second Survey with the results of the first Survey conducted just prior to the effective date of the Truth in Lending Act and Regulation Z indicates that there has been a significant improvement in the knowledge of consumers concerning the cost of their credit purchases and their borrowing for personal, family and household needs. The proportion of consumer borrowers who had no knowledge of the interest rates they were paying has declined substantially since Truth in Lending has been in force. Furthermore, for the more common types of consumer credit, those borrowers who believe they know the interest rates they are paying now appear to have a more realistic estimate of the actual rates than they did before Truth in Lending.

Only 13 percent of the consumers who purchased homes and acquired new first mortgages or refinanced their first mortgages during the period since Truth in Lending became effective reported they did not know the interest rate they were paying as compared with 27 percent in the Survey conducted just prior to the effective date. Similarly, of those consumers taking out personal cash loans, the proportion reporting that they did not know the interest rate they were paying dropped from 43 percent in the 1969 Survey to 28 percent in the 1970 Survey. In 1969, nearly three-fifths of those who had purchased major appliances or furniture on instalments reported that they did not know the interest rate they were being charged while in 1970 this proportion has been reduced to a little over two-fifths. Declines in the proportion of consumer borrowers not knowing the interest rates they were being charged were also reported by consumers who financed home improvements on credit or purchased automobiles on credit, but the declines in the proportion of "don't knows" for these types of credit transactions were less dramatic than for the other types of credit.

The increase from the 1969 to the 1970 Survey in the number of consumers who believed they knew the annual percentage rates they were paying was also accompanied by an increase in the proportion reporting interest rates in line with prevailing rates for most types of credit transactions. For those consumers with personal loans, only 12 percent reported that their annual percentage rate was as high as 10 percent in the 1969 Survey while more than one-fourth of the borrowers reported that high a rate in the 1970 Survey. A rate of 10 percent or more was reported in 1970 by about two-fifths of the consumers who had bought appliances or furniture on credit as compared with only one-sixth of those who had reported such purchases in the 1969 Survey. The comparison is similar for annual percentage rates on other types of credit transactions, with what appear to be unrealistically low rates reported less frequently in the 1970 Survey and higher, more realistic, rates reported more frequently than in the 1969 Survey. It should be noted that the upward shifts from the 1969 to 1970 Surveys in the rates reported on first mortgage financing appears to be primarily a reflection of the general upward trend in mortgage interest rates rather than any change in the knowledge of consumers.

The increase in consumer knowledge about the interest rates they are paying on their credit transactions appears to have occurred generally among most income groups and educational levels. Among all of the income groups, the proportion of "don't know" answers to the interest rate questions either declined substantially from 1969 to 1970 or showed little change. The only exception was for consumers with incomes from $5,000 to $10,000 who undertook home improvements and they reported an increase in the proportion of "don't know" answers, from 39 percent in 1969 to 46 percent in 1970.

The upward shift from 1969 to 1970 toward more realistic annual percentage rates reported by consumer borrowers was consistently reflected in all income groups. This shift was generally more pronounced among the higher income groups, except for consumers with personal loans in which case the upward shift was most noticeable among those with incomes of less than $8,000.

The improvement from 1969 to 1970 in consumer knowledge of interest rates was also general among the different educational levels. There was a decline in the "don't know" responses for most of the educational groups and an upward shift in the interest rates reported was apparent for all groups for all major types of credit transactions.

The increase in consumer awareness of the interest rates they pay appeared to be most widespread for the credit purchase of appliances and furniture and for personal loans Consistent improvement was noted among all income and educational groups. This can be regarded as a favorable development, since these are very common consumer credit transactions. Nevertheless, lack of knowledge is still quite common in these areas. The 1970 Survey shows that two-fifths of the consumers with credit purchases of appliances and one-fourth of those with personal loans still reported that they did not know the interest rate they were paying. Furthermore, two-fifths of the consumers who had a personal cash loan in the 1970 Survey reported an interest rate of 9 percent or less, about the same proportion as in 1969. Since it is unlikely that very many consumers would be able to obtain cash loans at such rates, it must be concluded that most of those reporting such rates are not aware of the annual percentage rates they are paying.

Consumers with retail charge accounts also showed a significant improvement in their knowledge of the interest rates paid on such accounts from 1969 to 1970. The proportion reporting that they did not know the interest rate they were paying on their retail charge accounts declined from nearly one-half in 1969 to one-third in 1970. Furthermore, the proportion reporting interest rates in the most likely range of 9 to 18 percent rose from two-fifths to three-fifths. Such shifts in response were shown by all of the income groups and all educational levels.

In the 1970 Survey, as in 1969, consumers were asked whether they had heard of a Federal law requiring that consumers be given certain information regarding the terms of their credit transactions and if they knew the name of this law. In the 1970 Survey, 57 percent of the consumers said they had heard of such a law as compared with 45 percent in 1969. However, in both years only one-fifth of those who had heard of the

Truth in Lending law knew the name of the law. The knowledge of the existence of such a law was substantially more prevalent among those with income of $10,000 and over and among those with some college than among the other income and educational groups.

Those who had heard of such a law were asked to indicate what they thought were the major provisions of the law. The large majority of consumers, 70 percent, continued to respond that the law provides for disclosure of interest rates or some other form of disclosure. However, nearly 18 percent in 1970 believe the law is directed to protecting consumers against excessive interest rates or some other credit practice. This proportion was slightly larger than the comparable figure for 1969. There was a moderate decline from 1969 to 1970 in the proportion of consumers who said they didn't know the provisions of the law. In both Surveys, the proportion of "don't know" answers declined as income and the educational level increased.

COMPLIANCE

The enforcement of the Truth in Lending Act is spread among nine Federal agencies. For the most part, Federal agencies that have general supervisory authority over a particular group of creditors were also given Truth in Lending enforcement responsibility over those creditors. Enforcement for all remaining creditors. except in those States which have an exemption from the Act, is the responsibility of the Federal Trade Commission. Consequently, the Commission has the bulk of the enforcement task.

Information received from the Federal agencies, other than the Federal Trade Commission, indicates no significant problems in the enforcement of Regulation Z. These agencies point out that the level of compliance is high which is probably attributable to the fact that creditors under the jurisdiction of these agencies are accustomed to operating under regulations and close supervision. For the most part, compliance is determined by those agencies during the regular periodic examinations of the creditors under their jurisdiction.

The Federal Trade Commission has informed the Board of its impression that large creditors who have their own legal staff, or can afford to hire outside legal counsel, usually are in full or substantial compliance. However, there still remain indications that many smaller creditors—particularly retailers—have not complied. The Commission reports that many of these creditors are either apathetic about their noncompliance or are fearful of contacting the Commission for assistance because of the desire not to reveal that they are in violation of Federal law. In order to get a more precise idea of the extent to which creditors under its jurisdiction are complying with Truth in Lending, the Commission has authorized a survey designed to determine the extent of compliance by both large and small creditors. Both types of creditors are asked to send in specimen copies of disclosure forms from which the creditor's compliance is determined. The Commission's staff anticipates that the results of this survey will be made public early in 1971.

The Federal Trade Commission uses a number of different means to educate creditors subject to its jurisdiction, as well as enforce compliance among them. The headquarters' staff devotes its attention to issuing broad guidelines, rendering informal interpretations, and effectuating compliance on the part of national and major multi-state creditors of all kinds. In the 11 field offices, Consumer Protection Specialists are employed who examine local creditors for the purpose of determining compliance with Truth in Lending. In addition, an average of two attorneys works full time in the enforcement effort in each of the 11 field offices. The Commission indicates that the field offices have a program of wide-scale monitoring of advertisements placed in the local press, supplemented by subscriptions to every major newspaper in the territory covered by each field office.

The Commission has developed informal working liaison agreements with 12 States for assistance in enforcing compliance with the Truth in Lending Act. These States are Alabama, Alaska, Idaho, Kansas, Montana, New Hampshire, Oregon, Rhode Island, South Dakota, Vermont, Virginia, and West Virginia. When apparent violations occur within one of these States, those attributed to creditors regulated by the State are referred to the State authorities for correction.

The Commission reports that since July 1, 1969, it has opened 36 formal investigations. Eighteen formal complaints have been acted upon by the Commission and nine final consent orders have been issued. One of the 18 formal complaint cases was issued against a lender, while the other 17 were issued against sellers of merchandise on credit.

The Board continues to seek uniformity in the interpretation and application of Regulation Z among the enforcement agencies. To this end, the Board furnishes copies of its correspondence relating to new or unusual problems to the other Federal enforcement agencies, as well as to the officials in the four States that have received exemption from the Truth in Lending Act.

24

Problems Encountered by the President's Committee on Consumer Interests

Frank E. McLaughlin

The author feels that the three-way dialogue between government, industry, and consumers regarding consumer affairs could stand considerable improvement. He feels that the dialogue can never really be worthwhile if industry adopts an excessively defensive attitude toward consumer affairs but is hopeful that American industry, an industry built on imagination and ideas, can recognize and respond to its responsibilities to the consumer.

This is an odd time to be talking about the problems of and the various needs for consumer protection I have encountered while working in the Office of the President's Special Assistant for Consumer Affairs. If the 91st Congress takes action on the hearings already held on consumer-related bills, much of what I have to say about problems encountered will be largely irrelevant to future operations of the Office of the President's Assistant or a successor office. The President's message to Congress proposes the establishment of a new Office of Consumer Affairs in the Executive Office of the President.[1] This office would have permanent legislative standing, an expanded budget, and greater responsibilities. It will greatly affect the practices, problems, and procedures of the office which I represent.

Reprinted from *Economics of Consumer Protection* (Danville, Ill.: The Interstate, 1971) pp. 53-59. Reprinted by permission.

PROBLEMS DUE TO ORGANIZATIONAL STRUCTURE

At present, the Office of the President's Special Assistant for Consumer Affairs exists by virtue of an Executive Order which directs the Office to study consumer interests and problems and make recommendations to the President.[2] In addition, it has been changed to work with federal agencies in coordinating plans and programs affecting consumers and to work with federal, state and local governments, private organizations, and individuals in areas of consumer interests. However, the President's Message recognized and touched candidly on the weaknesses of the offspring of this Executive Order when he stated "this position has been created by Presidential order rather than by statute, however, and it is neither as visible nor as effective as it should be."[3]

The President was referring, among other things, to the fact that the Office of the Special Assistant for Consumer Affairs simply has not had the staff nor technical resources to deal with the hundreds of issues affecting consumer interests. These issues need investigation, thoughtful consideration, proposed solutions (voluntary or legislative), and vigorous advocacy before industry groups, administrative agencies of government, and Congress. The Office of the Special Assistant for Consumer Affairs has been hampered, over its life, in responding to the needs for consumer protection by virtue of the fact that there have been *too many issues* and *too few people* to deal with them. Critical issues brought to the Special Assistant for Consumer Affairs by individual consumers, consumer groups, the Congress, the press, industry, and others have been so numerous that the time available to deal with each individual issue inevitably produces a sense of frustration and a feeling that justice has not been done to the importance of the issue. The establishment of a statutory office with an expanded budget would go a long way towards curing this lack "horsepower."

BUSINESS RESPONSE TO CONSUMER ISSUES

Another problem we have encountered in responding to the needs of consumers is attributable to the traditional reaction of many industry representatives towards discussion of the very existence of a consumer issue or irritation. An article of last fall[4] traced seven specific stages of industry response to a consumer problem. The traditional phases of reaction included denying the existence of the problem, blaming the problem on marginal companies cutting corners to survive, criticizing those who proclaim the existence of the problem, hiring a public relations firm to launch a campaign, working to blunt proposed legislation, launching a fact-finding committee to see whether a problem really exists, and, finally, deciding to actually do something about the problem.

I think that we can verify the existence of these reactions on many consumer issues, if they do not, in fact, appear on *every* consumer issue. I would hasten to point out, however, that this reflex series of reactions is tending to become more of an historical curiosity. More and more associations, individual companies, and company spokesmen are speaking out candidly and strongly on the need for the corporation to base more of its decision-making on the promotion and protection of the public interest. I feel that this emerging attitude is, in a large part, attributable to the recognition that traditional reactions to consumer issues may not work anymore—if indeed they ever "worked" at all. The handling of the fair packaging and labeling legislation is a good illustration of what I mean.

Prior to enactment of the Fair Packaging and Labeling Act, industry took the position in public and private discussions and before Congressional Committees that packaging and labeling of consumer commodities were adequately regulated through existing federal and state law. This position was taken at a time when agency and industry files were bulging with complaints about the confusing array of package sizes and quantity declarations, poorly identified products, ambiguous and misleading size characterizations, slack-filled containers, and misleading savings claims. Occasionally, an isolated manufacturer might admit the existence of abuses or problems in packaging and labeling. On the whole, through several years of congressional hearings, the industry's position denied there was a problem. Yet throughout the hearings, the volume and the character of packaging and labeling complaints were moving the federal establishment towards some type of legislation. This situation stimulates a mental image of the Washington representative or lobbyist continually calling the New York Office to say "We're doing fine, we didn't lose any yardage today."

If no problem existed, then there was no need for top management to ask Congress to give industry time to suggest and experiment with voluntary methods of solution. In addition (and of more significance to industry), there was no need for Congress to consider giving voluntary compliance processes further chance. All the while, more and more consumers scratched their heads and began to wonder if "large economy size" really meant economy in all instances; if they were really getting 10 cents off their regular price, and if there was any point in trying to calculate cost per ounce among the confusing array of different sizes of competing brands of packaged consumer commodities. Instead of admitting the existence of packaging and labeling irritations and coming up with creative solutions, thereby winning the admiration of the consumer and Congress, industry purchased a little time.

When time and events did converge to produce the Fair Packaging and Labeling Act, the buyers of time justified their positions and actions by declaring that they had been victorious in the end in that a gutted bill had been passed.[5] On the other hand, Senate supporters of the new legislation took the position that the act was comprehensive and strong and that industry could hardly claim victory when it had sought the defeat of each and every provision of the act.[6] Quite some time has passed since the enactment of the Fair Packaging and Labeling Act. Already, we have heard consumers and consumer advocates point out the weaknesses of the act and demand that Congress make good on its promise to facilitate consumer purchasing of packaged and labeled consumer commodities.

What is perhaps of more significance on the legislative scene is that we have just heard another senator, speaking for the committee which produced the act, characterize the law as a "half-truth in packaging and labeling," and state the intention of the committee to cure the weaknesses of the legislation,[7] The senator specifically mentioned the likelihood of the use of unit pricing and a declaration of quality information being included in proposed legislation. Such legislation has already been introduced in various forms in the House of Representatives.

With the prospect of further packaging and labeling legislation, I think a number of questions are occurring to many representatives of the affected industry and other industries such as:

1. Is the industry's internal communications system responsible for the frequently reluctant posture assumed towards consumer problems and the need for solution of consumer problems?

2. Is the apparent advantage of obtaining a delay in legislation and regulation offset by damage to industry's public image and the likelihood of subsequent and more stringent legislation propelled by the drives of consumerism?

3. Is it preferable to recognize the existence of problems and to propose creative voluntary solutions rather than to supinely await a legislatively imposed solution to a problem which industry will not admit exists?

4. If, because of the nature of the problem or because of existing legislation, it is not possible to arrive at a solution through voluntary procedures, would it not be in industry's long-term best interest to approach the government with suggestions for a legislative solution?

GOVERNMENT-INDUSTRY DIALOGUE

Unfortunately, a characteristic of the government-business dialogue on the subject of voluntary action to protect consumers is that meaningful discussions are usually held only in a time of crisis. The crisis may be imminent congressional consideration of a consumer bill, implementation through regulation and orders of a consumer bill by a regulatory agency, or the pending promulgation of an official government policy and position on a consumer problem. At such points, it becomes absolutely necessary to discuss problems and issues fully and frankly and to agonize over potential solutions which may, at other times, be uncomfortable to think about. The problem with this approach is that crises are not the ideal environment for arriving at solutions which are equitable to all parties concerned. As one of my employers used to say "If you want something bad, that's usually the way you get it."

Inability of government and industry to hold frequent and meaningful dialogues on consumer problems is attributable to other factors in addition to the human desire to postpone or avoid frustrating deliberations on difficult issues. The plain and disturbing fact of the matter is that frequently the representatives of an association or company are poorly informed about the marketing, advertising, labeling, or production factors which are at the basis of the particular consumer complaint. Such a discussion is not likely to probe the limits of voluntary industry correction of consumer abuses or the proper attributes of an effective legislative response to the problem. Solutions for a consumer problem frequently are hampered by the fact that the people who know the potentialities and problems of a particular segment of industry—the people who keep the business moving—are not sufficiently involved in the government-industry dialogue on the particular problem. These people should take a greater interest and participate more frequently in the initial discussions of consumer problems between government and industry. It may violate the tenets of standard trade association practice, but in my experience, discussion of consumer issues and problems between government and industry have been much more fruitful whenever the industry's operating executives themselves have the opportunity to sit in on the discussions.

CONSUMER INVOLVEMENT

President Nixon's consumer message recognized another long standing impediment to proper protection of the consumer.[8] The President recommended that Congress enact legislation which would extablish a consumer advocate to appear before federal regulatory agencies, in judicial proceedings, and in government councils. Consumers comprise the largest interest group in our economy. Yet there has, indeed, been a long standing recognition, which until recent years produced little action, that this group has been poorly represented in many phases of government.

The regulators both in government and industry have recognized the problems that attend the making of rules for a silent third party, the consumer. Both, up to now, can be faulted for their failure to make the consumer's role in this process of interaction more vocal. The consumer, too, is at fault for not having previously exercised all of the responsibilities that go with citizenship in a democratic society.

With the tendency of Congress to delegate more and more discretion for rule-making to federal agencies, it becomes a citizen's duty to inquire into what decisions the agencies are making and to register his views on proposed actions. It is his right to be adequately represented in the quasi-judicial proceedings and hearings of the various regulatory and old-line agencies of government which routinely establish policy in the field of consumer interests. The President's message recognizes the need to stimulate the self-advocacy role of the consumer by also proposing that the government establish and publish a consumer's version of the *Federal Register.*[9] Such a publication would apprise the consumer of pending decisions on major consumer policy issues and stimulate the involvement and reaction of the consumer to such proposals.

The job of advocating the consumer view and public interest at the hearing level would, under the President's proposal, be carried out by a corps of consumer advocates in the Justice Department. If the Congress is willing to act on these proposals, involving direct consumer involvement and legal advocacy of the consumer's point of view, I believe major impediments to proper consumer protection will be removed.

Much has been said in recent years concerning the nneed to stimulate the development of consumer product performance, safety, and labeling standards. The point has been made in congressional and other forums that the traditional voluntary mechanisms for establishing product standards have not routinely provided for the representation of the consumer's interest in the deliberations preliminary to establishment of the standard. The standards development and testing agencies, such as the American National Standards Institute and the American Society for Testing and Materials, have responded constructively to the need for more consumer involvement. They have run into problems, however, concerning identification of interested and knowledgeable consumer spokesmen who have the technical competence and necessary financial resources, for travel expenditures, to participate in the deliberations related to the development of the consumer standard. In my judgment, more attention should be given by all segments of industry to procedures which would insure proper consumer representation in the work of these standard-making bodies.

SUMMARY

There are a number of irritating impediments to providing the consumer with responsive consumer protection measures in the voluntary and legislative sectors. In brief, it can be said that this three-part dialogue between government, industry, and consumers regarding consumer issues could stand considerable improvement. I submit that there is no reason for government, industry, or the consumer to be satisfied with the system of interaction that now prevails. It can be greatly improved.

I see no reason for industry to adopt an excessively defensive attitude toward problems affecting the consumer. American industry is an industry of ideas. I have no doubt that industry can devise the measures to correct consumer problems once the problems are recognized and good will is directed towards their solution. In this regard, I do not believe that it is fair to say that voluntary correction *never works*. It is more accurate to say that the voluntary system *might work* but that it is not now functioning properly. The voluntary system, voluntary standardization, and other voluntary corrective measures are "on trial." It does not require the perspective of a prophet to predict that mandatory standards may be the order of the day after that "trial."

The outcome of the trial of the voluntary system is easy to predict so long as defensive attitudes impede the recognition of problems and bar discussion of their solution; as long as there are government liaison officials in industry who believe that communications consist of knowing which office to call after a problem reaches critical proportions and of knowing how to keep government officials from "bothering" industry policy-makers the rest of the time; as long as there are those who think that voluntary solutions can be arrived at without resort to the consumers' views; as long as there are people in industry and government who believe that their causes are advanced by a "war of words" in the trade and public press; as long as the idea prevails that the government would never "buy" a proposed voluntary solution to a correctable problem; as long, in brief, as there are those who believe that the "status quo" is preferable to all else—even to progress.

I do not want to end this chapter on a mournful note. I believe that the problems which I have discussed *are* being explored much more openly than ever before. I think

Congress is anxious to act on consumer issues and enact procedures aimed at insuring *more* responsive and *more* equitable treatment of consumer problems and vexations. I feel that the desire of all the affected parties to treat consumer problems more objectively and more equitably will reach major milestones in the near future.

REFERENCES

1. Message from the President of the United States, *Congressional Record,* 91st Congress, first session, House of Representatives, October 30, 1969.
2. U.S. President, Executive Order 11136, *Federal Register,* Vol. 29, No. 4 (January 3, 1964), p. 129.
3. President's Message, *op. cit.*
4. "How Business Responds to Consumerism," *Business Week* (September 6, 1969), pp. 94-108.
5. For example, see the *New York Times,* October 20, 1969, p. 1 and October 21, 1966, p. 65.
6. *Congressional Record,* 89th Congress. second session, U.S. Senate, October 19, 1966, pp. 27563, 27602-27606.
7. Senator Frank Moss, Opening Statement in *Fair Packaging and Labeling,* Hearings before the Consumer Subcommittee, Committee on Commerce, U.S. Senate, 91st Congress, second session, March 23, 1970, p. 65.
8. President's Message, *op. cit.*
9. *Ibid.*

25

Federal Role in Consumer Affairs

Virginia H. Knauer

The Special Assistant to the President for Consumer Affairs presents the case for the administration's Consumer Representation Act, S. 3240, to the Senate Subcommittee on Executive Reorganization and Government Research.

Mr. Chairman, I welcome the opportunity to appear here today to discuss establishment of a statutory Office of Consumer Affairs. I recognize that the several bills now before this committee provide several alternatives. I am pleased to have the opportunity to explain why we believe the approach of S. 3240, the administration's Consumer Representation Act, is the best approach.

You, Mr. Chairman, and your committee are to be commended for scheduling hearings on these proposals in the early days of this session of the Congress, so that Congress can act to establish an Office of Consumer Affairs at the earliest possible date.

Stronger Consumer Representation Needed

My experience as director of the Consumer Protection Bureau in Pennsylvania and now as Special Assistant to the President for Consumer Affairs leaves no doubt in my

Reprinted from *Federal Role in Consumer Affairs,* (Hearings before the Subcommittee on Executive Reorganization and Government Research of the Committee on Government Operations, United States Senate, 91st Cong., 2d Sess., on S. 2045, S. 3097, S. 3165 and S. 3240, January 20, 1970), pp. 245-251.

mind of the great need for stronger consumer representation and protection on both the State and National level. Frankly then, gentlemen, I am heartened that there are numerous bills before you on this issue. I consider this indicative of the degree of congressional interest in prompt action to establish an effective statutory office at the Federal level.

I am proud that the Nixon administration is the first administration in history to propose establishment of a statutory office to represent the consumer at the highest levels of the Federal Government. As you know, President Nixon personally urged this legislation in his October consumer message to the Congress as part of a far-reaching general administration program to protect the consumer's interests.

Consumer "Copelessness"

The need for such an office as the administration proposes stems directly from the present and rapidly increasing complexity of the marketplace and its products; laws and practices which have not always kept pace or been truly reflective of the individual consumer's ability to bargain on equal terms with the seller; limitations on his ability to represent himself adequately, or to secure satisfactory relief. The result has been the consumer's increasing feeling of alienation; indeed, of "copelessness."

Senator Ribicoff. You have invented a new word.

Mrs. Knauer. Yes. New frustrations every day, Senator.

Senator Ribicoff. The trouble is you know a new word for the bureaucracy. There are so many words that people don't understand, and I have often—I recall when I was at HEW just pleading with everybody in the whole agency to go through all their brochures and their directives to see if they couldn't reduce them to words that every reader could understand.

Okay, go ahead.

Billions of Dollars in Consumer Fraud

Mrs. Knauer. The rapidly growing complexity of products and marketing practices, coupled with the consumer's inability to know, to be represented, and to secure redress, creates a fertile field for the growth of deceptive practices and outright consumer fraud. Such practices can—and do—result in actual financial loss to the consumer reaching into the billions of dollars. Through unfair competition, such practices hurt the merchant who is fair. They undercut the free enterprise system, which is built on the premise that the consumer, by his decisions in the marketplace, directs the marketplace. When the consumer in unable to carry out that responsibility by making rational decisions, our national economy suffers.

At the same time, Government's efforts to serve the consumer have not in every case kept pace with the changing times. Government programs and services have grown without pattern throughout the Federal bureaucracy, creating increasing potential for duplication and overlaps, or gaps in the services consumers need. Yet, there has been no permanent, clearly defined consumer representation at the policy-decision level, or central coordinating force. Even when the consumer has turned to Government, he has not known exactly where to turn. He has felt further confused and voiceless.

Equal Rights for Consumer and Seller

The problems of the consumer have now come to the fore. The voice of the consumer—and a consumer who is increasingly organized—is being heard to insist on rights equal in the marketplace to those of the seller, and to insist on more direct representation in Government.

This administration is resolved to bring the consumer into his rightful place. The comprehensive administration package proposed by President Nixon to alleviate the consumer's problems has as its keystone the bill before you today.

It provides for the establishment of a statutory Office of Consumer Affairs in the Executive Office of the President which would have the central responsibility for coordination of all Federal activities affecting consumers and which would insure that the consumer's viewpoint be heard in the policymaking councils of Government.

On study you will find that the administration bill gives the Office of Consumer Affairs the power and functions to encompass all necessary activities. This office has been designed to utilize the already existing mechanism of Federal programs, and the existing expertise, wherever possible, without creating yet another cumbersome bureaucratic structure which ultimately adds to the problem rather than solves it.

In order to utilize existing expertise, this bill also provides for the establishment of a Consumer Protection Division in the Department of Justice with responsibility for advocacy in administrative and judicial proceedings. The Consumer Protection Division this bill creates also would have major responsibilities in providing increased protection for consumers under another bill in the administration consumer package, the Consumer Protection Act.

Four Bills Compared

I believe that it would be helpful at this point to compare and contrast the different approaches of the bills, which the subcommittee has before it today.

All four bills share the same basic objective in that their primary purpose is to promote the effective representation of consumer interests both inside and outside of Government. They all give the central responsibility to coordinate consumer programs and to resolve differences on consumer problems to one main consumer office or bureau.

S. 3097 and S. 2045 are similar to S. 3240 in their recommendation of the establishment of a statutory Office of Consumer Affairs in the Executive Office of the President. The Director would be appointed by the President with the advice and consent of the Senate S. 3165 would establish, however, an independent agency, the Bureau of Consumer Protection. The Director would be appointed by the President with the advice and consent of the Senate for a 15-year term.

S. 2045 and S. 3165 provide for the establishment of a Consumer Counsel who would appear and intervene before the courts and regulatory agencies to represent the consumer's interest. S. 3097 also gives the Office of Consumer Affairs this advocacy function. Mr. Richard McLaren, Assistant Attorney General, will, in his testimony, explain why this function would be best handled by the Consumer Protection Division in the Justice Department as proposed in the administration bill, S. 3240.

Better Federal-State Cooperation Under S. 3240

S. 3097, S. 2045, and S. 3165 provide for the establishment of consumer centers in major population areas throughout the country. S. 3240 does not contain this provision because we believe that local consumer problems can best be handled by the appropriate State and local consumer agencies. In our view, the encouragement and technical assistance which would be furnished by the Office of Consumer Affairs to State and local agencies under S. 3240 would be sufficient to enable these agencies to deal effectively with their local consumer problems. This would be in keeping with our policy of promoting better federal-State cooperation.

No Consumer Advisory Council is provided for in S. 3165 and S. 2045. We believe that the functions and contributions of this Council are indispensable for a truly effective representation of the consumer's interests. Therefore, S. 3240 provides for the establishment of a 20-member Consumer Advisory Council. As you know, Senator, that is eight more than is presently provided for.

Product Testing

S. 3097 gives the Secretary of Commerce the authority to test products intended for sale to consumers. We believe that the approach in the administration's proposed Consumer Product Testing Act of 1969, which is S. 3286, coupled with the testing provisions applicable to the Consumer Protection Division in the Justice Department by S. 3240, constitute the best approach to the immense problem of the testing of products intended for consumer consumption.

S. 3240 does not provide for the mediation or final arbitration of consumer complaints by the Office of Consumer Affairs as does S. 2045 and S. 3165. While the administration-proposed Office of Consumer Affairs has the flexibility whereby it can encourage voluntary settlements, it is recognized that this is too vast an area for this office to attempt to effectively handle. Therefore, the office is authorized to transmit these complaints to the appropriate regulatory agencies. It is also interesting to note that S. 2045 and S. 3007 do not provide for action on consumer complaints against Government, only for those against business: whereas S. 3240 covers action on complaints against both business and Government.

S. 2045 also does not provide for the presentation of the consumer viewpoint in Government policy formulation. The administration considers this to be of primary importance and accordingly gives to the Office of Consumer Affairs a major role in the formulation of Government policy affecting the consumer.

In considering all of the various approaches provided in these four bills, it is our conviction that S. 3240 embodies the most effective and comprehensive proposals for increased consumer representation.

Office Needed That Can Advise President Effectively

I believe all are generally agreed that what is needed is not simply the creation of yet another Government office, this time with the consumer's name tacked on the door. We need an office that can effectively advise the President on consumer matters. We need an office in a position to most effectively assure that the consumer is represented in policy decisions at the highest levels and to alert Government officials at all levels of the potential impact of their decisions on consumer's interests. We need an office in a position to help establish priorities for Government action in consumer issues, to spotlight unresolved problems, foresee potential problem areas in the future and act to resolve them before they can fester into a national economic sore. We need an office with central responsibility for coordinating all Federal activities in the consumer protection field, an office which can be in an effective position to resolve conflicts and convene meetings of the heads of Federal agencies. We need an office which can serve as catalyst and innovator, then be in a position to see that the program is activated all up and down the line.

Historic Step Proposed by Administration

To give the consumer only more Government in his name would ultimately be a disservice to the consumer. What he needs is better Government service. With this as criteria for a consumer office, this administration thoroughly considered the various alternatives for the actual organization of the office.

This administration believes it is vitally important that the Office of Consumer Affairs be permanently established. Although the previous administration had created the position of Special Assistant to the President for Consumer Affairs and a President's Committee on Consumer Interests, it had done so only by Executive order. That, of course, meant the office existed solely at the discretion of the President. For what an Executive order creates, an Executive order can take away. What this administration is proposing then, is a most historic step—the creation by law of a permanent voice for the consumer at the highest level of Government.

For ultimate effectiveness, the administration has proposed that the Office of Consumer Affairs be established within the Executive Office of the President.

No other location for the office will so effectively permit it to speak to the President, and for the President. From no other location will the office be able so effectively to bring the consumer's interests to bear on national policy decisions than from within the Executive Office. From no other location will the Office be able so effectively to help establish priorities or serve as the central coordinator for all Federal activities in the consumer protection field and resolve conflicts. In short, creation of a statutory Office of Consumer Affairs within the Executive Office will give that office maximum prestige, visibility, and effectiveness.

Disseminating Generic Information

In addition to its coordination function under the administration bill, another important function of the office would be the development of programs for disseminating generic information concerning consumer items which the Government purchases for its own use. It would carry on further studies as to how the skill and knowledge of Government purchasers can be shared with the public in a fair and useful manner. This is another historic step taken by the administration in making this generic information accumulated by the Government available to consumers.

The office would also have the function of conducting investigations, hearings, conferences and surveys anywhere in the United States concerning the needs, interests and problems of consumers. This would enable the Office to gather information from a wide range of sources and to focus attention on the specific consumer problems that arise in various sections of the country. Using this information the Office would encourage and coordinate the research conducted by Federal agencies leading to improved consumer products, services and consumer information.

Full protection of the consumer cannot be reached without the cooperation of private enterprise. Therefore, the Office of Consumer Affairs would work with and encourage the business community in its efforts to promote and protect the consumer's interests.

Consumer Register

In order to increase the amount of information readily available to consumers, the Office would encourage and coordinate the development of information of interest to consumers from Federal agencies. It would publish and distribute periodicals and other printed material which will inform consumers of matters of interest to them. There has been no central coordination in the past of the vast amount of consumer information which is available through the various Federal agencies. A new and very useful publication will be that of a Consumer Register. This will include notices of hearings, proposed and final rules and orders, and other useful information, translated from its technical form into language which is readily understandable by the layman. This information is presently included in the Federal Register, but in legal terminology which the majority of consumers do not understand. This has hampered them in their efforts to participate in the present Federal administrative process.

A necessary adjunct to consumer protection is consumer education. The administration-proposed Office of Consumer Affairs would be responsible for encouraging, initiating, coordinating, evaluation, and participating in consumer education programs and consumer counseling programs.

In order to promote increased Federal-State cooperation, the office would encourage, cooperate with, and assist State and local governments in the promotion and protection of consumer interests.

Consumer safety is an area of primary concern to the Office of Consumer Affairs. The administration bill provides that the Office would make a continuing evaluation and surveillance of consumer product safety and make recommendations to the President on needed improvements.

In the handling of consumer complaints, the Office would receive, evaluate, and transmit to the appropriate agencies complaints concerning actions or practices which may be detrimental to the consumer interest. It would cooperate with the Consumer Protection Division in the Department of Justice in carrying out its functions under the act.

Annual Report to the President

In the continuance of its close relationship to the President, the office would submit recommendations to the President on measures and priorities for improving Federal programs and all activities affecting consumers, and assist, as the White House representative, in the legislative and administrative hearing process. An annual report would be made directly to the President on ways to improve the effectiveness of consumer programs and on significant developments affecting the interests of consumers.

New Powers For Consumer Justice

Under the administration bill these many functions of the Office of Consumer Affairs would now become statutory powers established by congressional authority. As such, they are new powers giving to the Office of Consumer Affairs a much broader range than it has had in the past, so that it can truly take a leadership role in the crusade for consumer justice.

We hope Congress will act speedily and favorably on S. 3240, the Consumer Representation Act.

26

Government-Consumer Interest: Conflicts and Prospects

Richard H. Holton

The specialized professional seller meets the amateur
part-time buyer in the market place. Exposed to this imbalance and faced with a flood of products, the consumer is
disadvantaged. It may be that if there is an anti-business
attitude in the country, it might be based in part on latent
consumer dissatisfaction in the market place.

One of the paradoxes in the area of business-government relations at present is that while income per capita is at an all-time high and still rising, we are nevertheless encountering a substantial new wave of interest in consumer problems. Significant consumer legislation has recently been passed, more is under consideration, and still more may be waiting in the wings. Apparently a rising standard of living will not serve to paper over some imperfections in consumer markets which must be bothering the public in general, or at least Congress in particular.

In the public discussions of these consumer problems it seems odd that the work done by those economists and market researchers who have studied consumer demand is of such limited value in considering the issues involved or in understanding the need for improvement. Economists' studies of consumer demand have focussed primarily on consumption functions, both in the aggregate and for particular products. Market researchers have understandably concentrated on the economic and behavioral factors determining the demand for particular products, especially on those factors which are

Reprinted from *Changing Marketing Systems,* 1967 Winter Conference Proceedings of the American Marketing Association, Series no. 26, pp. 15-17. Reprinted by permission.

relevant for decisions by the marketing manager. By and large, it is only because of an accidental by-product here and there that this work has shed any light on the public policy issues in the discussion of consumer legislation.

I would submit that our understanding of the issues involved and our ability to anticipate new problem areas on the consumer front are enhanced if we look on the problem as being primarily a matter of imperfections in the state of information in consumer markets, and of costs of improving on the state of information. These imperfections in information vary greatly among individual consumers, and (for any individual consumer) there is great variation among the many kinds of goods and services on the market. Thus in this case as in others, it is a mistake to talk about "the" consumer or "the" purchasing decision in any generalized way.

In one model of consumer markets, we can assume consumers have full and perfect knowledge of all the alternative means of disposing of their income, including saving it. With that assumption of full and perfect knowledge, consumer expenditures (to drop any concern about savings for the moment) would be allocated among the available goods and services in some particular way. If we drop the assumption of perfect knowledge, the consumer must then spend some time and effort if not money in improving his state of information about the prices and characteristics of the alternative goods and services available on the market. We can assume that if, in this case with imperfect state of information, the consumer spends his money in a different pattern than he would if information were complete and perfect, in a sense his welfare is still maximized. It is maximized because he must have made the decision to buy the things he did rather than to seek out more information. It was his judgment, then, that the marginal cost of additional search would have been greater than the increase in satisfaction deriving from a more informed allocation of his expenditures among the available goods and services.[1]

The pattern of discussion of consumer issues these days seems to suggest that the consumer feels that the market for consumer goods. insofar as he individually is concerned, is imperfect if he buys goods and services which he would not have bought had he "known better," i.e., if the state of information had been better. Consumers no doubt recognize that they cannot be expert buyers of everything, so they do not expect to have full and perfect information. But can we not say that consumers are probably most unhappy in those instances where there is the grossest distortion of their buying behavior because of incomplete and imperfect information?

The consumer's information about the prices and quality of the alternative goods and services he might buy comes from at least the following sources: 1) his own experience, 2) word-of-mouth from friends and acquaintences, 3) advertisements, 4) retail clerks, 5) labels and other point of purchase sources, 6) consumer publications such as *Consumer Reports,* and 7) formal classes in school, especially high school home economics courses, and 8) certain government publications. Each of these sources is inadequate in one respect or another and we need not take time to inventory these. I would like to focus particularly, however, on one's own experience with a product or class of products as a means of providing information for the purchasing decision.

Typically the individual who is interested in fending off any additional consumer legislation argues that the consumer is protected quite adequately already by competition itself. If consumers find the product of any particular seller unsatisfactory, that seller cannot survive in the market place. As we all know, the rhetoric on this matter is often very colorful indeed. Rarely is it pointed out, however, that the kind of competitive system referred to assumes that consumers learn rather quickly which brands or which firms they prefer. In fact, however, much depends on the rapidity of this learning process.

To be more specific, the consumer may have gained quite satisfactory information from his own experience in the case of those items which he buys frequently, whose quality and performance characteristics are apparent either before he buys or after he has used the item once, and which exhibit a rate of technological change which is slow relative to the frequency of purchase.[2] Several of the items normally found in the supermarket might meet all three conditions for a particular consumer. But at the other end of the spectrum are a substantial number of goods and services which fail to meet one or more of these criteria. Automobile tires are a clear case in point. Here the frequency of purchase is low, the quality is not apparent (at least not in any very satisfactory way) even after the tire has been used and discarded, and the rate of technological change is fast relative to the frequency of purchase. But other items of this sort could be cited: automobiles themselves, appliances, some clothing items, casualty insurance, life insurance, medical care, appliance and automobile repair, and home maintenance services all come to mind. Funeral services can also be mentioned as an especially interesting case; I leave it to your own imagination to determine whether we can say that the quality of the service is apparent either before or after purchase and whether the rate of technological change is slow or fast relative to frequency of purchase. I trust we can all agree, however, that the frequency of purchase for the individual consumer is low.

In those cases where the three conditions are met, the process of learning can be rapid and quite complete. When the conditions are not met, the learning process may never be "complete" in any very satisfactory sense. The rate of technological change can so alter the body of information to be acquired by the prospective buyer that past information already learned will be obsolete.

The rebuttal to the above line of reasoning is in part that the consumer has access to the other sources of information as a means of improving the buying decision; he does not have to rely exclusively on his own experience with the item in question. If the consumer engages in sufficient search and research, he can acquire the information needed to make a wise choice in the market.

One of the problems is, however, that the consumer typically buys such a large number of individual items over the course of a year, let us say, that he simply does not have time to become an expert buyer of everything. He faces an allocation problem, namely in the allocation of his own time. He must decide how to divide his time between the buying search and the many other ways in which he might spend his time. Within the time he allots for buying search, he must decide how to allocate time among the alternative goods and services. He might be able to become an expert consumer of a few thing, but for many goods and services he will be quite amateurish, and understandably so.

The seller, meanwhile, is usually much more a specialist, either in one product or more commonly in a relatively narrow range of products. Furthermore, the seller's volume of any one line is likely to be great enough to support some time and talent devoted to shaping the consumer's choice. This leads to a kind of imbalance, so to speak, in the market for consumer goods: the part-time, amateur buyer faces a full-time, professional seller. This is a slightly exaggerated way to put it, but the image is reasonably accurate. It is little wonder, then, that the consumer often feels that he is at something of a disadvantage in dealing with the seller.

The low income consumer is often in a particularly weak position in the market place; for him, the imperfection of the sort we are concerned with here is likely to be especially great.[3] Because of his low income, the rate at which he is exposed to particular purchasing decisions is corresponding low, so the learning process would be slower because of this fact alone. But in addition, he is less well educated and therefore less well equipped to seek out information in the first place or to understand it well if he were to find it. If he lives in a Watts, he may find that the retailers to which he has easy access geographically do not include those with the lowest prices. This lack of information, coupled with either a reluctance or an inability to articulate his questions about a product, makes him easy prey to the expert door-to-door salesman. Perhaps the brand loyalty of low income people, and their preference for major brands, reflect the lack of information and/or an ability to cope with that information. The major brand label is in effect a proxy for information.

If we see the so-called "consumer problem" as being especially difficult in those instances where frequency of purchase is low, performance characteristics are not apparent, and technological change is rapid, and if we recognize that the consumer must allocate his time in the search process, I would submit that we can understand a bit better a number of the developments in consumer affairs over the past few years. Tire standards have been developed; all three conditions permitting rapid and satisfactory learning by the consumer have been absent in the tire market without the standards. Truth-in-packaging was a matter of concern perhaps not because the supermarket items most affected were not high frequency items, with characteristics apparent and subject to slow technological change but rather because the consumer needed help in coping with the volume of information available to him in the supermarket. With several thousand items on the shelves in the modern supermarket, there is obviously a huge amount of information available on the labels. Those opposing truth-in-packaging as unnecessary because the consumer already was being provided with ample information missed this essential point. And those people pressing for truth-in-packaging on the grounds that the consumer needed more information likewise missed the point. Given the consumer's problem of allocating his time, what was needed was not so much more information as such but more information presented in a manner facilitating price and quality comparisons. The same statement might apply to the truth-in-lending debate.[4]

Automobile insurance and even life insurance is now coming in for considerable attention on the consumer front. Again, the learning process for the individual consumer is rather slow for reasons which are fairly apparent. Medical care and pharmaceuticals have also been drawing criticism. Jessica Mitford's book on the high cost of dying brought to light the imperfections in the market for funeral services. Recently, too, the ICC has investigated the movers of household goods: here again the individual consumer learns very slowly, largely because of low frequency of purchase of this particular service. The news releases of the Federal Trade Commission give ample testimony to the problems encountered in home maintenance markets; firms specializing in aluminum siding and aluminum storm doors and the like seem to appear with distressing frequency on the FTC docket—again, a low frequency purchase.

One possible explanation of the increased interest in consumer affairs might be that the problem of consumer information is probably getting worse rather than better over time, largely because the American consumer is increasingly well off. His rising income may mean that he can afford the luxury of not shopping carefully.[5] If this is so, the nature of competitive discipline in the market place might be shifting to emphasize expertise in advertising and merchandising, since people might now be less inclined to make careful price and quality comparisons. This shift is only conjectural, but it would seem to have a certain logic. One hears that the rate of technological change is increasing: if so, the consumer's knowledge once acquired becomes obsolete more quickly than in the past. Furthermore, an increasing portion of the technological change in consumer goods may be below the threshold of perception. Thus the consumer increasingly must rely not on his own perception of performance, but on what others, notably the advertisers, tell him about the performance of the item. If there is anything to this notion, we should reconsider the common complaint about automobiles and consumer durables in general, namely that "they don't make 'em the way they usta." Maybe that should be turned around to say that consumers don't buy the way they used to; when incomes were lower perhaps the price and quality shopping was more carefully done and perhaps the quality of the product was more apparent to the consumer at the time of purchase because the product was technologically simpler.

The business community is well advised to give more attention to the question of consumer discontent. We have no accurate measure of the extent and nature of consumer dissatisfaction. The number of complaints which consumers register with retailers and manufacturers is low as a percentage of total retail transactions. But how much do we all grumble about one kind of purchase or another without registering a complaint? This consumer grumbling may be the seedbed of discontent which brings forth an enthusiastic reception for the writings of a Vance Packard or a Ralph Nader, regardless of the validity of the points such authors make. We might well reflect further on the proposition that if there is an anti-business attitude in the country, it might be based in substantial part on latent consumer dissatisfaction in the market place.

REFERENCES

1. See George J. Stigler, "The Economics of Information," *Journal of Political Economy,* LXIX (June, 1961), pp. 213-225.

2. See Joe S. Bain, *Industrial Organization,* (New York: John Wiley & Sons, Inc., 1959), p. 214, for comments on the role of consumer information in product differentiation.

3. See David Caplovitz, *The Poor Pay More: Consumer Practices of Low Income Families,* (New York: Free Press of Glencoe, 1963).

4. For a fuller discussion of the conflicting views of consumer markets, see Raymond A. Bauer and Stephen A. Greyser, "The Dialogue that Never Happens," *Harvard Business Review,* (November-December, 1967), p. 2 ff.

5. My colleague, Louis P. Bucklin, reports in a recent working paper, however, that well-to-do housewives are likely to visit more, rather than fewer, food stores than housewives from the lower income groups. This finding might or might not be inconsistent with the hypothesis that over time consumers have come to be less careful shoppers.

27

The Federal Trade Commission and the Regulation of Advertising in the Consumer Interest

Dorothy Cohen

Behavioral science research has uncovered various facets of consumer behavior that have significance in setting standards for protection from advertising abuse. This article suggests that the Federal Trade Commission take note of the behavioral characteristics of the consumer and amend its regulatory framework accordingly.

It is the purpose of this article to review the present means by which the Federal Trade Commission regulates advertising for the protection of the consumer, as well as the adequacy of the criteria which underlie the regulatory process. Further, it is suggested that additional measures be taken that would increase the effectiveness of the advertising regulatory process.

In implementing its responsibility to regulate advertising for the protection of consumers, the Federal Trade Commission has developed informal decision criteria. In broad terms, the Commission's judgments have been consistent with an "economic man" concept of consumer purchase behavior. It views the consumer as an informed,

Reprinted from *Journal of Marketing,* vol. 33 (January 1969), pp. 40-44. Reprinted by permission.

reasoning decision maker using objective values to maximize utilities. This is essentially a normative concept.

The basic assumptions of the Commission's regulatory design or criteria are maximization of the consumer's utilities and rational choice. A necessary ingredient to fulfill these assumptions is full, accurate information. The Commission, therefore, protects the consumer by identifying and attacking information which is insufficient, false, or misleading. These deficiencies are uncovered by relating the objective characteristics of a product, as determined by the Commission, to its advertising representations.

The Commission, therefore, operates under the legally and economically acceptable premise that the consumer is to be assured full and accurate information which will permit him to make a reasoned choice in the marketplace. Nonetheless, examination of the results of the Commission's activities utilizing this concept reveals the existence of several gaps in its protection. For example, the poor are not always protected from excessive payments because of lack of information about true cost or true price. The health and safety of the consumer are not always assured, since information concerning the hazards of using particular products is not always available. The belief that added protection is needed was reinforced by a report of the Consumer Advisory Council to President Johnson which states "that although this is an era of abundance ... there is also much confusion and ignorance, some deception and even fraud...."[1]

The need for added protection does not necessarily suggest discarding the Commission's regulatory framework, because a more effective structure currently does not exist. The elimination of the present regulatory design would in fact create a void in the consumer protection network. It does suggest, however, that steps should be taken as a basis for stronger protection in the future. The current movement to improve regulation through stressing full disclosure, while serving to eliminate some deficiencies, is not sufficient.[2] The Consumer Advisory Council's report, for example, in summarizing the outlook for the future, observes:

> Technological change is so rapid that the consumer who bothers to learn about a commodity or a service soon finds his knowledge obsolete. In addition, many improvements in quality and performance are below the threshold of perception, and imaginative marketing often makes rational choice even more of a problem.[3]

Full disclosure of pertinent facts is one step in improving the protection network. Additional steps are needed to assure that the consumer understands the significance of the facts. It has been noted, for example, that the consumer is selective in his acceptance of information offered. This selectivity is due, in part, to a difference between the objective environment in which the consumer "really" lives and the subjective environment he perceives and responds to.[4] The consumer reacts to information not only with his intelligence, but also with habits, traits, attitudes, and feelings. In addition, his decisions are influenced significantly by opinion leaders, reference groups, and so on. There are predispositions at work within the individual that determine what he is exposed to, what he perceives, what he remembers, and the effect of the communication upon him.[5]

It has been noted that appeal to fear (emphasizing the hazards of smoking or of borrowing money) may not deter the chronically anxious consumer, nor will it necessarily protect his health or pocketbook. Valid communications from a non-authoritative source may not be believed, whereas questionable communications from an authoritative source may be readily accepted. Thus, the extensive use of "sufficient" truth may take on an aura of non-believability and be rejected. Attempts to avoid conflicting evidence may result in ignoring the information completely.

The Commission's efforts to provide the consumer with economic information concerning value are not completely effective, since the consumer does not measure value in economic terms alone. Brand loyalties create values in the eyes of the consumer as does the influence of social groups and opinion leaders within these groups. His desire to attain certain levels of aspiration may lead the consumer to be a "satisficing animal . . . rather than a maximizing animal,"[6] that is, one who chooses among values that may be currently suitable, rather than those which maximize utilities. In order for the Commission to improve the consumer protection network, it must reflect an understanding of the behavioral traits of consumers.

Adapting the regulatory design to handle behavioral traits is no easy task. An examination of a behavioral model of consumer performance reveals the existence of many intervening variables, so that the creation of standards for this non-standardized consumer becomes exceedingly difficult. Moreover, current knowledge of the consumer as a behavioralist is far from complete. Indeed, the feasibility and success associated with the practical uses of this model are dependent upon future research.

It is, therefore, recommended that attention be directed toward current and future research in the behavioral sciences to devise means for amending the advertising regulatory framework. This would lead to improvements in the communication process and the elimination of protection gaps. The application of behavioral characteristics to the regulatory model is not intended as a panacea, but is a suggestion for improving some regulatory ailments. In broad policy terms the Commission can initially do little more than establish closer contact with the consumer and analyze behavioral data which may be relevant to the regulation of advertising. Suggestions for improved administrative procedures are limited to applications of current behavioral knowledge of the consumer. Future research may suggest more precise administrative action, for increased knowledge of the consumer's buying behavior should lead to the development of more effective mechanisms for his protection.

RECOMMENDATIONS

The following specific recommendations are suggested as guidelines for future governmental activities relative to consumer advertising.

Bureau of Behavioral Studies

A Bureau of Behavioral Studies should be established within the Federal Trade Commission (similar to the Commission's Bureau of Economics) whose function would be to gather and analyze data on consumer buying behavior relevant to the regulation of advertising in the consumer interest.

Consumer Complaint Offices

The Federal Trade Commission should establish "consumer complaint" offices throughout the United States. One method of gathering more information about the consumer is to provide closer contact between the Federal Trade Commission and the public. Complaints about advertising abuses may originate with consumers, but these have been at a minimum; and lately the Commission has accentuated its industry-wide approach to deceptive practices. Although the industry-wide approach is geared toward prevention and permits the FTC to deal with broad areas of deception, it minimizes the possibility of consumer contact with the Commission. In 1967, awareness of this fact resulted in an action in which the Commission's Bureau of Field Operations and its 11 field offices located in cities across the United States intensified its program of public education designed to give businessmen and consumers a better understanding of the work of the agency.[7]

If the Commission is to operate satisfactorily in the consumer interest, it must develop a closer relationship with consumers. Most consumers are still uncertain about the protection they are receiving, and the Federal Trade Commission appears to be an unapproachable body with little apparent contact with the "man-on-the-street."

Consumer complaint offices would identify the Federal Trade commission's interest in the consumer and act as a clearing house for information. Consumers could be informed about steps to take if they believe they have been deceived, what recourse is open, and how to secure redress for grievances. The Commission could secure evidence about deception direct from consumers. Moreover, the complaints of these private individuals might be based on noneconomic factors, permitting clearer delineation of the behavioral man and the ways in which he might be protected.

Priority of Protection

The Federal Trade Commission should establish a definitive policy of priority of protection based on the severity of the consequences of the advertising. While appropriations and manpower for the Federal Trade Commission have increased in recent years, they are still far from adequate to police all advertising. Therefore, the ability to protect is limited and selective. In its recent annual report the Commission did indicate, however, that it had established priorities:

> A high priority is accorded those matters which relate to the basic necessities of life, and to situations in which the impact of false and misleading advertising, or other unfair and deceptive practices, falls with cruelest impact upon those least able to survive the consequences—the elderly and the poor.[8]

Nevertheless, in the same year the Commission reported that approximately 20% of the funds devoted to curtailing deceptive practices were expended on textile and fur enforcement (noting that the Bureau of Textiles and Furs made 12,679 inspections on the manufacturing, wholesaling, and retailing level).[9]

Priority may be established in two ways. First, it may be considered relative to the harmful consequences of deceptive advertising. This approach could suggest, for example, that the Federal Trade Commission devote more of its energies to examining conflicting claims in cigarette advertising than to examining conflicting claims in analgesic advertising (which seems to focus on the question of whether one pain reliever acts faster than the other). Exercising such priorities might accelerate the movement toward needed reforms (such as the current safety reforms in the automobile industry) by pinpointing the existence of inadequately protected consumer areas.

A second method of establishing priority could be to delineate the groups that are most susceptible to questionable advertising. This is where the behavioral model may play an important role. Sociologists are trying to discover common aspects of group behavior, and research has disclosed that each social class has its own language pattern.[10] Special meanings and symbols accentuate the differences between groups and increase social distance from outsiders.[11]

Disclosure of special facets of group behavior should be helpful to the Commission in designing a program of protection. As noted earlier, the poor cannot be adequately protected by the disclosure of true interest rates because their aspirations may provide a stronger motivating influence than the fear of excessive debt. Knowledge of the actual cost of borrowing would offer no protection to the low-income family which knows no sources of goods and credit available to it other than costly ones. Nor would higher cost of borrowing deter the consumer who, concerned mostly with the amount of the monthly payment, may look at credit as a means of achieving his goals. In fact, the Federal Trade Commission concluded, in a recent economic report on installment sales and credit practices in the District of Columbia, that truth-in-lending, although needed, is not sufficient to solve the problem of excessive use of installment credit for those consumers who are considered poor credit risks and are unsophisticated buyers.[12]

The problems of the poor extend beyond the possible costs of credit. They include the hazards of repossession, the prices paid for items in addition to credit costs, and the possibility of assuming long-term debt under a contractual obligation not clear at the outset. It is possible that behavioral studies may disclose a communication system that would be a more effective deterrent to the misuse of credit than the disclosure of exorbitant interest rates. Until then, the Commission should give priority to investigations where the possibility of fraudulent claims, representations, and pricing accompany the the offering of credit facilities to low-income groups. For example, advertisements of "three complete rooms of furniture for $199.00, easy payments" continue to appear despite the Commission's ruling that "bait and switch" tactics are unfair. Thus, the possibility exists that the low-income consumer may be "switched" to a much more expensive purchase whose costs become abnormally high due to the exorbitant interest rates included in the "easy payments." In its monitoring and review of advertising the Commission's staff should give precedence to investigations of such "bargain, easy payments" advertising, since much of it is especially designed to attract the low-income groups.

Improvement of the Communication Process

The consumer's cognitive capacity (the attitudes, perceptions, or beliefs about one's environment) and its effect on the communication process should be reflected in designing advertising controls so that the inefficient mechanisms can be improved or eliminated.

Currently the concept of full disclosure is being expanded as the major means of offering the consumer additional protection. This is particularly evident where the objective is to dissuade the consumer from the use of or excessive use of a product or service. Little attention is paid, however, to determining whether the selective consumer is taking note of these disclosures.

An examination of behavioral man reveals that he is less "perfect" than economic man. His values are not based on objective realities alone, nor are his choices always what may be objectively considered as best among alternatives. In legislative design the regulatory authorities should come to grips with the question of whether protection of the consumer includes "protection from himself." There are indications that the latter concept is considered a legitimate area for regulatory activities—as evidenced in legislation affecting cigarette advertising and in some elements of the truth-in-lending and truth-in-packaging bills.

While questions may be raised about the legitimacy of interfering with the consumer's "freedom of choice," there is evidence that the methodology devised for this interference is deficient. In the current regulatory design, the proposed method of securing these different kinds of protection is the same, although the kinds of protection offered to the consumer may differ. For example, the consumer is currently protected against deceptive advertising by laws requiring that he be provided with truthful disclosure as to the product and its features. Where authorities believe that the advertising claims of certain products or services should be minimally used or completely avoided, the consumer is again protected by non-deceptive "full disclosure" as to the product and its features. Yet a quick review of consumer behavior and persuasibility reveals that a strategy designed to change or dissuade must, of necessity, differ from a strategy designed to reinforce. The consumer may be quite willing to accept information which supports his beliefs or preconceptions and yet be unwilling to accept evidence which refutes these same beliefs. Moreover, research has disclosed that adherence to recommended behavior is inversely related to the intensity of fear arousal. Intense fear appeal may be ineffective since it arouses anxiety with the subject which can be reduced by his hostility toward the communication and rejection of the message. It has also been noted that the tendency toward dissonance reduction can lead to failure to understand the information disclosed. Thus "full disclosure" cannot be a completely effective control mechanism when its main purpose is to protect the consumer from using a particular product or service, for the consumer may simply ignore these disclosures.

Based on current research, one approach the Commission might take toward an improved program of dissuasion would be to reinforce the negative information through an authoritative source, such as the Commission itself. Although the agency has a number of publications—*Annual Report, News Summary, Advertising Alert*—none of these is specifically geared to provide the consumer with information. A monthly report to consumers, initially available at "consumer complaint" offices, might serve as an effective mechanism for denoting the existence of hazardous products, excessive claims, questionable representations, and so forth. Specifically, this report could detail information of particular interest to consumers concerning advertising abuses that had been curtailed, cease and desist orders, questionable advertising practices currently under investigation, and so on. It is also suggested that this printed publication occasionally be supplemented by reports through a more pervasive medium—television.

It is not recommended that the Commission become a product-testing service, since the latter implies governmental control over competitive offerings and could place excessive restrictions on freedom of choice. Instead the report is to be considered a communication device, designed to insure that consumers take more note of available information on the premise that the information emanates from an authoritative governmental source.

Behavioral Criteria

The Federal Trade Commission should use behavioral as well as economic criteria in evaluating consumer interest. Subjective as well as objective claims should be examined in determining whether a "tendency to deceive" exists. Due to insufficient knowledge of consumer behavior, an accurate blueprint for defining products in terms of consumer choice is not available. Future research may present more precise propositions about consumer behavior which would facilitate the development and implementation of behavioral criteria. However, currently there are areas wherein the adaptation of behavioral factors in establishing criteria for advertising regulation may provide for more adequate protection in the consumer interest.

Assuming it were possible to provide the consumer with complete information based on economic criteria, the individual may still be unable to exercise informed choice. A recent report by the National Commission on Food Marketing stated: "Given complete price information, the help of computers and all the clerical help needed, it is impossible to say which retailer in a particular community has lower prices."[13] Moreover, as noted earlier, individuals do not choose on the basis of price appeal alone.

Advertising today, to a great extent, stresses noneconomic or promotional differences. Products are denoted as being preferred by groups, individuals, society, motion picture stars, sports leaders, and the average man. Since consumers may make their selections on the basis of these promotional representations, adequate protection requires that advertisements be subject to as close an examination for deceptive representation as they are for deceptive price claims.

Insufficient emphasis has been placed in the advertising regulatory design on the importance of testimonials in influencing consumer choice. In the examination of the selective consumer it has been noted that his choice is influenced by a desire for group membership and by the opinion of leaders within these groups. It has also been noted that the consumer engages in selective exposure and selective perception, suggesting that when the consumer finally does accept an "opinion leader," the latter exerts significant pressure on the consumer's choice.

The use of testimonials in advertising takes account of this fact of consumer behavior, but the regulatory design does not. Those who are deemed to be opinion leaders and dominant members of groups are selected and paid for their "testimonials." Moreover, where the selected figure does not perform well, for example, on television, an actor is used to replace him. The consumer may be deceived into believing an "opinion leader" is evaluating a product or service. These opinions may be used by the consumer to substantiate the suitability of this particular item in his own value structure.

Currently, the basic legal requirement is that testimonials be truthful. However, if someone declares that he prefers "Brand X," validation of this statement is necessarily subjective. Adequate consumer protection requires more stringent regulations which should extend into evidence of truthfulness of this testimonial and disclosure as to the way in which it was secured. It is suggested that in using a testimonial no substitute attestors be allowed; and if payment has been made for the endorsement, the advertisement should so state. If evidence is available that the individual does not use the product (such as a cigar recommendation by a non-cigar smoker), his testimonial should not be permitted.

SUMMARY

In its efforts to protect the consumer against advertising abuse, the Federal Trade Commission has developed a protective network in the consumer interest primarily based on economic standards. There are gaps in this protection network, which result from the fact that the consumer does not appraise his interest solely in economic terms. Rather, the consumer develops patterns of buying behavior that reflect the influence of non-economic values and the individual's cognitive capacity. The Federal Trade Commission should take cognizance of this "behavioral" man in its consumer interest activities.

It is recommended that the Commission become more familiar with and establish closer contact with the consumer through a Bureau of Behavioral Research, consumer complaint offices, and through the distribution of consumer publications to disclose advertising irregularities. In addition, it is recommended that the Commission adapt regulatory criteria to current knowledge of the behavioral man in order to assure that federal regulation of advertising is accurately functioning in the consumer interest.

REFERENCES

1. *Consumer Issues '66,* A Report Prepared by the Consumer Advisory Council (Washington, D.C.: U.S. Government Printing Office, 1966), p. 1.
2. See The J. B. Williams Co., Inc. and Parkson Advertising Agency, Inc. v. F.T.C., 5 *Trade Regulation Reporter #72,182* (Chicago, Ill.: Commerce Clearing House, Inc., August, 1967); and several aspects of truth-packaging and truth-in-lending legislation.
3. Same reference as footnote 1, at p. 6.
4. Herbert A. Simon, "Economics and Psychology," in *Psychology: A Study of a Science,* Simon Koch, editor, vol. 6 (New York: McGraw-Hill Book Co., Inc., 1963), p. 710.
5. Joseph T. Klapper, "The Social Effects of Mass Communication," in *The Source of Human Communication,* Wilbur Schramm, editor (New York: Basic Books, Inc., 1963), p. 67.
6. Same reference as footnote 4, at p. 716.
7. Federal Trade Commission, *Annual Report,* 1967, p. 67.

8. Same reference as footnote 7, at p. 17.

9. Same reference as footnote 7, at pp. 30 and 81.

10. Leonard Schatzman and Anselm Strauss, "Social Class and Modes of Communication," *American Journal of Sociology,* vol. 60 (January, 1955), pp. 329-338.

11. Tamotsu Shibutani, "Reference Groups as Perspecitves," *American Journal of Sociology,* vol. 60 (May, 1955), p. 567.

12. *Trade Regulation Reporter* #50,205 (Chicago, Ill.: Commerce Clearing House, Inc., July, 1968).

13. *Organization and Competition in Food Retailing, Technical Study No. 7,* a report prepared by the National Commission on Food Marketing (Washington, D.C.: U.S. Government Printing Office, 1966), p. 169.

Part Four

Business and the Consumer

In Part Four, business and consumerism is examined, with contributions by practitioners, academicians, and bureaucrats. The first section presents consumerism as a challenge to the business community, especially to the marketer. In the second section, the focus is on how business responds to consumerism. Self-regulation by industry is examined in the following section. The concluding section of Part Four recommends various courses of action to bridge the multifaceted gap among government, business, and consumers regarding the protection and advancement of consumer interests.

Peter Drucker sets the stage in the opening section: he begins his address with the blunt statement that the very existence of consumerism is a mark of the failure of the total marketing concept—the failure to anticipate consumer desires. Drucker concludes that the consumer movement actually is an opportunity for marketing and pleads with marketers to regard both consumerism and government not as enemies but as resources. David L. Rados focuses on the "right to (product) safety" in the second selection, indicating the changes that have occurred in product liability law and their implications for business. Rados notes how governments at all levels have responded to consumerism with laws that in-

creasingly say "Let the seller beware!" (*caveat venditor*). In the
third contribution, Hans B. Thorelli reports on Sweden's voluntary
informative-labeling system and shows what can be learned from
the Swedish experience. Thorelli observes that ample opportunities
exist for coordinating the elements of a consumer information
system without tight central control.

The second section begins with a special report by *Business
Week* that points to functional and dysfunctional reactions of the
business community to various phases of consumerism, notably
major consumer protection legislation. The report notes that it is
time for business to face up to the reality of consumerism. The
second selection, "The Dialogue That Never Happens," by Raymond A. Bauer and Stephen A. Greyser, examines the nature,
assumptions, and conflicts of the dialogue between businessmen—
especially marketers—and their critics. The authors confront the
question: Can business and government leaders resolve the problem
of talking past one another instead of to one another? Their
analysis helps explain the conflicting views expressed by government and business spokesmen in other articles in this and previous
sections. The third selection explores various consumer proposals
which are bringing about changes in the business community. The
selection sums up recent changes in the corporate response to
consumerism. As such, it shows that business is beginning to face
up to the reality of consumerism.

Self-regulation by industry is treated in the two articles which
comprise the third section of Part Four. Donald F. Turner,
Assistant Attorney General in charge of the Antitrust Division,
United States Department of Justice, comments on the shortcomings of private joint action as a device for protecting consumers. In the second article, Professor Louis L. Stern discusses the
limitations of government and business in consumer protection
efforts and raises the question of whether self-regulation can or
should deal with social issues.

Selections which conclude Part Four include contributions by
President Nixon, the American Bar Association Commission to
Study the Federal Trade Commission, the Chamber of Commerce
of the United States, Professor E. T. Grether, and Professor
Frederick D. Sturdivant.

In the first selection, a Message from the President of the
United States, President Nixon proposes new legislation—a
"Buyer's Bill of Rights"—to assure that the consumer receives
"what he is, in every way, fully entitled to." The American Bar

Association, in the second selection, recommends new initiatives to make the Federal Trade Commission a more effective enforcement agency. Next, the Chamber of Commerce of the United States suggests a combination of positive business-government actions to meet today's consumerism issues.

Professor Grether focuses on the changing consumer-seller relationship in the fourth selection. Grether discusses the implications of an emerging *caveat venditor* and proposes courses of action for firms and government bodies to take in order to maintain viable competition free from the extremes of *caveat emptor* and *caveat venditor.* In the last selection Frederick Sturdivant directs himself toward the problems faced by the ghetto shopper and offers a program for remedial action.

PART FOUR, CONTENTS

28

Consumerism: the Opportunity of Marketing

Peter Drucker

The author begins with the blunt assertion that the very existence of consumerism is a mark of the failure of the total marketing concept—the failure to anticipate consumer desires. He concludes that the consumer movement actually is an opportunity for marketing, and he pleads with marketers to regard both consumerism and government not as enemies but as resources.

We have asked ourselves where in the marketing concept consumerism fits or belongs. I have come to conclusion that, so far, the only way one can really define it within the total marketing concept is as the shame of the total marketing concept. It is essentially a mark of the failure of the concept.

One of your speakers has defined marketing as "looking at the world from the seller's end"—and that's one way of looking at it. And that's the way we have been practicing it. But there is another definition of marketing, which is to look at the business from the buyer's end. And that is consumerism, and we haven't practiced it. Or we would not today have it thrown up—thrust at us—as a challenge and a threat and as an attempt to limit, to penalize, to restrict economy activity.

A good many of my friends in business have been telling me over the years that consumerism is an invention of the politicians, and that there is no support for it in the marketplace. And I am willing to believe that up to a point. But I've been around

An address before the Marketing Committee of the National Association of Manufacturers, April 10, 1969. Reprinted by permission of the National Association of Manufacturers.

long enough to know that politicians don't flog dead horses—they can't afford to. They are in a much more competitive business than we are, and if there is no support for something they go elsewhere very fast. And so I am afraid that we have to accept the fact that the politicians respond to a fairly general and fairly deep feeling on the part of the public and that they have identified here an exposed, raw, throbbing nerve.

And I am told by my friends that the various legislative measures proposed by this or that advocate of consumerism are not going to help any, they are going to make things worse—and I've been around long enough to believe that.

I know that if one waits for the politician to find a solution, it is almost always the wrong one because politicians, by definition, react to the headlines. And that's always treating the symptoms and leaving the basic condition untouched. But that also means that the people whose business it is to concern themselves with a problem have simply not lived up to their opportunities and have waited for the politicians to react to "a scandal." Scandals make for very poor laws—that's been known for 3,000 years—and so one doesn't wait for them.

And so the fact that consumerism today is an issue, and a live one, and one that isn't going to go away, is in a way a very real indictment. . . .

Consumerism means that the consumer looks upon the manufacturer as somebody who is interested, but who really doesn't know what the consumer's realities are. He regards the manufacturer as somebody who has not made the effort to find out, who does not understand the world in which the consumer lives, and who expects the consumer to be able to make distinctions which the consumer is neither able nor willing to make.

How much time do you expect the housewife to have to find out?

Let me say, as an oldtimer around here, when I look at our advertising I know perfectly well why the consumer doesn't trust us. Not because we scream so much, but because we are talking about things that are meaningless to the consumer. Again and again and again I see the advertising that says, "Our clever, ingenious engineers have suspended the laws of gravity to bring you a pocket comb." Well, let me say that the housewife ain't no engineer, thank God, but she has been around for a long time and she isn't stupid. And so she says, "If it was that hard to make this gimmick, it won't work anyhow." And she is right most of the time.

It is our job to make things simple so that they fit the reality of the consumer, not the ego of our engineers. I've long ago learned that when most manufacturers say "quality," they use the engineers' definition, which is: "Something that's very hard to make and costs a lot of money." That's not quality, that's incompetence. . . .

We have not realized that the very abundance, the very multiplicity of choices creates very real problems of information and understanding for the consumer. We have not looked at our business from his, the consumer's, point of view.

The great problem today is lack of information. When you talk to the young people. you find that a great deal of their restlessness stems clearly from absence of information about the enormous, challenging, and perhaps even threatening variety of career choices available to them. When 30 or 40 years ago there were almost none. And there business has done not a *good* job, but the *only* job, compared to local government.

Yet the largest number of jobs is not in business. Business is a minority employer of educated people; it is still the largest employer of *un*educated people. Local government is the largest employer of educated people; and you try to find out any information about the jobs—*e.g.,* those that Commissioner Grant [Mrs. Bess Myerson Grant, Commissioner of Consumer Affairs for the City of New York.] has in her Consumer Affairs Department of New York City—and you will have a hard time. You can find out how to become a policeman or a fireman, but that's about all . . .

Very bluntly—and I am not saying anything some of you haven't heard me say before—we have been craven, timid in taking responsibility for our impact. Several years ago, I sat with the general counsel of one of the big automobile companies, and we went over the then-new automobile safety bill. When we were all through, he opened his bottom drawer, pulled out a folder and said. "You know, that's a bill we worked out here 12 years ago on this problem. There is nothing in the Nader bill we haven't in our bill." I said why didn't you go any further ten years ago, and he grinned and said, "You know perfectly well why not. We all immediately said we can't possibly acquaint the American public with the fact that there are automobile accidents." Yet the American public had, by 1950, caught on to that fact—or don't you think so?

In other words, when one sees an impact, one does not say, "The public is not clamoring." One does not listen to one's public relations vice president. (I'm not so sure one ever listens to him, but certainly not on this occasion.) What one says is, "If there is no clamor now, this is an opportunity."

I am concerned because I know that it isn't true that the American automotive industry didn't *do* anything about automotive safety. They did almost all the work we have on safe-driving training and on safe highways. Ford began in 1948, '49, '50 to install seat belts. When it turned out that the public didn't want them, it rapidly withdrew and dropped them. And now, 15 or 18 years later, we are the villains.

The public utility companies—I know half a dozen of them—have for 30 years been trying to get permission from their regulatory commissions to use low-sulfur, low-smoke fuels to free the air from pollution. But the commissions were concerned only with low power rates, and always said, "No, you can't charge extra for the cost of it." And now we blame the power companies.

I'm concerned because the pharmaceutical companies have for many years known that their very achievements make it impossible for the physician to know drugs anymore, and yet they haven't dared to say so, or to take the initiative in creating their own information for the physicians. Now they have a bill in California which I am afraid will become national, which lets, in effect, a group of bureaucrats and laymen determine what drugs doctors can prescribe. This is much more serious interference with the doctor-patient relationship—and with the drug companies—than any publication of a formulary ten years ago could have produced, when some of the companies had one and didn't dare bring it out because they were afraid that the physicians might criticize them. By now the younger physicians know perfectly well that they don't know pharmacology anymore; it's much too complex.

In the first place, if one sees an impact, one doesn't say there is no public clamor, nobody really wants it, we won't get paid for it. One says, "What do we have to do to make it possible to do the intelligent thing when the darn thing boomerangs?" As eventually it always does; it has never yet failed.

Impact one is responsible for. And if it means that one starts lobbying for safety legislation, no matter how unpopular this may be in the board rooms in Detroit, that's what one does. No one has ever lost anything except perhaps a few moments of unpleasantness in the club. And I think we have seldom learned this. And where we have learned it, let me say, without any exception, we have anticipated the problem, we have written whatever legislation was to be written.

It is simply not true that the politician doesn't listen to the businessman, or that the public doesn't listen to the businessman. This is simply myth. Whenever we have said. "This is a problem, we are the experts, we have thought it through, this is what needs to be done," well, we haven't gotten 100 percent always of what we sought, but we have gotten 96-1/8 percent, and that's good enough most times. But if one waits until there is a scandal and then one starts lobbying, one is automatically in poor shape.

And that brings me to the other problem—why consumerism is a weakness, why it has arisen in this form.

It is terribly hard for businessmen, terribly hard, harder than for anybody else, to understand that government is a resource. And that unless you start out this way, you are going to end up defending; and all one can do by fighting rearguard actions is to die a little more slowly. Government is a resource. Whether you like it or not, it's here. Commissioner Grant said, in so many words, "We don't know a darn thing. We are bewildered, we are lost, we need you, we want somebody who listens to our problems and we need your expertise." And just judging from what went on around the cocktail bar none of us heard her, and this is very typical.

We start out with the assumption that government won't let us. We start out with the good old German proverb which, roughly translated, says "Don't go near your prince unless he absolutely insists on it." There is something to it, but unfortunately we can't hide any more. And if one can't hide any more, then one has to become the prince's favorite courtier. There's no alternative.

Again and again, my friends and clients tell me they can't do this, they can't do that. So I get to Washington and I go to the commission or to the Congressional committee and do you know that I have never yet found a single case where the general counsel of my client and his public relations vice president were right. Not once. Nine times out of ten the commissioner down at the ICC looks at me and he says: "That problem, we have never heard of it. We have no rule on it." And I say "Well, can my client go ahead?" and the commissioner says, "Look, have you read the Organic Act?" and I say "No" (and he kind of says why haven't you, and he's quite right and I now read organic acts before I go down). Then he says: "The Organic Act says that we cannot approve anything in the commission unless it's a tested practice. So you see, as the act says, we can't approve anything in the commission unless it's a tested practice. So you see, as the act says, we can't approve something you haven't done. You go ahead and do it for five years; don't tell us—do it, find out whether the damn thing works and come back and we'll approve it." And so they did.

Above all, let me say, this is true of Congress. Our attitude toward Congress is a very peculiar one. And I am going to be nasty. We have let ourselves be infected in our attitude towards Congress by the New Deal, and nobody has the New Deal attitude towards Congress as badly as the businessman. The attitude is that the Congressman is a stupid enemy. That is also the arrogant attitude of the executive branch. And we have taken it on full measure. And it is arrogance and it is stupid.

Even if it were true, it wouldn't be intelligent to act on it because we depend on the Congressmen. But it also *isn't* true. What is true is that, in our very complex world, Congress is understaffed, is underinformed, has an impossible assignment. Compared to the 5,000 research men Mr. McNamara could call into his office with one stab on the button, the Armed Services Committee, which is the mostly highly staffed Congressional committee, has 18 people on it, and everybody thinks its highly overstaffed.

Yet, while they are expected to deal with terrifically complex work, they are dependent on a monopoly on information of the experts of the Executive Department, and they are therefore more than eager for reliable information. And yet we never go to them until we want something from them. And usually something that by that time has already been on the front page—the constituencies have been organized, the Polish-American Veterans have passed a resolution, and then we want them to say "No," and they don't understand even what it's all about. All they do know is that we never come to them unless we want them to do something that is difficult, disagreeable and dangerous for them to do. And then we wonder why we don't get very far.

Instead, it's our job to know people in Congress not from the point of view of what can they do for us, but what can we do for them? Here are public servants, not every one of them a genius but most of them probably capable of making a better and easier living elsewhere. The American elected official in Washington works very long hours as a rule—not everybody, but most of them.

What do they need from us? There are a great many things they don't understand, questions they have, things that puzzle them in our very complex world. Yet few businessmen have ever said, "I will go and make it my business not to lobby, not to spend a lot of time, but simply to ask 'What can I do for you? Is there anything I happen to know that might help you? Is there anything you might want to find out? Is there anyting you don't understand?' " Anyone who has said these things has found that if and when he needed a friend he had one. Because he had, to put it very simply, built a little brand loyalty. And I'm sure that what applies to product brand loyalty applies to all brand loyalty.

My sage and mentor in the retail business, 40 years ago, said, "There ain't no brand loyalty that two-cents-off can't overcome." And he was absolutely right. That applies, and should apply, to all brand loyalty. Still it holds until someone offers the "two-cents-off."

And so the attitude, "government won't let us," is an essential root cause of consumerism. The attitude is that government is an enemy instead of a fact, whether we like it or not, that we have no responsibility toward it—we just keep it away. Whereas the truth is that government today needs the informed public as a resource, as an input, as somebody concerned with the needs of government—not as a flatterer, but as somebody who will say, "Well, you're all wet down there."

Our trouble in the black ghetto—the retail merchant's problem—is one that in polite society one doesn't mention: pilferage runs 25 percent or more. That's a main reason why prices are high in the ghettos. This is nothing very new—we've had it for hundreds of years in all slums, black or white. If we could lick that problem, we could do something about prices in the ghettos. If we don't lick it, I assure you we won't do anything. Yet do you really think anybody has told our good Commissioner Grant that simple fact of life? I doubt it. And that's not her fault; that's our fault. It's our fault not to have been a resource.

And so the attitude of "government won't let us" is perhaps the root cause and unless we somehow manage to overcome it and say "What can we do now?" before there is trouble—to alert government to things we see, to find out what's in their minds but also for them to find out what's in our minds and our experience—we're going to have more and more trouble.

Let me try to summarize:

In this present world, we have two pulls—very strong. One is the pull of consumption. If you look at the economy these last 20 years, what has kept it going and has prevented major depressions in the developed countries has been the insatiable appetite of the consumer. Again and again and again we slid into what was, by all signs, a major recession, only to find that the consumer today has the affluence to shift a good bit of his income from savings to consumption. They have learned to do it, and by maintaining or ever increasing consumption they have prevented a recession.

Let me put it differently for those of you who are economists: For the last 20 years, the consumer in the developed countries has again and again and again changed the multiplier between investment and consumption. Not in the direction in which economic theory would expect him to go, but in which economic theory always also thought he could not go. Because the economist has always believed that consumers cannot over short periods, and will not, rapidly change the proportion of income that goes into consumption as against savings, and vice versa. This consumer pull has kept us going.

There is at the same time today a second pull, among the young people particularly, which is anticonsumer. How serious it is one sometimes doubts when one listens to, or realizes that anti-consumer folk songs would not be possible without electric guitars. I love those songs against technology played on the newest electronic devices. But still, you have those pulls.

We clearly have an interest in the consumer pull. Society also wants the desire of people for goods or services and the increasing ability to shift consumption patterns, as it wants the increasing freedom of individuals to consume comparatively little in the way of goods and much more in the way of certain services, and vice versa. The *freedom* of the consumer is the exciting marketing fact of our situation—not, as the kids think, the manipulation of the consumer.

(The kids, let me say, unfortunately listen to their elders. It isn't true that they rebel. They now listen to the people who got their Ph.D. during the depression. So what their elders think and what they report is 30 years out of date—but that's the way it goes; I don't complain. All I can say is, I'll let my children worry about the rebellion of their children. That's their problem, not mine.)

We have an interest in maintaining this freedom, and therefore, we have an interest in a strong and active consumer movement. Don't make the mistake of thinking this is an enemy. This is the most hopeful thing for us around. How do we really use it, how do we really challenge it, how do we really help it? We have to stop seeing the consumer as a threat and look upon him as an opportunity.

We have a similar dichotomy in our attitude toward government. There is that tremendous constant increase of governmental power—but there is also an increase in disenchantment with government. This is true in all age groups, but incidentally it is strongest among the young. It doesn't mean that they are for business, but they are no longer for government. It doesn't follow anymore for them that you're either for government or for business. They can also say, "a plague on both your houses." Let me say that we have an interest, therefore, in the acceptance of institutions, both government and business.

The great challenge for this generation is how to make institutions perform—not how to tear them down. And therefore our great challenge is how do we make government capable of doing its job—not how do we defend ourselves against it.

I started out by saying that the place of consumerism in the total marketing concept, if any, is the shame of marketing. Let me finish up by saying that consumerism actually should be, must be, and I hope will be, the *opportunity* of marketing. This is, let me say, what we in marketing have been waiting for. Let's not be afraid of it; let's use it. Let's say, "What can we do *with* it?" And let's also learn the lesson from it—that if we don't start; if we don't with our knowledge and our position of power, ten years earlier, live up to the level of our knowledge and our vision and of our intelligence, these things are going to be turned against us.

The question is: Can we anticipate and lead and initiate them constructively—or will we have to spend the rest of our lives fighting rearguard actions which one can never win and in which one can only lose more and more and, above all, lose more and more of the excitement of the initiative of the challenge of the work we are in—the work we think is satisfying, the work we know is and should be productive?

29

Product Liability: Tougher Ground Rules

David L. Rados

In today's sophisticated markets, the approach to product liability increasingly is not "Let the buyer beware!" but "Let the seller beware!" Consumerism has become an important political force, and governments at all levels have responded with laws that hold manufacturers more directly responsible for product deficiencies. In recent decisions the courts, too, have favored consumers to a far greater extent than they once did; the number of successful suits against manufacturers and the size of the awards have increased greatly. To protect themselves, manufacturers need to reexamine their design and production systems from a product safety point of view, check their advertising claims, and make sure their product liability insurance gives adequate coverage.

In the U.S. economy, the powerful forces of competition and consumer demand compel manufacturers to produce products with a high measure of consumer satisfaction. And, in spite of some legislation and regulation, these forces are still of first important political force. As a result, there have been numerous investigative hearings

But something new has been added. In recent years consumerism has become an important political force. As a result, there have been numerous investigative hearings

Reprinted from *Harvard Business Review,* vol. 47, no. 4 (July-August 1969), pp. 144-152. Reprinted by permission.

by national and state governments; many new consumer laws have been proposed, and several important ones already have been passed. Also, the number of product liability suits and the size of the judgments have increased greatly.

More and more the discipline of the competitive marketplace is being buttressed by the discipline of the law. And these new legal forces are particularly important in the field of product liability because, in spite of their threat of considerable expense for the unwary company, they are not well known among executives.

This article will discuss the changing law of product liability and indicate some of the ways in which management can respond. But let us start with a sketch of the climate in which consumer protection has flourished.

NEW CONSUMER CLIMATE

The new attitudes about consumer problems stem from a high level of consumer education and affluence. The consumer knows more and is able to buy more wisely, but he faces bewildering problems in evaluating products. He must judge differences of technology, function, price, and promotion on the basis of commercial as well as noncommercial information that is occasionally misleading, often irrelevant, and always imperfect. The consumer earns more and is able to buy a higher standard of living. But he is frustrated because the products he buys do not perform as he has been led to expect.

His awareness of this frustration has been heightened by the considerably publicity given to product safety and effectiveness over the past several years. There have been hearings on automobile, tire, and drug safety. Other industries have either received unfavorable publicity from a product error, like the emission of harmful X rays from TV sets, or are scheduled for investigative hearings, such as those planned for the auto insurance industry. Lengthy and well-publicized debates on consumer protection legislation have added to consumer apprehension about product safety and manu- facturers' probity.

The past several years have also seen the passage of bills on truth in lending, truth in packaging, meat inspection, and poultry inspection. Moreover, the correlation between cancer and cigarette smoking continues to receive attention and has recently been the subject of "Stop Smoking" advertising campaigns by the American Cancer Society and the American Heart Association. And the now common ritual by which auto manu- facturers call back unsafe automobiles reinforces consumer apprehension about auto safety in general. The rise in consumer expectations and the heightened concern with product safety are most clearly seen in the rise of the consumer protection movement.

Problems for the Manufacturer

The manufacturer is having his difficulties as well. The market that is supposed to influence his products is relatively inarticulate in its quality demands. The product quality offered to the consumer depends on the demand for quality, and this in turn depends on how well informed consumers are.

To make a reasoned purchase, the consumer must be able to state his needs and compare those needs with the offerings in the market. But the amount of technical knowledge alone needed to evaluate say, a color TV set is formidable. And even if he had the necessary background, the consumer would not have the test and performance data he needs. Thus the technical complexity of products has reduced the number of knowledgeable consumers and therefore has produced a less articulate demand for different levels of quality.

There are still other pressures on the manufacturer. Product complexity raises difficulties in controlling the quality of design and manufacture. There are, of course, many sophisticated quality control techniques, but offsetting pressures encourage the erosion of quality—e.g., the pressure to hold down costs.

Today's markets, moreover, are markets on the move. They must be reached quickly; competitive moves must be matched or bettered; new methods of product differentiation must be attempted. All these factors put pressure on the manufacturer to take less care than he would like. The pressure is particularly pronounced in companies with a strategy of continual product innovation because controlling quality is most difficult during the development and introduction of new products, especially when competitive tactics demand quick reactions.

TOUGHER COURTS

To appreciate the current state of the law, it is necessary to understand how a hypothetical case might have proceeded a decade ago.

In the first place, the manufacturer would not have waited to be sued. Starting at the time of sale, he would have tried to limit his legal liability, using a sales agreement containing disclaimers and narrow express warranties. For example:

The manufacturer of a power lawn mower might have given the purchaser of each of his mowers an express warranty that the machine was free of defects. This warranty would have formed a part of the sales contract and, like all contractual provisions, would have been binding on the producer.

But he would not have stopped at this point. He would first have limited his liability to replacing defective parts and then stated that this was the only warranty being offered (meaning that he would do nothing more than replace defective parts). Under such a limited warranty he would not have been required to pay for, say, injuries caused by a defective part.

But he still might have been sued. Assume a buyer had bought the mower, used it, and been injured by it. In bringing the manufacturer to court, the injured buyer— the plaintiff—could have proceeded either in contract or in tort law. In contract law he might have argued that, regardless of the express warranty, the manufacturer was bound by an implied warranty that his product was reasonably fit to mow lawns and that a mower which can cause an injury is not fit. Thus the manufacturer had broken a provision of the contract and would have to compensate the plaintiff.

The manufacturer would have replied that there was no "privity" (direct contractual relationship) between him and the plaintiff. He would have argued that the plaintiff's business was with the retailer who sold the mower, not with him; and the court would have agreed. In the absence of privity, the plaintiff could not have collected for violation of the contract. He would first have had to sue the retailer, who in turn would have sued the manufacturer.

The plaintiff might also have taken action against the manufacturer in tort (the law of personal injury), arguing that, regardless of whether there was any contract between them, the manufacturer had a duty to prospective users of his mowers to design and produce safe mowers and that he had failed to take reasonable care in fulfilling that obligation. In other words, he would have argued that the manufacturer had been negligent.

But proving negligence is often difficult. If the manufacturer could have proved, for instance, that the product had been blameless even if the product was actually unsafe. Let us suppose a piece of scrap metal in the housing of the mower had worked loose, flown out of the housing, and caused the injury. If the manufacturer could prove that his production and inspection processes were thorough and performed with care and that part of the production process in which the housing was assembled was highly mechanized, he could be held blameless. The presence of the scrap metal would be treated as an accident, for which no one was responsible.

Today, warranties, disclaimers, privity, and negligence still dominate product liability law as legal doctrines, but as defenses against adverse judgments they are much weaker.

Warranties & Disclaimers

The attempt to limit liability is less successful now than it has been in the past. As one example, claims in advertisements, sales promotion literature, labels, instructions, and oral sales presentations are likely to be held as legally binding on the manufacturer as an express warranty if the purchaser relied on the claims in making his purchase.

The value of disclaimers has also been lower since the landmark Henningsen case:

In May 1955 Claus Henningsen picked up a new Plymouth from the authorized Chrysler dealer in Bloomfield, New Jersey—Bloomfield Motors, Inc. He and his wife Helen used the car around town for several days, and then on May 19 Mrs. Henningsen drove to Asbury Park.

On the return trip, while driving along New Jersey Route 36 at approximately 20 miles per hour, she heard a loud noise "from the bottom, by the hood," and the stirring wheel spun out of her hands. The car swerved sharply to the right, into a highway sign and then into a brick wall. The car, driven only 468 miles, was a total loss. Mrs. Henningsen sustained painful but not crippling injuries.

What has caused the accident? Mrs. Henningsen had been driving in a safe manner, according to the testimony of a bus driver who had seen the accident. Was Chrysler to blame? The front end of the car was so badly damaged that experts could not say what had gone wrong. One of these experts, an insurance inspector, could only say that "something down there had to drop off or break loose." This meant that it was impossible to prove negligence on Chrysler's part.

The Henningsens sued in contract and won. Chrysler appealed, arguing that when Henningsen bought the car, he had signed a disclaimer that limited Chrysler's liability to the replacement of defective parts. The New Jersey Supreme Court was unimpressed by this argument. Such disclaimers, standard on all automobile contracts, were "a sad commentary on the automobile manufacturers' marketing practices," because customers had no chance to bargain on the point, and yet they signed away any personal injury claims that might arise because of the defects.

"It is difficult to imagine a greater burden on the consumer," the court said. Such disclaimers are so indefensible as to be "inimical to the public good" and therefore invalid as a matter of law. Chrysler could not avoid its legal obligation to make automobiles of good enough quality to serve the use for which they were intended.

The case really turned on whether the disclaimer was the *only* warranty applying. The judge ruled it was not and, in striking down the disclaimer, held that the manufacturer and dealer were obligated (under an implied warranty of merchantability) to market reasonably safe cars.[1]

Decline of Privity

Historically, as the organization of the economy became more complex and the legal ties joining producer with ultimate consumer lengthened, the absence of privity often blocked recovery by injured parties.

The first exceptions to the basic rule (that there can be no recovery in contract in the absence of privity) came in cases involving food and beverage products, then in any products intended to affect human life, such as food, drugs, firearms, and so on. In 1916 came the landmark decision:

> The plaintiff, a canny Scot named MacPherson, was injured when defective wooden spokes on a wheel of his new Buick collapsed. Buick argued that MacPherson had bought the car from a dealer, not from Buick, and therefore that Buick's obligations did not extend to him. But Buick was found to have been negligent in failing to inspect the wheel before mounting it. The judge ruled Buick was responsible for defects that could be attributed to negligence, regardless of how many middlemen and dealers stood between Buick and the ultimate buyer, that is, regardless of the narrow confines of contract privity.[2]

The Henningsen case, 43 years later, completed the demise of the privity rule. In that case, it was impossible to prove negligence because the front end of the car was to provide the needed evidence. As in the MacPherson case, there was no privity of contract between Henningsen and Chrysler. Again the court overruled the privity argument, but this time in the absence of proof of the manufacturer's negligence.

The significance of these two decisions (and a host of supporting decisions over the years) has been to seriously weaken lack of privity as a defense against product liability suits.

Implied Negligence

Perhaps the most radical change in product liability law concerns negligence, as courts move rapidly toward adopting a new doctrine—strict liability in tort—under which an injured plaintiff can recover *whether or not the manufacturer is to blame.*

Here is an account of the landmark case:

A certain Mr. Greenman saw a Shopsmith combination power tool demonstrated in a dealer's store in California. After he had read a promotional brochure, Greenman decided he wanted the tool for his home workshop, and Mrs. Greenman dutifully gave it to him for Christmas. Two years later Greenman bought the attachments that enabled the tool to be used as a lathe. He wanted to make a chalice. After he had worked the block several times without difficulty, it suddenly flew out of the machine and struck him on the forehead, inflicting serious injury.

Somewhat tardily he hauled both the dealer and the manufacturer, Yuba Power Products, Inc., into court. Greenman and Yuba were not in privity, of course; for that matter, neither were Mrs. Greenman and Yuba. This defense was swept aside by the court. Using expert witnesses, Greenman was able to prove that the set screws used to hold the part of the tool together were inadequate, so that the normal vibration of the lathe caused the tailstock to shift away from the lathe head, allowing the block to fly out. Greenman was also able to prove that he had read the promotional brochure and relied on its claims that the product was rugged.

With this evidence the jury could decide on the basis either of negligence or of warranty. If it found Yuba had been careless in design or manufacture it could find negligence; if it held that the promotional brochure represented an express warranty, it could find breach of contract. Like all juries, this one did not reveal how it reached its decision, but it did decide to grant damages to Greenman.

Yuba appealed to the California Supreme Court, and lost again. But that court added something new. It stressed that Yuba's apparent breach of warranty and negligence were basically irrelevant to Greenman's case. Even if it had not been negligent, Yuba would still be liable. "A manufacturer is strictly liable in tort when an article he places on the market, knowing that it will be used without inspection, proves to have a defect that causes injury to a human being."[3]

The Greenman decision was quickly extended by another California Supreme Court decision, which held that a manufacturer could not escape strict liability in tort by proving its suppliers or dealers were responsible for the defect involved.[4] Moreover, the court also found the *retailer* strictly liable in tort for injuries caused by the defective product.

Since these decisions, the doctrine of strict liability in tort has been adopted by more and more states, particularly many of the influential industrial states, such as New York, New Jersey, Ohio, Michigan, and Illinois. The doctrine has also been applied to new situations, such as leasing, where one rent-a-car agency was held strictly liable in tort for an injury caused by defective brakes in one of its cars.

Onus on Manufacturer

What does strict liability in tort mean? It has two meanings, one legal, the other social and economic:

The legal meaning is simply that the burden of proving blame or fault has been removed from the plaintiff. Thus it has become far easier to recover damages from manufacturers. Although Yuba was apparently negligent in constructing the Shopsmith, the court did not concern itself with fault. It decided merely who should bear the cost of the injury. This clearly was not to be the "powerless" consumer.

A quote from the Greenman decision illustrates the social and economic meaning of strict liability: "The purpose of [strict liability in tort] is to insure that the costs of injuries resulting from defective products are borne by the manufacturers that put such products on the market rather than by the injured persons who are powerless to protect themselves."

Social conscience today is far more concerned with victims of injury than it was during the nineteenth century, when the basic rules governing product liability were formulated. Strict liability embodies a belief that the cost of accidents should be passed from the few (victims) to the many (consumers) in the form of higher prices and that the agency to accomplish this is the manufacturer. It also reflects the belief that strict liability will encourage greater care by the manufacturer and hence will yield fewer accidents.

Other Trends

The Henningsen and Greenman cases unquestionably effected a major change in product liability law. Other changes also appear to be taking place, although their significance is not easy to predict.

Loss of Value. Greenman sustained an injury. So did Henningsen and MacPherson. What happens when there is no physical injury but just a loss of value? One controversial case gives a hint:

> Mr. Daniel Santor bought a "Grade #1" Gulistan rug manufactured by A. and M. Karagheusian, Inc., a well-known rug producer. After being installed, the rug developed a strange line. Santor telephoned the dealer who assured him the line would wear away. But instead of improving as time went on, the situation became worse, and two additional lines appeared.

> Finally Santor decided to take legal action. As the retailer from whom he had bought the rug had moved out of state, Santor proceeded against the manufacturer, with whom, of course, he was not in privity. The court held that strict liability in tort would apply and granted Santor recovery for the loss of value of the rug (i.e., the difference between the rug's present value and its value were it unmarked).[5]

While other courts have reached similar conclusions, particularly in two cases involving poor performance of tractors, the application of strict liability to loss of value cases has not yet been widely adopted. In fact, the California court that ruled for Greenman does not apply strict liability in tort to such cases. Most courts have been reluctant to apply strict liability to loss of value, but some legal scholars argue there is no logical reason to allow recovery for personal injury and deny it for loss of value.

Negligent Design. One new cause for action is negligence in design. While strict liability without fault has been emphasized in this article, most product liability cases are still based on allegations of negligence; that is, the plaintiff must prove the product was defective and unreasonably dangerous when it left the manufacturer's hands. This can be difficult to establish, particularly when the product has passed through the hands of several middlemen and has a long life. But if the plaintiff can prove faulty design, at one stroke he proves that the manufacturer was negligent and that the product was unsafe when it left his hands. For this reason, design negligence suits have multiplied in recent years.

Advertising Claims. Courts have long looked on certain types of claims made in advertising and in labels as express warranties. Thus if a windshield advertised as shatterproof breaks when hit by a pebble, the injured plaintiff may recover even though he and the manufacturer are not in privity. But now the reach of advertising copy is broadening, as this recent case demonstrates:

> A car owner by the name of Inglis proved in court that he had relied on American Motors' advertising claims that his Rambler would be trouble-free, economical in operation, and manufactured with high-quality workmanship. His hopes were frustrated, however. The trunk door was out of line, could not be opened and continually squeaked and rattled; the trim around the door was torn, the doors were out of line and squeaked and rattled; the door handles were loose; the steering gear was improperly set; the oil pump was defective; the brakes squeaked and grated; the engine leaked substantial quantities of oil; and loose parts inside the car fell out from time to time.

> Unable to obtain satisfaction from his dealer, he took the case to court. The court ruled that where there was difference between the advertising claims and the product's actual performance, there was no "sound reason [why] he should not be permitted to . . . recoup his loss."[6]

Here again, there was no injury, only frustrated expectation. The difference is that the advertising copy was held to be an express warranty, that is, part of the bargain between Inglis and American Motors. Because American Motors did not live up to its end of the bargain, it had to make good the car's loss of value.

Extension of Liability. The reach of liability is extending in two new directions. We have seen how the doctrine of privity in product liability has been obliterated, enabling both purchaser and user of a defective product to recover. The Uniform Commercial Code[7] extends these protections not only to the purchaser, but to his immediate family, members of his household, and guests.

Liability is also beginning to reach beyond the manufacturer to his suppliers. Thus:

> When an American Airlines plane crashed because of an allegedly faulty altimeter, the court decided that the cause of action would be against Lockheed, the plane's manufacturer, and not the manufacturer of the altimeter.[8] But the court divided on the issue; and in a subsequent case involving a defective truck part, an Illinois court did extend strict liability in tort to component manufacturers.

So far no advertising agency has been held negligent in the preparation of copy, but such action can be reasonably expected. Even industry associations and testing laboratories, which are organizations remote from the injured consumer, may soon have to face actions. Assume, for example, that a manufacturer markets a product that conforms to standards developed by his industry's trade association. What happens if the product subsequently injures a person because the standard was insufficient? It is probable that, under the right conditions, the trade association will be held liable.

IMPACT & ACTION

We have seen that several factors have contributed to the fast-growing strength of the consumer movement during the past several years. But the solutions to consumer dissatisfaction are not developing quickly; and as the conditions that have powered the development of consumerism become even more salient, it seems likely that the pressure for more consumer protection will increase.

What is the impact of these changes in the law on business operations? What can management do to minimize the risks of being sued?

The impact of these changes will be greatest on two types of companies:

1. Those who through poor design or careless manufacture have failed to maintain minimum quality standards and consequently are placing unsafe products on the market.

2. Those who are introducing large numbers of new products.

The first is already in danger, for the reasons outlined earlier. *Caveat emptor,* "Let the buyer beware" has been replaced by *caveat venditor,* "Let the seller beware"—or, even better, "The seller must take care."

But, no matter how careful, the company developing large numbers of new products is also in a difficult position. Large firms sometimes have 50 or 100 products in various stages of development. Tight control over the safety of working models and prototypes is difficult. So is quality control of models developed for market tests. Errors in design or manufacture may not in fact show up during short tests, in which case the manufacturer must expose himself by placing thousands or millions of his product on the market before serious flaws are discovered.

Even assuming successful development and performance of test models, the manufacturer must move to pilot plant or full-scale manufacture of the product. Here, the newer the product, the more likely it will be to develop bugs. But even dealing with minor variants of present products does not ensure perfect production from the start.

Hence manufacturers who adopt growth strategies based primarily on product innovation run the biggest risks. What are these risks?

One is the risk of unfavorable publicity resulting from product liability cases or from government investigations. While General Motors will not comment on whether sales of the Corvair suffered from its well-publicized design negligence cases, many executives in the industry believe they have. Such publicity also serves notice to other plaintiffs and encourages them to press their suits.

Second, the cost of developing and introducing new products will increase. Design and pre-introduction testing must now be more thorough; advertising and labeling must be tested for clarity and comprehensiveness; and field tests must be monitored closely. These kinds of activities will increase development time and certainly will raise costs.

Third, should the product fail and cause injury there will be costs of litigation and possibly adverse judgments. Since such suits usually are surrogates for a much larger number of possible suits, most are appealed, further raising costs. And while such suits are pending, the acceptability of the product remains in question.

Finally, in the present climate it is clear that any business touched by publicity concerning poor quality of its products will be exposed to the possibility of congressional investigation and regulatory legislation.

But what can management do? That is the crucial question.

Safety Audit

The first step is to collect information—the diagnostic step.

Management should begin by identifying the products most likely to contain safety-related defects. It can review complaint letters and warranty claims, study problems that competitors have had with similar products, study its own market research about consumer experiences with its products, and review evaluations of its products by outside testing agencies. These steps will help to identify the products on which action should first be taken.

Once potentially unsafe products and lines are identified, an analysis can be made of their safety. Safety engineers should review design and manufacturing procedures to make sure quality control and testing are adequate from start to finish. Careful study should be made of possible ways in which the product can fail, with the aim of correcting serious flaws at the time of redesign. There must be clear, effective communication between the design sections and manufacturing as to acceptable tolerances, drawings, and assembly instructions.

Systems Analysis

The second, or action, step is to adopt the systems approach that has been so useful in creating safe military products.

This includes the assignment of responsibility for a safety program to a specific individual with responsibility for the safety of the design concept, production and testing procedures, and inspection. He should also be responsible for determining whether safety tests are realistic in terms of consumer use patterns.

Such programs can be expensive, so executive judgment must be exercised to ensure that the trade-offs between added costs and reduced risks of poor design and manufacture are properly made. But such programs do not yield only higher costs. Many businesses that have attempted safety and quality analyses have found they had been overlooking opportunities for low-cost improvements in their products and cheap ways of reducing costs. Thus:

> Before it offered its five-year auto warranty, Chrysler Corporation analyzed its engineering, design, and manufacturing procedures with great thoroughness. As a result, significant quality improvements were made in every manufacturing area. The results were wholly beneficial to the company, to say nothing of Chrysler's customers.

The source of a safety-related product defect may lie almost anywhere in the product cycle from initial conception to use by the user. Thus in planning the improvement of product safety the responsible executive must not overlook any areas of importance. Here are five major areas.

Product Design. Design is a fertile source of product liability cases. Not only is it difficult to control design activities under the best of conditions, but the whole area is relatively neglected to begin with. Moreover, *liability arising from poor design is a business risk which is not insurable.*

What can be done? One obvious move is to check the product against any developed safety standards, either by industry (or trade) group or by government group. The law demands that the manufacturer demonstrate his expertise by producing safe products. If his product has fewer safety features than normal in his industry, this may be used to show failure to exercise the care and skill of an expert.

It is important to anticipate potential hazards and either design them out of the product or warn the user of the hazard and how it can be avoided. This type of check as well as other safety and reliability checks could be performed by formal design review committees—something that many companies have already done. If the proposed product fails to meet their approval, these committees can call for further design checks, such as *failure mode analysis,* a procedure of systematically postulating the most likely ways in which the product can fail, with the aim of reducing or eliminating failures likely to cause injury to users. In many cases it also proves useful to keep complete records on design procedures, particularly relating to reasons for accepting one design feature and rejecting another.

Manufacturing. Well-run companies take considerable pains to ensure that their products conform to specification and the percent of defectives is held in control. The matter of product liability, therefore, should be a major concern to such companies. This concern impresses on production personnel the need to remedy situations that might lead to unsafe products. Remember also that a company can be held liable for errors of suppliers. (MacPherson was able to collect from Buick although the defective part, the wooden wheel, was purchased from an outside supplier. Buick was negligent in not carefully inspecting the purchased part.) Hence quality control and inspection are important for both purchased materials and materials fabricated in-house.

As with safety analysis, quality control analysis is not entirely a burden; it often uncovers opportunities for companies to do a better job at lower cost. And if the improvement in the product is promotable, the benefits may include a stronger market position.

Communications. Designing and producing a safe product is not enough, however. Instructions, labels, advertising copy, and even oral sales presentations must be designed and produced with equal care.

Instructions should be written in clear, simple language; sometimes it will pay to test them for clarity and comprehensibility. Labels affixed to the product itself are important in many kinds of products because original instructions get lost, particularly when the product has a long life. Informative labels, preferably securely attached to the product, with data on potential dangers and basic operating characteristics (load limitations, maximum performance limits, and so on) are useful in such situations.

Advertising and sales presentations must be screened for unwarranted claims. Most large companies already require ad copy to be screened by their legal department. Few take the same pains to ensure that the representations of their salesmen are equally restrained.

Liabilities arising from excessive claims in marketing communications are most serious in the areas of consumer packaged goods and other mass produced goods. (Henningsen recovered in part because of the inequality in bargaining power between himself and Chrysler.) On the other hand, the sale of capital equipment to presumably sophisticated buyers able to protect themselves is far less likely to be challenged because of sales claims that promise too much. It is possible, however, that even here a plaintiff may recover if he can prove that he relied on sales puffery in making his purchase and operating decisions.

Marketing Research.   Marketing executives are becoming more and more aware of the importance of actions that take place after the sale is complete. For example, more attention is being paid to why orders are cancelled and to how the consumer justifies his purchases to himself immediately following the purchase. Also, studies are being conducted to learn how consumers actually use products, in order to generate new ideas for related products and to better satisfy consumer use patterns.

This trend should be reinforced by the demands placed on the manufacturer by product liability. Particularly with a product that is potentially or inherently dangerous, the manufacturer no longer can assume that his responsibility ends with the sale. He must find out how his customers view the product and, specifically, how they are using it. And if there are potential dangers. he must take steps to prevent accidental or even careless use from causing injury.

Product Liability Insurance.   No matter how much care the manufacturer takes to produce safe products, the possibility of product liability cannot be completely eliminated. But product liability insurance can be used to cover the remaining area of risk.

Today's manufacturer usually acts as insurer not only for himself but also for the members of his distribution channels, his consumers, and perhaps even innocent bystanders. As a result, the volume of product liability insurance has increased sharply in the past ten years. While the amount being written is hard to estimate because product liability insurance is usually lumped into a general casualty policy, one estimate is that premiums for such insurance are $60 million annually and climbing fast. Some drug manufacturers are said to carry as much as $100 million of product liability insurance.

Most large companies already have coverage against liability actions, though few top executives know exactly what it covers. Fewer small companies have such insurance; but because adverse judgments could easily wipe out their entire net worth, they now are probably purchasing such insurance at a faster rate than large companies.

It is particularly important for an executive to understand what such insurance actually covers. Typically it covers injury or destruction of property arising from use of the product. Typically it does not cover:

Business risks, chiefly the failure of a product to perform its intended purpose due to poor design.

The costs of withdrawing a whole class of defective products from the market.

Injury to the product itself, its repair, and its replacement.

Defects which could have been foreseen or detected through proper checking and testing.

LET THE SELLER BEWARE

This article has indicated the changes that have occurred in product liability laws. The courts have become increasingly impressed by the need to protect consumers from defective products. Both contract and tort law have undergone rapid change in the attempt to satisfy this need. Where contract liability has proved inadequate, it has been supplemented by tort law. This blend of contract and tort law has resulted in the increasing use of strict liability in tort in product liability suits.

It has been argued that consumers should have freedom of choice in the market-place, including freedom to make the wrong choice. But consumers now have less freedom to make an unsafe choice. Consumers are increasingly to be protected from the voluntary consumption of unsafe products.

The court decisions mentioned in this article illustrate the development of new law and also make clear the message to the producer: Let the seller beware.

REFERENCES

1. Henningsen v. Bloomfield Motors, Inc., 161 A. 2d 69 (1960).
2. MacPherson v. Buick, 111 N.E. 1050 (1916).
3. Greenman v. Yuba Power Products, Inc., 377 P. 2d 897 (1963).
4. Vandermark v. Ford Motor Company, 391 P. 2d 168 (1964).
5. Santor v. A. and M. Karagheusian, Inc., 207 A. 2d 305 (1965).
6. Inglis v. American Motors Co., 209 N.E. 2d 583 (1965).
7. See Edward L. Schwartz, "Uniform Commercial Code" (Thinking Ahead) HBR September-October 1953, p. 23.
8. Goldberg v. Kollsman Instrument Corp., 191 N.E. 2d 81 (1963).

30

Consumer Information Policy in Sweden — What Can Be Learned?

Hans B. Thorelli

Almost all Western nations now have private or public consumer information programs. Sweden has a particularly rich experience in the product information area. In this article special emphasis is placed on Sweden's voluntary informative-labeling system which is relatively unknown in the United States. The author suggests that the consumer-conscious U.S. industry might well consider developing a similar consumer information system.

In several respects Sweden and the United States are remarkably similar; in others the two countries are quite different. Among the similarities are the two highest standards of living in the world, an emphasis on materialistic motives among their citizens, a considerable historical experience with consumer information programs, and a sophisticated and extensive current debate on consumerism. The differences include those of overall size, homogeneity of income, race, outlook, and behavior patterns and the nature of experience with consumer information programs. In view of these conditions of both congruence and divergence, it seems natural to ask: What can be learned from the Swedish experience?

This article reports on consumer information programs in Sweden implemented by

Reprinted from *Journal of Marketing*, vol. 35 (January 1971), pp. 50-55. Reprinted by permission.

independent bodies which have no economic interest in the sale of the market offerings about which they provide information. In the United States, the best example of such an organization is Consumers Union (CU). As this example demonstrates, the main U.S. effort in the consumer information area has been made by private organizations, although the Wool Products Labeling Act and the "Truth in . . ." laws demonstrate the force of public initiative. By contrast, the Swedish experience consists primarily of the governmental programs enumerated below.

The State Institute for Consumer Information

Tracing its roots to World War II, the State Institute for Consumer Information (Konsumentinstitutet, KI) was established in 1957 "to promote the improvement of the working efficiency in homes, both private and collective, and to encourage the production and consumption of good and practical consumer goods."[1] To accomplish these goals, the law continues, the Institute is to conduct investigations, engage in research, and disseminate information concerning technical, economic, hygienic, and other problems related to the home and housekeeping. In 1969 KI operated on a budget of approximately one million dollars. The government-appointed Board consists of representatives from economic interest groups, the state bureaucracy, and Parliament, and its staff is heavily science-and home economics-oriented.

Comparative testing is the principal KI activity. In 1968, its journal *Advice and Discovery (Rad och Ron)* reported the results of 15 major tests, ranging from vacuum cleaners to fish sticks. *(Consumer Reports* publishes 60 to 70 such tests annually.) The periodical has approximately 100,000 subscribers, comparable to the 1.8 million of *Consumer Reports* relative to total population. One half of the journal's contents relates to questions of general consumer interest other than tests.

Test results are printed with brand names and list prices. Properties considered of significance in helping the consumer to reach a purchasing decision are usually discussed by way of introduction. Unlike CU, no overall judgment of particular brands is given. Individual characteristics of the brands and models tested are listed rather than graded. (Exception: qualitative characteristics, for which scales such as good-fair-bad are almost unavoidable.) In this respect KI and CU procedures are rather similar, although different from several continental countries where each property is given a qualitative grade. Brands are, however, tabulated next to each other to facilitate comparison by readers themselves. KI states that the needs and preferences of individuals are too numerous and varied to compare two brands, each with its own set of properties, in terms which are applicable to all consumers. While individual test reports have occasionally been controversial, KI's seriousness of purpose cannot be doubted.

For various reasons, CU traditionally has been highly reserved in its relations with producers. KI feels freer in its relations with industry, does not view the producer as suspect, and is, in fact, anxious to prevail on his expertise. Both CU and KI will ask producers about the characteristics and sales of different models; KI will also consult them on test methods. However, producers do not get the opportunity to react to advance copy of KI's test reports.

Critics maintain that the Institute is not sufficiently concerned with market factors as regards the products and models selected for testing, and the criteria used in the evaluations. They also charge that its reports lack adequate publicity and do not appear in sufficiently popularized form. Yet the press in recent years has given KI reports a fair amount of coverage.

Swedish Institute for Informative Labeling

Of special interest is the Swedish Institute for Informative Labeling (Varudeklarationsnamnden, VDN), founded in 1951. VDN is a world leader in the area of general purpose informative labeling. While VDN is in principle a private organization, its amended bylaws of 1957 were confirmed by the government as well as by the VDN foster parent, the Swedish Standardization Commission.[2]

VDN's principal objectives are to promote the increased use of standardized informative labels by consumer goods producers (Fig. 1), and to increase the awareness of such labels among consumers. In addition, the Institute assists in the preparation of standardized methods of measuring performance (so-called SMMP), selects the properties to be labeled for each product, grants the right of qualified firms to use VDN labels, and insures that the licensees adhere to the performance standards stated on the label.

VDN is actually half private and half public. In 1968, industry furnished 30% to 50% of VDN's $300,000 budget mainly in the form of license and control fees. The balance of its budget is provided by standing and special-purpose government grants. The government appoints the Institute's chairman in addition to a few other Board members. The remaining Board members are comprised of representatives of consumer interests (housewives, coops, unions, home economics teachers) and producer groups (industry, trade, farmers). VDN operates like a private organization outside the public bureaucracy, although it could hardly afford to disregard the latter.

By February, 1969 VDN had completed 144 product specifications and had issued 901 licenses. This figure is larger than the cumulative accomplishments of the corresponding bodies in Great Britain, Germany, Holland, Denmark, Finland, and Norway, and in this respect the record is indeed impressive. It is quite modest, however, when related to the total number of consumer products and brands that exist in a market that is almost as highly developed as the United States. Many industries have hesitated to join these plans, even though producers everywhere have a significant influence on them.

Before VDN adopts a label format for a generic product, a draft specification of properties to be declared and methods to be used in their measurement is circulated among consumer and trade groups, testing laboratories, and experts. After confirmation by the VDN Board, producers and distributors may be licensed to use the new label. Unlike most of its sister organizations in other countries, VDN does not find it necessary to have a brand tested before a license is issued. Each licensee has to conduct the tests necessary to determine his individual ratings for various properties labeled. After the product is on sale, VDN will have random copies tested by neutral laboratories. If ratings are found to be below label declarations, VDN will warn the licensee; it can also withdraw his license. Revocation has never been necessary; the

---

VDN—VARUFAKTA

Design: Focus de Luxe, No. 20300

Materials: Stainless steel containing 18% chromium, 8% nickel. Knife blades of stainless steel with 14% chromium, hardened. Handles of polyamide plastic (nylon).

Resistance to Chemical Attack:
   Note. All stainless steel may be attacked by the substances in certain foodstuffs. The higher the content of chromium, the greater will be the resistance to attack. See "Instructions for Care" and note the composition of the alloy under "Materials." The stainless steel used for tableware contains at least 12% chromium, and may have as much as 18% chromium and 8% nickel—although hardened knives have at the most 14% chromium.

Handle's Resistance to Washing:
   Withstands washing by machine with a water temperature of 85° and drying in hot air at 100°
   *Strength of the anchorage after such washing: 5
   After washing by hand in water at 60°   5
   For normal household use a strength of 3 or 4 is sufficient. For restaurant and institutional use the strength should be 4 or 5.

*Bending Strength (spoons and forks):   5
   For normal household use a strength of 2 or 3 is sufficient. For restaurant and institutional use the strength should be 4 or 5.

*Durability of the Cutting Edge: 5
   The higher the figure, the less risk there will be of marking (discolouring) chinaware.

*Scale 1-5, with 5 representing the greatest strength or durability.

Instructions for Care: See back of label.
Manufacturer: AB GENSE, Eskilstuna.

FIGURE 1.   VDN label for Gense brand stainless steel cutlery.

small percentage of discrepancies between products and their label declarations have been promptly corrected.

   Several people tend to equate the informative labels issued by VDN, and the quality marks which trade associations and government agencies in many nations use to designate the overall quality of a product. However, three major differences exist between these consumer information devices. While VDN labels do incorporate public health and safety standards, other minimum standards regarding materials or performance are generally not required. Quality marks are based on the notion that a product meets or exceeds certain specifications. VDN labels preserve individuality, in that brand ratings will tend to differ on various characteristics. Generally, quality marks only separate marked from unmarked brands. Labels explicitly account for brand ratings on different characteristics; this is usually not the case with quality marks. Labels and marks have an important point of strength in common in providing point-of-purchase information.

Other Consumer Information Agencies and Devices

The single most important characteristic of a market offering is its price. In an age of great price variations by locality as well as by type of outlet, this factor has proved the Achilles heel of consumer information. KI gives list prices only in its comparative test reports; VDN labels are concerned only with nonprice characteristics. The provision of price information is one of the objectives of the State Price and Cartel Office (Statens Prisoch Kartellnamnd, SPK, established in 1957), which conducts periodic price surveys. Most of its studies are at the macro level, however, and refer to products generically rather than by model and brand, or to types of stores rather than specific outlets. Only in a few—albeit significant—cases has SPK undertaken price surveys coordinated with the comparative tests of KI, or accounted for individual stores located in specific communities. Thus far the impact of SPK on consumers has been more to stimulate price consciousness than to provide price information regarding relative value in the purchase of specific products. By not supplying the rationale of varying prices, SPK may in fact add more confusion to the market place than it eliminates.

Several large supermarkets and department stores have established so-called consumer corners, in which shoppers can consult *Rad och Ron* and SPK surveys, as well as numerous other educational guides and brochures by public and private agencies. These corners have been pioneered by consumer co-ops (Kooperativa Förbundet). which otherwise have taken a surprisingly mild interest in consumer information. Occasionally, such corners will be staffed by a home economist specializing in consumer information. While these consumer corners have not been a great success, KI itself operates a much-used field advisory service in Stockholm. On the other hand, experiments in the establishment of a network of local consumer groups to be sponsored primarily by unions and co-ops have met with limited response. The experience thus far has been that while such groups can be made to prosper when provided with centralized ideas and funds, they tend to fail when left to their own devices.

Consumer Council (Konsumentrådet, KR) is a government commission created in 1957 to sponsor behavioral and economic research on consumer questions, articulate the consumer viewpoint before government bodies, and support and coordinate the consumer information programs of KI, VDN, and SPK. Weaknesses in management have made KR relatively ineffective as a research sponsor. Until 1969, it had done little to stimulate a systems approach to consumer information among KI, VDN, and SPK. That year, KR sponsored an extensive comparative test of color TV sets and their prices and commissioned KI, SPK, and a state testing laboratory to conduct the research. The report created considerable furor in both industry and the press. While it seems that some of the interpretations made in the report were without solid foundation in the laboratory tests, some of the criticism was certainly exaggerated. Nevertheless, the incident illustrated the weaknesses of KR as a coordinating agent.

Sweden is the home of the ombudsman concept. The 1809 Constitution provided for two ombudsmen who were to protect the citizen in civil and military affairs. After a decade of debate, Sweden got a consumer ombudsman (konsumentombudsman, KO) on January 1, 1971, which was provided for in the new law regulating improper marketing practices. While the prime purpose of the new law is consumer protection rather than information, it is worth mentioning here. It is foreseen that a major activity of the KO office and associated bodies will be the redefinition of what constitutes misleading information in advertising and sales promotion and attendant vigilant surveillance of the field.

THE LEFT TWIST AND CURRENT PROPOSALS

Until 1968, there had been remarkably little political conflict concerning the development of existing consumer information programs in Sweden. In principle, all democratic parties agreed that there was a need for such information and for public support of such programs. No such unanimity exists concerning the most recent proposals in the consumer information field; this fact may need some explanation.

For decades the philosophy of the Swedish Social Democratic party was almost indistinguishable from other Social Democratic and Labor parties in Western Europe. During the last two or three years, however, the ideology of this dominant party has undergone a dramatic radicalization, resulting in what Swedes aptly refer to as the Left Twist of the local political scene.

This trend is symbolized by Premier Olof Palme, whose favorite theme is that freedom is equality in all areas, from after-tax income to public education. The Left Twist is particularly evident in the mass media, but also pervades other aspects of society. The state radio-TV monopoly is staffed largely with left-wing personnel whose views manage to come through in programming. In addition, the voice of the leading Stockholm daily—formerly liberal—is now largely that of its socialist majority of journalists. The author believes, on the basis of a dozen visits to Sweden, that an atmosphere has been created in which the bourgeoisie has become too timid to voice its views on such matters as the epidemic spread of drugs, the virulent criticism of the United States, and the rapidly accelerating government influence on the economy.

This influence is manifested by an array of new measures, such as the creation of a government supertrust which controls a dozen large state industries, giving them a virtual carte blanche to expand into any economic activity they please. Other measures include the introduction of case-by-case credit controls, the appointment of government members to the management of all commercial banks, and the creation of state monopolies for most school books and all official print. Some 20 years after the abolishment of wartime price controls, prices on all goods were "frozen" as of the end of October, 1970. A proposal now being considered would compel the closing of "excess" gas stations. Naturally, these and other extensions of statism have been accompanied by considerable antibusiness, antimarketing, and particularly, anti-advertising fanfare.

Current proposals for an all-comprehensive State Consumer Board are an outgrowth of this political climate. All consumer protection, education, and information activities would then be centralized under the keynote "household-centered consumer policy." Coordination would be obtained by the Board taking over the functions of not only KR, KI, and SPK but also VDN. Socialization of the VDN informative-labeling activity would mean the end of commercially independent private initiative in Swedish consumer information. In addition, the proposals foresee the Board guiding and communicating with local and regional consumer-oriented public bodies for what could be called "producer jawboning." It will be noted that the proposals are largely organizational and centralistic. As yet there is little official documentation regarding the specific activities of the Board beyond absorbing the functions of the existing bodies. It has been officially stated, however, that VDN labels must be made easier for the average consumer to understand and that they be made obligatory. Furthermore, consumer information is to be directed more toward the choice between different products and services than toward the evaluation of different brands of the same product. Finally, it was stated that "producer jawboning" will involve, as a minimum, "analysis of business policy and contacts with firms and public authorities as regards such matters as price, assortment, product development, service, and promotion policies."[3]

A vocal group of women socialists have articulated their views of the matter in greater detail. Some of them urge the imposition of compulsory testing and, presumably, approval by government experts, prior to the introduction of any new product or brand. Others talk about a compulsory government quality authentication scheme under which approved products would be awarded a green or gold label depending upon how experts view their quality. Thus, before they could meet the test of the market, products would first have to withstand the test of the bureaucrats.

WHAT CAN BE LEARNED FROM THE SWEDISH EXPERIENCE?

The Swedish experience confirms what representatives of Consumers Union will tell you: that the self-evident basis of any consumer information system is the comparative testing of goods and services. This is an exacting and not always exciting job. It has two main problems: (1) The development of reliable and valid testing methods, preferably adopted by national or international standardization bodies; and (2) the presentation of test results in a form which is both useful and interesting to consumers. The author believes it is fair to say that KI has received more recognition for its work on standard test methods than has CU. On the other hand, CU undertakes many more tests than KI. In regards to readability and relevance. *Advice and Discovery (Rad och Ron)* can be placed in approximately the same category as *Consumer Reports.* It may be noted in passing that the work of comparative testing bodies would be greatly accelerated by the development of standard testing methods (SMMP) by other organizations, such as university, government, and industry laboratories.

An objective tester will admit that test methods rarely are perfect, and that interpretations of results are often open to criticism. Furthermore, it is extremely difficult to make overall recommendations from results which are based on many different criteria without the injection of a heavy dose of subjectivity. The establishment of proper relative weights for each characteristic might be done by opinion surveys, but this process would clearly be very expensive. Even so, the problem would remain that what might be suitable to the mass of consumers might be unsuitable to any given individual. Also, not every consumer wishes to read test reports; some consumers want short-cut information available at the point of purchase. This is why Sweden pioneered the informative labeling system, and why agencies in other nations such as France have gone even further by simply attaching a quality mark to products much similar to the old Good Housekeeping Seal in the U.S. In general, five lessons can be learned from the Swedish experience in regard to informative labeling:

1. That informative labeling is equally dependent on the development of credible testing methods as is comparative testing;

2. That great effort must be exerted to prevent labels from becoming too technical to be of interest and help to the consumer;

3. That voluntary labeling plans do not sell themselves to either industry (without whose support such plans would not yield any labels) or, for that matter, to consumers;

4. That large investments must be made in the general promotion of a labeling program to industry, trade, and consumers;

5. That inasmuch as the individual store will carry only one or a few brands of a product, there should be brochures available reproducing all the labels of a given product, thus minimizing the necessity to shop around.

The overall reach of consumer information programs in Sweden, as in the United States, is confined largely to the well-educated middle class. Thus, in quantitative terms, the reach is one of respectable modesty whether programs are publicly or privately sponsored. It should not be concluded that the market potential for consumer information supplied by independent bodies is small. But clearly, greater effort at popularization of the information is needed. In addition, there is almost certainly a strong need for simpler forms of information such as credible quality marks (one need only consider the success of the Woolmark.) These efforts at popularization and simplification have as their natural counterpart basic consumer education in high schools or, at least, in-school training in systematic decision making. The urge to make good decisions, and knowledge about how to make them, should facilitate popular use of consumer information.

The most important thing one may learn from the recent proposals in Sweden is that like many other policy instruments, consumer information is a sword with two edges. It is customarily thought that consumer information can be used to improve the operation of a free market and to promote consumer sovereignty. However, it may also be used as a tool for regulating markets in ways considered desirable by government planners but not necessarily by consumers themselves. In a democratic society there is as much danger of consumer manipulation by hidden informers as there is by hidden persuaders. Indeed, the danger is greater in the case of the informers, since they are immune from the realities of competition which provide a check on the persuaders.

Contrary to these same proposals, past Swedish experience suggests that ample opportunities exist for coordinating the elements of a consumer information system without tight central control. While a concerted effort is needed to develop standard testing methods, it is not necessary for all comparative testing, informative labeling, and quality marketing activities to be controlled by a single office. Indeed, such programs appear to thrive in systems which are characterized by a perpetual interplay of competition and cooperation, independence and coordination. Those consumers who would rather make their own decisions than have a central body act as their product planners and buying agents would prefer a decentralized system. In such systems independent organizations—private as well as public—carry on partially overlapping, partially distinct programs. Presumably, freedom of choice in the market for goods and services presupposses some freedom of choice in the market for consumer information

REFERENCES

1. Rules and Regulations of KI, Article 2 (Public Laws and Regulations of Sweden, 1964, No. 349). A four-page information pamphlet about KI is available in English from Konsumentinstitutet, Ralambsvagen 8, S112 59 Stockholm, Sweden.
2. VDN has published several information brochures in English; e.g., "Whose Choice?" (1963), "The VDN System of Informative Labelling" (1964). Address: VDN, Taptogatan 6, S115 28 Stockholm.
3. Translated from the suggested organization chart of the State Consumer Board, a chart appearing in the Progress Report of the Royal Commission on Consumer olicy, *Synpunkter på den framtida konsumentpolitiken* (Ministry of Commerce mimeos. H1969:5).

31

How Business Responds to Consumerism

Business Week

No previous time has witnessed so many proposals for government regulation of business practices affecting consumers. Many of these proposals cause much anguish to some businessmen. To others, they signal the opportunity to improve products and presentations and to adopt a positive program focusing on the interests of the consumer. This article describes the frustrations of the businessman as he evaluates the many ploys open to him.

First Banana. "Hey, did you hear about the man who crossed a parrot with a tiger?"
Second Banana: "No what did he get?"
First Banana: "I don't know. But when it talks, you better listen!"

Whatever else consumerism is, it's beginning to look like a tigerish sort of parrot, and business, it seems, would do well to listen.

Some businesses are not only listening, they are doing something. Appliance makers are starting to print their warranties in clear English. Auto makers are trying to get new cars to customers with all the screws tightened and all the weatherstripping in place. Textile manufacturers are looking more closely at the clothes their products end up in, to make sure the fiber is really suited to the suit.

Every class of manufacturer whose product ends up sold at retail—from foods and finance service to toys and tires—is thinking, more or less intensively, about what to do when Ralph Nader, or Consumers Union's Walker Sandbach, or Senator Warren

Reprinted from *Business Week,* (September 6, 1969), pp. 94-108. Reprinted by permission.

Magmuson (D-Wash.), or Representative Benjamin Rosenthal (D-N.Y.), or another of the growing corps of influential consumer protectors comes knocking at the door.

Impetus

Few businessmen make any secret of it. Fear is the spur. Banks and finance companies have had a taste of consumer credit regulation and worry that they may some day be held responsible for the reliability of products financed through notes they have bought. No one has to teach Detroit the power of safety crusades, performance, pricing, and warranty revision may come next. Overnight, the delicate credibility of the toy and baby-food industries could be destroyed all over the country. Cosmetic and drug manufacturers, regulated for years, are uncomfortably aware that what they have swallowed so far may be only the beginning.

Read, for example, a recent press release issued by the Democratic Study Group, an informal alliance of liberal congressmen. After warming up with an indictment of the Nixon Administration in the field of consumer protection, the group lists no fewer than 30 separate desired pieces of legislation to regulate business in its relations with the public: IC laws dealing with product safety (including drugs, toys, tires, fish, eggs, and medical devices); five on consumer information (package labeling and pricing, product testing); six on deception and fraud; three on consumer credit: and six others that range from electric power reliability standards to the guarantee of reasonable access to liability insurance.

New Weapons

A laundry list compiled by the Chamber of Commerce of the U.S. is even longer: 86 major bills before the Congress, and more dumped into the hopper every day.

The Nixon Administration itself, despite the Democrats' criticism, is readying a package of consumer-oriented legislation. In a recent speech, Mrs. Virginia Knauer, the President's consumer adviser (who has turned out to be just as tart-tongued as her Democratic predecessors), outlined the first bill in the program: an act that enables consumers economically injuired by fradulent or deceptive marketing practices to pool their small claims and bring "class actions" in the Federal courts. The proposed law is similar to several already introduced in Congress. Nader says such a bill is potentially the most powerful weapon that could be put in the hands of consumers.

If anyone, at this late date, thinks that all this is just so much political wind, he should glance at the major legislation of the past few years:

The National Traffic & Motor Vehicle Safety Act, which took on the whole automobile industry.

The Fair Packaging & Labeling Act, which passed over the strenuous objection of the mammoth food industry.

The Consumer Credit Protection Act, which vitally touches the banking and finance industries as well as every retail organization that grants credit.

If one thing can be said for the lawmakers, it is that they are not afraid to tackle the biggest. Consumerism is powerful politics. Senator Magnuson used consumerism as a key issue in his successful drive for re-election last year. His theme: "Let's keep the big boys honest."

Senator Frank E. Moss (D-Utah), who recently won a signal victory over the cigarette makers, is considered by Republican strategists to be vulnerable next year in his bid for re-election. He recently scheduled a public hearing in connection with his campaign to tighten the Truth-in-Packaging Law. Where did he hold the hearing? Salt Lake City, of course.

Bandwagon

Among politicians, consumer protection is becoming institutionalized, just as defense, taxation, space, oil, and banking. Staff assistants to senators are making careers of consumer protection; they spend much of their time keeping up their bosses' interest with a stream of clippings, reports, studies, gossip, draft bills, draft speeches.

Some legislators need no encouragement. For each session of Congress through the years, Representative Leonor K. Sullivan, a serene and comfortable lady who represents a Democratic district in St. Louis, has introduced an omnibus package of amendments to the Federal Food, Drug & Cosmetic Act (this year's version, all 120 pages of it, is designated H. R. 1235). She watches with equanimity as her bill dies in the Interstate & Foreign Commerce Committee. But every so often, bits and pieces of it turn up in other bills that do get passed, and she is perfectly prepared to continue submitting variations of her bill to the end of her Congressional career.

Furthermore, anyone in the business community who expects the Republicans to capture the Senate next year and overturn the consumerist establishment should reconsider. The consensus in Washington is that consumer protection is no longer the exclusive concern (if it ever was) of the liberal Democrats. Conservatives of the stripe of Senator John Tower (R-Tex.) are becoming interested. Votes, it seems, are votes, and everyone is a consumer.

Boiling Point

There's an explanation why consumer issues have become good politics. In the very broadest sense, consumerism can be defined as the bankruptcy of what the business schools have been calling the marketing concept.

For all the millions of words written on the subject in the last 20 years, the marketing concept is a fairly simple idea: The proper way to run a business, and especially a consumer-goods business, is to find out the customer's wants and needs, felt and unfelt. The next step is to work back through the chain from customer to manufacturer, and design and produce a product that fills those needs and wants better than anything else on the market. With proper attention to efficient production, good distribution, attractive packaging, and effective promotion, the manufacturer should have few troubles.

But the whole system, which has worked brilliantly since the mid-1950s, is precariously balanced on one assumption: that the consumer is capable of exercising intelligent choice, and inclined to exercise it. The consumer it is said, "votes with her pocketbook."

More and more people are beginning to believe that the assumption is not at all self-evident. Dr. Peter F. Drucker, the management consultant, lectured the marketing conference of National Assn. of Manufacturers last April in these terms: "Consumerism means that the consumer looks upon the manufacturer as somebody who is interested, but who really doesn't know what the consumer's realities are. He regards the manufacturer as somebody who has not made the effort to find out, who does not understand the world in which the consumer lives, and who expects the consumer to be able to make distinctions which the consumer is neither able nor willing to make."

In atomic physics, there is the concept of critical mass—a point at which enough fissionable material is present to support a violent reaction. The U.S. consumer economy is at the point of critical mass, and consumerism is the explosion. A great many things have come together at once.

Product complexity. "The product," complains John J. Nevin, the head of Ford Motor Co's central marketing staff, "is getting more complex as we are building it better. We've kept pace with complexity, but we haven't licked it." Few consumers can peer under the hood of an eight-cylinder, air-conditioned, power-assisted automobile and understand what is there.

The business boom. The country's productive capacity is beginning to gape at the seams under the pressure to get the goods out on the market at any cost. Last fall, the New York Times reported that 5% of certain classes of women's wear needed some repair by retailers before they could be placed on sale. Says one Detroit executive: "Things have moved so fast—from 6-million cars to 9-million in less than a decade. How do you increase repair stalls fast enough?"

The marketing boomerang. In a sense, consumer marketing and advertising have been too successful. Convinced that quality and convenience are forever on the rise, that the technical genius of industry can work miracles, that the new is always better, that the computer can solve anything, the customer expects a lot that cannot be delivered. "We are suffering," says Herbert M. Cleaves, senior vice-president of General Foods, "from a revolution of customers' rising expectations. The consumer never had it so good, but he wants to know 'what have you done for me lately?' " Marketing overkill is even harming products that do perform well. "They've been screaming about how good their products are for so many years, people no longer believe them," says Morris Kaplan, technical director of Consumers Union.

Full employment. It's a truism that no one wants to be an auto mechanic or repairman anymore. There are better and easier jobs in the factories. And present repairmen are so beset by customers that they can't take the trouble they used to. Says John C. Bates, director of General Motors' service section: "It's not that they don't do the work, but that they don't cater to the consumer anymore. If you get respect, you don't complain. Ten years ago, management in a dealer's repair shop had pretty good control over his people. As labor shortages developed, there's been an abrogation of control."

Anomie, or the feeling of disorder and isolation, the sense, in short, that a bad situation has no bottom. The white, suburban, middle class, which constitutes the principal market for goods and services, believes that government is cold and unresponsive, that taxes are too high, that Negroes are too aggressive, that the Vietnam war will never end. The middle class is at its collective wit's end. And now the last refuge, the goods and services the suburbanite buys with his devalued dollars to support the good life, seems to have let him down.

Together, the discontents have produced the broadest consumer protection movement in U.S. history, a movement that is not only concerned with protecting consumers against physical harm and outright fraud, but that also attempts to guarantee performance, efficacy, and to regulate the total relationship between buyer and seller. In legal terms, emphasis has moved from torts to contracts.

"There is a lack of balance in the consumer's capacity to deal equally with the guy who's got an item to sell," says Senator Gaylord Nelson (D-Wis.) one of the most active consumerists in Congress. The aim is to redress that balance.

One applicance executive ticks off on his fingers the big issues that are coming up: safety, of course, and the problems of product recall; some machinery for the resolution of customer grievances; improvement and standardizations of product warranties; provision of a lot more information to the consumer on what he is buying and how well it will perform.

FACING UP TO REALITY

"The most encouraging thing," says General Electric Co's associate counsel, Winston H. Pickett, "is that businessmen are taking consumerism seriously and addressing themselves to it on a systematic and continuous basis." Adds a key man in a powerful Senate committee: "People are changing; or at least everyone is willing to play the game and make the right pronouncements."

Both men were addressing themselves to the No. 1 problem: How should business respond to the consumer challenge? The question—and its various answers—are likely to occupy a lot of high-priced time for a good many years to come. And that in itself is a problem. "We're not a huge company." says E. G. Higdon, president of Maytag Co., "and we don't have a lot of loose management with nothing to do. The consumerism boom is putting the time pressure on some of our top people. You don't go out and employ someone to go to Washington and sit down and listen. You have to send someone who knows this business, who is capable of representing us adequately, and who can come back with the proper information to let us form our own opinions."

Actually, the business response to government regulation has been fairly predictable over the years, and falls into several stages.

Deny everything. Nearly everyone goes through a phase of shock when hallowed business practices are questioned, and this is the automatic reponse.

Blame wrongdoing on the small, marginal companies. In any industry where fragmentation and ease of entry are the rule, the argument is popular that the major companies are blameless, but that the small outfits must cut corners to survive.

Discredit the critics. "Hell," says one Congressional staff man, "I've had publishers worried about circulation sales investigations down here peddling stuff on the Communist nature of consumerism based on 1942 documents."

Hire a public relations man. A big campaign to modify public opinions is allurling. But, as one PR man says, "there's no sense in a PR campaign if you have nothing to say."

Defang the legislation. Trade associations and Washington law firms are specialists in this, and it is often effective, at least for a while. It worked for the tobacco industry in 1965. It also worked in respect to the Truth-in-Packaging Law.

Launch a fact-finding committee to find out whether anything really needs to be improved in the way the company does business. The food industry is deeply involved in this now.

Actually do something, whether you think you are guilty or innocent. Carl Levin, a PR man who runs the Washington office of Burson-Marsteller, cites the case of his client, Reserve Mining Co., the big taconite processor in Minnesota. Reserve has been critized for dumping ore tailings into Lake Superior. "Reserve thinks it's right," says Levin. "But if everyone's wearing a mini-skirt, you wear one too. Whether it's a real public interest or merely what the public thinks is its interest, it must be taken into account. They're trying to do something short of closing down the plant."

More and more businessmen are convinced that the rewards—or the avoidance of penalties will come only in the later stages of this cycle. Says GE's Pickett: "You're going to do something voluntarily or involuntarily. These aren't fancied grievances. The dimensions are a matter of dispute, but not the existence of them."

How does industry answer these complaints? Consider the case of the food industry. Regulation is certainly nothing new, and the processors have been living with minimum standards of health and cleanliness for decades. But in the early 1960s, the proposals to regulate labeling on consumer packages cropped up. By the time the Fair Packaging & Labeling Act was passed in 1966, the grocery industry had earned a reputation for primitive intransigence that would have shamed a 19th Century railroad baron.

But packaging was only the beginning. Some of the laveling regulations are just being promulgated, and the industry is under attack on additives and plant inspection.

Introspection

In 1967, the Grocery Manufacturers Assn. commissioned a study by McKinsey Co. to try to get some new ideas. A number of alternatives were discarded, including a massive public relations campaign and an expensive continuing opinion survey to find out what is bugging the consumer. What finally came out of it all was the Comsumer Research Institute, run by James Carman, a business administration professor from the University of California.

CRI is a foundation sponsored by major manufacturers that sell through super-markets, by the National Assn. of Food Chains, the National Assn. of Wholesale Grocers of America, by several large ad agencies, and a group of magazines with a healthy interest in food advertising.

The studies themselves—planned or actual—vary in stature. Some of them merely put out brush fires, such as a study now in the works on cents-off deals in super-markets.

A project in the planning stage is socalled "unit-pricing." Several bills now in Congress would require retailers to stamp the price per ounce, or pound, or foot on packages. "We want to do some decent research," says Carman. "How much would it cost? Would it change the way goods are priced physically; that is, would the actual price-stamping have to change? Would it promote more or fewer pricing mistakes?"

Carman's biggest expenditure area is in consumer information studies. For example, one scholar is looking at the state of consumer testing and grading programs in Europe in an effort to determine whether a similar program would make sense in an American environment. Another project will study what product information consumers actually use.

Feedback

Carman's sponsors very much want to know what's bugging consumers. So far he has no answer.

The U.S. Chamber of Commerce thinks it has a method that might work. The Chamber has designed a program that it is trying to sell to its local affiliates. The proposition: a series of local meetings between business and consumers designed to get some kind of feedback on dissatisfaction—and get some action on injustice.

There are other schemes. One of the original alternatives to Carman's institute was a national market research study proposed by A. Edward Miller, at the time (1967) president of Alfred Politz Research, and now president of World Publishing Co. Miller's scheme involved a $100,000 study, jointly paid for by government and industry to isolate the areas of consumer discontent.

Miller also proposed a continuing study, called the Consumer Index of Buying Satisfaction, to provide both the regulators and the regulated with something better than letters of complaints as a clue to consumer dissatisfaction.

CRI is the packaged-goods producers' principal effort at the moment. Individual companies, of course, are doing more. General Foods, for example, early this year set up the Center for Applied Nutrition, which is charged with research into the problem of nutrition and hunger. It is no secret that one of the issues of increasing interest to the consumerists is whether convenience foods are more or less nourishing than food the housewife prepares herself, and whether consumers thing they are getting more sustenance than they really are.

LIKELY NEW TARGETS

The major dialogue in the business community is taking place not on the food industry but among the durable goods makers, which are less accustomed to severe regulation.

They are, to put it bluntly, in a sweat. The areas that are bugging them are warranties, repair, reliability, consumer grievance mechanisms, and product safety. And the principal argument is how fast to move to head off unwelcome regulations.

The battleground is over industry-wide product standards and product certification. Are they desirable? Are they prudent? Are they anti-competitive? The National Commission on Product Safety, appointed by the President, distrusts self-regulation and is pushing for federal standards and surveillance. The commission has gone so far as to enlist the Antitrust Div. of the Justice Dept. In May, Arnold B. Elkind, chairman of the commission, asked Assistant Attorney General Richard W. McLaren for an advisory letter on the antitrust implications of self-regulation. In June, McLaren replied, and his very cautious response has provided ammunition for the warring points of view.

In July, for example, the commission announced that Justice does not think voluntary safety standards necessarily violate the laws, but that setting such standards "would appear to be a task more appropriately entrusted to a governmental body than private groups of manufacturers."

True, McLaren said that, but the statement was taken out of a context that bore on quite a different point. Donald L. Peyton, managing director of the United States of America Standards Institute (USASI), a private organization supported by trade associations to promulgate voluntary standards, has photocopies of McLaren's letter and the safety commission's press release. He implies that Elkind distorted McLaren's views to frighten industry away from self-regulation.

But a careful reading of McLaren's statement reveals that Elkind need distort nothing: The general tenor of McLaren's opinion is that self-regulation could be extremely dangerous.

Dilemma

There's nothing surprising in that. The anti-competitive aspects of voluntary codes have been recognized for years. A product standard rigged to favor one or two producers, or a certification program too costly for small manufacturers, is very likely in violation of the antitrust statutes.

Juel Ranum, board chairman of the Assn. of Home Appliance Manufacturers, an organization that is doing more than most in the area of performance standards and consumer grievance, puts the fears of industry very explicitly indeed: "The one thing I haven't heard in Washington is what a politician would do if a company in his particular area were threatened by standards that it was unwilling or unable to meet. This is a real dilemma, because if the standards are to mean anything, they will have to raise the level, not lower it. At the present time, if we as an industry attempted to write a standard that every single manufacturer could not meet now, it would be absolutely construed as a violation of antitrust laws, as an attempt to drive some companies out of business."

The danger is no illusion. USASI's Peyton admits: "I can get GE and Westinghouse to reduce current leakage. But the standard would put 50 manufacturers out of business."

Nevertheless, USASI (the name will soon be changed to American National Standards Institute because the Federal Trade Commission thinks the present name sounds deceptively like an arm of the U.S. government) believes that voluntary certification is both safe and feasible, despite the opposition or lethargy of some of its members. Says one of Peyton's associates: "We have a consumer council loaded with consumer-oriented manufacturers, some of whom are sitting on it to make sure that no standards are written on his industry."

Yardsticks

USASI recently launched a national certification program that will offer something of a breakthrough in self-certification for performance.

Peyton would like to see graded standards, which would get an industry off the antitrust hook by finding room for manufacturers of every degree of efficiency and size. "There's nothing illegal, immoral, or fattening about component performance levels for a whole industry," he says. "Why not have performance points as well as price points and market the product accordingly?"

One reason, says a testing engineer, is that it is harder to do than most people in or out of Washington think. "Take tires. Quality grade labeling is an almost impossible situation. Everyone's been working on it, but the chore is beyond man's knowledge and they're a year past the deadline for Commerce Dept. regulations."

There are other reasons why people in industry doubt USASI's success. Companies joining the certification program must satisfy USASI that product liability insurance covered USASI. Testing costs are also higher under the program because the testing laboratory that actually administered the certification standards would have to post a bond with USASI for the life of the program plus 10 years. To be legal, the certification must be open to any company. Says one observer: "Suppose a company that's not an association member came along and asked for the USASI seal. He hasn't contributed a nickel to the association's certification program, which includes expensive advertising to acquaint the public with its value. The first time a Hong Kong air-conditioner importer comes along, USASI is down the drain."

Debate

USASI is not the only institution pushing reluctant manufacturers to adopt some form of self-certification. Hoffman Beagle, president of Electrical Testing laboratories, one of the oldest independent testing labs in the business, thinks that self-certification sponsored by an industry association can work.

He has made it work in a few cases. For example, the aluminum window manufacturers administered their own program for years, but found that the inspection system left something to be desired. In 1963, Beagle's laboratory took over policing of the standards, including random sampling of production. "We have in all our programs sole authority without recourse to determine the facts of compliance. If we gig someone, it costs them money."

Beagle is puzzled by the consumerist issue. "You think the woods would be full of new clients these days," he says. "But it's not so." He doesn't think cost is the reason.

"I have yet to find an industry where a viable certification program could not be instituted at a cost per unit that leaves the pricing structure unaffected," Beagle says.

Others disagree. Baron Whitaker, president of Underwriters' Laboratories, which certifies electrical safety, puts his finger on a fundamental paradox in trying to graft consumer protection measures onto a sophisticated market economy. "If you put in extra safety features or extend product life, the cost has to come out of somewhere. There's no Santa Claus."

Delicate Balance

To understand exactly what all this means in terms of competing in a cutthroat market, maintaining dealer margins, and maintaining pricing points in the volume segments of a business, listen to John W. Craig, senior vice-president of the appliance division of Admiral Corp.: "Does attention to the consumer cost money? Certainly it does. You get nothing free any more. The only solution is cost-improvement programs. Our engineering, purchasing, and manufacturing departments have annual requirements set up calling for taking a certain amount off manufacturing costs without interfering with performance, features, or reliability."

In the face of that kind of optimism, a lot of marketing men can only grin wryly. In most hardgoods industries—including the automobile business, where it has been raised to a high art—cost control and engineering adjustments are matters of a fraction of a cent. The whole point: to bring in the product somehow at a competitive price level in the face of rising costs. The trick is to do it without losing much of the quality or durability. A major program of improvement in response to consumerist demands plays havoc with such a delicately balanced system. It is the lucky company that can raise its price enough to cover the costs and still meet competition.

Herd Instinct

These competitive pressures are precisely why whole industries try to act together on new standards, as Senator Magnuson points out in his book, The Dark Side of the Marketplace: "When asked why they had not incorporated the $2 instinctive release on their wringer washing machine, one company admitted that even such a small expenditure that would require some alterations in production would require a higher price, giving competitors an edge in a low-income market, where every dollar-off counts. . . . Recently, an automotive engineer told me that many in the auto industry were secretly glad that a law was passed, mandating the use of the safety features by all companies, for competition had long prevented their adoption by one company alone."

The problem of how to satisfy everyone in the system at once pops up everywhere you look.

The problem of repair, for example, is both knotty and expensive. GE has erected a huge edifice to solve it: factory service branches which now account for 80% of its major appliance service calls.

Detroit Revs Up

The auto industry naturally is in the biggest bind. Ford is gearing up its HEVAC (heating, ventilation, air conditioning) laboratory, which will experiment with modular design for car climate control systems, among other things. The reason: air-conditioning is the company's biggest warranty headache, and it shows up early enough to be covered by even the shortest warranty period.

For the first time, too, Ford is asking its engineers to consider ease and accessibility of repair when they design a car, especially at the lower-priced end. The luxury models, whose owners presumably don't care one way or the other, will still emphasize style over fast—and cheap—repair. "Lee Iacocca [executive vice-president of Ford] can't stand exposed screw heads," says one man, "so there are none in the Continental." When you want to fix a car, it's nice to be able quickly to find the screws that hold it together.

The experiment with Maverick, which is billed as a repair-it-yourself car, is another indication of Ford's direction. The owner's manual is not all that easy to follow, but the company claims the last Ford with such a manual was the 1931 Model A Ford car.

GM is experimenting with a program, still in the pilot stage, in which an inspector selects a new car at random from a dealer's lot and drives it. GM calls it the "Would-I-buy-this-car test."

Sharper Focus

The auto companies are paying a lot of attention to the "short-term" quality problems, the ones that show up in the first 10 days of a car's life: vent leaks, faulty door handles, and the like. Building quality through basic engineering and design is more difficult and more time-consuming. But Ford's Nevin points out that even the little repairable items may represent basic design failure. "Take a vacuum or electrical system where there is routinely a 5% defect rate. Maybe the plant simply can't build the part to that design."

Finally, there is the problem of customer relations. GM's Bates believes that the attitude of people dealing with consumers has a lot to do with customer satisfaction. So early this year the company began a series of meetings for dealer employees on owner relations that eventually clocked 37,000 employees. GM is also setting up incentive programs for mechanics. It makes contributions to a fund for mechanics with the best repair records, based on how often or seldom a customer who has just had his car fixed has to return for another go-around.

Satisfying the consumerists isn't all headache by any means. Celanese figured out a set of end-use licensing standards for its Fortrel and Arnel fibers that is widely known in consumerist circles. Celanese got into the program because it was a late starter in an industry dominated by Du Pont's brand names, and it felt it had to invest real money in building confidence in its merchandise. The lure: the ad budget Celanese spends to support the products of everyone from the mill to the cutter that makes the clothing. To get Celanese's money, everyone has to conform to the standards the company has established.

A HAZY OUTLOOK

In the struggle over the new consumerism, businessmen are often angry, and even more often bewildered. But by and large they don't appear to be cynical.

If they were, the record shows that probably the safest course would be to let Congress pass any sort of regulatory bill it pleased, then sit back and watch the regulators fail to enforce it.

Consider, for example, the Fair Packaging & Labeling Act—"Truth-in-Packaging"—enacted in 1966. It will come as a surprise to many people who remember the publicity generated by the bill's passage that, despite the redesign of a host of supermarket packages to conform with the act's provisions, some parts of the law are still not officially in effect.. The effective date for drug and cosmetics packages is now Dec. 31. Food packaging regulations went into effect only two months ago.

In some instances, even the official dates may prove unrealistic. One section of the act, for example, charges FDA with promulgating regulations governing "cents-off" deal labels on packages. FDA has yet to issue such regulations. Exactly why is in some dispute. A Senate Commerce Committee staffer believes that FDA, with all its other problems, simply assigned a low priority to the intricacies of promotional labeling. But other observers maintain that the agency simply found the task beyond its capabilities, that it just doesn't know enough about high-powered packaged goods marketing to draw up meaningful rules.

Trials and Errors

To do it justice. FDA had made a number of efforts to stretch its limited resources.

Two years ago, the agency launched an experiment in self-inspection with General Foods to see whether food manufacturers could manage the surveillance of food processing on their own. The experiment was conducted in GF's modern plant in Dover, Del., and covered two products—a gelatin dessert (a "low risk" product) and a custard ("high risk").

The program has undergone a series of modifications, and will be terminated this month. The result: "It worked not as well as we both had hoped," according to GF's Herbert Cleaves. The problem was the endless paperwork involved in reporting to Washington—a chore to produce, and certainly a chore to read. Cleaves thinks that "with refinements" self-certification can be made feasible in the food industry. if the biggest and most modern food processors could take some of the strain off FDA, it would have more resources to police smaller operators.

Despite imaginative ideas like these, however, an internal study group set up by FDA recently declared that the agency "had been unable to develop the kind of concerted and coordinated efforts needed to deal adequately and simultaneously with problems of pesticide residues, food sanitation, chemical additives, microbiological contamination, drug and device safety and efficacy, hazardous household products, medicated animal feeds, and myriad other problems." In short, said the study group, "we are currently not equipped to cope with the challenge."

Frustrations

The Federal Trade Commission is not in much better shape. It is an agency, as Louis M. Kohlmeier, Jr., points out in his new book, The Regulators, that was designed by Congress to be the national expert on monopoly and economic concentration and has ended up as the national authority on phoney chinchilla-farming schemes. As a matter of fact, to any business reporter who regularly sees FTC's fat packets of new releases cross his desk, it sometimes seems that the commission's major activity is enjoining infractions of the fur-labeling act in Bent Spoon, North Dakota.

What has happened, of course, is that FTC has over the years been saddled with responsibility for a variety of consumer protection measures—mainly involving deception and fraud—which it is not really equipped to handle.

The load on FTC is so great, and the administrative machinery so cumbersome, that it is the despair of the commissioners; Mary Gardiner Jones, a liberal Republican commissioner, asserts that the commissioners, no matter how well intentioned, have no time to get out into the business world to see what's going on, and certainly no time to think about a rational and imaginative regulatory policy regarding the marketing of consumer goods.

The result is a very real frustration, even for businesses facing the threat of regulation. Both the home appliance manufacturers and the auto people have been waiting a year for the final draft of FTC's promised report on warranty practices.

What makes them impatient, of course, is the pending warranty legislation in Congress. Early drafts of both the House and Senate bills are tough, and, in the opinion of many in industry, almost impossible to live with. They include not only requirement for a full parts-and-labor express warranty if any guarantee of product performance is offered at all, but a section requiring compulsory arbitration of warranty grievances. The specter of compulsory arbitration over the repair of a $10 toaster makes the appliance men's hair curl. So they are counting on the FTC report to put matters in somewhat better perspective.

Similarly, the synthetic fiber and textile industry is discouraged over the delay in reporting on the amendment to the Flammable Fabrics Act. The amendment, ramrodded by Senator Magnuson, was passed 18 months ago. The Secretary of Commerce was supposed to define the extent and nature of the textile fire hazard by end-use of the fabric and report recommendations to the industry. Only two small sections of the report have been issued, and the industry is still waiting for the rest. "They just haven't done their homework," says an executive of one big fiber producer.

Uncertainties

More than one businessman has said in exasperation—though never on the record—that thoroughgoing enforcement of existing laws would in some ways be preferable to the arbitrary system of random prosecution. Business sits around for lightning to strike. "It's an awful way to try to build an intelligent policy of response to legislation," one man complains.

Then, too, Kohlmeier argues in his book that the regulatory agencies are more concerned with protecting the interests of the regulated industries than with the needs of the consuming public. His argument is persuasive, particularly in regard to the Interstate Commerce Commission, which has consistently maintained a floor under freight rates, and the Federal Communications Commission, which is generally regarded to have botched the allocation of television frequencies.

Businessmen faced with specific new regulation, however, don't always believe they have a friend at the regulatory agency. They may not be afraid of the regulators now but they are genuinely scared about the potential for regulation in the age of consumerism. Ralph Nader predicted recently that within the next decade some businessmen will end up in jail if their products injure a consumer.

32

The Dialogue That Never Happens

Raymond A. Bauer and Stephen A. Greyser

Can business and government leaders resolve the problems of talking past one another instead of to one another? This article suggests that two different views of the consumer world explain the communications gap between businessmen—especially marketers—and their critics. The nature of these two views, why they exist, and what can be done to resolve the problem are discussed here.

In recent years government and business spokesmen alike have advocated a "dialogue" between their two groups for the reduction of friction and the advancement of the general good. Yet, all too often, this is a dialogue that never happens. Rather, what passes for dialogue *in form* is often a sequence of monologue *in fact*, wherein each spokesman merely grants "equal time" to the other and pretends to listen while preparing his own next set of comments. Obviously, this is not always the case, and, if taken literally, it tends to minimize some real progress made. Our aim here is to try to facilitate and stimulate that progress by exploring what lies behind the dialogue that never happens and by suggesting what can be done—on both sides—to develop more meaningful and effective business-government interactions.

Authors' note: This article is based on a speech given by Professor Bauer to the 1967 National Conference of the American Marketing Association in Toronto in June. We gratefully acknowledge the assistance of Robert D. Moran, Harvard Business School Doctoral Candidate, in the development of and research for the article.

Reprinted from *Harvard Business Review*, vol. 45, no. 6 (November-December 1967), pp. 2ff, Reprinted by permission.

In this context, we link "government spokesmen" with "critics." Naturally, not all in government are critics of business, and vice versa. However, almost all critics seek redress of their grievances via government action and seek government spokesmen to present their views "in behalf of the public."

Our primary focus will be held in the field of marketing—particularly selling and advertising—which is perhaps the most controversial and most frequently criticized single zone of business. Marketing seems to be the area where achieving true dialogue is most difficult and where business and government spokesmen most seem to talk past each other.

Before examining why this takes place, let us look at two comments on advertising that illustrate the lack of dialogue. The first comment is that of Donald F. Turner, Assistant Attorney General in charge of the Antitrust Division of the Justice Department:

> There are three steps to informed choice: (1) the consumer must know the product exists; (2) the consumer must know how the product performs, and (3) he must know how it performs compared to other products. If advertising only performs step one and appeals on other than a performance basis, informed choice cannot be made.[1]

The other comment is that of Charles L. Gould, Publisher, the San Francisco *Examiner:*

> No government agency, no do-gooders in private life can possibly have as much interest in pleasing the consuming public as do . . . successful companies. For, in our economy, their lives literally depend on keeping their customers happy.[2]

DOUBLE ENTENDRES

Who do business and government spokesmen talk past each other in discussing ostensibly the same marketplace? We think it is because each has a basically different model of the consumer world in which marketing operates. This misunderstanding grows from different perceptions about a number of key words.

The first word is *competition.* The critics of business think of competition tacitly as strictly price differentiation. Modern businessmen, however, as marketing experts frequently point out, think of competition primarily in terms of product differentiation, sometimes via physical product developments and sometimes via promotional themes. The important thing is that price competition plays a relatively minor role in today's marketplace.

Some of the perplexity between these two views of competition has to do with confusion over a second word, *product.* In the critic's view, a product is the notion of some entity which has a primary identifiable function only. For example, an automobile is a device for transporting bodies animate or inanimate; it ordinarily has four wheels and a driver, and is powered by gasoline. There are variants on this formula (three-wheeled automobiles) which are legitimate, provided the variants serve the same function. Intuitively the businessman knows there is something wrong with this notion of the product because the product's secondary function may be his major means of providing differentiation (an auto's looks, horsepower, and so on).

Then there is the term *consumer needs*, which the business critic sees as corresponding to a product's primary function—for example, needs for transportation, nutrition, recreation (presumably for health purposes), and other things. The businessman, on the other hand, sees needs as virtually *any* consumer lever he can use to differentiate his product.

Next, there is the notion of *rationality*. The critic, with a fixed notion of "needs" and "product," sees any decision that results in an efficient matching of product to needs as rational. The businessman, taking no set position on what a person's needs should be, contends that any decision the customer makes to serve his own perceived self-interest is rational.

The last addition to our pro tem vocabulary is *information*. The critic fits information neatly into his view that a rational decision is one which matches product function and consumer needs, rather circularly defined as the individual's requirement for the function the product serves. Any information that serves that need is "good" information. To the businessman, information is basically any data or argument that will (truthfully) put forth the attractiveness of a product in the context of the consumer's own buying criteria.

Exhibit I summarizes our views of these two different models of the consumer world. We realize that we may have presented a somewhat exaggerated dichotomy. But we think the models are best demonstrated by the delineation of the pure views of contrasting positions, recognizing that both sides modify them to some extent.

VIEWS OF HUMAN NATURE

A review of our "vocabulary with a double meaning" and the two models of the consumer world show that the critic's view is based on a conviction that he knows what "should be." In contrast, the businessman's view is based on militant agnosticism with regard to "good" or "bad" value judgments which might be made (by anyone) about individual marketplace transactions.

The businessman's view of human nature may be the more flattering, perhaps

EXHIBIT I

TWO DIFFERENT MODELS OF THE CONSUMER WORLD

Key words	Critic's view	Businessman's view
Competition	Price competition.	Product differentiation.
Product	Primary function only.	Differentiation through secondary function.
Consumer needs	Correspond point-for-point to primary functions.	Any customer desire on which the product can be differentiated.
Rationality	Efficient matching of product to customer needs.	Any customer decision that serves the customer's own perceived self-interest.
Information	Any data that facilitate the fit of a product's proper function with the customer's needs.	Any data that will (truthfully) put forth the attractiveness of the product in the eyes of the customer.

excessively so. Certainly, the marketer's notion of "consumer sovereignty" compliments the consumer in attributing to him the capacity to decide what he needs and to make his choice competently even under exceedingly complex circumstances. It also sometimes challenges him to do so. This perhaps undeserved flattery glosses over some obvious flaws in the market mechanism. It is rooted in the belief that this mechanism, even though imperfect in specific instances, is better than administrative producers for regulating the market.

The critic takes a far less optimistic view of human nature—both the consumer's and the seller's. He thinks that the seller often (sometimes intentionally) confuses consumers with a welter of one-sided argumentation. Such information, in the critic's eye, not only lacks impartiality, but usually focuses on secondary product functions and is not geared to consumer needs.

Both sets of assumptions are, we think, at least partially justified. Customers do have limited information and limited capacity to process it. This is the way of the world. Furthermore, there is no reason to believe that every seller has every customer's interest as his own primary concern in every transaction, even though in the long run it probably is in the seller's own best interest to serve every customer well.

All of this disagreement comes to focus on a point where both business and government are in agreement; namely, modern products are sufficiently complex that the individual consumer is in a rather poor position to judge their merits quickly and easily. The businessman says that the customer should be, and often is, guided in his judgment by knowledge of brand reputation and manufacturer integrity, both of which are enhanced by advertising. The critic argues that the customer should be, but too seldom is, aided by impartial information sources primarily eveluating product attributes.

These conflicting views of vocabulary and human nature are reflected in several specific topic areas.

BRANDS & RATING SERVICES

One of these areas is the relationship of national branding to consumer rating services, the latter being a traditional source of "impartial information" for consumers. Somehow the crux of this relationship seems to have escaped most people's attention: consumer rating services are possible *only because of* the existence of a limited number of brands for a given product. In order for a rating to be meaningful, two conditions are necessary:

1. *Identifiability*—the consumer must be able to recognize the products and brands rated.

2. *Uniformity*—manufacturers must habitually produce products of sufficiently uniform quality that consumer and rating service alike can learn enough from a sample of the product to say or think something meaningful about another sample of the same product which may be bought in some other part of the country at some later time. This is a seldom-realized aspect of national branding.

It is generally assumed by both groups that the "consumer movement" is basically opposed to heavily advertised branded goods. The stereotype of *Consumer Reports* is that it regularly aims at shunting trade away from national brands to Sears, to Montgomery Ward, or to minor brands. Yet the one study made of this issue showed that, contrary to the stereotype, *Consumer Reports* had consistently given higher ratings to the heavily advertised national brands than to their competitors.[3]

Ideological Blindness. What we have here is an instance of the consumer movement and brand-name manufacturers being ideologically blinded by different models of the market world. The consumer movement concentrates on the notion of a product having a definable primary function that should take precedence over virtually all other attributes of the product. True, some concessions have recently been made to aesthetics. But, on the whole, the consumer movement is suspicious of the marketing world that strives to sell products on the basis of secondary attributes which the consumer movement itself regards with a jaundiced eye.

The evidence available to the consumer movement is that, in general, national advertising is *not* accompanied by poorer performance on primary criteria. But the consumer movement fails to realize that it *takes for granted* the central claim for advertised branded products—namely, that by being identifiable and uniform in quality, they offer the customer an opportunity to make his choice on the basis of his confidence in a particular manufacturer.

But the manufacturers of nationally branded products and their spokesmen have been equally blind. First of all, we know of none who has pointed out the extent to which any form of consumer rating must be based on the identifiability and uniformity of branded products. The only situation where this does not apply is when the rating service can instruct the consumer in how to evaluate the product—for example, looking for marblizing in beef. However, this is limited to products of such a nature that the customer can, with but little help, evaluate them for himself; it cannot apply to products for which he has to rely on the technical services of an independent evaluator or on the reputation of the manufacturer.

Moreover, except for such big-ticket items as automobiles, consumer rating services usually test products only once in several years. In other words, they rate not only a *sample* of a manufacturer's products, but also a sample of his performance *over time.* Thus, if one "follows the ratings" and buys an air conditioner or a toaster this year, he may buy it on the rating of a product made one, two, or three years ago. Similarly, if one buys a new automobile, he depends in part on the repair record (reported by at least one rating service) for previous models of that brand.

In large part, then consumer rating services are devices for rating *manufacturers!* This is not to say they do not rate specific products. Sometimes they even draw fine distinctions between different models from the same company. But in the course of rating products, they also rate manufacturers. What more could the manufacturer ask for? Is this not what he claims he strives for?

Basic Dichotomy. More to the point, what is it that has kept the consumer movement and brand-name manufacturers from paying attention to this area of shared overlapping interests? Neither will quarrel with the exposure either of factual deception or of product weaknesses on dimensions that both agree are essential to the product. This is not where the problem is. The problem is that the manufacturer *sells* one thing and rating services *rates* another.

The concept of a "product" that dominates the thinking of rating services and the thought processes of those who suggest more "impartial evaluation information" for consumers (e.g., Donald Turner of the Department of Justice and Congressman Benjamin Rosenthal of New York) is that a product is an entity with a single, primary specifiable function—or, in the case of some products such as food, perhaps a limited number of functions, e.g., being nutritious, tasty, and visually appealing. The specific goal of many proposed ratings—with their emphasis on the physical and technical characteristics of products—is to free the customer from the influence of many needs to which the market addresses himself, most particularly the desire for ego-enhancement, social acceptance, and status.

The marketer, oddly enough, tends to accept a little of the critic's view of what a product is. Marketing texts, too, speak of primary and secondary fuctions of a product as though it were self-evident that the aesthetic ego gratifying, and status-enhancing aspects of the product were hung on as an afterthought. If this is true, why are Grecian vases preserved to be admitted for their beauty? And why did nations of yore pass sumptuary laws to prevent people from wearing clothes inappropriate to their status?

We shall shortly explore what may lie behind this confusion about the nature of products. First, however, let us examine another topical area in which similar confusion exists.

'Materialist Society'

The selling function in business is regularly evaluated by social commentators in relationship to the circumstance that ours is a "materialist society." We could say we do not understand what people are talking about when they refer to a materialist society, beyond the fact that our society does possess a lot of material goods. But, in point of fact, we think *they* do not understand what they are talking about. Let us elucidate.

At first hearing, one night conclude that criticism of a materialist society is a criticism of the extent to which people spend their resources of time, energy, and wealth on the acquisition of material things. One of the notions that gets expressed is that people should be more interested in pursuing nonmaterial goals.

The perplexing matter is, however, that the criticism becomes strongest on the circumstance that people *do* pursue nonmaterial goals—such as ego enhancement, psychic security, social status, and so on—but use material goods as a means of achieving them. Perhaps the distinctive feature of our society is the extent to which *material* goods are used to attain *nonmaterial* goals.

Now there are many ways in which societies satisfy such needs. For example, there are ways of attaining status that do not involve material goods of any substance. Most societies grant status to warriors and other heroes, to wise men who have served the society, and so on. Often the external manifestation of this status is rigidly prescribed and involves signs whose material worth is insignificant: a hero wears a medal, a ribbon in his lapel, or a certain type of headdress, or he may be addressed by an honorific title.

However, in societies that value economic performance, it is not uncommon for material goods to be used as status symbols. Indians of the Southwest, for example, favor sheep as a symbol even to the extent of overtaxing the grazing lands and lowering economic status of the tribe. As a practical matter, this might be more damaging to the welfare of the Navaho than is the damage that many low-income Negroes do to their own individual welfares when, as research shows, they insist on serving a premium-priced brand of Scotch.

Many of the things about which there is complaint are not self-evidently bad. Art collecting is generally considered a "good thing." But take the worst instance of a person who neurotically seeks self-assurance by buying art objects. Clinically, one might argue that he would do himself a lot more long-run good with psychotherapy even though, when one considers the resale value of the art objects, he may have taken the more economical course of action. Similarly, it is not self-evident that the promotion of toiletries to the youth as a symbol of transition to manhood is inherently cruel—unless the commercials are especially bad! It is clear, however, that there is no societal consensus that the transition to manhood should be symbolized by the use of toiletries.

What seems to be the nub of the criticism of our society as a materialist one is that simultaneously a great number of nonmaterial goals are served by material goods, and there is no consensus that this should be so. Behind this is our old friend (or enemy): the concept of a product as serving solely a primary function. In the perspective of history and of other societies, this is a rather peculiar notion. Who in a primitive society would contend that a canoe paddle should not be carved artistically, or that a chief should not have a more elaborate paddle than a commoner?

Much of the confusion over the words on our list seems to be a residue of the early age of mass production. The production engineer, faced with the task of devising ways to turn out standardized products at low cost, had to ask himself, "What are the irreducible elements of this product?" This was probably best epitomized in Henry Ford's concept of the automobile, and his comment that people could have any color they wanted so long as it was black. Clearly, Ford thought it was immoral even to nourish the thought that a product ought to look good, let alone that it should serve various psychic and social functions.

But all this was closely related to the mass producer's effort to find the irreducible essence of what he manufactured. This effort broke up the natural organic integrity of products, which, at almost all times in all societies, have served multiple functions.

Many writers have called attention to the fact that in recent times our society has passed from the period of simpleminded mass production to that of product differentiation on attributes beyond the irreducible primary function. As yet, however, we do not think there is adequate appreciation of the impact of the residue of the early period of mass production on thinking about what a product is. In that period even very complex products were converted into commodities. Since each performed essentially the same primary function, the chief means of competition was pricing.

Products as Commodities

At this point, we shall argue that the thinking of those who criticize the selling function is based on a model for the marketing of commodities. This factor does not exhaust the criticisms, but we believe it is at the core of present misunderstandings over the concepts on which we have focused our discussion.

On the one hand, to the extent that products are commodities, it is possible to specify the function or functions which all products in that category should serve. It follows that a person who buys and uses such a commodity for some purpose other than for what it was intended has indeed done something odd, although perhaps useful to him (for example, baseball catchers who use foam-rubber "falsies" to pad their mitts). In any event, it is possible both to specify the basis on which the commodity should be evaluated and the information a person is entitled to have in order to judge that product. A person searching for a commodity ought first to find out whether it serves this function and then to ask its price.

On the other hand, to the extent that products are *not* commodities, it is impossible to expect that price competition will necessarily be the main basis of competition. Likewise, it is impossible to specify what information is needed or what constitutes rational behavior. Is it rational for a person to buy toothpaste because its advertiser claims it has "sex appeal"? Presumably people would rather look at clean than dingy teeth, and presumably people also like to have sex appeal—at least up to the point where it gets to be a hazard or a nuisance.

But it does not follow, insofar as we can see, that ratings—or grade labeling—should discourage product differentiation or the promotion of products on a noncommodity basis. If the consumer were assured that all products in a given rating category performed their primary functions about equally well, could it not be argued that those attributes which differentiate the products on other functions would then become increasingly interesting and important? Or, to be more specific, what makes it possible for "instant-on" TV tuning to be promoted—other than a presumed agreement, by both manufacturer and consumers, that the TV set performs its primary function little better or worse that its competition?

This is a facet of competition not appreciated by the opponents of grade-labeling, who have argued that it would reduce competition. Perhaps it would be more helpful if the opponents of grade labeling first gathered some evidence on what has actually happened to competition in countries where grade labeling has been introduced. (The head of one major relevant trade association recently told one of us that he knew of no such research.)

Toward More Information

Readers will note that we have indulged in considerable speculation in this article. But most of the issues on which we have speculated are researchable. Relatively little, for example, is really known about how businesses actually see themselves carrying out "the practice of competition," or even about the actual competitive mechanisms of setting prices. Furthermore, in all of this. there is no mention of the *consumer's* view of these various concepts or of his model of the marketing process. To be sure, we can be reasonably certain of some things. For example, we know that consumers do regard products as serving needs beyond the bare essentials. Yet it would be helpful to know far more about their views of the overall marketing process.

What we propose as a worthwhile endeavor is an independent assessment of the consumer's view of the marketing process, focusing on information needs from his point of view. Thus, rather than businessmen lamenting the critics' proposals for product-rating systems and the critics bemoaning what seem to be obvious abuses of marketing tools, both sides ought to move toward proposing an information system for the consumer that takes into account *his* needs and *his* information-handling capacities while still adhering to the realities of the marketing process.

For those who have the reading habit, it will be obvious that this proposal is but an extension of the conclusions reached by members of the American Marketing Association's Task Force on "Basic Problems in Marketing" for the improvement of relations between marketing and government.[4] In brief, along with suggested studies on the influence of government policies and programs on corporate marketing decisions, a special study was recommended in the area of consumer-buyer decision making and behavior:

> It is of the highest importance to investigate the impacts of the host of governmental regulations. facilities, aids and interventions upon the quality and efficiency of consumer-buyer decision making.[5]

The report went on to state that, particularly in light of the generally recognized drift from *caveat emptor* toward *caveat venditor*, "abundant basic research opportunities and needs exist" in the area of government impact and consumer-buyer behavior.

What Can Businessmen Do?

Certainly there is a crying need for more information and, as we have tried to illustrate, for fresh analytic thinking on almost all of the issues on which government and business are butting heads. We have elaborated on the different models of how the marketplace does, and should, work because we think their existence explains the largest part of why marketers and their critics often talk past each other, even when they have the best intentions of engaging in a dialogue. The other part is explained by the relative absence of facts. As we have noted, the consumer's view of the market-advertising process and his informational needs represent an important (and relatively unprobed) research area.

Returning to the "dialogue," we should add a further problem beyond that of business and government spokesmen talking past one another. Inasmuch as many on both sides see themselves as representing their colleagues' views, partisanship becomes mixed with the aforementioned misunderstanding, since such partisanship is likely to address itself to stereotyped views of "the other side," the comments become irrelevant. That many well-qualified first-hand commentators are regarded as self-serving by their critics is a point aptly made by Denis Thomas. Equally apt is his corollary observation that those "who view business . . . from a suitably hygienic distance lose no marks for partiality even if their facts are wrong."[6]

How then can effective interactions take place? Obviously, the key parts will be played by:

1. Thoughtful business and government leaders.

2. Marketers and their critics who take the time to consider and to understand (even if they do not agree with) each others' premises and assumptions.

3. Those who engage in meaningful dialogue oriented to fact finding rather than fault finding.

4. Those on both sides who address themselves to solving the problems of the real, rather than the presumed, public.

These constructive parts are not easy to play, but there are many who are trying, and succeeding, as these three examples illustrate:

The Department of Commerce has taken a series of measures, including the formation of a National Marketing Committee, to play a positive "activist" role in business-government relations; marketers are involved in what goes on rather than, as has occurred in many previous government situations, being informed after the fact.

William Colihan, Executive Vice President of Young & Rubicam, Inc., proposed at the University of Missouri's Freedom of Information Conference that marketing undertake a major consumer education job to "make the marketing system benefit the nonaffluent, the undereducated."[7] This 20% of adult consumers represents, he feels, both a public responsibility and a marketing opportunity.

John N. Milne of Toronto's MacLaren Advertising Company Limited spelled out eleven specific major economic, social, ethical, and communications research projects to provide a "factual basis for an objective assessment of advertising, to replace emotional pleas." Business, government universities, and projects in other nations would serve as sources and beneficiaries of data "so that advertising's usefulness to all segments of society can be assessed and improved."[8]

Beyond the parts played by thoughtful business and government people, we see a distinctive role for schools of business in bringing about meaningful interaction. Business schools are a unique resource both in their understanding of the business system and in their capability to conduct relevant research. Other faculties, at least equally competent and objective in research, generally do not have the depth of understanding of why things are the way they are—a necessary precursor to relevant study. We hasten to add that grasping how something *does* operate implies no consent that this is how it *should* operate, now or in the future.

Both in research and as participants (or moderators) in dialogue, business school faculties can play a significant role.

Business and government should sponsor the necessary research. The particular need for business is to recognize that the era of exclusively partisan pleading must end. In our judgment, the American Association of Advertising Agencies' sponsorship of research on consumer reactions to advertising and advertisements is a splendid model.[9] The findings are by no means exclusively favorable to advertising. But they make more clear where problems do, and do not, lie. And academic "insurance" of the objective conduct of the research and presentation of findings should bring about a degree of governmental acceptance and set the standard for any subsequent research.

We can use more of this, and more of it is beginning to take place. A dialogue is always most profitable when the parties have something to talk about.

REFERENCES

1. Statement made at the Ninth Annual American Federation of Advertising Conference on Government Relations held in Washington, D.C., February 1967.
2. Ibid.
3. Eugene R. Beem and John S. Ewing, "Business Appraisers Consumer Testing Agencies," HBR March-April 1954, pp. 113-126, especially p. 121.
4. See E. T. Grether and Robert J. Holloway, "Impact of Government upon the Market System," *Journal of Marketing,* April 1967, pp. 1-5; and Seymour Banks, "Commentary on Impact of Government upon the Market System," ibid., pp. 5-7.
5. Grether and Holloway, ibid., pp. 5.
6. *The Visible Persuaders* (London, Hutchinson & Co., 1967), p. 11.
7. *Freedom of Information in the Market Place* (FOI Center, Columbus, Missouri, 1967), pp. 140-148.
8. Speech given at the Annual Conference of the Federation of Canadian Advertising and Sales Clubs, Montreal, June 1967.
9. For a description of the research and a review of the major results, see Stephen A. Greyser, editor, *The AAAA Study on Consumer Judgment of Advertising—An Analysis of the Principal Findings* (New York, American Association of Advertising Agencies, 1965), and Opinion Research Corporation. *The AAAA Study on Consumer Judgment of Advertising* (Princeton, 1965); the findings and their interpretation are the subject of the authors' forthcoming book, *Advertising in America: The Consumer View* (Boston, Division of Research, Harvard Business School, on press).

33

Seller Beware — Consumer Proposals Bring About Changes in American Business

John A. Prestbo

MORE FIRMS ADD OFFICIALS TO DEAL WITH THE PUBLIC; BUT COMPLAINTS CONTINUE

BETTY FURNESS IS SKEPTICAL

The U.S. consumer movement is getting a lot of publicity. But is it getting anything else?

Businessmen aren't kowtowing to consumer militants, throwing their profits to the winds or vying with one another to appoint Ralph Nader to their boards. Nevertheless, consumerism does seem to be winning some recognition—albeit grudging recognition in some cases—from the business community. And many executives throughout the country are busily, and noisily, initiating programs aimed at appeasing complaints and demands of American buyers.

Item: More than a dozen major companies in the past 18 months have appointed top-level officers to new positions solely concerned with consumer affairs. Some of these officials, such as those at Chrysler, Pan American Airways and RCA, are vice presidents. Others possess an array of imposing titles, such as Swift & Co.'s "director of public responsibility."

Item: More and more companies are installing toll-free telephone lines for the use of consumers who wish to bypass dealers and other intermediaries and lodge com-

Reprinted from *Wall Street Journal* (June 21, 1971). Reprinted by permission. John A. Prestbo is a Staff Reporter of the *Wall Street Journal*.

plaints directly at headquarters. Other firms are advising consumers through advertising to forward their complaints to headquarters in writing.

Item: Some companies are changing their corporate structures and revamping their business methods to accommodate consumers. Ford Motor Co. recently put its service division on a par with its sales division. Matthew S. McLaughlin, Ford's marketing chief, says the management of the service division will give district service managers "more time to handle repair and service problems at a local level." And many supermarkets are adopting unit-pricing systems to show shoppers the cost of items per ounce, quart or other measure of different sized packages.

Item: Some firms are openly berating other companies on behalf of consumer causes. Bohack Corp., a New York supermarket chain, quit carrying Lady Scott tissues when Scott Paper Co. began placing 175 tissues in a box that formerly contained 200. While Scott says it's only alternative was to raise prices—a move it deemed undesirable—Bohack tells its customers that Scott's action is deceptive because the paper company's competitors continue to put 200 tissues in similarly sized boxes.

Too Big to Ignore

"Consumerism is finally becoming too big an issue for business to ignore," says Stephen A. Greyser, a Harvard Business School professor. The professor's words are borne out by a number of statistics. The White House Office for Consumer Affairs says the number of complaints it receives now runs about 2,500 a month, compared with 1,500 a month a year ago. The Federal Trade Commission says consumer complaints directed to that agency have risen 50% since last July to an annual rate of 20,000.

Furthermore, public-opinion surveys indicate an increasingly negative attitude toward big business. For example, Social Research Inc. recently found that 60% of the people it polled in the Chicago area thought that "big business forgets the public welfare." This figure compares with 40% in 1964.

A few companies are beginning to admit that these complaints and attitudes are, at least to some extent, justified. "We were having a meeting discussing consumerism about 18 months ago and a marketing vice president wondered out loud who the complaint-handling department belonged to," recalls an official of RCA. "He was told, apparently for the first time, that it was his." Today, however, RCA says its executives are more attuned to consumers, largely because of pressure from Robert W. Sarnoff, its chairman and president.

Pan Am's Problem

Other large companies are realizing that sheer size has caused problems with consumers. "In recent years we've become so used to dealing with big airplanes and big numbers of people that things have gotten dehumanized," admits John Barnes, staff vice president for consumer action at Pan Am. And Elisha Gray II, chairman of Whirlpool Corp., says that "when you make or handle products numbering in the millions and involving budgets and sales of millions or billions of dollars, it's pretty easy to lose sight of the fact that you have to satisfy your customers one at a time."

This isn't the first time that consumerism has challenged U.S. business. In the early 1900s and again in the 1930s, social critics led campaigns against fraud, deceit, price-fixing and unsafe or unwholesome products. Such complaints persist; but today's consumer movement, which began building in the late 1950s, is more concerned with the quality of products and services and with the ability of the individual consumer to cope with giant companies and increasingly complex and technical products.

Modern consumerism is often lumped indiscriminately with population control, minority hiring and other issues confronting the business community. But many consumer activists share a surprisingly narrow view of what the consumer movement wants: safe, reliable products and services that perform as advertised and that are repaired or remedied promptly when they fail. In addition, the activists say, consumers want more detailed information about goods and services to enable intelligent comparison before a purchase is made.

Are companies sincerely trying to meet these demands? Or is the business community's response to consumerism merely an attempt to pull the wool over the public's eye? Betty Furness, formerly a special assistant for consumer affairs under President Johnson and now chairman of the New York State Consumer Protection Board, has one opinion: "Frankly, the more money and ingenuity these companies spend telling us how much they care about us, the more skeptical I am that they're actually doing anything that will result in better treatment of consumers."

Harvard's Prof. Greyser agrees that "a lot of companies' new-found concern for consumers could be palaver." The professor adds, nevertheless, that he thinks some firms are making meaningful responses to consumers—despite the fact that they may be motivated more by a desire to stave off legislation than by altruism. "Nothing's widespread yet," Prof. Greyser says, "but a little program in this company and another one in that company all add up to what I think are some solid gains for consumers."

But whatever the motive, some companies have undertaken major overhauls in the name of consumerism. One example is Grolier Inc., a large publisher of reference books, which last year began to revamp its door-to-door sales operations because of growing consumer complaints about fast-talking salesmen. One new Grolier policy, begun last fall, is to doublecheck every order with the purchaser before it is shipped.

"We have a person from our credit department, rather than a salesman, call each customer back and spend 15 to 20 minutes going over the contract to make sure he understands," Grolier's president, William J. Murphy, explains. "We want to catch any misrepresentations by over-zealous salesmen, and if we can't resolve any misunderstandings we cancel the order right on the phone and return the customer's down payment."

Grolier goes even further. Its headquarters in New York calls a random 10% of its customers eight weeks after an order is shipped in order to solicit reactions to the company's books—and to its salesmen. Additionally, revised Grolier contracts now invite dissatisfied customers to make collect calls to the New York office to register their complaints.

Such reforms have been costly for Grolier. Several hundred salesmen quit or were fired as a result of the new policies, resulting in severance pay claims and other termination costs. This exodus in turn contributed to a 16% first-quarter decline in

Grolier's U.S. book sales this year and a drop of $800,000 in pre-tax profit in the same period.

Mr. Murphy, however, is optimistic. "The impact (of the new policies) is pretty much behind us," he says. He also says he believes the reforms will pay off in good will for the company.

Grolier's response to consumerism is, for the moment, far more extensive than that of many other large companies. Many firms, however, are making genuine attempts to improve communication between their clients and themselves. One such institution is New York's giant Chase Manhattan Bank.

"People have always had a friend at Chase Manhattan Bank, but too often they had to get shunted from office to office before they found one that could or would help them," says Marjorie P. Meares, who became Chase's first consumer-affairs officer early last year. "Now, people who call in are connected with my department first. If they have a complaint or problem that we can't handle, we put them in touch with the person who can. We really aren't doing anything more for the consumer than we used to, but I'd like to think we're doing it a little faster and more consistently."

A Panel Discussion

In some instances, responses to consumerism are being effected on an industry-wide basis. For example, the Association of Home Appliance Manufacturers, the Gas Appliance Manufacturers Association and the American Retail Federation last year established the Major Appliance Consumer Action Panel to serve as an independent court of last resort for unresolved consumer complaints. The eight panel members were chosen from outside the industry and, with the exception of travel expenses, aren't reimbursed for their work.

Most customer complaints are resolved at a lower level, but those cases in which the customer and manufacturer are unable to agree come before the panelists for review at monthly meetings. "The stickier cases sometimes take several months to settle," says Mrs. Virginia F. Cutler, chairman of the panel and head of the department of family economics and home management at Utah's Brigham Young University.

While consumer advocates hail the panel as an example to be followed by other industries, Mrs. Cutler's group doesn't always rule in favor of the consumer; in fact, about 40% of the panel's decisions thus far have favored the manufacturer. "We turned down one fellow who wanted a new air-conditioner to replace one he'd just bought that burned out," Mrs. Cutler says. "We found that he lived in an old house that wasn't properly wired for any kind of air-conditioner. He knew about the wiring, so we figured it was his responsibility to have inquired whether an air-conditioner would work in his house."

The panel, however, has its limitations. "We can't enforce our decisions—only recommend them to the manufacturers," Mrs. Cutler says. Nevertheless, in more than 100 mediations, the panel's recommendations have only twice been declined.

In another area of the business community a 50-member National Advertising Review Board, sponsored by three advertising industry trade groups and the Council of Better Business Bureaus, will be set up this fall to handle complaints about false and deceptive advertising. A statement describing the group's planned activities declares that if the board decides an ad is misleading but can't persuade the advertiser to change it, "the matter will be turned over to the Federal Trade Commission, or other appropriate government agency, and the board's findings will be publicized."

Liberalizing Guarantees

In other consumer-related moves, some companies are liberalizing their guarantees and warranties. Some makers of color-television sets have extended their warranties on solid-state models to a year from 90 days, and at least one manufacturer, RCA, is experimenting with two-year free-labor warranties. And in the automotive world, Ford and General Motors have added special 90-day warranty coverage of potentially expensive services such as wheel-alignment and balancing, brake adjustments and tightening of loose bolts and other parts.

Maytag Co. now places information tags on all its products. The tags tell prospective purchasers a number of product-related facts: where the specific model fits into Maytag's line, what features it has, how much electricity it uses, what is needed for installation, special safety precautions to be followed, and information on warranty coverage. According to Betty Furness, Maytag's information tags represent "the greatest single response that any company has made to a legitimate consumer demand."

Corporate response to consumerism, of course, has a long way to go before consumer advocates are entirely satisfied. In the meantime, however, reputable concerns are more frequently imparting product information to potential customers. The food industry is a case in point. CPC International Inc. recently began printing the nutritional content of its Skippy peanut butter on the labels of Skippy jars. And Jewel Cos., a Chicago-based food-store chain, says that by late summer all of its private-label foods with limited shelf lives will be openly marked with the dates they are to be removed from sale.

34

Consumer Protection
by Private
Joint Action

Donald F. Turner

When does cooperation between manufacturers in setting
safety and performance standards constitute an antitrust
violation? Even aside from this vexing question, the author
takes a dim view of the prospects of private, collective
action in setting performance and safety standards actually
benefiting the consumer—he fears many manufacturers,
faced with the competitive situation, will set their standards
on the lowest common denominator.

My assignment today is to comment on the inadequacies of private joint action as a device for protecting consumers. You have no doubt expected that in passing I would express some views on the antitrust dangers in private joint action of this kind. I shall of course do so. However, while there is a close correlation between the inadequacies of private group action and the antitrust risks, absence of antitrust risks does not necessarily mean that private joint action adequately serves the public interest. I feel it necessary, therefore, to go somewhat beyond purely antitrust considerations.

I can conveniently begin the discussion with an analysis of the *Radiant Burners* case, which, though raising only one comparatively easy antitrust issue, could well have raised a good many more. Let me briefly summarize the allegations of the plaintiff's complaint in that case, allegations which the Supreme Court held were sufficient to charge a violation of the Sherman Act. The plaintiff sued the American

Reprinted from *1967 New York State Bar Association Antitrust Law Symposium* (New York: Commerce Clearing House, Inc., 1967), pp. 36-46. Reprinted by permission.

Gas Association and assorted members, including both gas distributors and manufacturers of gas equipment and appliances. The plaintiff charged an unlawful combination to exclude from the market gas appliances not receiving a seal of approval from
AGA's testing laboratories. AGA's testing laboratories, according to the complaint,
purported to test the utility, durability and safety of gas burners and other equipment.
Yet, it was asserted AGA approval was not based on "valid, unvarying, objective
standards" and that AGA could and did make determinations arbitrarily and
capriciously as to whether a given gas appliance had passed its tests. Plaintiff alleged
that its own gas burners, denied the seal of approval, were more safe and more
efficient, and at least as durable, as burners which the AGA had approved.

The alleged consequences were described as follows:

> Plaintiff avers that it is not possible to successfully market gas equipment, including
> its Radiant Burner, unless AGA approved because AGA and Utilities (a) refuse to
> provide gas for use in equipment not AGA approved, (b) refuse or withdraw
> authorization and certification of dealers who handle gas burners or equipment not
> AGA approved, (c) prepare and circulate false and misleading reports that equip-
> ment not AGA approved is unsafe, unreliable, or lacking in durability, (d) Utilities
> discourage prospective purchasers from buying or installing equipment not AGA
> approved and refuse to permit its display in public areas of their offices and (e)
> induce municipalities and government agencies to pass ordinances which require
> that no gas burner or equipment shall be used within their limits unless such gas
> burner or equipment bears the seal of approval by AGA.

As you know, the District Court dismissed plaintiff's complaint for failure to state a
claim upon which relief could be granted; and the Court of Appeals affirmed, holding
that no *per se* violation of the antitrust laws was alleged, and that in the absence of
such an allegation the plaintiff was required to allege general injury to the competitive
process and harm to the public at large. The Supreme Court unanimously reversed in a
per curiam opinion, holding that the collective refusal to supply gas for use in
plaintiff's burners fell into the category of restraints that are unlawful in and of
themselves, and that plaintiff need establish only his injury in order to recover.

In view of the fact that plaintiff was allegedly excluded from the market by a
collective refusal to deal, *Radiant Burners* raised no novel antitrust points. But suppose
that there had been no allegation of a collective refusal to deal on the part of the gas
distributor members of the AGA. It seems clear to me that serious antitrust problems
would have remained. Failure to obtain AGA's seal of approval would tend to exclude
a manufacturer's product from all or a substantial part of the market for the following
reasons:

a. The existence of municipal and other ordinances prohibiting the use of
non-approved equipment within the limits of their jurisdictions;

b. The high likelihood of individual refusals by AGA's gas distributors to supply
gas for use in non-approved appliances; and

c. The high likelihood that denial of the seal of approval would impose upon a
manufacturer a serious competitive disadvantage in the advertising and other
promotion of his wares.

Given these exclusionary effects, I think the complaint in *Radiant Burners* still stated a cause of action. An allegation that plaintiff's products were arbitrarily and capriciously denied a seal of approval would support a claim that the AGA and its various members were carrying on a combination plainly in unreasonable restraint of trade. Certainly where competitors are involved in an organization granting a seal so important to business success—and even, I believe, where competitors are not involved—the group is under an obligation to insure that its decisions to grant or withhold the seal are fairly made. Cf. *Silver v. New York Stock Exchange,* 373 U.S. 341 (1963). Moreover, they are under a duty to insure that the testing procedures and the seal of approval are available to all interested manufacturers on non-discriminatory terms. It should not be limited to members only; it should not be limited to American manufacturers only.

Moreover, where a seal of approval or promulgation of standards has such practical exclusionary effects, it seems to me that the group must, at the least, establish appropriate procedures for the formulation of standards for approval; and serious questions are raised as to whether particular bases for exclusion are appropriate for private group action at all. Let us look again to the facts alleged in the *Radiant Burners* case. I point in particular to the following:

a. There was an inferable conflict among appliance manufacturers as to the minimum standards that had to be met before the seal of approval was given.

b. There was no indication that the ultimate purchasers of gas appliances had any representation in the formulation of standards (although the gas distribution utilities might arguably have represented the comsumers' interest at least in part).

c. The AGA's seal of approval required the meeting of minimum standards not only on safety but also on "utility" (which I take to mean efficiency) and durability.

Such circumstances raise at least two dangers:

(1) Due to diverse manufacturer interests, the standards procedure might be used by a dominant group of manufacturers to handicap or exclude competitors for any one of several wholly unacceptable reasons—that the competitor is a price cutter or that he has developed a new product which threatens a serious invasion of established producers markets; and

(2) Due either to diverse manufacturer interests or conflict of interest between manufacturers and consumers, the standards might cut off from the ultimate consumer product options that a substantial number of them would very much like to have.

A good case might well be made for safety standards which kept unquestionably unsafe products off the market, at least until there has been an opportunity for legislative action. (See my remarks before the Northwestern Fifth Annual Corporate Counsel Institute, October 14, 1966.) Indeed, one might assume that no consumer wants an unsafe gas burner in view of the potentially disastrous consequences that are involved. I might note, however, that even on safety standards a point could well be reached where the added cost of further enhanced safety would arguably be too high; that is, where the risk to be guarded against is so remote that many consumers would prefer to disregard it rather than pay the price.

But whatever the case for safety standards, questions of efficiency and durability are quite different. Why deprive consumers who know what they are about from purchasing a less efficient or less durable stove at a lower cost if they wish to do so? As I said a few months ago in discussing agreements among competitors to eliminate certain product options:

> For many consumers, the extra quality is not worth the extra price; others may not be able to afford the more expensive product at all. If there are sellers willing to supply them with cheaper merchandise, which they wish to buy, this is simply what competitive allocation of resources is designed to permit. An agreement to remove from the market alternatives which some buyers want and which some sellers are prepared to supply is not "improving" competition but interfering with it.

To restate this in terms of our present subject, it is not "protecting" consumers to deprive them of safe product options which they, fully aware of all the facts, prefer to buy.

The dangers that a standards procedure or seal of approval may be used by a dominant group of manufacturers to unreasonably handicap their competitors and/or to drive desired product options off the market are of course reduced by affording to all affected groups an opportunity to make their views known and to have some voice in the ultimate results. They are reduced if non-member manufacturers as well as member manufacturers participate, and if consumers have effective representation. But if there are substantial differences among these diverse groups, is there any completely satisfactory way of determining on what basis decisions are to be made? Is each manufacturing member to have one vote; or plural votes depending upon his sales? How many votes should consumer representatives have? The short of the matter is that the problems raised by conflicting interests of this kind cannot be appropriately solved by any voting procedures within the private group. It seems to me that they can only be resolved satisfactorily by establishment of an impartial tribunal of some sort to make the ultimate determination. But if this is so, have we not really said that the kind of standards which the group is attempting to impose are of such a nature that the responsibility should be given, at least ultimately, to a governmental body?

The dangers I have described—unreasonable exclusion of competitors and/or unwarranted elimination of product options—would also be minimized by adopting, instead of a single standard or single seal of approval, a grading scheme based upon general acceptable testing standards. In *Radiant Burners,* for example, the AGA could have simply made testing reports on safety, efficiency and durability of the various products submitted to it. This would have given consumers a large amount of highly useful information, but would leave them free—insofar as their local distribution utilities did not interfere—to assign their own weights to price and performance characteristics. Moreover, if AGA had confined its activities to the publication of testing reports, this would have forced local governments who wished to establish some control over gas appliances to make for themselves an appropriate legislative determination of what minimum performance standards should be met.

I have said that this method of procedure would tend to minimize the dangers, but of course it would not wholly eliminate them. There still may be serious good faith dispute on whether particular characteristics of a product are of enough significance to warrant testing and grading. But I would guess that this problem would be of serious proportions in only a comparatively few cases.

So far, I have been discussing the inadequacies of private group action to protect consumer interests largely in terms of correlative antitrust risks. It is obvious, however, that the absence of antitrust risks does not mean that private group action is an adequate or appropriate means of doing the job. To illustrate this let me return for the moment to problems of safety. While members of an industry might conceivably push safety requirements to an excessively high level, the much more likely danger is probably the reverse, namely that the diverse interests of various private producers will be accommodated in such a way that safety standards will tend to be based on the lowest common denominator. Either that, or the standards will be set at such a point that one or more manufacturers will simply refuse to adhere.

The main conclusion to be drawn from all of this is that the prospect for satisfactory private solution of the problems of protecting or helping consumers is directly dependent upon the extent of conflicts of interests among the groups affected. The greater the conflicts of interest—either among competing manufacturers, or between manufacturers and parties with whom they deal—the more likely it is that private group action will prove comparatively unsuitable as a device for protecting consumers from products they do not want or should not be allowed to have. The more the conflicts of interest, the more likely that private group action will either harm the kind of competitive and consumer interests which antitrust law can protect, or simply prove inadequate for establishing the kind of standards that the public interest would dictate. I realize of course that legislation, with or without implementation by an administrative agency, is not without problems of its own. But it is the only appropriate solution where serious conflicts of interest are involved and where the general public interest seems likely to require higher standards of consumer protection than will evolve from private joint action.

This by no means eliminates all room for private activity. There is no doubt that there are wide-spread opportunities for legitimate and highly beneficial collective private activity in the area of voluntary formulation of and adherence to standards. There are some 300 standards-writing organizations in the United States which have developed more than 13,600 standards. The annual rate of publishing new and revised standards exceeds 3,000. More than 400 of these standards have been developed under procedures established by the United States Department of Commerce. I would not pretend to know very much about the details, and if I did it would be risky for me—for obvious reasons—to cast any general blessings on these troubled waters. But I can make a few comments. There are many situations in which standardization is in the interests of all concerned, and diversity is minimal. No serious criticism can be directed at the private formulation of standards designed to reduce clearly excessive and pointless proliferation of product variety. No one's interests are served by having an infinite variety of sizes of nuts and bolts. There are many other instances in which product variety—in terms of size, weights, shapes, and the like—has proliferated not in response to any felt consumer need or demand, but by accident or for such reasons as the desire of competing manufacturers to do something distinctive. If flour manufacturers put out packages in all one-ounce variations from 4 to 104, almost certainly at least some consumers will randomly select packages of each size that is on the market. But this hardly reflects a "consumer demand" in the ordinary sense of the word. Group action to reduce the number of package sizes would almost certainly be beneficial. It would help the buyer in making comparisons among the products of competing manufacturers, and help protect him against deception and just plain befuddlement.

There are other advantages that are obtainable in appropriate circumstances by standardization of consumer goods. By ensuring that different brands will be equally satisfactory in important functional respects, standards may well lessen the influence of advertising and promotional activities unrelated to actual product differences, and thereby lower the barriers to effective entry by new producers. Standardization may lead to significant reductions in production and distribution costs. Standards which facilitate interchangeability of parts may promote competition by increasing the sources of supply available to the consumer and, by the same token, the markets available to competing producers.

Yet, again, the existence of these actual or potential advantages is not determinative. I don't have to tell you that standardization can be misused. It can and has been used to facilitate non-competitive pricing. *C-O-Two Fire Equipment Co. v. U.S.,* 197 F. 2d 489, 493 (9th Cir. 1952).

Moreover, even where it is generally agreed that standardization to reduce excessive product variety would be desirable and in everyone's interest, there may be serious conflicts of interest which make appropriate private solutions difficult if not impossible to achieve. A possible example is a current dispute on lumber standards, a dispute which I gather has been going on for some time. While I am not acquainted with all of the facts, I understand that a principal difficulty involves comparability of green and dried lumber. More particularly, the question is whether a green 2 X 4 should be bigger than a dry 2 X 4 in order to be called a 2 X 4, and if so, by how much. The consumer is obviously interested in a standard that accurately reflects the comparability of wet and dry lumber. If all producers were similarly situated there would be no problem. Manufacturers equally capable of producing both would normally have no evident interest in distorting the standard to favor the purchase of one or the other unless the industry's structure and behavior are imperfectly competitive in some significant respect. Absent significant imperfections, the producers would presumably endeavor to establish as accurately as possible the normal shrinkage of green lumber and set standards such that a green 2 X 4 would be the same size as a dry 2 X 4 once it became dry.

Suppose, however, that the producers are not similarly situated, that a large number of small producers have no drying facilities and therefore sell green lumber only. Suppose further that only a very few large producers possess drying facilities. If this is so, a conflict of interest among the two groups immediately arises. The producers of green lumber have a strong interest in obtaining a standard which creates no gap or a minimal gap between a green and a dry "2 X 4." Competitive interests of producers of dry lumber would lead them to favor a standard creating as wide a gap as possible. It seems clear that the private interest of neither of these two groups should be decisive in the formulation of the standards. Yet with such diversity of interests, it would be only fortuitous for any conceivable voting scheme to produce what appears to be the proper result, namely a standard which accurately reflected average shrinkage.

This example illustrates again the proposition that the problem of protecting or helping consumers requires a decision-making procedure independent of private interests wherever there are significant conflicts, a procedure which perhaps can be established effectively under private aegis in some instances but which probably implies a governmental solution on all matters of wide-spread significance.

I close with one further illustration. At first blush, an agreement among competing manufacturers purporting to eliminate "deceptive" advertising would appear to involve no problems whatsoever. Yet a careful study of the joint action among cigarette companies on advertising of tar and nicotine content demonstrates amply that even such an agreement has its pitfalls. The original agreement among cigarette companies to abandon advertising of tar and nicotine content was tolerated if not blessed on the following reasoning: Actual differences in tar and nicotine content among cigarettes appeared to lack significant relation to health which many if not most consumers supposed that they had; *ergo,* eliminating such advertising saved consumers from buying cigarettes with the lower tar and nicotine content in the mistaken belief that they would be benefited thereby. However, there is now considerable doubt, to say the least, that this is an appropriate way of looking at the matter. Abandonment of such advertising eliminated or at least sharply reduced the incentive for cigarette manufacturers to lower tar and nicotine content to levels that might be medically significant. Moreover, numerous decisions in the area of false and misleading advertising have rested on the proposition that consumers are entitled to disclosure of facts that they are interested in even though their preferences seem wholly irrational. More specifically, those cases suggest that consumers were and are entitled to information which would enable them to pick cigarettes with the lowest tar and nicotine content, simply because they prefer to do so.

I here pass no judgment on these questions. I do suggest that private agreement among competing manufacturers is not the best way to decide them. I cite the case as a further indication of matters to be concerned about when private parties act jointly for the purported purpose of protecting the consumer.

35

Consumer Protection Via Self-Regulation

Louis L. Stern

What should be the roles of government, business, and consumers in consumer protection? The author discusses the limitations of government and business in consumer-protection efforts. He also raises the question of whether self-regulation can or should deal with social issues.

Consumerism, like marketing, is becoming a broadened concept.[1] It encompasses "health services, public utilities, transportation, and automobile safety, and urging consumer representation, consumer education, and antipoverty programs."[2] The new consumerism includes concern for distortions and inequities in the economic environment and the declining quality of the physical environment.[3] Mary Gardiner Jones expressed it this way:

> What is new today about consumerism is the fact that consumers' concerns today are much more directly focused on the human values and environmental considerations involved in today's economic decisions than they are on the more strictly "economic" problems of obtaining the highest quality goods at the lowest possible price.[4]

Accordingly, it has been suggested that during the 1970s the Federal Trade Commission (F.T.C.) will "by an imaginative, vigorous interpretation of this broad language (Section 5 of the F.T.C. Act) take cognizance of every type of business practice which offends the current social mores."[5]

Reprinted from *Journal of Marketing*, vol. 35 (July 1971), pp. 47-53. Reprinted by permission.

It is generally agreed that consumerism is here to stay. This is the implicit assumption or explicit conclusion of the business community. In the words of the Chamber of Commerce of the United States,

> But whatever the causes, it is of paramount importance to recognize that the consumer movement is well established and is likely to gain strength in coming years.[6]

Therefore, attention is now turning toward various forms of response to the consumer movement. Indicative of this direction is the creation of the Consumer Research Institute by the business community to objectively study consumer problems and evaluate alternative responses. Listed below are examples of questions that are being raised concerning organization, techniques, and policies:

1. Is it socially wiser to accept the present state of consumer dissatisfaction than to pay the cost of reducing consumer dissatisfaction?

2. Can industry reform itself without government pressure?

3. Which is likely to be most effective and economical, Better Business Bureaus, trade association complaint bureaus, or corporate divisions of consumer affairs?

4. Should consumers be encouraged toward self-protection through class action suits?

5. Can public policies be market tested?

6. What is the best positioning of consumer representation?

7. Can consumer education suffice to eliminate market abuse?

The following basic issues underlies these questions: What should be the role of private versus government effort to protect consumers? Buskirk and Rothe stated that, "The relative role the government will play, and that which industry should play, is a critical aspect in the resolution of the consumerism issue."[7]

Because consumer issues will be attended to in one way or another, government versus private regulation is a vital subject. This article addresses itself to that subject. It examines the difficulties of private and public regulation and suggests means of improving both. It interprets consumer interests in the broad manner indicated above.

GOVERNMENT REGULATION

There are several objections to government regulation. One objection is that it may lead to further and repressive regulation. Regulations seldom fade away; instead, they proliferate. As each refinement or clarification comes into force, business ingenuity probes to discover the minimum requirements necessary for compliance. Then new regulations are formed to close the loopholes which have been found. The process continues with additional and ever more confining rules until innovation is choked and business operating costs are increased. In short, government regulation tends to become progressively intrusive and destructive of incentive.

A second objection to government regulation concerns lack of uniformity of application. Differences from case to case in interpretation of regulations may appear inexplicable and inequitable. Perhaps worst of all, they are unpredictable. On the other hand, uniform application of regulations without consideration of individual circumstances also raises objections, especially from small firms.

Regulations are sometimes unevenly enforced. Because the F.T.C. and the Department of Justice have limited resources, they cannot hope to prosecute all violators of the law. The F.T.C., which is the principal government agency concerned with consumer protection, receives a small budget ($19.5 million in 1970)[8] in comparison to the job it faces. Moreover, the size of its staff is decreasing relative to the size of the U.S. economy. Merely to keep pace with the growth in disposable personal income since 1962, the F.T.C. would have needed a staff of 2,000 people by 1970 compared to the 1,270 people it actually had.[9] In addition, the F.T.C. has assumed new responsibilities under the Fair Packaging and Labeling Act (1966) and the Consumer Credit Protection Act (1968). The relatively few F.T.C. investigators have time to observe only a small proportion of the total number of firms, products, markets, and transactions.

Uneven enforcement is certain to be regarded as unfair if the prosecuted actions were committed in response to competitive necessity. Compound a sense of unfairness with suspicion that government agencies are more interested in developing the dark areas of the law than in enforcing the lighted areas equally, and objection to government regulation is to be expected.

A basic objection to government regulation is that the F.T.C. functions as both prosecutor and judge. Since the commissioners direct the thrust of agency effort and authorize the issuance of complaints, it is unrealistic to expect them to rule impartially when the cases are argued.

There are other criticisms that are being raised. Regulatory actions often take many years to conclude. Sometimes regulatory actions is not initiated until the objectionable behavior has been terminated. In addition, the F.T.C. is charged with lassitude, cronyism, and incompetence; with responding only to business and Congressional pressure groups; failure to aggressively detect consumer abuses; and failure to allocate its energies toward really important issues.[10]

Government regulation is a mixed blessing. It serves to represent public ideas. It serves to clarify, define, and make explicit acceptable and unacceptable norms of conduct. It is simultaneously a last resort and a precipitator of action. In addition, it is insensitive, inept, and burdensome. It is fashioned by compromise and twisted by interpretation.

SELF-REGULATION

Self-regulation is an obvious alternative. It is repeatedly called for by businessmen and government authorities.[11] However, what does experience show? Until the passage of the Fair Labeling and Packaging Act (1966), the food industry did virtually nothing to eliminate package-size proliferation or higher-priced large "economy" sizes. The gasoline industry promoted a wide variety of contests or sweepstakes in some of which the winners were controlled geographically or chronologically.[12] The detergent industry had to be forced into developing bio-degradable detergents, and then pressured into removing phosphates and enzymes from their products. The automobile industry produces useless bumpers of variable heights. Sixty percent of the commercial AM and FM radio stations and 35% of the commercial television stations do not support the code of the National Association of Broadcasters.[13]

The record is *not* as one-sided as the listing above. If space permitted, an industry-by-industry analysis might be attempted, but value judgments would still be involved. In any event, it is difficult to discover the whole truth of a company or industry situation. Pollution is a case in point. The public relations field has jumped on the antipolution "bandwagon" to such an extent that a substantial credibility gap exists.[14]

Nevertheless, it can be said that many individual companies and various associations have undertaken pro-consumer activities. These activities range from the proposal of codes "that acknowledge business responsibility to protect the health and safety of consumers, improve quality standards, simplify warranties, improve repair and servicing quality, self-police fraud and deception, improve information provided consumers, make sound value comparisons easier, and provide effective channels for consumer complaints,"[15] to concrete actions to implement such goals.

But voluntary action is seldom adequate. No matter how willingly some companies may observe voluntary guidelines, there are other companies that must be coerced to observe them. The other companies may not pull an industry to their level of ethics, but neither are they so few, or so insignificant, that they can be ignored. In fact, "It isn't just the fringe operators who are guilty, ... it is too often the nation's most reputable companies."[16]

Enforceability

To be meaningful, self-regulation must be enforceable and industry-wide. It must punish or prevent violations of regulatory norms. To do so requires collective action in the form of a boycott against the offender (if he refuses to reform). But boycotts in restraint of trade are illegal under the Sherman Act regardless of how meritorious or beneficial the motives or results may be. In fact, the courts are so dogmatic on this point that the Supreme Court of the United States proclaimed:

> Even if copying were an acknowledged tort under the law of every state, that situation would not justify petitioners in combining together to regulate and restrain interstate commerce (in order to prevent copying).[17]

One cannot help but feel that the Sherman Act needs to be amended by Congress or judicial interpretation to permit meritorious restraints of trade. If amended by Congress, the determination of which restraints are meritorious should be left to the F.T.C. and the courts. The procedure would be to require prior approval and periodic reapproval of proposed restraints by the F.T.C. If, after open hearings, the F.T.C. cannot distinguish between meritorious (from the public's point of view) restraints of trade and self-serving restraints of trade, then surely the restraints are not of much consequence to begin with. If a half-open door policy toward restraints of trade complicates the enforcement task and increases court loads, so be it. That is the price for freeing private energies on behalf of the consumer interests. Self-regulation cannot be fully effective without enforcement power.

PRODUCT STANDARDS

One of the most common areas of self-regulation is product standards. Because of recognition of their potential for public gain. Several thousand voluntary product standards are now in existence. Product standards may concern safety or healthfulness, size and style variations (thereby reducing production and distribution costs and consumer confusion), or quality or performance. Product standards are least desirable in the latter roles since consumer needs and preferences vary the most in this respect and can alternatively be served by mandatory informative labeling.[18]

The principal danger of product standards is that they may slow product improvement and innovation, or deny reasonable product alternatives to consumers. (In addition, producers may tend to manufacture the minimum quality possible consistent with meeting the standard.) These effects, in turn, may restrict market entry and lessen competition, thus protecting the dominant procedures and the status quo rather than consumers' interests. On the other hand, even though product standards are formed solely in the consumers' interests, even safety, they cannot be enforced by collective action. For example, an association of gas pipeline companies, gas distributors, and gas appliance manufacturers adopted a seal of approval for appliances. Safety of operation was a primary criterion in granting the seal of approval. Although the case was clouded by the use of additional test criteria and allegedly discriminatory testing procedures, the court's decision centered upon the refusal of the association to supply gas for use in nonapproved appliances. The boycott was declared illegal (if proved to exist) regardless of consumer peril.[19]

The law bends over backward, so to speak, to protect competition regardless of the immediate consequence to consumers. Accordingly, voluntary standards are only as effective as the willingness of industry members to accept them and the extent to which consumers rely upon them. Naturally, the least ethical producer is least likely to be bound by a voluntary standard, and the industry is more or less helpless to do anything about it. The best the industry can do in concert is to attempt to persuade buyers to accept only products conforming to the standard and to persuade the government to make the standard mandatory. Members of the industry may unilaterally attempt to force the deviant firm into line, but they run the risk of being accused of implicit agreement in doing so.

Is there a way out of the dilemma of trying to protect consumers in the short run while preserving the long-run benefits of freedom? In the writer's opinion, the answer is to: (1) provide maximum consumer involvement in the writing of product standards; (2) provide for automatic review of standards at frequent intervals; (3) permit the sale of products not conforming to the standards provided that the nonconforming products are labeled with the relevant standards and the manner and extent to which they do not conform to those standards; and (4) *permit collective action among firms to boycott any firm whose products conform to neither the industry standards nor the labeling requirement.*

Health or safety considerations might require that some standards be conformed to without exception. In most cases, however, the proposed privilege of deviating from product standards would guarantee the right to innovate. It would also enable firms to better serve specialized market segments for which the standards might be inappropriate. The fact that deviations from product standards would have to be prominently labeled would place some products at a competitive disadvantage for the sake of improved market information. However, the extent of the disadvantage would be limited by the merits of the deviation from the standard and the extent to which consumers felt a need for relying upon the standard.

PROMOTIONAL PRACTICES

Promotional practices are of equal or greater importance to consumer welfare than product standards. Hence, as with product standards, self-regulation is both prevalent and contentious, and the issue again becomes the purpose and effectiveness of such self-regulation.

Promotional practices raise questions of (1) amount (waste, competitive barrier, omnipresence); (2) cultural effects (media control, social values, unbalancing of competition between private goods and social goods); (3) function (to inform or only persuade); and (4) taste. Even the basic principle that consumers should not be deceived, though readily agreed upon, is disputed in interpretation. For example, how many readers would agree with various members of the F.T.C. that: (1) it is unfair or deceptive to withhold useful information (such as gasoline octane ratings, automobile mileage per gallon, or product test life); (2) irrelevant or emotional appeals are misleading and deceptive; and (3) promotional claims are deceptive unless proven? Three successive presidents of the United States have proclaimed the right of consumers to be informed, yet manufacturers do not acknowledge and fulfill a corresponding obligation to provide information—certainly not negative information.[20]

Nonperception

Aside from being constrained by the Sherman Act, the difficulty of self-regulation of promotional practices is two-fold: On the one hand is nonperception, and on the other it is nonresponsibility. The first problem is simply a failure to perceive any injustice in questionable practices. For example, a soap manufacturer may distort a competitor's test marketing program. He may arrange with a wholesaler to buy up a sufficient amount of the test product to inflate the sales measurement. Simultaneously, he may adopt the test product advertising theme and begin to implement it nationwide. As a result, the competitor may be falsely encouraged to "go national" with the new product. Since most of the huge introductory promotional expenditures will be incurred at the start of the campaign, a large loss will be sustained before it becomes apparent that the product is failing. If the product does succeed, its success will be minimized and undermined by the pre-emption of the copy theme. The perception problem is that both companies may regard these occurrences as simple competitive gamesmanship.

Another example of misperception (by buyer and seller) is the claim of price reductions or performance advantage "up to" a stated amount. Advertisers are well aware of the legal requirement to be objectively honest in advertising. Furthermore, it is illegal to make statements which by themselves are true, but which, when taken as a whole, are likely to deceive. [21] Yet literally true "up-to" statements which probably convey the impression that the price-cut or performance-gain to be expected by the buyer is of the "up to" amount are widespread. Whether such statements are deceptive could easily be resolved through appropriate research. It illustrates the potential value of a government-funded institute to study consumer behavior and the impact of advertising and marketing upon society. [22]

The point is that there are many advertisements and marketing practices in general that are objectionable to many people, but which raise no compunctions among some sellers. Such abuses as the advertisement in poor taste, the unsolicited merchandise, the engineered contest, the shrinkage of package weight, the unsubstantiated claim, and the negative-option sale plan are all defended by sellers who perceive no wrong in them. Their insensitivity may be profit-motivated or philosophical, but in either case it is not conducive to effective self-regulation.

Levitt suggests that a primary reason for businessmen's insensitivity to social responsibility, even though it may be in their long-run interest, is their total commitment to achieving day-to-day profit maximization. [23] The blindness caused by "keeping one's nose to the grindstone" is exacerbated by a steady diet of "chauvinistic patter" from business journals written according to what their editors think businessmen want to hear. Other observers have suggested that businessmen's nonperception of the social environment is due to the narrow direction of consumer research toward improving product, package, and promotional appeals; in short, their research has been too sales-oriented. [24]

Nonresponsibility

The second aspect of the problem of promotional practices is nonresponsibility; that is, sellers recognize the wrong but accept no responsibility for it. A classic case is beer and soft drinks. With society becoming ever more concerned about waste disposal, these two industries are selling more of their product in nonreturnable glass containers. Thirty-six percent of all glass shipments in 1969[25] were for nonreturnable bottles of beer and soft drinks compared with 7.5% of such shipments in 1959.[26] The beverage industries, including liquor and wine, but excluding milk, are responsible for 50% of all glass container waste.

When companies are confronted with this abuse of social interest (which is aggravated by consumption of beverages away from home), they reply that they are only serving the public's preference for nonreturnable containers. To their way of thinking, it is the public's responsibility, not theirs. (The cigarette industry uses the same rationale, although additional factors are involved.) Indeed, the responsibility is shared by consumers as individuals and through their governments; however, the first responsibility belongs to the bottlers. Just as producers have a concerted interest relative to consumers in lobbying activities, so too, producers have concerted responsibilities.

Businessmen who reject the concept of social responsibility may do so in order to maximize profits, or because they feel a lack of mandate from society to take specific actions. That the profit consideration may be declining in importance is indicated by the statement of B. R. Dorsey, president of Gulf Oil Corporation, who declared that " 'maximum financial gain, the historical number one objective' of American business, must move 'into second place whenever it conflicts with the well-being of society.'" [27] The second reason, namely, the lack of public mandate, may also be overcome; that is, a concern for democratic process may be upheld via attitude research. However, a deeper question remains: Should the attitudes of an ill-informed and untrained public be controlling?

ALTERNATIVES

Although the line between nonperception of wrong and nonacceptance of responsibility may be difficult to distinguish, the absence of effective self-regulation is clear. Why? One reason is that self-regulation is stymied by the Sherman Act barrier against collective use of pressure upon offenders. Only the removal of the legal barrier to enforceable self-regulation will provide the necessary test of whether enforceable self-regulation can obviate the need for more government regulation.

Resistance to the idea of enforceable self-regulation is based upon fear that self-regulation may be perverted to industry benefit at the expense of consumers or prospective competitors. This fear can be allayed by requiring prior F.T.C. approval of proposed regulations and periodic reapproval. Such fear can be further allayed by including a counter balance to the possibility of business or political influence over the F.T.C.'s judgment. This counter balance would include:

1. Separation of the prosecuting and adjudicating functions of the F.T.C., and placing the later function under a newly established system of trade courts;[28] and

2. Providing competitors, consumer organizations, and other government agencies the right to seek injunctions from the above trade courts against any form or application of self-regulatory activity which is deemed unfair or socially harmful.

A significantly lesser form of self-regulation would be for trade associations to attempt to prosecute offenses under existing law. This approach might include the initiation of trade practice conferences in order to spotlight questionable activities within the industry and generate trade practice rules or guides. There are three major weaknesses to this approach. First, although the F.T.C. Act broadly prohibits unfair methods of competition and unfair or deceptive acts in commerce, it does not authorize private suits. The Lanham Act does authorize private suits, but applies only to false descriptions or representations in commerce. Second, while Congress could authorize private suits under the F.T.C. Act, neither this Act nor the Lanham Act reaches the potential of enforceable self-regulation for implementing social responsibilities. For example, as currently interpreted, neither law interdicts the sale of hand guns, "high-powered" cars, or telephone solicitation. Third, industries tend to have a "live and let live" attitude. Companies with high ethical standards seldom are inclined to report, much less take action against, the dishonest or offensive members of an industry.

CONCLUSION

The more technology advances, the more deeply will marketing become involved in social issues. The argument that business has no responsibility but to satisfy consumer wants is an open invitation to government regulation. In the short run, consumers do not always fully comprehend the private effects of their wants (witness disbelief of smoking hazards) let alone the social effects (say of D.D.T., nonreturnable containers, or private urban transportation). Nevertheless, reality cannot be denied, and wisdom eventually prevails. When business does not accept social responsibility in fact as well as in survey response,[29] public regulation is eventually forced upon it.

Self-regulation cannot repeal human nature, and a free enterprise system cannot survive without a vigorous profit incentive. On the other hand, neither can a free enterprise system remain healthy if "the responsiveness of a firm to the consumer is directly proportionate to the distance on the organization chart from the consumer to the chairman of the board."[30] What is needed is a greater sensitivity to changing public demands upon business.

In order to harness the potential of self-regulatory effort, the Congress, the F.T.C., and Department of Justice must make enforcement possible when it is clearly in the public interest. However, the opportunity for enforceable self-regulation by no means assures unqualified success for this approach. A continuing threat of increased government regulation will always be necessary to make self-regulation work. Government regulation, in turn, needs consumer advocates to make it function effectively. Hence, consumer protection is a sort of tripod affair. If business is to keep the tripod in balance, self-regulation will have to grow accordingly.

The more educated society becomes, the more interdependent it becomes, and the more discretionary the use of its resources, the more marketing will become enmeshed in social issues. Marketing personnel are at the interface between company and society. In this position they have a responsibility not merely for designing a competitive marketing strategy, but for sensitizing business to the social, as well as the product, demands of society.

REFERENCES

1. Philip Kotler and Sidney J. Levy, "Broadening the Concept of Marketing," JOURNAL OF MARKETING, vol. 33 (January, 1969), pp. 10-15.
2. National Goals Research Staff, *Toward Balanced Growth: Quantity With Quality* (Washington, D.C.: United States Government Printing Office, 1970), p. 133.

3. George S. Day and David Aaker, "A Guide to Consumerism," JOURNAL OF MARKETING, vol. 34 (July, 1970), pp. 12-19.
4. Address by Mary Gardiner Jones, Federal Trade Commissioner, before the Manufacturing Chemists Association, New York, November 25, 1969.
5. Address by Joseph Martin, Jr., General Counsel, Federal Trade Commission, at a conference sponsored by California Business Seminars, Inc., Los Angeles, California. September 23, 1970.
6. Chamber of Commerce of the United States, Council on Trends and Perspective, *Business and the Consumer—A Program for the Seventies* (Washington, D.C.: Chamber of Commerce of the United States, 1970), p. 10.
7. Richard H. Buskirk and James T. Rothe, "Consumerism—An Interpretation," JOURNAL OF MARKETING, vol. 34 (October, 1970), p. 63.
8. From an address by Mary Gardiner Jones, Federal Trade Commissioner, before the Sixth Biennial World Conference of the International Organization of Consumer Unions, Baden, Vienna, Austria, June 29, 1970.
9. Same reference as footnote 8.
10. Edward F. Cox, Robert C. Fellmeth, and John E. Schulz, *'The Nader Report' on the Federal Trade Commission* (New York: Richard W. Baron, 1969). See also "The Regulators Can't Go On This Way," *Business Week,* no. 2113 (February 28, 1970), pp. 60-73; and Louis M. Kohlmeier, Jr., *The Regulators; Watchdog Agencies and the Public Interest* (New York: Harper and Row, 1969).
11. Significant articles in this area include Robert B. Hummer, "Antitrust Problems of Industry Codes of Advertising, Standardization, and Seals of Approval," *Antitrust Bulletin,* vol. 13 (1968), pp. 607-618; H. Richard Wachtel, "Product Standards and Certification Programs," *Antitrust Bulletin,* vol. 13 (1968), pp. 1-38; Harvey J. Levin, "The Limits of Self-regulation," *Columbia Law Review,* vol. 67 (March, 1967), pp. 603-642; and Jerrold G. Van Cise, "Regulation—By Business or Government?" *Harvard Business Review,* vol. 44 (March-April, 1966), pp. 53-63.
12. See *Investigation of "Preselected Winners" Sweepstakes Promotions,* hearings before the Select Committee on Small Business, House of Representatives, 91st Congress, 1st Session, 1970.
13. Maurice Christopher, "Work Added by New Guidelines Strains NAB Codes' Resources," *Advertising Age* (March 15, 1971), p. 93.
14. See E. B. Weiss, "Management: Don't Kid the Public With Those Noble Anti-Polution Ads," *Advertising Age* (August 3, 1970), p. 35; and Stanley E. Cohen, "Anti-Pollution Claims May Prove Pandora Trouble Box for Advertisers," *Advertising Age* (September 14, 1970), p. 110.
15. Same reference as footnote 2, p. 143.
16. "The Editorial Viewpoint, *Advertising Age* (March 30, 1970), p. 14.
17. *Fashion Guild v. F.T.C.,* 312 US 457, 458 (1941).
18. Louis L. Stern, "Consumer Protection Via Increased Information," JOURNAL OF MARKETING, vol. 31 (April, 1967), pp. 48-52.
19. *Radiant Burners, Inc. v. Peoples Gas Light and Coke Co.,* 364 U.S. 656 (1961).
20. For alternative concepts of information see same references as footnote 2, pp. 139-140.
21. *Bennett v. F.T.C.,* 200 F2d 362; *P. Lorillard Co. v. F.T.C.,* 186 F2d 52.
22. See Dorothy Cohen, "The Federal Trade Commission and the Regulation of Advertising in the Consumer Interest," JOURNAL OF MARKETING, vol. 33 (January, 1969), pp. 40-44; and "Nobody Understands Marketing Economy, Sen. Moss Says; Proposes a New U.S. Institute," *Advertising Age* (February 15, 1971), p. 14.
23. Theodore Levitt, "Why Business Always Loses," *Harvard Business Review,* vol. 46 (March-April, 1968), pp. 81-89.
24. For example, see Peter F. Drucker, "The Shame of Marketing," *Marketing/Communications,* vol. 297 (August 19, 1969), pp. 60-64.
25. *Modern Packaging Encyclopedia* (New York: McGraw-Hill, Inc., 1970), p. 19.
26. *Modern Packing Encyclopedia* (New York: McGraw-Hill, Inc., 1961), p. 41.

27. Reported by Alfred L. Malabre, Jr., "The Outlook," *Wall Street Journal* (March 22, 1971), p. 1.

28. See "F.T.C.'s Elman, in Parting Shot, Advocates 'Radical Structural Reform of Agencies,' " *Wall Street Journal* (August 12, 1970), p. 4.

29. See Arthur M. Lewis, "The View from the Pinnacle: What Business Thinks," Fortune, vol. 80 (September, 1969), pp. 92-95, and 207-208.

30. Address by Virginia Knauer, Special Assistant to the President for Consumer Affairs, before the Federal Bar Association, Washington, D.C., September, 1970.

36

Buyer's Bill
of Rights

President Nixon

To the Congress of the United States:

The history of American prosperity is the history of the American free enterprise system. The system has provided an economic foundation of awesome proportions, and the vast material strength of the nation is built on that foundation. For the average American, this strength is reflected in a standard of living that would have staggered the imagination only a short while ago. This constantly rising standard of living benefits both the consumer and the producer.

In today's marketplace, however, the consumer often finds himself confronted with what seems an impenetrable complexity in many of our consumer goods, in the advertising claims that surround them, the merchandising methods that purvey them and the means available to conceal their quality. The result is a degree of confusion that often confounds the unwary, and too easily can be made to favor the unscrupulous. I believe new safeguards are needed, both to protect the consumer and to reward the responsible businessman.

I indicated my deep concern for this matter in my special message to the Congress of October 30, 1969. At that time I urged the Congress to enact a legislative program aimed at establishing a "Buyer's Bill of Rights." This proposal found little success in the 91st Congress. But putting the remedies aside has not sufficed to put the problems aside. These remain. They must be dealt with.

Accordingly, I am again submitting proposals designed to provide such a Buyer's Bill of Rights by:

This is a reprint of Message from the President of the United States to the 92d Cong., 1st Sess., HR Document no. 92-52, February 25, 1971.

Creating by Executive Order a new Office of Consumer Affairs in the Executive Office of the President which will be responsible for analyzing and coordinating all Federal activities in the field of consumer protection;

Recognizing the need for effective representation of consumer interests in the regulatory process and making recommendations to accomplish this after full public discussion of the findings of the Advisory Council on Executive Organization;

Establishing within the Department of Health, Education, and Welfare a product safety program. The Secretary of Health, Education, and Welfare would have authority to fix minimum safety standards for products and to ban from the marketplace those products that fail to meet those standards;

Proposing a Consumer Fraud Prevention Act which would make unlawful a broad but clearly-defined range of practices which are unfair and deceptive to consumers and would be enforced by the Department of Justice and the Federal Trade Commission. This act, where appropriate, would also enable consumers either as individuals or as a class to go into court to recover damages for violations of the act;

Proposing amendments to the Federal Trade Commission Act which will increase the effectiveness of the Federal Trade Commission;

Calling upon interested private citizens to undertake a thorough study of the adequacy of existing procedures for the resolution of disputes arising out of consumer transactions;

Proposing a Fair Warranty Disclosure Act which will provide for clearer warranties, and prohibit the use of deceptive warranties;

Proposing a Consumer Products Test Methods Act to provide incentives for increasing the amount of accurate and relevant information provided consumers about complex consumer products;

Resubmitting the Drug Identification Act which would require identification coding of all drug tablets and capsules;

Encouraging the establishment of a National Business Council to assist the business community in meeting its responsibilities to the consumer; and by

Other reforms, including exploration of a Consumer Fraud Clearinghouse in the Federal Trade Commission, increased emphasis on consumer education and new programs in the field of food and drug safety.

NEW OFFICE OF CONSUMER AFFAIRS

The President's Committee on Consumer Interests has made important gains on behalf of the American consumer in the past two years.

It has brought a new and innovative approach to the problem of keeping the consumer informed and capable of handling the complex choices presented to him in today's commercial world. One such measure involves the dissemination of information which the United States Government, as the nations' largest single consumer, collects on the products it uses. In my message of October 30, 1969, I announced that I was directing my Special Assistant for Consumer Affairs to develop a program for providing the buying public with this information.

On the strength of her recommendations, on October 26, 1970, I signed Executive Order 11566 which establishes a means for making available to the public much of the product information which the Federal Government acquires in making its own purchases. A Consumer Product Information Coordinating Center has been established in the General Services Administration with continuing policy guidance from my Special Assistant for Consumer Affairs to make these data available to the public through Federal information centers and other sources throughout the country.

In addition, the Committee on Consumer Interests has made significant strides in developing Federal, State and local cooperation in consumer programs, encouraging establishment of strong State and local consumer offices, and advising on the enactment of effective consumer laws and programs.

Nevertheless, further cooperation among Federal, State and local governments is essential if we are truly to insure that the consumer is properly served. Therefore, I am asking my Special Assistant for Consumer Affairs to intensify her efforts on behalf of the consumer at the State and local level. I am directing her to conduct regional meetings with State officials concerned with consumer issues, with consumer groups, and with individual consumers to discuss common problems and possible solutions.

But I believe the greatest overall accomplishment of this office has been to give the consumer new assurance of this administration's concern for his and her welfare in the marketplace. In manifesting this concern during the past two years, the responsibility of the President's Committee on Consumer Interests has grown, as has its impact on consumer problems. I have therefore signed today a new Executive Order creating a new Office of Consumer Affairs in the Executive Office of the President. I am appointing my Special Assistant for Consumer Affairs to be Director of this new office. This change reflects the increasingly broad scope of responsibilities assigned to the Special Assistant for Consumer Affairs and will increase the effectiveness of the Office. The Office will advise me on matters of consumer interests, and will also assume primary responsibility for coordinating all Federal activity in the consumer field.

Finally, while I am deeply concerned with obtaining justice for all consumers, I have a special concern to see justice for those who, in a sense, need it most and are least able to get it. Therefore, I am directing my Special Assistant for Consumer Affairs to focus particular attention in the new Office on the coordination of consumer programs aimed at assisting those with limited income, the elderly, the disadvantaged, and minority group members.

A CONSUMER ADVOCATE

In my message of October 30, 1969, I pointed out that effective representation of the consumer requires that an appropriate arm of the government be given the tools to serve as an advocate before the Federal agencies. I proposed then that this function be performed by a Consumer Protection Division created for the purpose and located within the Department of Justice. That proposal was not acted on.

Since that time my Advisory Council on Executive Organization has completed its Report on Selected Independent Regulatory Agencies. This report makes sweeping recommendations on the reorganization of those agencies for the purpose of helping them better serve the interests of the consumer.

One specific recommendation involves the creation of a new Federal Trade Practices Agency dealing exclusively with matters of consumer protection. This Agency would result from a general restructuring of the Federal Trade Commission. The report specifically suggests that a consumer advocate might be placed within the Federal Trade Practices Agency.

I believe that this is a better approach than the creation of still another independent agency which would only add to the proliferation of agencies without dealing with the problems of effectiveness to which the Advisory Council report addresses itself.

As I indicated at the release of the Advisory Council's report, I am delaying legislative proposals on these issues pending full public discussion of the findings and recommendations of the Council. I urge that those who comment on the Advisory Council recommendations also focus on the manner in which the consumer interest can best be represented in Federal agency proceedings. I further urge the Congress to view the problems of consumer advocacy and agency structure as part of the general problem of making the Federal Government sufficiently responsive to the consumer interest.

After April 20, when comments have been received, I will make the recommendations I consider necessary to provide effective representation of consumer interests in the regulatory process. If the Congress feels it must proceed on the matter of consumer advocacy prior to receiving my recommendations, then I strongly urge and would support, as an interim measure, the placement of the advocacy function within the Federal Trade Commission.

A PRODUCT SAFETY ACT

Technology, linked with the American free enterprise system, has brought great advantages and great advances to our way of life. It has also brought certain hazards.

The increasing complexity and sophistication of many of our consumer goods are sometimes accompanied by the increasing possibility of product failure, malfunction, or inadvertent misuse resulting in physical danger to the consumer.

Therefore, I propose legislation providing broad Federal authority for comprehensive regulation of hazardous consumer products.

This product safety legislation will encompass five major responsibilities which would be assigned to a new consumer product safety organization within the Department of Health, Education, and Welfare. Through this organization the Secretary of Health, Education, and Welfare will:

1. Gather data on injuries from consumer products;
2. Make preliminary determinations of the need for particular standards;

3. Develop proposed safety standards with reliance on recognized private standards setting organizations;

4. Promulgate standards after a hearing and testimony on the benefits and burdens of the proposed legislation; and

5. Monitor industry compliance and enforce mandatory standards.

The mechanisms which will be included in this bill provide for full participation on the part of private organizations and groups in the development of standards.

NATIONAL ATTACK ON CONSUMER FRAUD

Consumer fraud and deception jeopardize the health and welfare of our people. They cheat consumers of millions of dollars annually. They are often directed against those who can least afford the loss and are least able to defend themselves—the elderly, the handicapped, and the poor.

At the same time, the honest businessman is damaged by fraud and deceptive practices every bit as much as the consumer—and perhaps more. He is subjected to the unfair competition of the unscrupulous businessman, and he loses money. He is subjected to the opprobrium of those who have suffered at the hands of unscrupulous businessmen, and he loses the goodwill of the public. For it is a fact, however unfortunate, that in the area of business especially, the many are commonly judged by the actions of the few.

Efforts to eliminate these unethical business practices have not been successful enough. It is commonly profitable for unscrupulous businessmen to operate in defiance of the enforcement authorities, to accept whatever penalties and punishment are incurred, and to continue to operate in spite of these. The penalty is just part of the overhead. I want these practices brought to an end.

With this message I am committing this administration to a full and forceful effort to see that they are brought to an end.

Consumer Fraud Prevention Act

I am again submitting and I urge prompt attention to a bill to make unlawfull a broad but clearly defined range of practices which are deceptive to consumers. The legislation would provide that the Department of Justice be given new powers to enforce prohibitions against those who would victimize consumers by fraudulent and deceptive practices.

It would give consumers who have been victimized by such practices the right to bring cases in the Federal courts to recover damages, upon the successful termination of a government suit under the Consumer Fraud Prevention Act.

I am also recommending civil penalties of up to $10,000 for each offense in violation of this act.

The Department of Justice has created a new Consumer Protection Section within the Antitrust Division, which has centralized the Department's enforcement in the courts of existing statutes designed to protect the consumer interest. Thus the

Department of Justice is prepared to enforce promptly the proposed Consumer Fraud Prevention Act.

Federal Trade Commission

While there is a need for new legislation to insure the rights of the consumer, there is also a need to make more effective use of the legislation we already have, and of the institutions charged with enforcing this legislation.

A principal function of the Federal Trade Commission has historically been to serve as the consumers' main line of resistance to commercial abuse. In the past year the Commission, under new leadership, has been substantially strengthened. A major organizational restructuring has produced within the Commission a Bureau of Consumer Protection, a Bureau of Competition, and a Bureau of Economics. An Office of Policy Planning and Evaluation has been created to establish a more effective ordering of priorities for the Commission's enforcement efforts.

In order to make FTC procedures more responsive to the needs of consumers, responsibilities of the eleven Commission field offices have been extended to include trying cases before hearing examiners in the field, negotiating settlements, conducting investigations, and referring complaints to the Commission. Six Consumer Protection Coordinating Committees have been established in selected metropolitan areas.

I am submitting today legislation which would provide the FTC with the authority to seek preliminary injunctions in Federal courts against what it deems to be unfair or deceptive business practices. The present inability to obtain injunctions commonly results in the passage of extended periods of time before relief can be obtained. During this time the practices in question continue, and their effects multiply.

The proposed bill would expand the jurisdiction of the Commission to include those activities "affecting" interstate commerce, as well as those activities which are "in" interstate commerce.

Finally, I recommend that the penalty schedule for violation of a Commission cease-and-desist order be adjusted from a maximum of $5,000 per violation to a maximum of $10,000 per violation.

Guarantees and Warranties

A constant source of misunderstanding between consumer and businessman is the question of warranties. Guarantees and warranties are often found to be unclear or deceptive.

In 1970, I submitted a proposal for legislation to meet this problem. I am submitting new legislation for this purpose.

This proposal would increase the authority of the Federal Trade Commission to require that guarantees and warranties on consumer goods convey adequate information in simple and readily understood terms.

It would further seek to prevent deceptive warranties; and it would prohibit improper use of a written warranty or guarantee to avoid implied warranty obligations arising under State law.

Consumer Fraud Clearinghouse

My Special Assistant for Consumer Affairs is examining the feasibility of a consumer fraud clearinghouse—a prompt exchange of information between appropriate Federal, State and local law enforcement officials which can be especially helpful in identifying those who perpetrate fraudulent, unfair and deceptive practices upon the consumer and deprive the honest businessman of his legitimate opportunities in the marketplace.

Upon her recommendation, I am asking the FTC to explore with State and local consumer law enforcement officials an effective mechanism for such an exchange.

CONSUMER EDUCATION

Legislative remedies and improved enforcement procedures are powerful weapons in the fight for consumer justice. But as important as these are, they are only as effective as an aware and an informed public make them. Consumer education is an integral part of consumer protection. It is vital if the consumer is to be able to make wise judgements in the marketplace. To enable him or her to do this will require a true educational process beginning in childhood and continuing on.

The Office of the Special Assistant for Consumer Affairs has established guidelines for consumer education suggested for use at the elementary and high school level. Those guidelines have been sent to every school system in the country, and their reception has been encouraging. I believe they mark an effective step toward developing an informed consumer. The Office has also begun the development of suggested guidelines for adult and continuing education with particular emphasis on special socio-economic groups and senior citizens.

Now, in order to expand and lend assistance to Consumer Education activities across the nation, I am asking the Secretary of Health, Education, and Welfare, in coordination with my Special Assistant for Consumer Affairs, to work with the nation's education system to (1) promote the establishment of consumer education as a national educational concern; (2) provide technical assistance in the development of programs; (3) encourage teacher training in consumer education; and (4) solicit the use of all school and public libraries as consumer information centers.

I am also asking the Secretary of Health, Education, and Welfare, in coordination with my Special Assistant for Consumer Affairs, to develop and design programs for the most effective dissemination of consumer information, and particularly to explore the use of the mass media, including the Corporation for Public Broadcasting.

ADDITIONAL PROPOSALS

Consumer Remedies

As we move to shape new consumer legislation, I believe we must also review all consumer remedies. Although this is primarily a matter of State and local responsibility, I believe that the problem is also of national concern. Accordingly, I am asking the Chairman of the Administrative Conference of the United States to join with other interested citizens representing a broad spectrum of society to undertake a thorough study of the adequacy of existing procedures for resolving disputes arising out of consumer transactions.

The study would (1) focus particularly on the means of handling small claims and explore methods for making small claims courts more responsive to the needs of consumers; (2) examine existing and potential voluntary settlement procedures, including arbitration, and potential means of creating incentives to voluntary, fair settlements of consumer disputes; (3) address the difficult and troublesome questions presented by mass litigation; (4) examine problems and solutions at the State as well as the Federal level; and (5) draw on the experience of other nations in improving consumer remedies.

The purpose of this study will be to gather those facts needed to determine the means of gaining the greatest benefit to consumers with the least cost to production processes and to the country. I urge Federal, State, local and private bodies to cooperate in this effort. I also ask that recommendations to the President, the Congress, the courts and the general public be made within the shortest practicable time.

FOOD AND DRUG PROGRAMS

Events in the past year have reconfirmed the need for urgent action to insure thorough and effective quality control through the Food and Drug Administration over the food Americans consume and the drugs they take.

In my message of October 30, 1969, I called for stronger efforts in the field of food and drug safety.

At that time I announced that the Secretary of Health, Education, and Welfare had intitiated a thorough study of the Food and Drug Administration. As a result of that study, a number of management reforms have contributed to a more effective functioning of the FDA.

Food. During the past two years consumer concern about the quality of certain foods in this nation has become acute. I have instructed the Food and Drug Administration to develop new and better methods for inspecting foods—domestic and imported—to insure that they are entirely free from all natural or artificial contamination. In addition, a major study is under way reviewing the safety of all food additives. Finally, because too many Americans have no understanding of the most basic nutritional principles, the Food and Drug Administration has developed programs of nutritional guidelines and nutritional labeling. Different approaches to labeling are presently being tested for method and effectiveness.

Drugs. In the past year the Food and Drug Administration has been engaged in an extensive program to insure the effectiveness of the drugs Americans use. Decisions have been made on some 3,000 drugs marketed between 1938 and 1962 and representing 80% of the most commonly prescribed drugs.

In addition, the Food and Drug Administration will expand its research efforts aimed at insuring that all drugs available on the market are capable of producing the therapeutic effects claimed for them.

I have resubmitted legislation requiring the identification coding of drug tablets and capsules to prevent those poisonings which result from the use of drug products of unknown or mistaken composition.

A Consumer Product Test Methods Act

Consumers are properly concerned with the reliability of the information furnished them about the goods they buy, and I believe they have a right to such information.

Accordingly, I again propose legislation aimed at stimulating product testing in the private sector. Under this legislation, the Secretary of Commerce, through the National Bureau of Standards, in consultation with my Special Assistant for Consumer Affairs, would identify products that should be tested. Competent Federal agencies would identify product characteristics that should be tested and would approve and develop, where necessary, testing methods to assess those characteristics. Suppliers of goods would be permitted to advertise their compliance with government approved testing standards. In addition, interested private organizations may receive accreditation indicating their competence to perform the approved tests, and the use of an accredited organization in testing a product may be advertised.

National Business Council for Consumer Affairs

Most businessmen recognize and accept their responsibility to the consumer, and in many cases they have voluntarily undertaken efforts to assure more fully that these responsibilities are met throughout the business community.

To emphasize and encourage such voluntary activity, a National Business Council for Consumer Affairs will be organized by the Secretary of Commerce. It will work closely with my Special Assistant for Consumer Affairs, the Federal Trade Commission, the Justice Department and others as appropriate in the further development of effective policies to benefit American consumers.

The Council will be a vehicle through which Government can work with business leaders to establish programs for accomplishing the goal I stated in my 1969 message on consumer protection of fostering "a marketplace which is fair both to those who sell and those who buy." And it will encourage everyone who does business to do an even better job of establishing competitive proces for high quality goods and services.

CONCLUSION

In submitting the foregoing proposals, I want to emphasize that the purpose of this program is not to provide the consumer with something to which he is not presently entitled; it is rather to assure that he receives what he is, in every way, fully entitled to. The continued success of our free enterprise system depends in large measure upon the mutual trust and goodwill of those who consume and those who produce or provide.

Today, in America, there is a general sense of trust and goodwill toward the world of business. Those who violate that trust and abuse that goodwill do damage to the free enterprise system. Thus, it is not only to protect the consumer, but also to protect that system and the honest men who have created and who maintain it that I urge the prompt passage of this legislative program.

THE WHITE HOUSE, *February 24, 1971*   RICHARD NIXON

37

Consumer Protection: Proposals for New Initiatives

ABA Commission to Study the Federal Trade Commission

The American Bar Association Commission to Study the
Federal Trade Commission criticizes the effectiveness of the
FTC in the area of consumer affairs and recommends broad
changes to reorder FTC priorities and the allocation of its
resources.

Our study of the FTC's existing programs has indicated a serious misallocation of
resources and a confusion of priorities. The only solution for this which can prevent
similar distortions from occurring in the future is for the FTC to set up its own
apparatus to define and to keep current a unified plan in the consumer area. Past
efforts to do this have produced no effective results. The primary requisite for
planning is adequate information about what consumer problems are, quantitatively
and qualitatively. This can be achieved through analysis and classification of complaints received by the FTC, and by consultation and coordination with all interested
groups, e.g., organized consumer groups, OEO Community Action Law Offices, U.S.
Attorney's offices, Better Business Bureaus and the NAACP Legal Defense and
Education Fund. Then the FTC must deploy its resources so that national problems
are handled at a national level through the promulgation of regulations or through

Reprinted from *Report of the ABA Commission to Study the Federal Trade Commission*
(Washington, D.C.: The Bureau of National Affairs, 1969), pp. 54-63. Reprinted by permission.

landmark proceedings, while regional enforcement efforts are carried out in a way which attains the maximum compliance per manhour of enforcement effort.

Achievement of these requisites, we believe, requires new initiatives on the part of the FTC. There are many routes to the goal. We will set forth herein three suggestions as a guide to the type of initiative the problems warrant.

First, a pilot project for a more intense study of retail marketing abuses and their prevention, which could carry out on a larger scale and a more sustained basis the embryonic effort of the District of Columbia pilot project. This pilot project could compile the information needed to classify and quantify consumer abuses, and demonstrate the most effective enforcement techniques. Second, there are substantial areas which have been largely neglected by the Federal Trade Commission, but which a pilot project might explore with an eye to FTC action under Section 5, or to federal legislation as necessary and appropriate. Finally, the addition of sanctions for which new legislation probably would be required could make the FTC a more effective enforcement agency across-the-board.

A.   PILOT PROJECT FOR PREVENTION AND STUDY OF RETAIL MARKETING ABUSES.

We recommend that the FTC establish special task force offices in 8 or 10 major urban areas in the United States which preferably would be independent of existing field offices. Each office would be staffed with an average of about ten lawyers and other professional personnel, and supporting clerical staff,[1] and their assignment would be to carry forward a model program to detect, proceed against, and at the same time study, classify, and report on problems of localized fraud against consumers. These programs would be designed to protect consumers generally, but emphasis would be on economic fraud and deception against particularly vulnerable groups—the poor, the uneducated, and the elderly.

Project content would vary from city to city. For example, in a city where state and local enforcement agencies are relatively active, and OEO Community Action Law offices or the U.S. Attorney's Office is energetically pressing legal actions against economic exploitation of consumers, the FTC's program should emphasize coordination with existing enforcement groups by referring complaints, operating as an information clearing house, working on consumer education, etc. Where other sources of enforcement against consumer exploitation are deficient, however, the FTC might experiment with a program that involves a greater emphasis on formal enforcement activities.

The project described below would be designed to operate for three years, after which a report would be submitted to Congress. If results warranted, the program might be continued thereafter. The nature of the program is outlined below.

(1) Detection

Information as to consumer abuse would be developed through establishment of one or more "consumer complaint" offices in each area, staffed by FTC personnel, which would make known throughout the community the willingness of the FTC to investigate alleged consumer frauds. Project members also would set up cooperative arrangements with other public and private legal service organizations. One reason for careful coordination is that formal investigation by the FTC, conducted by subpoena, could confer immunity on the firm being investigated under 15 U.S.C.A. §49. Before resorting to a formal investigation, it would be necessary for the FTC to be sure the matter would not be more appropriately pursued by federal or state agencies with criminal enforcement power.

In addition to local complaint offices, staff personnel would review newspaper and magazine ads and local radio and TV scripts for false advertising, study garnishment rolls and other court records to determine whether sellers may be taken oppressive advantage of the judicial process, and hold public hearings in the community to discuss economic abuses. The results of such studies then might be summarized and correlated with trends emerging in the letters currently received by the FTC from consumers complaining about fraud and deception.

(2) Enforcement Proceedings

Proceedings would be filed against companies where there is cause to believe they have engaged in serious consumer frauds in violation of Section 5. It is anticipated that many cases would be settled through decree or voluntary compliance, as is true with most FTC work. Where that is impossible or where a violation is particularly flagrant, cease and desist orders should be sought. Lawyers in the local office would be responsible for deciding whether to file a formal complaint, issue subpoenas, enter into a consent settlement, and, if necessary, try the case before hearing examiners assigned to sit in each local area where a project is established.[2] Since the staff of FTC hearing examiners has little work to do at present, a commitment of their time for this purpose would simply make use of resources currently being underutilized. Moreover, since most consumer fraud cases (e.g., bait-and-switch, false advertising, phony warranties, etc.) are relatively simple to try compared to the much more complicated cases that arise under anti-monopoly statutes, we expect that the young lawyers assigned to these local offices would be competent to handle these matters.

As we have previously noted, some consumer fraud situations are almost entirely local in character (for example, a single unconscionable contract between a seller and buyer); others can be dealt with effectively on a national basis (for example, false advertising, including bait-and-switch tactics, systematic abuse of holder in due course defenses, door-to-door sales frauds, etc.) Where the abuse is entirely local, the FTC office would be expected to establish liaison with and refer the matter to city or state authorities, or to a neighborhood law office. Where clearly national, of sufficient impact, and within its planning priorities, the FTC itself would act. Finally, in the vast intermediate area of questionable conduct, where there are both local and interstate aspects, the field offices would be expected to deal with and dispose of those matters unless there is reason to believe that existing state or private law enforcement is adequate to handle them. As we have already indicated, we doubt that the jurisdictional problem would be a bar to the FTC in dealing with these mixed intrastate-interstate schemes.

In addition to case-by-case enforcement, it would be expected that other techniques characteristic of FTC procedure—e.g., trade practice guides and rules, advisory opinions, extensive voluntary compliance arrangements, etc.—would be used, and also that existing guides in the fraud and deceptive practice area would be modified and updated on the basis of experience gained. Among other possibilities, the FTC might consider whether means could be found to encourage informal settlements of disputes between sellers and buyers—for example, by establishment of a community complaint board, appointment of a consumer ombudsman of establishment of a low-cost arbitration for refunds, financed by sellers in the community.

While all of these investigations of novel doctrines of law or experiments with new approaches could be undertaken by personnel at the Washington office, we believe it is only by involvement at local levels that reliable data can be obtained and realistic approaches designed and implemented.

(3) Coordination with Local Education and Enforcement Units.

In the long run, we recognize the desirability of having local enforcement agencies take over most of the task of coping with ghetto frauds and other localized abuses of consumers. We believe a federal presence is justified now, however, because consumer abuse is a serious problem and because local authorities, by their own testimony, are not capable, at present, of effectively coping with it. We note by the way that there seems to be no serious problem of resistance to federal activity; almost all state attorneys general seem to welcome federal law enforcement efforts in the consumer fraud area.[3]

A major emphasis of the program should be on cooperation with and the training of local enforcement personnel in order that they may ultimately assume responsibility in the local consumer abuse area. The FTC should continue its efforts to support adoption by the states of uniform state laws dealing with consumer frauds and deception, and should conduct seminars with state legislators to make available to the states relevant experience on the national level and in other states.[4] The FTC also might try to stimulate local units to engage more extensively in consumer protection education programs, through publication of written materials, TV programs, open meetings, and so forth. An obvious but important project would be simply to advise consumers of their rights under local court procedures. Faculties and students at local law schools, some of which are already engaged in clinical programs designed to study consumer fraud problems, also might be invited to become involved in a local consumer protection project.

(4) Reports and Studies

A major purpose of the proposed program would be to enlarge our knowledge of the types and extent of exploitation of consumers and of the most effective methods for combatting such exploitation. Essential to the acquisition of the requisite body of empirical data is the collection and analysis of economic and statistical information by professionals. The problems in the field of consumer protection are to a large extent economic and intelligent solutions require the full utilization of economic skills and insights. A substantial capability for economic data gathering and analysis therefore should be included in the pilot program.

One important by-product of the study function of the project should be comprehensive reports to Congress that illuminate the problems in these areas. Such reports would also address the question of the extent to which local enforcement agencies are adequately staffed and financed to protect the consumer interest. In that connection, criteria to determine adequacy of present enforcement efforts should be published, after consultation by the FTC with representatives of local agencies. Finally, the FTC should also consider whether and to what extent federal funding, through the model cities program or otherwise, ought to be made available to state and local consumer protection authorities.

(5) Substantive Proposals

As we envision it, the pilot program will not be confined to preparing reports or developing new procedures for dealing with consumer fraud, important as these functions may be. We expect that one major result of the program will be to develop new, substantive consumer protection law.[5]

There is no shortage of problem areas. Widespread concern has been expressed by many persons and groups about a number of commercial practices which may adversely affect legitmate consumer interests. If, after proper study, the Commission finds that remedial action is necessary, it should not hesitate to act.

For some practices, new legislation may be necessary to effect needed reforms. In these cases, the Commission should enlist the aid of Congress, the business community, private consumer groups and other federal agencies, in formulating and enacting new laws.

But new legislation may not be necessary to control all such practices. Imaginative use of Section 5 might bring many of these problems, or important aspects of them, within the jurisdiction of the FTC. Section 5 of the FTC Act is vastly flexible, and the boundaries of the phrase "unfair" practices, in terms of consumer protection, are still to be judicially determined.

We cannot consider and resolve the many problems of social and economic significance inherent in dealing with the various commercial practices that have come under attack in recent years. Indeed, this is one of the functions of the pilot program. But we cannot ignore the existence of these problems and some of the suggested solutions. Therefore, as examples of the type of problems to be attacked, and the type of questions to be considered in shaping solutions, we offer the following:

Presale Disclosure. Under what circumstances need disclosure be made about the product's capabilities or disabilities in order to avoid a sale which is deceptive or "unfair?" What attributes of what products should be described by a producer on a label or tag attached to a product?

Door-to-Door Sales. Are home solicitation sales inherently likely to involve deceptive sales practices? If so, can such deceptions be remedied without excessive costs to legitimate transactions? Under what circumstances, if any, and with what safeguards, should such rescission be permitted?[6]

Warranty Disclaimers and Limitation of Remedies Clauses.   What kinds of limitations of liability by the seller should or should not be permitted? How much freedom of bargaining should be retained by a buyer who would prefer knowingly to assume product risks himself? Should forms be prescribed to communicate clearly to buyers whatever choices a contract may contain? What does fairness require by way of conspicuousness for contract clauses that the consumer may not expect, or that affect substantial rights?

Deficiency Judgements.   In consumer transactions in which the seller retains a security interest, to what extent should he be entitled, as under general commercial law principles, to sue for a deficiency of the secured collateral upon resale does not compensate him for the total amount of the contract? To what extent do forced resales of consumer goods generate rather than avoid deficiency judgements? Are there alternative ways of handling these secured transactions which would protect all of the parties?

Holder in Due Course.   The holder in due course doctrine, developed for the sporadic assignment of negotiable instruments, among strangers, has never been used in the commercial assignment of accounts receivable. Is it appropriate to continue its use in the consumer filed, to shift the risk of unscrupulous sales practices from a knowledgeable finance company to an inexperienced consumer?

Garnishment.   The garnishment of a debtor's earnings is a frequent collection device for consumer sales in default. Is such a device an appropriate one, to enable an otherwise impecunious debtor to establish his eligibility for credit, or is it an abuse of process? Prejudgment garnishment, absent notice and a prior hearing, was recently held unconsittutional by the Supreme Court in *Sniadach v. Family Finance Corp.*[7] The Truth-In-Lending Act, and many state laws, prevent firing an employee whose wages have been subjected to a single garnishment. Is firing of garnisheed employees still common? Is further legislation necessary to protect wage-earners but still provide adequate creditor remedies?

(6) Conclusions

The benefits of this program would be immediate and long-run. The primary immediate benefit would be the suppression and deterrence of some of the most serious examples of local consumer fraud as a result of the coordinated Federal, state and local efforts.

The numerous long-range benefits would include:

The· collection of a body of empirical data necessary to evaluate properly the magnitude and nature of consumer fraud problems, and to assist in the evaluation of both pending and new legislative efforts.

The development of needed legislation on both Federal and state levels.

An expansion of the type of behavior that could be regulated within the limits of existing legislation.

The stimulation of state and local enforcement units to play more active roles in combatting consummer abuses, coupled with the education and training necessary to carry out the expanded role.

The significant contribution to a successful FTC recruiting program to attract able young lawyers who wish to become involved in contemporary social problems.

A gain in stature for the Federal government as a result of a concrete demonstration of concern about consumer fraud and a willingness to take effective action.

B.   SANCTIONS

(1) Preliminary Injunctions

Currently, a firm engaging in an unfair or deceptive practice may continue to do so until a Federal Trade Commission cease-and-desist order has become "final"; and the elapsed time between the initiation of a Commission investigation and denial of certiorari is likely to be at least two years.

Under Section 13 (a) of the Act, the Commission already has the power to seek preliminary injunctions in federal district court where the unfair or deceptive practice consists of false advertising of a food, drug, device, or cosmetic. Bills have recently been introduced which would amend Section 13 of the Act to cover other unfair or deceptive practices, and passage of such a measure is recommended.

So that the Commissioners need take no adversary position in the courts before adjudicating the case themselves, the power to seek preliminary injunctions should not be vested in the Commissioners. Rather, the General Counsel, after consulting with the chief of the bureau in charge of the case, should make this decision. If a preliminary injunction is granted, it should be effective only for a limited period so that the FTC would require to expedite the trial on the merits, unless the defendant chosses to waive this feature.[8]

(2) Private Recovery

We recommend that private rights of action for damages and injunctive relief be created for and on behalf of consumers and other persons who are injured by deceptive practices which are violations of Section 5 of the FTC Act. This private right of recovery, particularly to the extent that it does not depend upon the utilization of the FTC resources, would multiply the effectiveness of the enforcement mechanism and the seriousness of the sanction against violation.

Such actions could be brought in federal court, and the state courts could be given concurrent jurisdiction. Wherever the action is brought, the private party might rely for his right of recovery simply on violation of Section 5 to his injury. To make more meaningful to consumers these private rights, there might be created a type of consumer action which would require lowering or elimination of jurisdictional amounts or, alternatively, more permissive aggregation of claims to meet the jurisdictional amount.

A whole range of questions would need to be answered in defining the nature of the private right, but we do not regard the solution to these questions as within our jurisdiction. Should automatic or discretionary trebling of damages be permitted? Should the existence of an FTC cease-and-desist order constitute a prima facie case for the private party against the respondent subject to the cease-and-desist order? Should the private right arise only upon, and pursuant to, a finding of a violation by the FTC? Should it, instead, be restricted to actions based on settled interpretation of Section 5 by the FTC? Should the right accrue, not directly to individual consumers, but, instead, for their benefit, to some public authority like the FTC as parens patriae to collect amounts of which consumers have been defrauded, either to hold in the public fisc or to distribute among the defrauded private parties to the extent that they can be identified? As in Sherman Acts suits, Truth in Lending Act suits, or Civil Rights Act suits, should successful plaintiffs be awarded attorneys fees and, if so, in what amounts? Are safeguards on such actions required to avoid the filing of frivolous or nuisance cases?

REFERENCES

1. As noted previously, the pilot project in the District of Columbia, conducted to some extent along lines proposed here, used an average of 5 attorneys plus supporting staff. Since this proposed project incorporates additional responsibilities and activities, we believe a larger staff is necessary. We chose ten as a convenient average: in cities like New York, an effective project would need to be larger, while in other places less than 10 might be adequate.
2. This procedure would constitute an increase in authority delegated to staff over and above the present situation, but is consistent with propsals we have made in other sections of this report; see pp. 80 to 83 *infra*.
3. *Home Improvement Fraud Hearings 77.*
4. There are a number of uniform laws presently available to the states, but none has been widely enacted. Suggestions have emanated from the FTC, and from the Committee of State Officials on Suggested State Legislation of the Council of State Governments, and more will come from the National Commission on Product Safety. Recent suggestions from the Council of State Governments include bills on unsolicited merchandise (1969), false advertising (1965), retail installment financing (1963), and labeling of hazardous substances (1961). More generalized major bills are the Uniform Consumer Credit Code (UCCC), which covers both credit arrangements and sales, and incorporates some of the substantive suggestions made to the FTC above: the Uniform Deceptive Trade Practices Act which provides only a broad injunctive remedy but none in damages, and two sets of FTC recommendations. The first is the Unfair Trade Practices and Consumer Protection Law which includes treble damage actions, consumer class actions, criminal penalties, and preliminary injunctions among its remedies; and the abolition of the holder in due course doctrine among its substantive provisions. The FTC also recommends several "Proposals for Stimulating Competition as an Aid to Low-Income Consumers in the Inner Cities." These proposals include: granting subsidies, loans, insurance guarantees and tax incentives for ghetto business; developing management and clerical training programs for local

residents; instituting educational programs for low-income market retailers and low-income consumers; and finally that the states study the feasibility of federally financed insurance programs for retailers extending low cost credit to ghetto dwellers.

Each of these bills contains useful provisions, although their adaptability to various states depends upon the particular problems of that state and on existing consumer legislation there. The FTC, instead of adding to the confusion, should attempt to coordinate the activities of all groups who are dedicated to the enactment of effective state legislation. This should be a major part of the Federal-State Cooperation program described above.

5. The program is not designed to supplant the operations of the Federal-State Cooperation Office. We concur in what appears to be a general view of people active in this field that the Office furnishes valuable services, and its operations should be continued and expanded.

6. The Commission has recently taken action to curb door-to-door sales abuses. After finding that a door-to-door sales company used bait and switch and other unfair and deceptive practices to sell sewing machines, it issued an order requiring a three-day "cooling-off" period during which contracts negotiated in the customer's home could be rescinded. The FTC also ordered full diclosure in understandable terms that the sales contract would be assigned to a third party without recourse. Household Sewing Machine Co., No. 8761, (FTC Aug. 6, 1969). *See also* All-State Industries of North Carolina, No. 8738 (FTC April 1, 1969).

7. 395 U.S. 337 (1969).

8. It is possible that the FTC already has the power to seek preliminary injunctions in the Courts of Appeals against all unfair or deceptive practices, without need of further legislation. *See* FTC v. Dean Foods Co., 384 U.S. 597, 608 (1966).

38

Business-
Consumer
Relations

Chamber of Commerce of the United States

This statement is a call by the Chamber of Commerce of
the United States for businessmen to act forthrightly on
consumers' complaints and, more important, to anticipate
and act on future consumer problem areas and issues.

As American society changes, so do the wants and needs of consumers. In a world of ever-increasing complexity, consumers expect more help from both business and government—and greater understanding and fulfillment of the wants and needs that comprise consumer satisfaction. They also expect ever-higher performance levels of quality, safety, and integrity from business.

The aspirations of America's consumers are a challenge to business to respond positively to consumer problems, demonstrating with new meaning and visibility the traditional business concern for consumer satisfaction.

To meet this challenge effectively will require an increasing commitment by business, not only to act on today's consumer complaints, problems, and questions—but also to anticipate and act on future problem-areas and issues before demands arise for government action. This will require a greater understanding of the mutuality of interest among business, consumers, and government in safeguarding and expanding the consumer's freedom of choice in the marketplace as well as in fostering opportunities for business enterprises to compete, to innovate, to grow, and to provide for rising levels of living and satisfaction for consumers.

Reprinted from *Policy Declaration, 1970-1971*, Chamber of Commerce of the United States (Washington, D.C., 1970), pp. 9-12. Reprinted by permission.

The National Chamber Federation of business enterprises, local and state chambers of commerce, and trade and professional associations provides a singularly appropriate mechanism for implementing activities to achieve these objectives. The involvement of these business organizations in coordinated programs further to strengthen business-consumer relations is a significant demonstration of the business community's awareness, responsibility, and concern for consumer satisfaction and for its social obligations in a complex society.

To the greatest possible extent, business organizations should act voluntarily, expeditiously, and effectively on consumer problems, recognizing as well the role consumers themselves must play in advancing their own interests. In general, the involvement of government should be restricted to necessary protection of consumer health and safety and to the assurance of marketplace integrity. Additional government attention to consumer problems is warranted only after it is shown that voluntary business action is inadequate to the need.

Accordingly, we support an appropriate combination of business-government action, giving particular attention to the following:

1. Consumer Health and Safety. Consumers have a right to consideration of their health and safety in the design and manufacture of all consumer products. This responsibility is borne by both business and government, recognizing that safety also requires the proper use and care of products by consumers. The Chamber recognizes the need for appropriate legislation to safeguard consumers against unreasonable risks of injury, and encourages the systematic compilation of information about hazards and accidents involving consumer products, as well as efforts to better inform consumers about the safe use of products.

The Chamber encourages uniform, national consumer product safety standards in applicable industries through the continued use and strengthening of existing voluntary standards-making processes. The Chamber recognizes, however, a catalytic role for government in standards-making when appropriate, provided all concerned parties are afforded a full and fair opportunity to participate.

2. Product Servicing and Warranties. The Chamber supports efforts to maximize the quality of product servicing and repairs, recognizing that proper use and care of products is an important factor in their continued performance and serviceability. The Chamber supports simplification, clarity, modernization and compliance with warranties and guarantees on consumer products through voluntary industry measures. Action by the Federal Trade Commission or appropriate legislation to accomplish these goals would be acceptable alternatives only if it is shown that voluntary improvements have been inadequate to the need.

3. Ethics and Integrity. Consumers have a right to integrity in consumer services and marketing methods. This particularly embraces honesty as distinct from strict legality in all transactions. Both businessmen and consumers have an obligation to behave ethically and honestly in their marketplace dealings. Advertising should be truthful and informative.

Fraudulent and deceptive practices must be eliminated. The Chamber supports appropriate Federal, state, and local measures and activities to protect both consumers and ethical businessmen from such practices. Enactment by the states of uniform laws to deal with frauds and deceptions would be a desirable exercise of state authority. Government agencies, programs, and activities to attack frauds and deceptions should be effectively structured, empowered and funded. The Chamber opposes the principle of consumer class actions as ineffective, excessive and unnecessary.

Competitive freedom among businessmen promises maximum variety and freedom of choice for consumers. To assure the continuance of market competition, care must be exercised not to impose unnecessary restraints on competitive behavior that limit consumers' freedom of choice or that unduly restrict business reponsiveness to consumer wishes. Vigorous competition, practiced fairly and ethically, is essential to both consumer and business interests.

4. Consumer Information and Choice. Consumers have a right to maximum choice and to be fully informed in order to choose wisely. The Chamber encourages business to identify and analyze consumer complaints, misconceptions, or questions, and to provide positive and meaningful responses. Business and government should seek appropriate means to facilitate value comparisons by expanding information meaningful to consumers. Business and government should give strong support to consumer education programs which utilize the Nation's educational resources to sharpen consumer skills.

5. Consumer Voice. Consumers should be heard and heeded in the councils of both government and industry. Business should utilize the resources of individual companies, associations, chambers, better business bureaus, recognized consumer groups, and other appropriate bodies to establish suitable complaint mechanisms and thus assure that the complaints and concerns of consumers are directed to those persons or organizations best equipped to resolve them.

The Chamber supports statutory creation of an office to coordinate as appropriate the varied consumer programs, services, and activities of the Federal government as desirable in the interests of economy, efficiency, and improved communications. Consumer interests are most appropriately served when they are a consideration of all departments, agencies, bureaus, and branches of government. The consolidation of consumer programs, services, or activities within a single agency or department or any effort to assign exclusive representation of consumers to a single unit of government would prove detrimental to the interests of consumers and the economy as a whole.

Consumers have a right to the protection of their interests by government as well as by business. But everyone has an obligation to recognize that when government steps in there will be costs which must be weighed against possible benefits: Costs in the form of reduced freedom of choice; costs in the form of higher prices reflecting the increased expenses of doing business imposed by government regulation; costs in the form of higher taxes to finance added government activities. In deference, therefore, to the full range of both business and consumer interests, businessmen at all levels should work constantly to anticipate and preclude government involvement by assuring that consumer problems are tackled voluntarily, effectively, and expeditiously in order to maximize consumer satisfaction in the fullest sense.

39

From Caveat Emptor to an Emerging Caveat Venditor: Whither?

E. T. Grether

There are those today who allege that the market is dead. If so, then we have turned full circle from *caveat emptor* to *caveat venditor* in which sellers are subject to the discipline of social forces and values expressed through government regulations and their own conceptions of social responsibility.

This paper analyzes these charges and suggests courses of action for firms and government bodies to take to maintain viable competition free from the extremes of *caveat emptor* and *caveat venditor.*

The ancient maxim caveat emptor, "let the buyer beware," was enunciated in the 16th Century in a horse trade: "If he be tame and have ben rydden upon, then *caveat emptor.*"[1] Undoubtedly, many a buyer in a horse trade has lamented that this minimum warranty had not been enough.

CAVEAT EMPTOR AND THE COMPETITIVE MARKET ECONOMY

The enunciation of *caveat emptor* was an important opening phase in establishing what came to be the competitive system of free enterprise and free consumer-buyer

Reprinted from *Changing Marketing System,* 1967 Winter Conference Proceedings of the American Marketing Association, Series no. 26, pp. 174-177. Reprinted by permission.

choice, or the market-type economy. Eventually, but gradually, most of the resources of some western societies, including even the services of human beings, and basic natural resources came to be organized, coordinated and allocated through the competitive market system. And, from Adam Smith on, formal economic analysis both rationalized and expressed the presumed rationale of this system. There have long been economic theories of competition.

Now there are those nowadays who deny both the rationalization and the rationale of the competitive market system. In other words, the market, like some conceptions or visions of God allegedly is dead.[2] If this be true then also we have returned full circle from *caveat emptor* to a *caveat venditor* in which sellers are no longer subject to the discipline of the competitive market but instead to social forces and values expressed largely through governmental regulations, and through their own conceptions of social responsibility. To state things so simply and clearly is to expose the error in the view that the market is now dead. But it may well be that there is an inexorable drift away from the market as a regulator, i.e. that we are moving away from the free market *caveat emptor* to an emerging nonmarket *caveat venditor*.

Clearly, the simple required warranty "if he be tame and have ben rydden upon" is not enough for our modern industrial societies. Many, perhaps most, products and services in our complex, high level economy cannot be appraised by simple inspection or often even through ordinary use-experience. Automobiles, some university instruction, airline transportation, antibiotics, color TV, plastics, guided missile systems, electronic computers, synthetic materials, the sizes and contents of some packaged goods, inadequately explained credit terms, etc., etc., are beyond the ken of many or most users. Hence, traditional simple expressed or implied warranties have had to be extended either voluntarily or under public regulation.

But this extension has been in a legal environment, at least in the United States, that also requires independent rivalry and action. Hence, one cannot appraise business behavior in making and selling the enormously varied offerings of goods and services in our markets merely in terms of traditional ethics and mores. From this standpoint things would be much simpler if enterprises in the United States could join forces in cartels and work out group arrangements and controls as in some other parts of the world, or, if a governmental bureaucracy made the decisions for consumer-buyers, or, set strict rules for business behavior, or, if there were only one monopoly outlet for sale (as in the case of alcoholic beverages in some states). But by the same token things would be much duller, the offerings to consumer-buyers would be less varied, and most likely would include a lot more shoddy than now.

Our insistence upon our basic national economic policy of competition inevitably affects behavioral patterns and results in marketing. Since enterprises must go it alone, product innovation and product differentiation, and branding and trade-marking are greatly enhanced. Consequently, also, brand sales promotion and especially advertising become the key elements in an organic process of new product development and of independent rivalry. Actually, of course, this is not in itself new, but the modern technological and industrial and social environment makes a difference in degree almost one of kind. The branded products and myriad services in our markets today cannot be compared directly to the simple "commodities" of yesteryear with its low standard of living. Originally, goods were branded—literally—for identification in shipment. So too, were they packaged for protection in handling and storage. They were marked too, so that the worker who produced shoddy could be traced and identified. Modern brands and trade marks, and packages, still, of course, identify and help protect users. But the primary role of the modern trade-mark and brand in the United States is to allow the seller in independent rivalry, to channel a large portion of the benefits of his innovations—aggressive or defensive and of his expenditures in building and holding markets—to himself. Of course, in cartelized markets, much of this expenditure can be saved, especially the defensive expenditures to hold market positions and market shares. But this is not our way of doing things in this country. Consequently, there tends to be an enormous proliferation of products, outlets, alternatives for choice and especially of brands in our markets. Consequently both the alternatives for consumer-buyer choices as well as the difficulties of making wise choices are enhanced.

Clearly, in this context, it is of utmost importance that consumer-buyers be given accurate and adequate information about products and services to guide choices. "If he be tame and have ben rydden upon" obviously is not enough. Clearly too, when health and safety are at issue and intelligent choices cannot or will not be made by users, and competitors either independently or through acceptable programs of self-regulation (as F.T.C. Trade Practice Conferences or other lawful means) cannot or do not provide adequate warranties and information, then it is necessary under public auspices to spell out at the very least, the minimum standards essential to protect users, especially ordinary householders. But such requirements in our society, should not, except in very unusual situations, be extended to the point of becoming detailed prescriptions governing the production, marketing and sale of products and services. To do so, is to run backwards towards the types of onerous detailed regulation out of which the competitive market system evolved.

This conclusion in no sense points away from appropriate governmental regulation. Markets have never been entirely "free" or "unregulated." There is always the continuous interaction between the governmental or other external constraints, intended to "regulate" markets and the regulatory, disciplinary forces of competitive markets themselves. The market system is not a mechanical closed mechanism but an open ended system more largely biological in character than mechanistic. Hence, the basic issue for us today, as in the past, is the character of required public constraints appropriate to our needs and times. This assumes that one does not go along with those who hold that the rule of competition is over[3] or on the contrary, that we accept fully the dictum of the United States Supreme Court that "subject to narrow qualifications, it is surely the case that competition is our fundamental national economic policy, offering as it does the only alternative to the cartelization or governmental regimentation of large portions of the economy."[4] In my view, Mr. Justice Brennan erred when he stated that the qualifications on the rule of competition are only "narrow." On the contrary, the combined burden of public and private qualifications of competitive functioning are so heavy, as to lend some support to the views of those who hold that the market is dead and that antitrust enforcement of the policy of competition is a charade.[5] But it is sounder public policy to assume that free consumer choices and independent competition, among sellers, are or can be made, so acceptably effective as to be preferable to alternatives.[6]

But to accomplish this end, two basic requirements must be reconciled that can be in conflict. First, the complexities of many products, and the enormous variety of alternative brands and services require that accurate information be available to assist buyers. But second, our insistence upon independent, competitive rivalry makes it essential to allow play for the aggressive promotion and proliferation of brands, including the "puffing" of the merits of the branded goods.

Present laws and regulations, federal, state and local on the whole are adequate for curbing outright misrepresentation and falsehood, given the will and resources for enforcement. It will be recalled that the Wheeler-Lea Amendment to the Federal Trade Commission Act gave the Commission authority to proceed against "unfair or deceptive acts" without reference to injury to competition. Over half of the enforcement funds of the Commission are used to halt deceptive practices in advertising.

The gray zone of "puffing," however, and confusion created by brand proliferation produce much more difficult and subtle problems from a regulatory standpoint than outright deception, or a *per se* violation of antitrust. The issues here are not so much those of actual misrepresentation but of confusion and good taste. In this great area it is essential that public regulation tread softly and deftly because the requirement of independent pursuit of business objectives makes product differentiation, branding and brand promotion as of the essence. But in this great area, there are tremendous, additional unutilized opportunities for self-regulation without violating the *per se* rules of antitrust. It is in this area too, that social critics find abundant opportunity for their criticisms of the impacts of advertising and selling expenditures upon social and aesthetic values and judgments. An endeavor to resolve these issues by detailed oversight and regulation by government would create more serious problems than those resolved, except possibly where measurable health and safety factors are involved.

THE SUPREME COURT OF THE UNITED STATES AND THE ECONOMIC THEORY OF COMPETITION

One of the paradoxes in public policy in the regulation of competition in the United States has been the lack of application of the economic theories of competition, especially in antitrust enforcement. As late as 1955, the Report of the Attorney General's National Committee To Study the Antitrust Laws hedged the relatively innocuous section of the Report on "Economic Indicia of Competition and Monopoly" as follows: ". . . care must be exercised to recognize that the economists' use of a particular word does not necessarily carry any legal significance. . . . We caution that the theory (as 'workable' or 'effective' competition) does not provide a standard of legality under any of the antitrust laws. Legal requirements are prescribed by legislatures and courts, not by economic science. . . . This section of the Report is intended as an economic not a legal analysis of competition and monopoly."[7]

In the enforcement of the antitrust laws, economists have been used only to a small degree and typically for the statistical and clerical purposes of the lawyers in charge of cases.[8] And this has been true despite the fact (as noted) that the analysis of competition has been central in economic theory for decades, and that in antitrust research, "much of the most valuable and significant work in the field is . . . done by economists," not by lawyers.[9] The reasons for this state-of-affairs involve both the nature of much of pre-Chamberlinian economic analysis and the inherent conservatism of law and lawyers, and the case-by-case manner in which issues arise and are adjudicated. The tendency in the case-by-case approach is to relate to a slowly evolving body of precedent rather than to a more general body of theory, as in economic analysis. The classifications and distinctions of the economic theories of competition have often been scorned as meaningless or inapplicable (as some are in fact).

We seem, now, however, to be entering a new era in terms of the application of economic analysis in the enforcement of our national economic policy of competition. In the words of one commentator, "Beginning in 1962, . . . the Supreme Court began to recognize explicitly, and to come to grips with the problem of oligopoly power. Antitrust has not been the same since." The same commentator notes that in the *Philadelphia Bank* decision a rule of law is required to be more consistent with economic theory that with past precedent."[10] Thus, in a sense, Chamberlinian economic analysis, especially small group oligopoly analysis, has come out of the wings to the center of the stage. It will take many more cases and years for the full meaning to unfold. Another commentator has stated that "the discipline called 'economics' has come to antitrust. And all of the signs suggest very strongly that it is here to stay."[11]

IMPLICATIONS FOR AN EMERGING CAVEAT VENDITOR?

If economic analysis, and especially market structure economic analysis, and particularly, oligopoly or competition among the few, continues as a focal point in antitrust enforcement, the impact will be to reemphasize independent rivalry in American markets but in the context of the modern great corporation. Consequently, appraisals and public policies will continue to be in terms of both traditional ethics, mores and standards and the requirements of a pro-competition policy. There would be a relatively smaller application of standards of social performance and social responsibility in favor of tests of effects upon competition and market power, including so-called oligopoly power. In many instances, however, this will put the appraisal of business practices or arrangements in quite a different setting than that of traditional ethics or mores. For example, the ancient practice of reciprocity is viewed now not so much through the lenses of the traditional ethic of professional purchasing executives, or in terms of kinship with commercial bribery, but in terms of whether competition is substantially enhanced or weakened, under the wording of revised section 7 of the Clayton Act. Conglomerate acquisitions and growth by conglomerate diversification allegedly create a form of conglomerate market power or leverage which can be exercised in systematic, organized, coercive reciprocal trading relations.[12]

Many aspects of business policy and decision-making will have to be reexamined and rethought in the market structure framework, including various types of restrictive arrangements, consignment selling and price discrimination. It needs to be noted that the Supreme Court seems to have generalized the presumptions of some economic analysis and of some oligopoly models that oligopoly is "inherently undesirable," and hence it is necessary to stop the trend towards oligopoly.[13]

It is exceedingly interesting to speculate as to the fate of product differentiation and brand promotion and advertising in this setting. There is the possibility that product differentiation will be under even stronger suspicion as a barrier to entry, in accordance with some economic analysis.[14] Inevitably, advertising as the most prominent and public expression of product differentiation and promotion becomes the leading accomplice, especially because in much economic analysis competitive advertising often has been held to be wasteful. In the market structure setting, however, the charge would not be so much waste, as undue success, and hence undue market power and interference with entry and potential competition.

On the other hand, the current emphasis, if it continues, should serve to focus the search light of economic analysis, especially of welfare economics, on the total functioning of competition under diverse market structures much more realistically and in a more revealing manner than in the past. Hopefully, the result will be to sharpen and deepen the level of economic analysis in the great deficit area of oligopoly theory and of actual competitive functioning in our markets, especially with respect to product innovation and development, differentiation and brand promotion. Such an outcome in most fields should point away from highly detailed, positive prescriptions of business behavior in favor of more effective competitive market discipline. But it is likely that this outcome may very well be misinterpreted and sabotaged by some of the chief beneficiaries. Under these conditions, detailed tests of social performance, rather than tests of competitive market structure and performance may become dominant.

FINAL OBSERVATION

From my point of view what is needed is:

1. A deeper and wiser understanding on the part of both government and private enterprise as to the realistic nature of competitive functioning under modern technologies.

2. A willingness on both sides to accept and encourage market structure adjustment when necessary to maintain acceptably competitive market discipline.

3. For private industry to take full advantage of all independent and cooperative opportunities for self-regulation to assist consumer-buyers to make reasonable, efficient choices among alternatives without, however, reducing the vigor of competition.[15]

4. For legislatures and administrative tribunals to resist measures that would prescribe business practices in detail, except where health and safety in a measurable sense are involved, and private industry in competition or in cooperation is unwilling to provide for the necessary protection of consumer interests.[16]

Our insistence upon a policy of effective competition requires that we accept also in our society a certain amount of *caveat emptor* in the purchase of most goods. In most buying situations today, however, "if he be tame and rydden upon" is not enuf. But the requirements upon sellers must not be so burdensome and detailed as to destroy competitive motivation and incentives.

REFERENCES

1. See W. H. Hamilton, "The Ancient Maxim Caveat Emptor," *Yale Law Journal* XL (June 1931), p. 1136.
2. See e.g. A. A. Berle, *The American Economic Republic* (New York: Harcourt, Brace and World, 1963); J. K. Galbraith, *The New Industrial State* (Boston: Houghton Mifflin, 1967).
3. cf. Galbraith, *op. cit.,* p. 49.
4. *United States v. Philadelphia National Bank,* 374 U.S. 321, 372 (1963).
5. Galbraith, *op. cit.,* p. 197 and see footnote 6 below.
6. See e.g. the seminar discussion involving Galbraith, W. Adams, W. F. Mueller and Donald F. Turner, on "Are Planning and Regulation Replacing Competition In The New Industrial State," Select Committee on Small Business, U.S. G.P.O., Washington, D.C., 1967.
7. *Report of the Attorney General's National Committee to Study the Antitrust Laws* (1955), pp. 315, 316.
8. At one time, even, the use of economists was forbidden in antitrust enforcement.
9. H. L. Packer, *The State of Research In Antitrust Law,* Walter E. Meyer Research Institute of Law (1963), p. 9.
10. J. F. Brodley, "Oligopoly Power Under the Sherman and Clayton Acts—From Economic Theory to Legal Policy," *Stanford Law Review,* Vol. 19, (January, 1967), pp. 288, 298.
11. Editorial Foreword, *Antitrust Law and Economics,* Vol. 1, (July-August, 1967), p. 3.
12. See Brodley, *op cit.,* pp. 325-329 and J. D. Narver, *Conglomerate Mergers and Market Competition* (Berkeley and Los Angeles, California: University of California Press, 1967), pp. 112-114.
13. Broadley, *op. cit.,* p. 289 and elsewhere and *Brown Shoe Co. v. United States, 370* U.S. (1962).
14. See the classic volume of Joe S. Bain, *Barriers To New Competition* (Cambridge: Harvard University Press, 1956).
15. See e.g. Jerrold G. Van Cise, "The Hobson's Choice of Industry – Partnership with the Federal Government," 45th Annual Conference of Texas Industry, October 26, 1967.
16. Senator Philip A. Hart has stated that, "tight economic regulation of any sector of industry is justified only if absolutely necessary," Annual Meeting of the Federal Bar Association, Washington, D.C., May 3, 1967.

40

Better Deal
for Ghetto
Shoppers

Frederick D. Sturdivant

The violent assault on retail business in Watts, in the summer of 1965, showed how bitter and resentful many Negroes were toward stores serving the area. Numerous riots since then have demonstrated that the situation was not unique to Watts. A fundamental cause of this bitterness, the author believes, is the presence of an inefficient, unethical business community in ghetto areas. The poorest segments of our affluent society are being served by the least effective members of the nation's distribution system. A program to revolutionize the economic structure of these areas is needed, and such a program is proposed in this article. The program is based, not on consumer protection, insurance, or technical assistance principles, but on the concept of investment guarantees and credits to retailers who build branch stores in ghetto districts.

However remote and unreal the newspaper photos of large numbers of looters carrying furniture, groceries, appliances, and other merchandise through the streets of many of this nation's major cities may seem, their message for U.S. business is profound. "Such poverty as we have today in all our great cities degrades the poor," warned George

Author's note: The research for this study was partially supported by a National Defense Education Act grant and funds provided by the University of Southern California Institute for Business and Economics.

Reprinted from *Harvard Business Review,* vol. 46, no. 2 (March-April 1968), pp. 30-39. Reprinted by permission.

Bernard Shaw in 1928, "and infects with its degradation the whole neighborhood in which they live. And whatever can degrade a neighboorhood can degrade a country and a continent and finally the whole civilized world. . . ."[1]

Over the past two years an epidemic of this contagious disease has struck with great violence in Los Angeles, New York, Rochester, Chicago, San Francisco, Newark, Detroit, and other large U.S. cities. There is the threat of more riots to come. A major share of the responsibility for halting the epidemic and preventing further assaults on the structure of society rests with the business community.

No informed citizen questions the presence of large numbers of people living in poverty in the United States. Indeed, most Americans have tired of the debate which attempts to quantify and measure a state of existence that is too qualitative and miserable to be measured precisely. Many companies have participated in private and governmental programs by hiring and training individuals from disadvantaged areas.[2] In fact, efforts to deal with the dilemma of the underskilled and unemployed have represented the major thrust of the business, community's commitment to the War on Poverty. In some areas of high unemployment such programs have led to significant improvements in local conditions.

While few would question the importance of training and employing the disadvantaged, a fundamental point is generally ignored. *The most direct contact between the poor and the business community is at the retail level.* The greatest opportunity to assist and to revolutionize the daily lives of the poor rests in the retailing communities serving poverty areas.

While it is a great step forward to create jobs for the unemployed or to train men for better-paying jobs, such improvements can be nullified when the worker and members of his family enter the marketplace as consumers. Very little may be gained if they are confronted with a shopping situation that generally offers them higher prices, inferior merchandise, high-pressure selling, hidden and inflated interest charges, and a degrading shopping environment. Such conditions are closely related to the frustrations that have produced the spectacle of looted and burned stores throughout the nation.

A TALE OF TWO GHETTOS

The first of the terribly destructive and bloddy Negro riots took place in the south central section of Los Angeles in August 1965. In the aftermath of the nearly week-long Watts riots, which seemed to set the pattern for subsequent revolts around the country, it was apparent that retail establishments had been the primary target of the rioters. Of the more than 600 buildings damaged by looting and fire, over 95% were retail stores. According to the report of the Governor's Commission on the Los Angeles Riots, "The rioters concentrated primarily on food markets, liquor stores, furniture stores, department stores, and pawnshops."[3]

Manufacturing firms and other kinds of business facilities in the area, which in many cases contained valuable merchandise and fixtures, were virtually untouched, as were public buildings such as schools, libraries, and churches. Not one of the 26 Operation Head Start facilities in the Watts area was touched.

Even cursory survey of the damage would indicate that a "vengeance pattern" might have been followed. The various news media covering the riots reported many interviews which revealed a deep-seated resentment toward retailers because of alleged exploitation. The possibility that the rioters were striking back at unethical merchants was reinforced by the fact that one store would be looted and burned while a competing unit across the street survived without so much as a cracked window.

In the fall of 1965, facts and questions like these prompted a two-year study of consumer-business relations in two disadvantaged sections of Los Angeles:

1. As the center of the Los Angeles riots, Watts was an excellent place to begin the study. Consumers and merchants were very willing to discuss their experiences and to explore the causes of the riots. Civil rights groups and merchants' organizations were eager to cooperate with an "objective" research effort which would vindicate their respective points of view. In effect, there were a number of advantages in studying the conditions in Watts while the rubble still littered the streets and participants in the destruction were seeking to be heard.

2. But Watts by itself was not sufficient for an objective investigation. The basic retail structure of the area had been virtually destroyed, and it was impossible to contact many of the merchants who had been burned out by the rioters. In addition, feelings were so intense on both sides that the danger of distortion was greatly magnified. Since the population of the area was heavily Negro, the investigation might have become a study of exploitation of this minority rather than an analysis of the relations between business and the poor in general. Therefore, a second study area was selected—a disadvantaged section of the Mexican-American community in east Los Angeles.

In each area, more than 25% of the population fell below the government's $3,000 poverty line. In addition, each area had high unemployment (7.7% for Mexican-Americans and 10.1% for Negroes), a high incidence of broken homes (17.2% for Mexican-Americans and 25.5% for Negroes), and the many other household and community characteristics which are associated with ghettos.[4]

Over a period of two years, more than 2,000 interviews were held with consumers and merchants in these two poverty areas, numerous shopping forays were conducted, and price-quality comparisons were made with stores serving the more prosperous sections of Los Angeles and surrounding communities. Although there were a number of interesting differences between the findings in the two areas (the differences were based for the most part on cultural factors), the evidence points to two basic flaws in local retailing which were present in each of the areas:

1. The prevalence of small, inefficient, uneconomical units.

2. A tendency on the part of many stores to prey on an undereducated and relatively immobile population with high-pressure, unethical methods.

These findings, I believe, apply rather generally to the retail segments serving disadvantaged areas in U.S. cities. Let us look at each of them in more detail.

INEFFICIENT 'MOMS & POPS'

One of the cruelest ironies of our economic system is that the disadvantaged are generally served by the least efficient segments of the business community. The spacious, well-stocked and efficiently managed stores characteristic of America's highly advanced distribution system are rarely present in the ghetto. The marvels of mass merchandising and its benefits for consumers normally are not shared with the low-income families. Instead, their shopping districts are dotted with small, inefficient "mom and pop" establishments more closely related to stores in underdeveloped countries than to the sophisticated network of retail institutions dominant in most of the U.S. economy.

With the exception of one outdated supermarket, no national or regional retailing firms were represented on the main street of Watts before the 1965 riots. Following the riots, when 103rd Street was dubbed "Charcoal Alley," not even that lone supermarket remained. On Brooklyn Avenue, the heart of the poorest section in east Los Angeles, one found such establishments as Factory Outlet Shoes, Nat's Clothing, Cruz Used Furniture, Villa Real Drugs, and Chelos Market, ranging in size from 315 square feet to 600 square feet. Of the 175 stores in the shopping district (this figure excluded service stations), only 5 were members of chain organizations, and 2 of these firms traced their origins back to a time when the neighboorhood was a middle-class district.

Lacking economies of scale and the advantages of trained management, the "moms and pops" muddle through from day to day and, in the process, contribute to the oppressive atmosphere of such neighborhoods. Their customers generally pay higher prices, receive lower-quality merchandise, and shop in shabby, deteriorating facilities.

Inflated Prices and . . .

The most controversial of these conditions is pricing. The phrase, "the poor pay more," was popularized by Columbia University sociologist David Caplovitz's widely read book with that title.[5] Unfortunately, in addition to being an eye-catching title, it describes reality. While the small, owner-operated stores do not have a monopoly on high prices in the ghetto, they contribute significantly to the inflated price levels. Consumers in Watts, for example, can expect to pay from 7% to 21% more for a market basket of 30 items if they shop for groceries in one of the small local stores than would a family shopping in a supermarket in affluent Beverly Hills. Similar or even greater price differentials prevail in most merchandise categories.

Comparative pricing analyses of the disadvantaged areas and the more prosperous sections in a city are very difficult to make because of quality differences. When national brands are carried by a ghetto appliance dealer, for example, he generally stocks only the lower end of the line. Retailers in higher income areas usually concentrate on the middle and upper price ranges of the product line. Furthermore, off-brand merchandise tends to make up a substantial part of the ghetto dealer's line. Since these lines are not carried in other areas, direct price comparisons are impossible. In food stores, the problem is particularly acute with respect to meat and produce items. Commercial grades of meat are generally carried by ghetto stores, and visual comparisons reveal major qualitative differences in the produce carried, but precise measurements of these quality distinctions are impossible.

Depressed Looks

The physical setting also does little to enhance ghetto shopping. Resentment over the appearance of stores is deeply felt in Watts. I have encountered many reactions like these:

"The manager of that grocery store must think we are a bunch of animals," charged one middle-aged Negro woman with whom I talked. She continued, "The floors are filthy, there are flies all over the place, they handle our food with dirty hands and never say thank you or nothing that's nice."

Commenting on the shabby appearance of the stores on 103rd Street, one young Negro activist said, "The merchants don't give a damn about Watts. They take our money back to Beverly Hills and never spend a cent fixing up their stores."

While such charges are influenced by emotion, the reasons for the bitterness become understandable when one takes a walk down "Charcoal Alley" with its many vacant lots, one dozen or so vacant stores, two thrift shops, six liquor stores, one dime store, one drugstore, one pawnshop, one record shop, one appliance-dry goods store, and a few bars. Although the number and variety of stores along Brooklyn Avenue in east Los Angeles is greater, 53% of the stores are more than 20 years old and have had no apparent improvements made since their construction. Of these stores, 6% are in obvious need of extensive repair and remodeling.

PARASITIC MERCHANTS

While the deteriorated condition of shopping facilities obviously does little to attract shoppers from outside the area, the ghettos do act as magnets for high-pressure and unethical merchandisers who become parasites on the neighborhoods. Take New York, for example. Because of the predominance of parasitic merchants in the ghettos of Manhattan, Caplovitz describes business communities there as "deviant" market systems " in which unethical and illegal practices abound."[6]

The parasitic merchant usually deals in hard goods and emphasizes "easy credit." He stocks his store with off-brand merchandise, uses baitswitch advertising, offers low down payments and small installments, employs salesmen who are proficient at closing often and fast, and marks up his merchandise generously enough to assure himself of a very good return for his effort. Again, direct price comparisons are difficult because of brand differences, but *Exhibit I* reflects the higher prices paid by ghetto shoppers compared with store prices in a middle to lower-middle class suburb of Los Angeles.

EXHIBIT 1
GHETTO SHOPPERS PAY MORE FOR APPLIANCES

| | | Price | |
Product	Watts area	East L.A. area	Control area
1. Zenith portable TV (X1910)	$170	—	$130
2. Olympic portable TV (9P46)	$270	$230	—
3. RCA portable TV (AH0668)	$148	—	$115
4. Zenith portable TV (X2014)	—	$208	$140
5. Emerson portable TV (19P32)	$210	$200	$170
6. Olympic color console TV (CC337A)	—	$700	$630
7. Zenith clock radio (X164)	—	$ 42	$ 19
8. Eureka vacuum (745a)	—	$ 35	$ 30
9. Fun Fare by Brown (36" free standing gas range)	—	$200	$110

Note: Prices for items 1-4 are averages computed from the shopping experiences of three couples (Mexican-American, Negro, and Anglo-White) in three stores in each of the three areas. The three couples had nearly identical "credit profiles" based on typical disadvantaged family characteristics. The stores located in the Mexican-American and Watts areas were selected on the basis of shopping patterns derived from extensive interviews in the areas.

Items 5-9 are the only prices obtainable on a 24-item shopping list. One low-income Anglo-White couple shopped 24 randomly selected stores in the disadvantaged areas.

All prices are rounded.

Data gathered on markups further confirm the presence of exploitation. The major furniture store serving the Watts area and its unaffiliated counterpart in east Los Angeles both carried Olympic television model 9P46. This model wholesales for $104. The retail price in the Watts area store was $270, a markup of 160%, and $229.95 in east Los Angeles, a markup of 121%. The latter store also carried a Zenith model number X1917 priced at $269.95, or 114% above the wholesale price of $126.

Are such substantial markups justified because of the higher risks associated with doing business in a ghetto? It would seem that such risks are more than offset by the interest charges on the installment contract. The rates are highly volatile, but never low. A Mexican-American couple and a Negro couple with virtually the same "credit profile" shopped a number of furniture and appliance stores in the two disadvantaged areas as well as stores in the middle-class control area. An "easy payment" establishment serving south central Los Angeles applied the same high pressure tactics to both couples, who shopped for the same television set. The retailer charged the Negro couple 49% interest on an 18-month contract, while the Mexican-American couple really received "easy terms"—82% interest for 18 months!

Charges of this magnitude go well beyond any question of ethics; they are clearly illegal. In California the Unruh Retail Installment Sales Act sets the maximum rate a dealer may charge on time contracts. For most installment contracts under $1,000, the maximum service charge rate is 5/6 of 1% of the original unpaid balance multiplied by the number of months in the contract. Accordingly, the legal rate for the television set selected by the two couples was 15%.

While it is true that most ghetto merchants do not exceed the legal limits, their customers still pay higher credit charges because of the inflated selling prices on which the interest is computed.

How They Get Away With It

Parasitic merchants are attracted to disadvantaged areas of the cities by the presence of ill-informed and generally immobile consumers. Operating from ghetto stores or as door-to-door credit salesmen, these merchants deal with consumers who have little understanding of contracts or even of the concept of interest. Given their low-income status, one dollar down and one dollar a week sounds to the buyer like a pretty good deal. The merchants are not at all reluctant to pile their good deals on their customers with the prospect of repossessions and garnishments.

Comparative shopping outside his own neighborhood would, of course, provide a ghetto resident with a vivid demonstration of the disadvantages of trading with the local merchants. Unfortunately, the idea of comparing prices and credit terms is little understood in the ghetto. And for those residents who can appreciate the advantages of comparative shopping, transportation is often a barrier. In Watts, less than half of the households studied had automobiles. The public transportation facilities, which are inadequate at best throughout the city of Los Angeles are archaic. Infrequently scheduled, time-consuming, and expensive bus services are of little value to the area's shoppers.

In east Los Angeles, the Mexican-Americans have greater mobility; 73% of the households studied had an automobile, and bus services were better than in Watts. The Mexican-Americans also have relative proximity to modern shopping facilities. However, there are strong cultural ties that encourage residents to forgo shopping advantages offered in other areas. They choose, in effect, to be reinforced continually in the existing cultural setting by frequenting stores in the disadvantaged area where Spanish is spoken. Whether for reasons of transportation problems or self-imposed cultural isolation, the local merchant enjoys a largely captive market.

SHUNNING DEPRESSED AREAS

Not all merchants in disadvantaged areas are there for the purpose of exacting all they can from a neighborhood of undereducated and poor consumers. As noted before, many of the small shops offer their customers higher prices and lower quality because of inefficiency, not by design. The great villain, say the retailers, is the cost of doing business in disadvantaged areas. For example, it is said that small merchants normally cannot afford insurance protection. Of the merchants interviewed in Watts, fewer than 10% had insurance before the riots. Retailers in slum areas have always paid higher insurance rates. According to California's insurance commissioner, rate increases of 300% following the riots were not uncommon. In this respect, the riots throughout the country have only magnified the problem of good retail service, not relieved it.

Since so few small merchants attempt to insure their business, the major effect of the abnormally high rates is to deter larger organizations from investing in ghetto areas. An executive responsible for corporate planning for a retail chain would be hard pressed to justify building a unit in Watts or east Los Angeles when so many opportunities and excellent sites are available in fast growing and "safe" Orange County (in the Los Angeles area). A parallel could be drawn with building in the South Side of Chicago as opposed to the prosperous and rapidly expanding suburbs on the North Shore, or in virtually any central city slum area contrasted with the same city's suburbs. Large retailers not only are frightened away by insurance costs, but also point to personnel problems, vandalism, and alleged higher incidences of shoplifting in disadvantaged districts.

This is not to suggest that there are not profits to be made in such areas. Trade sources, especially in the supermarket industry, have pointed to unique opportunities in low-income neighborhoods.[7] The managements of supermarket chains such as Hillman's Chicago and ABC Markets in Los Angeles admit that, while there are unique merchandising problems associated with doing business in depressed areas, their profit return has been quite satisfactory. It might also be noted that companies that do a conscientious job of serving the needs of low-income consumers are highly regarded. For instance, interviewees in Watts were virtually unanimous in their praise for ABC Markets. Perhaps the most dramatic affirmation of the chain's position in the community came during the riots: not one of the company's three units in the area was disturbed during the week-long riots.

My interviews with executives of Sears, Roebuck and Co. and J. C. Penney indicate that these companies have been successful in adapting to changing conditions in transitional areas. Those of their stores located in declining neighborhoods have altered their merchandising programs and the composition of their work forces to adjust to the changing nature of the market area. The result has been profits for both firms.

Yet, in most cases, such opportunities have not been sought out by large retailers, but stumbled on; they have been happily discovered by older stores trying to readapt themselves in areas where the racial and economic makeup is changing. New stores are built only in trading areas where the more traditional competitive challenges are to be found. As one executive said, "Our target is the mass market, and we generally ignore the upper 10% and the lower 15% to 20% of the market." The upper 10%, of course, can be assured that Saks Fifth Avenue, Brooks Brothers, and a host of other such firms stand ready to meet their needs. The poor, however, are left with "moms and pops" and the easy-credit merchants.

A WORKABLE SOLUTION

Most critics of business-consumer relations in disadvantaged areas have called for legislation designed to protect consumers and for consumer education programs.

Indeed, laws designed to protect consumers from hidden and inflated interest charges and other forms of unethical merchandising should be passed and vigorously enforced. Consumer economics should be a part of elementary and secondary school curricula, and adult education programs should be available in disadvantaged areas. However, these approaches are hardly revolutionary, and they hold little promise of producing dramatic changes in the economic condition of the disadvantaged.

A crucial point seems to have been largely ignored by the critics and in the various bills introduced in the state legislatures and in Congress. This is the difficulty of improvement so long as the retailing segments of depressed areas are dominated by uneconomically small stores—by what I call an "atomistic" structure. Indeed, many legislators seem eager to perpetuate the system by calling for expanded activities by the Small Business Administration in offering assistance to more small firms that do business in the ghettos. Another common suggestion is for the federal government to offer low-cost insurance protection to these firms. This proposal, too, may do more to aggravate than relieve. If the plight of the ghetto consumer is to be dramatically relieved, this will not come about through measures designed to multiply the number of inefficient retailers serving these people.

Real progress will come only if we can find some way to extend into the ghettos the highly advanced, competitive retailing system that has so successfully served other sectors of the economy. To make this advance possible, we must remove the economic barriers that restruct entry by progressive retailers, for stores are managed by business-men, not social workers.

How can these barriers be removed?

Investment Guarantee Plan

Since shortly after the close of World War II, the federal government has had a program designed to eliminate certain barriers to investment by U.S. corporations in underdeveloped countries. In effect, the government has said that it is in the best interest of the United States if our business assists in the economic development of certain foreign countries. In a number of Latin American countries, for instance, the program has protected U.S. capital against loss through riots or expropriation. The investment guarantee program does not assure U.S. firms of a profit; that challenge rests with management. But companies are protected against the abnormal risks with building facilities in underdeveloped countries. If a guarantee program can stimulate investment in Columbia, why not in Watts or Harlem?

I propose a program, to be administered by the Department of Commerce, under which potential retail investors would be offered investment guarantees for building (or buying) a store in areas designated as "disadvantaged." A contract between the retail firm and the Commerce Department would guarantee the company full reimbursement for physical losses resulting from looting, burning, or other damages caused by civil disorders as well as from the usual hazards of natural disasters. In addition, the contract would call for compensation for operating losses sustained during periods of civil unrest in the area. To illustrate:

A Montgomery Ward store established in the heart of Watts would, under this program, be insured for the book value of the establishment against damages caused by natural or human events. If the firm emerged from a period of rioting without suffering any physical damages, but was forced the cease operations during the period of the riots, Montgomery Ward would be compensated for operating losses resulting from the forced closure.

Costs & Restrictions.   The costs to a company for an investment guarantee would be minimal in terms of both financial outlay and loss of managerial autonomy. An annual fee of 0.5% of the amount of insured assets would be charged. There is no actuarial basis for this rate; rather, the fees are charged to cover the costs of administering the program and building a reserve against possible claims.

There would be no restriction on either the size of the investment or the term of the guarantee contract. The contract would be terminated by the government only if the firm violated the terms of the agreement or if the economic character of the area improved to the point it was no longer classified as disadvantaged.

In addition to paying annual premiums, the participating companies would be required to conform to state and local laws designed to protect consumers (or minimum federal standards where local legislation is not in effect). A participating retailer found guilty of violating state law regarding, let us say, installment charges would have his contract terminated.

In effect, the ethical merchandiser would find no restrictions on his usual managerial freedom. So long as he abided by the law, his investment would be protected, and he would have complete freedom in selecting his merchandise, setting prices, advertising, and the other areas of managerial strategy.

Enlarged Investment Credit

The guarantee program would offer the manager maximum discretion, but it would not assure him of a profit. The guarantee phase of the program merely attempts to place the ghetto on a par with nonghetto areas with respect to investment risk. The final barrier, the high costs associated with doing business in such areas, would have to be offset by offering businesses enlarged investment credits. Credits of perhaps 10% (as compared to the usual 7% under other programs) could be offered as an inducement to outside retailers. Firms participating in the guarantee program would be eligible for such investment credits on all facilities constructed in disadvantaged areas.

The more generous investment credits would serve as a source of encouragement not only for building new facilities, but also for expanding and modernizing older stores that had been allowed to decline. For example, the Sears Roebuck and Penney stores located (as earlier mentioned) in transitional and declining areas would be likely targets for physical improvements.

Key to Transformation

Perhaps the most important characteristic of the investment guarantee and credit program is the nature of the relationship that would exist between the government and the business community. The government is cast in the role of the stimulator or enabler without becoming involved in the management of the private company. The program is also flexible in that incentives could be increased or lowered as conditions warrant. If the investment credits should fail to provide a sufficient stimulus, additional incentives in the form of lower corporate income tax rates could be added. On the other hand, as an area becomes increasingly attractive as a retail location, the incentives could be reduced or eliminated.

If implemented with vigor and imagination, this program could lead to a dramatic transformation of the retail segment serving ghetto areas. While size restrictions would not be imposed, the provisions of the program would be most attractive to larger retail organizations. Thus, the "atomistic" structure of the retail community would undergo major change as the marginal retailers face competition with efficient mass distributors. The parasitic merchants would also face a bleak future. The study in Los Angeles revealed no instance in which a major retail firm was guilty of discriminatory pricing or inflated credit charges. In addition, the agency administering the investment program could make periodic studies of the practices of participating firms, and use these investigations to prod companies, if necessary, to assure their customers of equitable treatment.

CONCLUSION

No one program will solve a problem as basic and complex as that of the big-city ghetto. A variety of projects and measures is needed. While the program I propose has great potential, its promise is more likely to be realized if it is supported by other kinds of action to strengthen local businesses. For instance:

Various "activist" groups have been bringing pressure on unethical retailers. In Watts, some limited efforts have been made to boycott retailers who do not conform to a code of conduct that has been promulgated. In Washington, D.C., a militant civil rights organization, ACT, has launched a national campaign to encourage bankruptcy filings by poor merchants; it has devised an ingenious scheme that could deal a severe blow to parasitic retailers.

In Roxbury, Massachusetts (a part of Boston), Negroes are organizing buying cooperatives. Such cooperatives have limited potential, but many people believe they can compensate for at least some of the problems of smallness and inefficiency which plague "mom and pop" stores in the area.

Some corporate executives are trying to help Negro businessmen develop managerial knowhow, Business school students have recently got into this act, too. A group of second-year students at the Harvard Business School, with the financial backing of The Ford Foundation, is providing free advice and instruction to Negroes running retail stores and other firms in Boston. The instruction covers such basic matters as purchasing, bookkeeping, credit policy, tax reporting, and pricing.

Some large stores are reportedly considering giving franchises to retailers in ghetto areas. Assuming the franchise are accompanied by management assistance, financial help, and other advantages of a tie-in with a large company, this step could help to strengthen a number of local retailers.

Some of the large-scale renewal projects undertaken by business have, as a secondary benefit, introduced residents of run-down areas to progressive retailing. In the 1950's, a 100-acre slum section of south Chicago was razed and turned into a 2,009-apartment community with a shopping center. In the shopping center were branches of various well-known organizations—Goldblatt's Department Store, Jewel Tea Supermarket, Walgreen Drug Stores, and others. Similarly, if a group of Tampa business leaders succeed in current plans to rebuild part of Tampa's downtown business district, such leading stores as Macy's, Jordan Marsh, Bon Marche, and Sears, Roebuck plan to open branches in the new buildings. In both cases, residents of the poor areas adjoining the shopping sections would be able to take advantage of progressive retailing.

Projects like the foregoing would be welcome allies of the program proposed in this article. For this program, despite its many great advantages, will not be easy to carry out. The major retailers attracted to disadvantaged areas will face many challenges. Studies will have to be undertaken to help them adapt successfully to local conditions. Creative and imaginative managers will be needed at the store level.

The new program should be good for retailers from the standpoint of profits. In addition, retail leaders should derive a great deal of satisfaction from demonstrating that U.S. enterprise is capable of contributing significantly to the solution of the major domestic crisis of the twentieth century. An efficient and competitive retail community in a ghetto would certainly discourage ineffective and unethical store managers in the area. And while the new program would not solve all of the problems of the nation's cities, it could do a great deal to reduce the injustices suffered by the poor and to eliminate the bitterness that feeds the spreading civil disorders.

REFERENCES

1. *The Intelligent Woman's Guide to Socialism and Capitalism* (Garden City, New York, Garden City Publishing Co., Inc., 1928), p. 42.
2. See Alfonso J. Cervantes, "To Prevent a Chain of Super-Watts," HBR September-October 1967, p. 55.
3. The Governor's Commission on the Los Angeles Riots, *Violence in the City—An End or a Beginning?* (Los Angeles, December 1965), pp. 23-24.
4. California Department of Industrial Relations, *Negroes and Mexican-Americans in South and East Los Angeles* (San Francisco, July 1966); these data understate both the income and unemployment problems since they cover the entire area and not just the poorest sections analyzed in this study.
5. New York, The Free Press, 1963.
6. Ibid., p. 180.
7. See, for example, "Supermarkets in Urban Areas," *Food Topics,* February 1967, pp. 10-22.

Appendixes

Appendix I
Significant Consumer
Protection Legislation
Enacted, 1872-1971

1872 *Mail Fraud Act of 1872* to make it a federal crime to defraud through the use of mail.

1906 *Food and Drugs Act of 1906* to regulate interstate commerce in misbranded and adulterated foods, drinks, and drugs.

1914 *Federal Trade Commission Act* to set up the Federal Trade Commission which, among other responsibilities, is to be concerned with "unfair methods of competition," such as deceptive advertising.

1938 *Federal Food, Drug, and Cosmetic Act of 1938* to strengthen the Food and Drug Act of 1906 by extending coverage to cosmetics and devices; requiring predistribution clearance of safety on new drugs; providing for tolerance for unavoidable or required poisonous substances; and authorizing standards of identity, quality, and fill of container for foods.

1938 *Wheeler-Lea Amendment* to amend the Federal Trade Commission Act of 1914 by making it possible to prosecute for deceptive advertising or sales practices.

1939 *Wool Products Labeling Act* to provide for proper labeling of the kind and percentage of each type of wool.

1951 *Fur Products Labeling Act* to provide that all furs show the true name of the animal from which they were produced.

1953 *Flammable Fabrics Act* to prohibit the shipment in interstate commerce of any wearing apparel or material which could be ignited easily.

1958 *Automobile Information Disclosure Act* to require automobile manufacturers to post the suggested retail price on all new passenger vehicles.

1958 *Food Additives Amendment* to amend the Food and Drug Act by prohibiting use of new food additives until promoter establishes safety and FDA issues regulations specifying conditions of use.

1959 *Textile Fiber Products Identification Act* to cover the labeling of most textile products not covered by the Wool or Fur Products Labeling Acts.

1960 *Federal Hazardous Substances Labeling Act* to require prominent warning labeling on hazardous household chemicals.

1960 *Color Additives Amendment* to amend the Food and Drug Act, allowing the FDA to establish by regulations the conditions of safe use for color additives used in foods, drugs, and cosmetics.

1962 *Kefauver-Harris Drug Amendments* to require drug manufacturers to file all new drugs with the Food and Drug Administration; to label all drugs by generic name; and to require pretesting of drugs for safety and efficacy.

1965 *Drug Abuse Control Amendments* to amend the Food and Drug Act by allowing the FDA to require all legal handlers of controlled drugs to keep records of their supplies and sales; to seize illegal supplies of controlled drugs; to serve warrants; and to arrest violators.

1965   *Fair Packaging and Labeling Act* ("Truth-in-Packaging") to regulate the packaging and labeling of consumer goods and to provide that voluntary uniform packaging standards be established by industry.

1966   *National Traffic and Motor Vehicle Safety Act* to authorize the Department of Transportation to establish compulsory safety standards for new and used tires and automobiles.

1966   *Child Safety Act* to strengthen the Hazardous Substances Labeling Act of 1960 by preventing the marketing of potentially harmful toys and permitting the Food and Drug Administration to remove inherently dangerous products from the market.

1966   *Cigarette Labeling Act* to require cigarette manufacturers to label cigarettes: "Caution: cigarette smoking may be hazardous to your health."

1967   *Wholesome Meat Act* to require states to upgrade their meat inspection systems to stringent federal standards and to clean up unsanitary meat plants.

1967   *National Commission on Product Safety Act* to establish a seven member commission to review household products that represent hazards to public health and safety and to file recommendations for necessary legislation.

1967   *Clinical Laboratories Act* to require all clinical laboratories operating in interstate commerce to be licensed by the federal government.

1968   *Consumer Credit Protecting Act* ("Truth-in-Lending") to require full disclosure of annual interest rates and other finance charges on consumer loans and credit buying including revolving charge accounts.

1969   *Fire Research and Safety Act* to provide funds to collect, analyze and disseminate information on fire safety; to conduct fire prevention education programs; and to conduct projects to improve efficiency of fire-fighting techniques.

1969   *Automobile Insurance Study Act* to provide for a 2-year comprehensive study and investigation by the Department of Transportation on the adequacy of state regulation of auto insurance and to evaluate industry rates, compensation, sales and policy discrimination practices.

1968   *Natural Gas Pipeline Safety Act* to authorize the Secretary of Transportation to develop minimum safety standards for the design, installation, operation and maintenance of gas pipeline transmission facilities.

1968   *Wholesome Poultry Products Act* to require states to develop inspection systems for poultry and poultry products which meet federal standards.

1968   *Hazardous Radiation Act* to require the Secretary of Health, Education and Welfare to establish performance standards for electronic products in order to limit or to prevent the emission of radiation.

1969   *Amend National Commission on Product Safety Act* to amend the National Commission on Product Safety Act in order to extend the life of the Commission so that it may complete its assigned tasks.

1969   *Child Protection and Toy Safety Act of 1969* to amend the Federal Hazardous Substances Act to protect children from toys and other articles intended for use by children which are hazardous due to the presence of electrical, mechanical, or thermal hazards, and for other purposes.

1969 *Public Health Smoking Cigarette Act of 1969* to extend public health protection with respect to cigarette smoking.

1970 *Amend the National Traffic and Motor Vehicle Safety Act of 1966* to amend the National Traffic and Motor Vehicle Safety Act of 1966 to authorize appropriations for fiscal years 1970 and 1971.

1970 *Prohibit Debt Adjusting in the District of Columbia* to prohibit the business of debt adjusting in the District of Columbia except as an incident to the lawful practice of law or as an activity engaged in by a nonprofit corporation or association.

1970 *Fair Credit Reporting Act* to regulate credit information reporting and use.

1970 *Council on Environmental Quality* to authorize the Secretary of the Interior to conduct investigations, studies, surveys and research relating to the nation's ecological systems, natural resources and environmental quality and to establish a Council on Environmental Quality.

1971 *Federal Boat Safety Act* to provide for a coordinated national boating safety program.

Appendix II
Selected Consumer Bills Introduced in the 92d Congress

INDEX

Savings accounts
Trading stamps
Unsolicited merchandise
Usury
Utility consumers' council
Warranties and guarantees

ADVERTISING

S. 1461. Truth in Advertising Act. to require the furnishing of documentation of claims concerning safety, performance, efficacy, characteristics and comparative price of advertised products and services.

S. 1753. National Institute of Advertising, Marketing, and Society Act. to establish the Institute, its primary objective being research of the impact of advertising and marketing upon society.

H.R. 3649. to amend the Communications Act of 1934 to prohibit the broadcasting of any advertising of alcoholic beverages.

AUTOMOBILES

A. General

S. 2582. to amend the National Traffic and Motor Vehicle Safety Act of 1966 to authorize safety design standards for school buses, to require certain safety standards be established for school buses, to require the investigation of certain school bus accidents, and for other purposes.

H.R. 453. to establish a commission to study the effects of highway safety and expense of changing the existing limitations on the weight and dimensions of motor vehicles using the highways of this nation.

B. Insurance

S. 945. Uniform Motor Vehicle Insurance Act. to regulate interstate commerce and to provide for the general welfare by requiring certain insurance as a condition precedent to using the public streets, roads, and highways in order to have an efficient system of motor vehicle insurance which will be uniform among the states . . . ; and for other purposes.

S. 946. Motor Vehicle Group Insurance Act. to promote the greater availability of motor vehicle insurance in interstate commerce under more efficient and beneficial marketing conditions.

H.R. 5220. to regulate interstate commerce by requiring certain insurance as a condition precedent to using the public streets, roads, and highways, and for other purposes.

H.R. 7514. National No-Fault Motor Vehicle Insurance Act. to require no-fault motor vehicle insurance as a condition precedent to using the public streets, roads, and highways, in order to promote and regulate interstate commerce.

C. National Traffic and Motor Vehicle Safety Act Amendments

S. 949. to amend the National Traffic and Motor Vehicle Safety Act of 1966 to add title to provide for motor vehicle safety collision standards.

S. 976. Motor Vehicle Information and Cost Savings Act. to amend the National Traffic and Motor Vehicle Safety Act of 1966 in order to promote competition among motor vehicle manufacturers in the design and production of safe motor vehicles having greater resistance to damage, and for other purposes.

(A*)S. 2357. Automobile Owners Information Act of 1971. to amend the National Traffic and Motor Vehicle Safety Act of 1966 to provide for the development of a consumer information program concerning the damage susceptibility and crashworthiness of passenger cars, and for other purposes.

H.R. 264. National Traffic and Motor Vehicle Safety Act Amendments. to amend the National Traffic and Motor Vehicle Safety Act of 1966 to include the design of motor vehicles within such Act, to authorize increased governmental inspection, to authorize certain testing facilities, and to require federal licensing for certain purposes of automobile dealers.

H.R. 1570. to amend the National Traffic and Motor Vehicle Safety Act of 1966 to require the establishment of certain standards relating to power-related windows.

H.R. 4107. to amend the National Traffic and Motor Vehicle Safety Act of 1966 to require motor vehicle safety standards relating to the ability of the vehicle to withstand certain collisions.

H.R. 8295. to amend the National Traffic and Motor Vehicle Safety Act of 1966 to require the establishment of standards to rear mounted lighting systems.

H.R. 8383. to amend the National Traffic and Motor Vehicle Safety Act of 1966 to add title to provide for motor vehicle safety collision standards.

CONSUMER AFFAIRS
(Establishment of Office and/or Agency)

S. 867. to create the Bureau of Consumer Protection and providing for the appointment of a director, and for other purposes.

S. 1177. to establish a *Council of Consumer Advisers* in the Executive Office of the President and to establish an independent Consumer Protection Agency in order to protect and serve the interests of consumers, and for other purposes.

S. 1205. to establish an *Office of Consumer Affairs* in the Executive Office of the President and a Bureau of Consumer Protection in order to secure within the federal government effective protection and representation of the interests of consumers, and for other purposes.

S. 2017. to establish an *Independent Consumer Council* as an independent nongovernmental organization to represent the economic interests of consumers of goods

*(A) denotes Administration bill.

and services made available to them through the trade and commerce of the United States before federal departments and agencies, to receive complaints and arbitrate voluntary adjustments thereof, to gather and disseminate information for the benefit of consumers, to authorize governmental assistance and support, and for other purposes.

S. 2064. to authorize the Office of Management and Budget and the Domestic Council to establish standards and procedures governing the operation of existing government advisory committees and the creation of new ones; to provide consumer representation on certain federal advisory committees to expand public access to advisory committee deliberations, and for other purposes.

H.R. 254. to establish a *Department of Consumer Affairs* in order to secure within the federal government effective representation of the interests of consumers; to coordinate the administration of consumer services by transferring to such department certain functions of the Departments of Commerce; Labor; and Health, Education, and Welfare; and other agencies; and for other purposes.

H.R. 671. to establish an independent agency to be known as the *U.S. Office of Consumers' Counsel* to represent the interests of the consumers of the nation, and for other purposes.

H.R. 3809. Consumer Protection Act. to establish an Office of Consumer Affairs in the Executive Office of the President and a Bureau of Consumer Protection in order to secure within the federal government effective protection and representation of the interests of consumers, and for other purposes.

CONSUMER EDUCATION

S. 404. Consumers' Education Act. to authorize the U.S. Office of Education to carry out certain activities concerning consumers' education.

S. 1981. Consumer Education Act. to authorize the U.S. Commissioner of Education to establish consumer education programs.

H.R. 3327. to provide for the establishment of a consumer education program designed to inform and give more adequate warning to elderly persons and others concerning the widespread existence, techniques, and dangers of home repair rackets and other forms of consumer fraud.

CONSUMER PROTECTION
(Fraudulent and Deceptive Practices)

S. 984. to authorize classes of persons injured by unfair consumer practices unlawful under the Federal Trade Commission Act to seek relief.

(A*) S. 1222. Consumer Fraud Prevention Act. Provides for a broad but clearly defined range of practices which are unfair and deceptive to consumers, for authority to the Department of Justice and the Federal Trade Commission to take action against such acts, for consumers to bring actions in federal courts after successful litigation by

*(A) denotes Administration bill.

Justice or proceedings before the Federal Trade Commission, and for other purposes.

S. 1378. Consumer Class Action Act of 1971. to provide implementation of the Federal Trade Commission Act, to give increased protection to consumers, and for other purposes.

S. 1823. 1971 Amendment to the Federal Trade Commission Act. to amend section 5 of the Act, to provide for private suits as individuals or a class against persons, partnerships, or corporations by reason of any unfair or deceptive acts or practices in commerce forbidden or declared to be unlawful by this section.

H.R. 262. Consumer Class Action Act. to amend the Federal Trade Commission Act to extend protection against fraudulent or deceptive practices, condemned by that Act, to consumers through civil actions, and to provide for class actions for acts in defraud of consumers.

CREDIT

A. General

H.R. 1472 to amend title 18 of the United States Code to prohibit the transportation or use in interstate or foreign commerce, with unlawful or fraudulent intent, or counterfeit, fictitious, altered, lost, stolen, wrongfully appropriated, unauthorized, revoked, or canceled credit cards.

B. Billing Practices

S. 652. Fair Credit Billing Act. to amend the Truth in Lending Act to protect consumers against careless and unfair billing practices, and for other purposes.

H.R. 243. A bill to amend the Truth in Lending Act to require that statements under open-end credit plans be mailed in time to permit payment prior to the imposition of finance charges.

H.R. 599. to provide for the protection of consumers by insuring fair and responsive billing practices on credit card accounts.

H.R. 1125. to amend the Truth in Lending Act to protect consumers against careless and erroneous billing, and to require that statements under open-end credit plans be mailed in time to permit payment prior to the imposition of finance charges.

H.R. 6994. to amend the Truth in Lending Act to prohibit the use of unfounded or veiled threats to aid in collection and to require that statements under open-end credit plans be mailed in time to permit payment prior to the imposition of finance charges.

C. Reporting

S. 968. to amend the Consumers Credit Protection Act to provide greater protection for consumers against unwarranted invasion of privacy.

S. 969. to protect the individual's right of privacy by prohibiting the sale or distribution of certain information.

H.R. 945. to enable consumers to protect themselves against arbitrary, erroneous, and malicious credit information.

D. Unsolicited Credit Cards

H.R. 3484. to safeguard the consumer by prohibiting the unsolicited distribution of credit cards and limiting the liability of consumers for the unauthorized use of credit cards, and for other purposes.

DRUGS

A. General

S. 2351. to establish the Federal Medical Evaluations Board to carry out the functions, powers, and duties of the Secretary of Health, Education, and Welfare relating to the regulation of biological products and drugs, and for other purposes.

B. Advertising

H.R. 4423. to make prohibitions against the advertising of prescription drug prices an unfair act or practice in commerce.

C. Identification

S. 476. Drug Identification Act of 1971. to protect the public health by amending the Federal Food, Drug, and Cosmetic Act to provide for an identification system for prescription drugs for human use.

(A*) S. 788. Drug Identification Act of 1971 to amend the Federal Food, Drug, and Cosmetic Act to establish a code system for the identification of prescription drugs, and for other purposes.

H.R. 492. to aid in the control of drug abuse by establishing a code for the identification of prescription drugs, to be printed on individual tablets or capsules.

H.R. 1235. Consumer Protection Amendments of 1971. Provides for authorizing a system of coding for prescription drugs, establishing a United States Drug Compendium, certification of certain drugs, requirement that all antibiotics be certified; and for other purposes.

H.R. 5036. to amend the Federal Food, Drug, and Cosmetic Act so as to require that in labeling and advertising of certain drugs sold by prescription, the "established name" of such drugs must appear each time the proprietary name is used, and for other purposes.

H.R. 8692. to amend the Federal Food, drug, and Cosmetic Act, as amended, to require that the label of drug containers, as dispensed to the patient, bear the established or trade name, the quantity and strength of the drug dispensed.

FEDERAL TRADE COMMISSION AMENDMENTS

S. 986. Consumer Product Warranties and Federal Trade Commission Improvements

**(A) denotes Administration bill.

Act of 1971. Title II strengthens the authority of the Federal Trade Commission and provides additional powers to enforce consumer protection.

(A*) S. 1219. Federal Trade Commission Act Amendments of 1971. Provides for increased authority of the Federal Trade Commission, and for additional powers to enhance such authority and make it more effective.

FOOD

A. General

S. 438. to amend the Federal Food, Drug, and Cosmetic Act, and for other purposes; contains provisions concerning serving of margarine and oleomargarine in public eating places.

S. 782. to amend certain provisions of the Federal Food, Drug, and Cosmetic Act; pertaining to flavoring extracts.

H.R. 204. to provide that poultry and meat products prepared from diseased animals shall be deemed adulterated.

H.R. 10817. to amend the Federal Food, Drug, and Cosmetic Act to provide for the annual registration and inspection of food manufacturers and processors.

B. Fish and Fishery Products

S. 296. to protect consumers and to assist the commercial fishing industry by providing for the inspection of establishments processing fish and fishery products in commerce, and to amend the Fish and Wildlife Act of 1956 to provide technical and financial assistance to the commercial fishing industry in meeting such requirements.

(A*) S. 700. Wholesome Fish and Fishery Products Act of 1971. Provides for regulating interstate commerce by strengthening and improving consumer protection under the Federal Food, Drug, and Cosmetic Act with respect to fish and fishery products, including surveillance and inspection of establishments processing fish and fishery products, and for other purposes.

S. 2573. to provide for inspection of foreign fish processing plants preparing fish for importation into the United States.

H.R. 979. to regulate interstate commerce by amending the Federal Food, Drug, and Cosmetic Act to provide for the inspection of facilities used in the harvesting and processing of fish and fishery products for commercial purposes, for the inspection of fish and fishery products, and for cooperation with the states in the regulation of intrastate commerce with respect to state fish inspection programs, and for other purposes.

C. Meat Inspection Act Amendments

S. 571. to amend the Federal Meat Inspection Act relating to the importation of meat and meat products into the United States.

*(A) denotes Administration bill.

S. 1085. to amend the Federal Meat Inspection Act to require that imported meat and meat food products made in while or in part of imported meat be labeled "imported" at all stages of distribution until delivery to the ultimate consumer.

H.R. 6955. to amend the Federal Meat Inspection Act to provide for more effective inspection of imported meat and meat products to prevent the importation of diseased, contaminated, or otherwise unwholesome meat and meat products.

D. Milk and Dairy Products

H.R. 58. to amend the public Health Service Act to protect the public from unsanitary milk and milk products shipped in interstate commerce, without unduly burdening such commerce.

H.R. 6716. to protect the public health and welfare by providing for the inspection of imported dairy products and by requiring that such products comply with certain minimum standards for quality and wholesomeness.

E. Standards for Imported Products

H.R. 1708. to require imported foodstuffs to meet standards required by the federal government for domestic foodstuffs.

F. Uniform System of Quality Grades

H.R. 1011. to provide for the development of a uniform system of quality grades for consumer food products.

FRANCHISES

S. 2399. Franchise Fair Practices Act. to require under the supervision of the Federal Trade Commission a full and fair disclosure of the nature of interests in business franchises, to provide increased protection in the public interest for franchisees in the sale of business franchises and to provide for fair competitive practices in the operation of franchise businesses and the termination of franchise agreements.

S. 2472. Fairness in Franchising Act. to supplement the antitrust laws of the United States by providing for fair competitive practices in the termination of franchise agreements.

GASOLINE

H.R. 664. to require disclosure of the specifications sold at retail.

MEDICAL DEVICES

S. 1824. Medical Device Safety Act. to protect the public health by amending the Federal Food, Drug, and Cosmetic Act to assure the safety, reliability, and effectiveness of medical devices.

H.R. 925. to establish the Federal Medical Evaluations Board to carry out the functions, powers, and duties of the Secretary of Education, and Welfare relating to the regulation of biological products, medical devices, and drugs, and for other purposes.

PACKAGING AND LABELING

A. General

S. 1540. to require a health warning on the labels of bottles containing certain alcoholic beverages.

H.R. 1235. Protects the public health by amending the Federal Food, Drug, and Cosmetic Act so as to amend certain labeling provisions of the food, drug, and cosmetic chapters to assure adequate information for consumers, including cautionary labeling of articles where needed to prevent accidental injury; and for other purposes.

H.R. 5806. Decorative Wood and Simulated Wood Products Labeling Act. to protect consumers and others against misbranding, false invoicing, and false advertising of decorative wood and simulated wood products.

H.R. 6551. to amend the Federal Food, Drug, and Cosmetic Act to require that cosmetics containing mercury or any of its compounds bear labeling stating that fact.

B. Care Labeling

S. 424. to require that certain articles of wearing apparel be permanently labeled with laundering and dry cleaning care instructions.

C. Cigarette Labeling

S. 1454. to amend the Federal Cigarette Labeling and Advertising Act to require the Federal Trade Commission to establish acceptable levels of tar and nicotine content of cigarettes.

H.R. 9891. to amend the Federal Cigarette Labeling and Advertising Act to require cigarette packages to bear a statement of the fire hazards presented by smoking.

D. Labeling

1. Drugs and pharmaceuticals

H.R. 1018. Drug Dating Act. to require that certain drugs and pharmaceuticals be prominently labeled as to the date beyond which potency or efficacy becomes diminished.

2. Durable products

H.R. 1019. Performance Life Disclosure Act. to require that durable consumer products be labeled as to durability and performance life.

H.R. 1374. Appliance Dating Act to require that certain durable products be prominently labeled as to date of manufacture, and for other purpose.

3. Perishable food

S. 2079. to amend the Fair Packaging and Labeling Act to require certain labeling to assist the consumer in purchases of packaged perishable or semiperishable foods.

H.R. 98. to amend the Fair Packaging and Labeling Act to require a packaged perishable food to bear a label specifying the date after which it is not to be sold for consumption.

4. Processed and packaged consumer products

S. 1985. to amend the Federal Food, Drug, and Cosmetic Act to require the labels on all foods to disclose each of their ingredients.

HR. 1017. Better Labeling Act. to require that certain processed or packaged consumer products be labeled with certain information; provides that processed food products shall be labeled to indicate nutritional content; that canned or frozen products shall be labeled to indicate net weight and drained weight; and that combination food items shall be labeled to indicate the major ingredients by percentage weight; all pursuant to regulations by the appropriate agencies.

5. Short shelf-life durable products

H.R. 1375. Durable Products Dating Act. to require that certain short shelf-life durable products be prominently labeled as to the date beyond which performance life becomes diminished.

E. Packaging Pollution Control Act

S. 282. to amend the Solid Waste Disposal Act in order to establish economic incentives for the return, reuse, and recycling of packaging to reduce the public costs of packaging and other solid waste disposal, to require national standards for controlling the amount and environmental quality of packaging, and for other purposes.

S. 1377. to reduce pollution which is caused by litter composed of soft drink and beer containers, and to eliminate the threat to the Nation's health, safety, and welfare which is caused by such litter by banning such containers when they are sold in interstate commerce on a no deposit, no return basis.

H.R. 5451. to discourage the production of one-way containers for carbonated and/or malt beverages so as to reduce litter, reduce the cost of solid waste management, and to conserve natural resources.

F. Unit Pricing

S. 868. to amend the Fair Packaging and Labeling Act to require the disclosure by retail distributors of unit retail prices of packaged consumer commodities, and for other purposes.

S. 928. to amend the Fair Packaging and Labeling Act to require the disclosure by retail distributors of unit retail prices of consumer commodities, and for other purposes.

PRODUCT SAFETY

A. Flammable Materials

S. 364. to strengthen enforcement of the Flammable Fabrics Act and to authorize appropriations for fiscal years 1971, 1972 and succeeding fiscal years in order to carry out the purposes of the Act.

H.R. 816. to prohibit the sale or importation of eyeglass frames or sunglasses made of cellulose nitrate or other flammable materials.

B. Glue and Paint Products

H.R. 1464. to amend the Federal Hazardous Substances Act to authorize the Secretary of Health, Education, and Welfare to ban glue and paint products containing toxic solvents.

C. Hazardous Products

S. 808. to amend the Federal Hazardous Substances Act to provide for more effective protection against the hazards caused by economic poisons.

S. 983. Consumer Product Safety Act of 1971. to protect consumers against unreasonable risk of injury from hazardous products and for other purposes.

(A*)S. 1478. to amend the Federal Hazardous Substances Act; to strengthen federal regulation of toxic chemicals.

(A*)S. 1797 Consumer Product Safety Act of 1971. to protect the public health and safety by reducing the risks of death, illness, and injury associated with the use of consumer products.

D. Power Mowers

S. 1685. Power Rotary Mower Safety Act. to provide for the establishment and enforcement of certain interim safety standards for power rotary lawnmowers.

PRODUCT TESTING

(A*) S. 1692. Consumer Product Test Methods Act. to provide incentives for increasing the amount of information available to consumers respecting consumer products; to assist consumers in making informed judgments by providing suppliers with test methods which they can voluntarily utilize to afford consumers reliable and meaningful information on the performance characteristics of consumer products.

SALES PROMOTION GAMES

H.R. 5038. to amend the Federal Trade Commission Act to make sales promotion games unfair methods of competition.

*(A) denotes Administration bill.

SAVINGS ACCOUNTS

S. 1848. Truth-in-Savings Act. provides consumer depositors with information to enable them to make a rational and intelligent decision about the investment of their funds in savings institutions.

TRADING STAMPS

H.R. 1192. to amend the Consumer Credit Protection Act to safeguard consumers in connection with trading stamp practices.

UNSOLICITED MERCHANDISE

S. 1167. to amend title 39, United States Code, as enacted by the Postal Reorganization Act, to prohibit the mailing of unsolicited samples of manufactured products.

H.R. 956. to amend titles 39 and 18, United States Code, to prevent a seller or publisher from mailing goods, materials, or publications (or a bill therefor) to any individual pursuant to a purchase order or subscription bearing such individual's name without first confirming that such individual in fact sent the order or subscription.

USURY

H.R. 821. to establish a national usury law.

UTILITY CONSUMERS' COUNSEL

S. 607. to establish an independent agency to be known as the United States Office of Utility Consumers' Counsel to represent the consumers of the nation before federal and state regulatory agencies with respect to matters pertaining to certain electric, gas, telephone, and telegraph utilities; and for other purposes.

WARRANTIES AND GUARANTEES

S. 425. to provide for the establishment of national standards for warranties made with respect to consumer goods distributed in or affecting interstate commerce, and for other purposes.

S. 986. Consumer Product Warranties and Federal Trade Commission Improvements Act of 1971. Title I provides minimum disclosure standards for written consumer product warranties against defect or malfunction.

(A*) S. 1221. Fair Warranty Disclosure Act of 1971. Provides for full disclosure of warranty terms, and for prevention of the sale of consumer products and services by the use of deceptive guaranties that affect commerce.

H.R. 261. to authorize the Federal Trade Commission to set standards to guarantee comprehensive warranty protection to the purchases of merchandise shipped in interstate commerce.

*(A) denotes Administration bill.

Appendix III
Major Government-Financed
Consumer Activities
in Nine European Countries
and in Canada

BELGIUM

Belgium Consumers Council. Established by Royal Decree on February 20, 1964. The Council is composed of a President, 9 members from consumer organizations, 3 members representing manufacturers and distributors, and 4 experts on distribution, product testing, or standardization. The Council is nominated by the Ministry of Economic Affairs for a period of 4 years. The objective of the Council is:

To document all problems of interest to the consumer.

To promote and encourage research work on consumption in general and in particular to those products and services that are important to the household economy.

To coordinate informational activities in behalf of the consumer.

To report to the Ministry of Economic Affairs, either on its own initiative or at the demand of the Government, the different points of view expressed on the Council.

Union Feminine pour l'Information et la Defense Consammateur. (UFIDEC) Made up of women within the Socialist Party and women within the cooperative movement. Does testing and publishes magazine. Heavily subsidized by the Belgium Government, UFIDEC also does some testing for the Common Market and acts as a lobbying group for consumers.

Note. The Ministry of Economics maintains a one-man liaison office with consumer organizations.

DENMARK

Danish Government Home Economics Council. Established by Act of Parliament in 1948. The Council functions under the Ministry of the Interior. The aims of the council are:

To promote good nutrition, good hygiene, and sound economics in Danish households.

Adapted from David Swankin and John Walsh, *Government Consumer Programs In Europe–Their Significance for the United States,* a staff report to the Consumer Advisory Council, Fall 1965.

389

Danish Housewives' Consumer Council. Private organization financed by subscriptions to its magazine (testing). In addition, the Council receives an annual grant from the Danish Ministry of Commerce.

Note. The Home Economics Council and the Consumer Council are represented on the Monopolies Control Board, and the Danish Standards Association.

FRANCE

Comite Nationale de la Consommation. This National Commission on Consumer Problems is under the French Ministry of Finance and Economic Affairs. It is composed of representatives of consumer organizations, manufacturers, distributors, education and government. It has recommended the establishment of a Consumers Institute which would do all kinds of consumer research, including product testing. That recommendation is now being considered.

Union Federale de la Consommation. French consumer organization which is partly financed through government subsidy. Publishes magazine, *Que Choisir,* The French equivalent of *Consumer Reports.*

Note. The following also do some work in consumer affairs and receive part of their financing from the Government: French family organizations (usually church-sponsored-provide social and welfare services to French families), Institut Pedagogique National (provides basic teaching materials for schools), French Association for Home Economics Information.

GREAT BRITAIN

The Consumer Council. Established by the British Board of Trade (Department of Commerce) in March 1963). The Council is composed of housewives, manufacturers, distributors, trade union representatives, and people experienced in community work. Members sit in their personal capacities, not as representatives of organizations. The functions of the Council are:

To inform itself about consumer problems and about matters affecting his interests.

To recommend action to solve such problems.

To provide advice and guidance for the consumer.

The Council is specifically prohibited from the preparation of comparative test reports, acting as a "consumer counsel," or law enforcement action. (The Council was abolished in 1970 as an economy measure.)

Citizens' Advice Bureau. Local offices established during the second World War to provide information on rationing and other wartime programs. Now provide a whole spectrum of informational and welfare services, including consumer services.

THE NETHERLANDS

Social-Economische Raad. This is a tri-partite body consisting of employers, trade union members and Government officials. Its purpose is to advise the Government on social and economic problems. Within this council, a specific *Board for Consumer Affairs* has been appointed. The new Board will make recommendations re consumer affairs to the parent organization. Future Government financing of consumer activities may depend upon the Board's recommendations. Members are drawn from consumer organizations (2), unions (3), women's groups (2), co-ops (1), family organizations (1), manufacturers (3), retailers (2), and wholesaler (1).

Note. The Dutch Ministry of Economic Affairs maintains a one-man Division of Consumer Affairs. This Division maintains contacts with outside consumer organizations.

NORWAY

Royal Ministry for Consumer and Family Affairs. This Ministry was established by Royal Decree in 1956. It represents the consumer interest in the central government. It has a staff of about 14.

The Norwegian Consumers' Council. An independent institution consisting of a Chairman and 7 members appointed by the Government. Members represent the following organizations: National Council of Women, Norwegian Housewives Association, the Women's Section of the Norwegian Farmers' and Smallholders' Association, the Norwegian Co-operative Union and Wholesale Society, and the Norwegian Federation of Trade Unions. The Council, financed largely by Government, publishes a magazine in which the results of consumer goods tests are published.

SWEDEN

Ministry of Consumer and Family Affairs, and International Aid to Developing Countries. This Ministry introduces bills and regulations concerning consumer interests.

National Consumer Council. Consists of a chairman and 14 members, all of whom are appointed by the Government. The Consumer Council is located in the Ministry of Commerce. A high ranking official of the Ministry of Commerce acts as a liaison between the Consumer Council and the Minister for Consumer Affairs. Three members of the Council represent business, 3 consumers, and 4 are specialists of various kinds. The Council represents the consumer interest in the Swedish Government, and gives grants to various organizations for testing, informative labeling, etc.

Institute for Informative Labeling. This Institute receives 45 percent of its funds from the Government. It sponsors an informative label (VDN) which is used on about 128 products sold in Sweden. A recent "Gallup poll" showed that about 45 percent of the Swedish people are acquainted with the VDN label. The Institute develops standards for various products, tests products against the developed standards and then rates them with a series of numbers.

The National Institute for Consumer Information. Government financed product testing and home economics institute. Publishes magazine (with test results) and puts on exhibitions of products throughout Sweden.

Note. Other organizations which receive government financing and do some work in consumer affairs are: State Research Laboratory (develops basic tests and standards), Swedish Standards Association, and the Swedish Society for Industrial Design.

SWITZERLAND

Federal Commission on Consumer Affairs. The Federal Commission, established last summer, will bring together business, consumer organizations, cooperatives, women's organizations, and others to chart a consumer program for Switzerland. The Government will accept recommendations from the Commission as to how Government funds can best be used to help consumers. Whether this will mean an emphasis on informative labeling or consumer goods testing is unknown yet. The Commission may also go into economic matters of concern to consumers, e.g., rising prices.

Swiss Institute for Household Economics. Established by various women's associations in 1948. This institute tests the technical qualities and performance of household appliances. It publishes a magazine in which test results are contained. It receives part of its financing from the Government.

WEST GERMANY

The Foundation for Goods Testing. Located in West Berlin, this is the official West German consumer goods testing institute (Stiftung Warentest). The Institute has a Board of Management, consisting of a housewife, a commercial scientist versed in business management, a commercial lawyer, an experienced administrator, and a political economist. An advisory body, consisting of 7 consumer members and 7 from industry, recommend products to be tested. In addition, consulting committees are established for each product tested.

Institute of Home Economics. This is a Federally-sponsored home economics research institute. It develops test methods for food products and home appliances and has a demonstration center in Stuttgard.

Verbrachen Zentralen. State and city financed consumer information centers. They are located in 11 major cities. They maintain demonstration centers, handle consumer complaints, and put on radio and TV shows.

Note. A one-man consumer liaison operation is maintained in the Ministry of Economics.

CANADA

The creation of the Canadian Consumer Council in 1968 reflected a growing awareness and interest in consumer problems, not only in Canada, but in most countries of the western world.

While individuals and organizations had for some time been urging such a development, the federal Department of Consumer and Corporate Affairs may in one sense be said to be an offspring of the Economic Council of Canada and the Special Joint Committee of The Senate and House of Commons on Credit (Prices) (the so-called Croll-Basford Committee). In 1966 the Economic Council was asked to study and advise the government on several topics related to the effective functioning of the Canadian economy, including such questions as consumer affairs, competition policy, and policy concerning trade marks, patents, copyright and industrial property. The consumer boycotts of that fall lent some urgency to their study, and in July, 1967 the Economic Council presented its first interim report on "Consumer Affairs and the Department of the Registrar General". One key recommendation of the Council was that a single organization take over "co-ordination, research and information activities, representation of the consumer interest, and the administration of a limited number of laws affecting both trade and financial matters". The Croll-Basford Committee, in its 1967 report, also supported the principle of an agency of departmental status to represent the consumer interest. In December, 1967 assent was given to Bill C-161, establishing a Department of Consumer and Corporate Affairs. One section of that Act provided for establishment of an advisory council to the Minister, as had been urged by the Economic Council:

> The Governor in Council may establish a consumer advisory council to advise or assist the Minister or to perform such duties and functions as the Governor in Council may specify, and may fix the remuneration and expenses to be paid to the persons appointed as members thereof.

Members of the Canadian Consumer Council were appointed by Order in Council in November, 1968 and met for the first time in early December. Subsequent meetings were held on February 17-18, April 28, June 23, September 29, and November 24, 1969.

At the time of the Council's first meeting, the Minister of Consumer and Corporate Affairs, the Honourable Ron Basford, offered the following guidelines as an aid to the launching of the Council's program:

> ... What we in Consumer Affairs are trying to do is right the balance a little and, in doing so, trying to make our mixed market economy work a little better than it does at present.

Reprinted from Canadian Consumer Council, *First Annual Report,* December 31, 1969.

On that basis, I believe it is possible for men and women drawn from various sectors of our economic life to come together here to discuss the problems facing the consumer and to reach agreement on how to adjust the balance of power between producer and seller. Any improvement that can be made to the consumer's position will make our economic system perform more effectively and thus help everyone.

Each of you has been chosen for your particular knowledge, in the belief that together you represent our society. I expect that your advice will be tendered on the basis of your personal experience and wisdom. I appreciate the fact that many of you are also leaders in your field and often act as spokesmen for a particular organization or section of the economy. However, you have not been chosen for your ability speak for a special group—be it producer or consumer—but rather you have been chosen on the basis of your own merit. I repeat, it is your personal advice that we are seeking. In my work, I can be governed by only one standard—the standard of the public interest. I know the same will apply to your work and to your deliberations.

In every statement that I have made about the operation of the Council, I have stressed the independence of its advisory role. In arranging for the establishment of the Council, I have provided for an independent staff and independent funds for research. When I seek your advice, or when you choose to offer your advice to me, I look for your thoughts, your ideas and your recommendations. . .

I expect that as an advisory body you will offer your advice to me in the first instance. However, I intend to make that advice widely known, and the Council should also feel free to do so in any way that it sees fit.

. . . You have the opportunity to explore the whole spectrum of consumer problems, to seek solutions and to recommend action. . .

. . . One of your main tasks is to improve the quantity and quality of the dialogue between producer and consumer.

These directives have been discussed from time to time by the Council, and a concept of the Council's role and function has emerged; the main dimensions of this concept are as follows:

1. The Council is designed to bring a wide variety of viewpoints to bear on issues of concern to consumers. It does not represent any single group or segment within our society.

2. The members of Council, although chosen in some cases because of their membership in certain groups, are not representatives of those groups. The views they express are their own, and are sought because of the individual's personal expertise or experience. The relevant criterion to be applied is that of the overall public interest.

3. The Council is an *autonomous* body, speaking independently of the views of government or other bodies. While cognizant of the problems of different jurisdictions, it does not consider itself limited in its interests by constitutional constraints.

4. The Council, while offering its advice and counsel first to the Minister, retains the right to publish its views in a form and manner which members themselves determine.

5. The fundamental goal of the Council's activities is to improve the consumer environment, and to remove those imperfections which operate contrary to the most efficient and productive allocation of resources.

Because of its nature, the Council has seen itself as being ill-equipped to deal with relatively narrow problems of a short-term or current nature. It has, therefore, confined itself to consideration of recurring and broader matters of public policy.

Budgetary considerations limited the Council to a small staff, and have significantly shaped the direction and nature of Council's activities. It has been Council's policy to contract out the bulk of its research requirements, and to work actively with and through other organizations which have greater resources for carrying out programs. One of our major roles is seen as helping bring together the many groups active in consumer affairs, providing a vehicle for communication and coordination of such activities. In addition, we have undertaken a number of specific activities ourselves.

In the view of Council members, one of the most significant problems in the field of consumer affairs in the lack of communication among consumers, business, government and other organizations with interests in the field. We have addressed ourselves as a matter of high priority to the difficult task of improving such communication, a task for which we feel the Council is uniquely suited by virtue of its composition.

Index